KEYNES

THE CLASH THAT DEFINED MODERN ECONOMICS

HAYEK

Nicholas Wapshott

W. W. NORTON & COMPANY

NEW YORK ■ LONDON

For information about permission to reproduce selections
from this book, write to Permissions, W. W. Norton & Company, Inc.,
500 Fifth Avenue, New York, NY 10110

For information about special discounts for bulk purchases, please
contact W. W. Norton Special Sales at specialsales@wwnorton.com or
800-233-4830

Manufacturing by RR Donnelley Harrisonburg
Book design by Ellen Cipriano
Production manager: Julia Druskin

Library of Congress Cataloging-in-Publication Data

Wapshott, Nicholas.
Keynes Hayek : the clash that defined modern economics /
Nicholas Wapshott. — 1st ed.
p. cm.
Includes bibliographical references and index.
ISBN 978-0-393-07748-3 (hardcover)
1. Free enterprise. 2. Subsidies. 3. Keynes, John Maynard,
1883–1946. 4. Hayek, Friedrich A. von (Friedrich August), 1899–1992.
5. Economists. I. Title.
HB95.W25 2011
330.15'6—dc23

2011029032

W. W. Norton & Company, Inc.
500 Fifth Avenue, New York, N.Y. 10110
www.wwnorton.com

W. W. Norton & Company Ltd.
Castle House, 75/76 Wells Street, London W1T 3QT

3 4 5 6 7 8 9 0

To Anthony Howard

CONTENTS

PREFACE

It was, perhaps, the most unusual episode in the long-running duel between the two giants of twentieth-century economic thought. During World War II, John Maynard Keynes and Friedrich Hayek spent all night together, alone, on the roof of the chapel of King's College, Cambridge.[1] Their task was to gaze at the skies and watch for German bombers aiming to pour incendiary bombs on the small picturesque cities of England.

In the spring and summer of 1942, in retaliation against British bombing of the medieval cities Lübeck, which sheltered a U-boat lair, and Rostock, home to the Heinkel bomber works, German planes bombed a string of English cities that held no strategic value. Exeter, Bath, and York endured flamestorms that put their ancient buildings at risk. The British headline writers came up with the phrase "The Baedeker Blitz" because it seemed the Luftwaffe planners were selecting British targets by consulting the German guidebook that rated cities according to their cultural worth. Though Cambridge held few important war industries, it warranted its place on the Nazi menu of devastation for its collegiate university founded in the Middle Ages.

Night after night the faculty and students of King's, armed with shovels, took turns to man the roof of the ornate Gothic chapel, whose foundation stone was laid by Henry VI in 1441. The fire watchmen of St. Paul's Cathedral in London had discovered that there was no recourse against an exploding bomb, but if an incendiary could be tipped over the edge of the parapet before it set fire to the roof, damage could be kept to a minimum. And so Keynes, just short of sixty years old, and Hayek, age forty-one, sat and waited for the impending German onslaught, their shovels propped against the limestone balustrade. They were joined by a common fear that they would not emerge brave or nimble enough to save their venerable stone charge.

It was particularly fitting that the two economists should defy the Nazi peril, for both, in different ways, had foreseen the coming of the national socialist tyranny and presaged the rise of Hitler. Keynes was a young economic don at King's when, at the outbreak of World War I, he was recruited by the Treasury, the British finance ministry, to raise money from Wall Street to finance the Allies' efforts. Once the war was brought to an end in 1918, Keynes was kept on to advise how best to squeeze reparations from the defeated Germans.

What Keynes found at the peace talks in Paris shocked him. While the victorious Allied leaders, sparked by vengeance, relished the misery they hoped to inflict on the German nation by severe financial penalties, Keynes saw the issue in a quite different light. He believed that to deliberately beggar a modern trading nation like Germany was to impose crippling poverty on its citizens, which would provide the conditions for extreme politics, insurrection, even revolution. Rather than bringing a just end to World War I, Keynes thought the Treaty of Versailles was planting the seeds of World War II. Back home, he penned *The Economic Consequences of the Peace*, a devastating indictment of the folly of the Allied leaders. The book was a best seller worldwide and propelled Keynes into the international limelight as an economist with the common touch.

Keynes's caustic eloquence was not lost on Hayek, a young soldier in the Austrian army on the Italian front who returned to find his home city of Vienna devastated and its people's confidence broken. Hayek and his family suffered from the precipitous inflation that soon beset the Austrian economy. He saw his parents' savings melt away, an experience that was to permanently harden him against those who advocated inflation as a cure for a broken economy. He was determined to prove that there were no simple solutions to intractable economic problems, and came to believe that those who advocated large-scale public spending programs to cure unemployment were inviting not just uncontrollable inflation but political tyranny.

Although both Keynes and Hayek agreed on the shortcomings of the Versailles peace treaty, they went on to spend most of the 1930s arguing over the future of economics. Before long, their disagreement included the role of government itself and the threat to individual liberties of intervening in the market. The debate was heated and ill-mannered and took on the spirit of a religious feud. When the 1929 stock market crash triggered the Great Depression, the two men provided competing claims on how best to restore health to the shattered world economy. Though the pair eventually agreed to disagree, their ardent disciples continued the fierce battle long after the two men died.

In September 2008, another Wall Street crash took place and another world financial crisis erupted. President George W. Bush, an ostensible adherent of Hayek's views on the sanctity of the free market, was faced with a stark choice: to watch while the market came to rest with a depression that might rival the one of nearly eighty years before, or to speedily adopt Keynesian remedies to spend trillions of borrowed government dollars to save the sinking economy from more harm. So alarming was the prospect of letting the free market do its worst that, with barely a second thought, Bush abandoned Hayek and embraced Keynes. The election of a new president, Barack Obama, oversaw further vast injections of borrowed money into the economy. But before the stimulus funds were fully spent, there was a violent popular reaction against incurring such unprecedented levels of public debt. The Tea Party movement rose to demand that the administration change its course. "Hank, the American people don't like bail-outs,"[2] Tea Party champion Sarah Palin scolded Treasury Secretary Henry Paulson in October 2008. Glenn Beck, the political commentator, revived the reputation of Hayek by drawing the attention of Americans to his neglected *Road to Serfdom*, and the long-forgotten Austrian rose to the top of the book sales charts. Keynes was now out and Hayek in.

Arguments over the competing claims to virtue of the free market and government intervention now rage as fiercely as they did in the 1930s. So who was right, Keynes or Hayek? This book is an attempt to answer the question that has divided economists and politicians for eighty years and to show that the stark differences between two exceptional men continue to mark the great divide between the ideas of liberals and conservatives to this day.

KEYNES

THE CLASH THAT DEFINED MODERN ECONOMICS

HAYEK

ONE

The Glamorous Hero

How Keynes Became Hayek's Idol, 1919–27

The greatest debate in the history of economics began with a simple request for a book. In the early weeks of 1927, Friedrich Hayek, a young Viennese economist, wrote to John Maynard Keynes at King's College, Cambridge, in England, asking for an economic textbook written fifty years before, Francis Ysidro Edgeworth's[1] exotically titled *Mathematical Psychics*. Keynes replied with a single line on a plain postcard: "I am sorry to say that my stock of *Mathematical Psychics* is exhausted."

Why did Hayek, an unknown economist with little experience, approach of all people Keynes, perhaps the best-known economist in the world? For Keynes, Hayek's request was just another item in his bulging postbag. Cambridge's economics prodigy retained no record of Hayek's request, though he was so conscious of the contribution he was making to posterity through his daring approach to the study of political economy that he had taken to hoarding each scribbled note and every last letter. His posthumously published papers, even when edited, fill thirteen volumes. Hayek, meanwhile, at the time seemed fully aware of the significance of his request. He treasured Keynes's bald reply and preserved it for the next sixty-five years as a personal memento and professional trophy. The postcard sits today in the Hayek archive at the Hoover Institution on the Stanford University campus in Palo Alto, California, tangible evidence that Hayek had instigated the first contact in what would become an intense duel over the role of government in society and the fate of the world economy.

Edgeworth interested Hayek because one of the subjects he explored at length was a topic that would come to engage both Keynes and Hayek: how scarce resources can best maximize the "capacity for pleasure." The forbiddingly titled *Mathematical Psychics: An Essay on the Application of Mathematics to the Moral Sciences*, published in 1881, was Edgeworth's best-known work. It anticipated a great number of the debates that would entangle economists over the next century, including notions of "perfect competition," "game theory," and, most important for the impending battle between Keynes and Hayek, the belief that an economy will reach a state of "equilibrium" with every able-bodied adult fully employed. Edgeworth was also an early expounder of theories about money and the monetary system, which by 1927 both Keynes and Hayek had already addressed at length. There was a pretext, albeit slender, that might have prompted Hayek to reach out to Keynes: Keynes had succeeded Edgeworth as editor of the *Economic Journal* in 1911.

But why Hayek should expect Keynes to possess what Keynes jokingly refers to as "my stock of *Mathematical Psychics*," as if he maintained a secret hoard of Edgeworth's forbidden works, is hard to fathom. Though Edgeworth was little remembered even among British economists, *Mathematical Psychics* was commonly available. While a profound division existed between the British school of economics, centered around the teachings of Keynes's mentor Alfred Marshall[2] at Cambridge, England, and the continental variety, which focused on the theories of capital investment (the money invested in a business) expounded in Vienna by Hayek's mentor Ludwig von Mises,[3] there was a good deal of contact, and a fair degree of misunderstanding, between the two camps. Marshallian economics was based on a commonsense understanding of the subject and how business worked in practice, emanating from the mercantilist tradition that had made Britain the most successful commercial nation in history. The notions of the "Austrian School" were more theoretical and mechanistic, deriving from an intellectual rather than a practical understanding of how business might work.

The Austrians mostly read English and were conversant if not persuaded by the English tradition; the English on the whole could not read German and largely ignored the works of Austrian and German theorists. But such was the bond between academics that national borders meant little. The trading of books and journals continued throughout the horrors of World War I, even when scholars found themselves on opposite sides of trench-dug borders. The philosopher Ludwig Wittgenstein, a friend of Keynes at Cambridge and a distant cousin of Hayek,[4] wrote to Keynes while serving in the Austrian army on the Italian front, "Could you possibly send [a new volume by the Cambridge philosopher Bertrand Russell] to me and let me pay for it after the war?"[5] Keynes duly obliged.[6]

Even if Hayek could not find a copy of *Mathematical Psychics* in the University of Vienna's extensive library, it was a stretch to imagine that his next port of call should be the world-renowned Keynes. Keynes was not merely a fellow of King's College, Cambridge, teaching economics to undergraduates. At age forty-two, he was famous worldwide because of his role as a British Treasury negotiator at the Paris Peace Conference, the precursor to the Treaty of Versailles, which brought the cataclysm of World War I to an end. By revealing to the wider public the intense xenophobia and nationalistic spite that had guided the Paris deliberations, Keynes had become a celebrated figure not only in Britain but also in Europe generally, particularly in the defeated nations of Austria and Germany.

Keynes's precocious understanding of economics and public

finance was so considerable that when Britain declared war in September 1914, he was recruited to negotiate an enormous loan from American creditors. The borrowing was vast not only because it funded Britain's worldwide war effort, in defense of an empire that covered half the globe, but also because American bankers did not trust the French and Italians to meet their repayments, leaving Britain to indemnify its allies. Keynes's efforts were so ingenious, and his charm so effective in cutting through bureaucracy, that when the war ended, Keynes joined the team to advise on how to make the Germans pay for causing so much death and devastation.

The war was the most destructive in history. At its root, the struggle between the Central Powers of Germany and Austria and the Allies, comprising Britain, France, Russia, and, eventually, the United States, was over territory and world trade. Within weeks the two sides had dug thousands of miles of shallow, dank trenches within shouting distance of each other, from which the two sides made suicidal sorties. The war marked the end of a chivalrous age and the dawn of the modern era. Cavalry and bayonet charges slowly gave way to tank battles, chemical weapon attacks, and aerial bombardment. After four terrible years, the Germans were starved into submission, and by the armistice in 1918 almost ten million in uniform lay dead, a further eight million were "missing," more than twenty-one million had been wounded, and nearly seven million civilians had perished. A generation of young Europeans had been slaughtered or maimed.

As Hayek recalled, Keynes was "something of a hero to us Central Europeans"[7] owing to his courageous condemnation of British, French, and American leaders for levying crippling reparations on those in the remnants of the defeated alliance. His damning account of the Paris talks, *The Economic Consequences of the Peace*, was published just months after the Versailles treaty was signed, and became an instant worldwide sensation. It contained irreverent assaults on the Allied leaders, including devastating portraits of the American president Woodrow Wilson, French prime minister Georges Clemenceau,[8] and the British prime minister David Lloyd George.[9] Keynes's predictions that the burdensome reparations would lead to political instability and extremist politics, and that they might spark another world war would turn out to be chillingly prescient. What Hayek did not know when he first attempted to engage Keynes was the full background to the young Cambridge don's very bourgeois rebellion.

Keynes was born into a family of academics. His father, Neville, wrote books on economics and was a Cambridge University administrator. His mother, Florence, was an intellectual too, an early graduate of the all-women's Newnham College, Cambridge, who became the first female mayor of Cambridge. Keynes enjoyed a more independent and original cast of mind than his mother and father. After attending Eton College, the foremost secondary school for the offspring of Britain's aristocrats, Keynes became an undergraduate at King's College, studying mathematics. He was soon adopted by his father's mentor, the white-whiskered Alfred Marshall, the leading light of English economics who had written the English-speaking world's definitive economics textbook, *Principles of Economics* (1890), in which he introduced basic economic concepts such as the notion that prices were arrived at when supply met demand and that the use of an object determined its value. Impressed by Keynes's brilliance, Marshall urged him to abandon math and channel his energies into economics.

At Cambridge, Keynes forged a number of intense friendships with a clique whose bohemian ideas would guide his thoughts and actions for the rest of his life. The Bloomsbury Group,[10] made up of soon-to-be-famous writers Lytton Strachey,[11] Virginia Woolf,[12] and E. M. Forster,[13] and visual artists Duncan Grant,[14] Vanessa Bell,[15] and Roger Fry,[16] and others, shared an admiration for the ideas of G. E. Moore,[17] a moral philosopher at Trinity College, Cambridge, who put great store on the value of personal friendships and aesthetics. The group rejected stuffy Victorian conventions, particularly its puritanical sexual morality, and members spoke in a private language to exclude others. The intertwined love lives of the group were its binding cement. They continued to live cheek by jowl in the London squares of the Bloomsbury neighborhood that lent the group its name and in their faux rustic homes in the southern English countryside.

Keynes was not handsome, nor did he consider himself attractive, but he enjoyed a commanding physical presence. He stood six foot six inches tall and had a slight stoop, which he had acquired as a lofty schoolboy. As soon as he left Eton he sported a full moustache. Most noticeable were his deep-set, warm and inviting chestnut eyes, suggesting wrapt attention. Both men and women fell in his thrall. His mellifluous voice seduced even those resistant to his charms. As Hayek remarked, "Those of us who had the good fortune to meet him personally soon experienced the magnetism of the brilliant conversationalist, with his wide range of interests and his bewitching voice."[18]

Keynes stood somewhat apart from the rest of the Bloomsburys, not because of his personal proclivities—he was an avid collector of modern pictures, a prolific and eloquent writer, and a promiscuous and unashamed homosexual—but because of his chosen field. While the others enjoyed a rarified artistic existence outside of conventional society, from which they could snipe at the established order with impugnity, Keynes's talent at economics made him in great demand from the wartime government. As his fellow Bloomsburys were not slow to point out, he had joined the very ruling class they despised. Like many in the group, Keynes had little time for the government's World War I aim of a clear and decisive victory and believed that to halt the daily carnage in the trenches the war should be brought to a swift close without victory on either side.

Barely had the war started when, in November 1914, Keynes found the extent of the bloodbath on the Western Front intolerable. "I am absolutely and completely desolated," he wrote to Strachey. "It is utterly unbearable to see day by day the youths going away . . . to slaughter. Five of this college, who are undergraduates or who have just gone down, are already killed."[19] As the war dragged on, the deaths of young friends brought the butchery home. "Yesterday came the news that two of our undergraduates were killed, both of whom I knew," he wrote to his sometime lover Duncan Grant. "And today, Rupert's death."[20] The news that the twenty-eight-year-old poet Rupert Brooke had died en route to the battlefield of Gallipoli shocked the nation, but it prompted particular sorrow among his friends at King's.

Notwithstanding his pacifist tendencies, Keynes was prepared to lend his intellect to the war effort, less because he was patriotic than because he became intrigued by the wartime public policy conundrums. Keynes played a more important role in the war effort than any other unelected official. And he was good at it. As his biographer R. F. Harrod[21] explained, "He occupied the key position at what was without challenge the centre of the inter-allied economic effort, he thought out the policy, and in effect bore the ultimate responsibility for the decisions."[22] It was an aspect of Keynes's life that set him apart from Hayek: while Hayek was consumed by economic theory for its own sake and maintained a deliberate distance from politics, Keynes was interested in the application of economics as a means of improving the lives of others.

As the war entered its second year, 1915, Keynes's attempt to reconcile his Treasury post with his belief that the war was immoral began to affect his Bloomsbury friendships. By early 1916, he came under pressure to join them in avoiding war service by registering as a conscientious objector.[23] The vituperative Strachey, who had lost the affection of Grant to Keynes, was the most blunt in making known his dislike of Keynes's occupation. After Edwin Montagu, the financial secretary to the Treasury, delivered a bloodthirsty tirade against the Germans, Strachey cut out a newspaper report of the remarks and placed it on Keynes's dinner setting with a covering note that read, "Dear Maynard, Why are you still in the Treasury? yours, Lytton."[24] Strachey told his brother James, "I was going to post it to him, but he happened to be dining at Gordon Square where I also was. So I put the letter on his plate. He really *was* rather put out." Strachey went on, "What was the use of his going on imagining that he was doing any good with such people? . . . The poor fellow seemed very decent about it, and admitted that part of his reason for staying was the pleasure he got from his being able to do the work so well. He also seemed to think he was doing a great service to the country by saving some millions [of pounds] per week."[25]

The pressure led Keynes to consider resigning, and he began spending a great deal of time defending his conscientious objector friends from prison sentences. But he remained convinced that his involvement in management of the war was right and that his contribution led to a more benign policy than were he to leave the work to others. When peace broke out in November 1918, he was glad he had resisted retreating to the quiet irresponsibility of King's College. But the war's end did not grant him a discharge from his public work. As one of the kingpins of British war policy, in January 1919 he set off to the Paris Peace Conference to advise Prime Minister Lloyd George on negotiating strategy.

Keynes had few illusions about the talks and approached them in the same way he justified his involvement in the management of the war: it amused him to be so intimately involved in the nation's affairs. He felt the outcome would be more just and less uncivilized, if not exactly civilized, if he were to take part. He felt guilt pangs for having fed the war machine thus far and hoped to expiate these feelings by making sure the treaty was fair. As his biographer Robert Skidelsky[26] put it, "He was looking for a way of making an act of personal reparation."[27]

The preeminent concern of the Allies was to ensure that "compensation will be made by Germany for all damage done to the civilian population of the Allies and to their property by the aggression of Germany by land, sea, and from the air."[28] The French, led by their wizened prime minister Georges Clemenceau, were the most obdurate in insisting that the beaten nations pay for the physical and human destruction they had unleashed. But the Allies soon found themselves in a bind. The more they demanded confiscation of German domestic assets and overseas investments, its coal and steel industries, its merchant marine fleet, and so on, the less Germany would be able to pay them in annual cash sums. The establishment of new nations, such as Hungary, Poland, and Czechoslovakia, who as members of the former German and Austro-Hungarian empires had sent their surpluses of goods to the imperial capitals, further diminished the conquered nations' ability to pay.

And there were other complications. One result of the conflict was the Bolshevik revolution in Russia, which had brutally overthrown the Menshevik democrats who had brought to an end the rule of Tsar Nicholas II and sued for peace with the Central Powers. If the Allies were not careful that the vanquished populations could afford to meet their demands, they might so undermine democracy in the defeated nations that communism would spread westward. Indeed, no sooner had Kaiser Wilhelm II been deposed in November 1918, when the defeat of Germany was seen to be inevitable, than the new democratic government was challenged by a coup led by the Marxist revolutionaries of the Spartacus League under Rosa Luxemburg.[29] The Allies nonetheless continued to make conditions ripe for extremists. While they squabbled among themselves over how much to levy on the German government in Weimar, they continued to enforce the blockade that had provoked the German surrender. Before long, a humanitarian disaster engulfed Germany and Austria, a condition of general misery that provided the perfect circumstances for revolutionaries to gather support.

In Paris, Keynes became a quiet champion for the vanquished nations. He argued that Germany should not be starved out of existence and went out of his way to ensure that Austria, in particular, should be treated more leniently, a fact that became widely known in Vienna, where the young Hayek had recently returned from the Italian front. Keynes befriended Dr. Carl Melchior,[30] a partner in the

Hamburg bank M. M. Warburg and the Germans' chief negotiator at Paris. In a secret meeting specifically forbidden by the Allies, the two men concocted a deal whereby food supplies would start making their way to Germany if the German merchant marine fleet surrendered to the Allies.

In May 1918, Keynes made a plea on behalf of the starving women and children of Austria. According to the minutes of the meeting that set up the Melchior deal, "Mr. Keynes states that he wished he could adequately picture the frightful conditions in Austria. People were starving on a large scale, and [the British] were already loaning them substantial sums to buy food. A large part of the population were without clothing. The people were in desperate straits and already were frightfully punished for their participation in the war."[31] It was Keynes's stand against the victors over the plight of the Austrians, as much as his opposition to the Versailles treaty, that ensured the heroic status awarded him by Hayek and his Viennese friends.

Keynes, believing the reparations would prove disastrous to the prospect of permanent peace in Europe, became increasingly miserable. "I've been utterly worn out, partly by work and partly by depression at the evil round me," he wrote to his mother. "The Peace is outrageous and impossible and can bring nothing but misfortune. . . . I suppose I've been an accomplice in all this wickedness and folly, but the end is now at hand."[32] He wrote to Grant, who had posed as a farm laborer to avoid the draft, that the Allied leaders "had a chance of taking a large, or at least a humane, view of the world, but unhesitatingly refused it."[33] He wrote to the chancellor of the exchequer, Austen Chamberlain, "The Prime Minister is leading us all into a morass of destruction. The settlement which he is proposing for Europe disrupts it economically and must depopulate it by millions of persons. . . . How can you expect me to assist at this tragic farce?"[34] Chamberlain, who had a week earlier expressed his "strong feeling that a continuation of your services for the present is of great importance,"[35] did not respond.

Keynes retreated from the Hotel Majestic, which housed the rest of the Treasury team, and sought sanctuary in an apartment adjoining the quiet and leafy Bois de Boulogne, in the west of the city. He suffered a nervous breakdown and wrote to his mother, "I spend more than half of my time in bed and only rise for interviews with the Chancellor of the Exchequer, [his ally in arguing against punitive reparations, South Africa Field Marshal J. C.] Smuts,[36] the Prime Minister [Lloyd George]. . . . I distinctly looked over the edge last week, and, not liking the prospect at all, took to my bed instantly."[37] Convinced there was little more he could do to bring sanity to the treaty, Keynes resigned, writing to Lloyd George, "I ought to let you know that on Saturday I am slipping away from this scene of nightmare. I can do no more good here. . . . The battle is lost."[38]

Fired up by what he had seen and heard in Paris, Keynes decided to put the experience to good use and within two weeks was ensconced in a farmhouse owned by Grant and his wife, Vanessa Bell, in Charleston, East Sussex, to calmly, comprehensively, ruthlessly, and often amusingly expose the dangerous absurdity of the victors' claims. He wrote *The Economic Consequences of the Peace* at a furious pace. His general point was that the peace talks were nothing of the sort. The lust for vengeance and a desire to see Germany permanently humbled for provoking what he described as "the European Civil War"[39] would likely lead to another world conflict. "Moved by insane delusion and reckless self-regard, the German people overturned the foundations on which we all lived and built," Keynes wrote. "But the spokesmen of the French and British peoples have run the risk of completing the ruin."[40]

Keynes wanted his readers to understand the full enormity of the crushing punishment meted out by the Allies and that Germany was incapable of fulfilling its treaty obligations. Taking his cue from Strachey's satirical *Eminent Victorians*, which debunked British idols such as the nursing heroine of the Crimean War, Florence Nightingale, Keynes caught the public imagination by traducing the personalities who met for a grim daily conference in President Wilson's drawing room in Paris. Clemenceau, "a very old man conserving his strength for important occasions . . . closed his eyes often and sat back in his chair with an impassive face of parchment, his grey gloved hands clasped in front of him."[41] The French prime minister's attitude was that "you must never negotiate with a German or conciliate him; you must dictate to him," and he believed that "a Peace of magnanimity or of fair and equal treatment . . . could only have the effect of shortening the interval of Germany's recovery and hastening the day when she will once again hurl at France her greater numbers."[42]

Keynes was similarly scathing about Lloyd George, though his mother persuaded him to omit a purple passage describing him as "this syren, this goat-footed bard, this half-human visitor to our age from the hag-ridden magic and enchanged woods of Celtic antiquity."[43] But Keynes kept in his accusation that Lloyd George had cynically called a general election in the midst of the Paris negotiations to ensure the victory of his Liberal government, and had then taken part in a bidding war with his Conservative rivals as to who would beggar Germany the soonest.

For Keynes, the devil of the treaty was, indeed, in the detail. Germany was to return coal-rich Alsace-Lorraine, which it had taken in the Franco-Prussian war of 1870, as well as the coal mining provinces of the Saar and Upper Silesia. Keynes judged that "the surrender of the coal will destroy German industry."[44] In addition, Germany would lose its navigable rivers, such as the Rhine, to an international body, and would lose its merchant fleet and much of its railway engines and rolling stock. He judged that "the industrial future of Europe is black and the prospects of revolution very good."[45]

Then came the reparations. Keynes revealed that France's main intention was to ensure that Germany was reduced to a nation of rustic paupers, while the French and Italians had a secondary aim: to bail out their bankrupt economies. Never mind that Germany was itself bankrupt, that bankruptcy had led to its surrender, and that it was in no position to raise the funds through taxation or borrowing. Keynes pointed to the vengeful Allied populations whose lust for revenge was so strong that "a figure for Germany's prospective capacity to pay . . . would have fallen hopelessly far short of popular expectations."[46] The sum the treaty insisted on was way beyond Germany's means. "Germany has in effect engaged herself to hand over to the Allies the whole of her surplus production in perpetuity."[47] Keynes's verdict was that the treaty "skins [Germany] alive year by year" and that the treaty would prove to be "one of the most outrageous acts of a cruel victor in civilized history."[48]

Delivered to the publisher, Macmillan, in November 1919, *Economic Consequences* was rushed into print the following month. Even Strachey, who since losing Grant to Keynes was hypercritical toward his friend's literary efforts, could not disguise his delight. "Dearest Maynard," he wrote. "Your book arrived yesterday and I swallowed it at a gulp. . . . As to the argument, it is certainly most crushing, most terrible."[49] Keynes replied, with tongue in cheek, that the book had been well received. "The book is being smothered . . . in a deluge of approval," he wrote. "Letters from Cabinet Ministers by every post saying that they agree with every word of it etc, etc. I expect a chit from the PM [prime minister] at any moment telling me how profoundly the book represents his views and how beautifully it is put."[50]

The jingoistic popular press accused Keynes of being pro-German and suggested he did not understand how important it was for Germany to be adequately punished. One paper recommended he be awarded the Iron Cross, Germany's ultimate award for valor. Chamberlain, Keynes's employer, accused him of disloyalty. "Frankly I am sorry that one who occupied a position of so much trust . . . should feel impelled to write in such a strain of the part his country played," he wrote. "I cannot help fearing that our international course will not be made easier by such comments."[51] The book, described by Harrod as "one of the finest pieces of polemic in the English language"[52] and by Skidelsky as "a personal statement unique in twentieth-century literature,"[53] was to transform Keynes's life. From then on he was much in demand by newspapers around the world for his comments on the treaty and anything to do with world trade and economics.

The book's sales told their own story. The first American edition of 20,000 sold out immediately. By April 1920 the tally was 18,500 in Britain, and 70,000 in the United States. It was translated into French, Flemish, Dutch, and Italian, as well as Russian, Romanian, Spanish, Japanese, and Chinese. By June, worldwide sales were over 100,000. Much to Keynes's delight, the book was translated into German. And it was the German edition that proved so popular in Vienna. As Hayek was to note, "His 'Economic Consequences of the Peace' had made him even more famous on the continent than in England."[54]

TWO

End of Empire

Hayek Experiences Hyperinflation Firsthand, 1919–24

Friedrich Hayek endured a war quite different from that of Keynes, sixteen years his senior. As a fifteen-year-old schoolboy at the outbreak of the conflict in 1914, Hayek was tall for his age, which led strangers to ask him why he had not enlisted. The von Hayeks were patriotic Austrians, perfect products of fin de siècle Vienna, who did not doubt the emperor's decision to fight alongside Germany. But it was not until March 1917, when he was nearly eighteen, that Friedrich, the eldest of three brothers, signed up to become an officer in the Austrian army.

His father, August, a medical doctor, was a university lecturer manqué who never overcame a feeling of failure at not achieving the status of full-time scholar. He consoled himself by lecturing part-time in botany at the University of Vienna. As in the Keynes clan, academia ran in the Hayek family. August's father, Gustave, was a secondary-school natural science teacher, and his father-in-law, Franz von Juraschek, was one of Austria's most prominent economists. August's frustrated ambition appears to have been passed on to Friedrich, who entered war service with the intention of becoming a university lecturer as soon as peace was restored. "I grew up with the idea that there was nothing higher in life than becoming a university professor, without any clear conception of which subject I wanted to do. . . . I even thought of becoming a psychiatrist,"[1] he recalled.

Unlike Keynes, who excelled at his studies, Hayek was a poor student and was twice removed from school, as he confessed, "because I ran into difficulties with my teachers, who were irritated by the combination of obvious ability and laziness and lack of interest I showed. . . . I consistently neglected my homework, counting on picking up enough during lessons to scrape through."[2] Much to his relief, Hayek discovered that naked intelligence put him near the top of his officers' training class. "In spite of a lack of any special natural aptitudes, and even in spite of a certain clumsiness, I emerged among the five or six heading the list of some seventy or eighty cadets,"[3] he remembered. By the time his training was complete, the war was entering its final year, which Hayek spent on the Italian front as a telephone officer. His life was endangered at least four times. Once, shrapnel nicked his skull. Another time he attacked a Jugoslav machine gun emplacement in full spate, which he drolly described as "an unpleasant experience."[4] He nearly hanged himself when parachuting out of an observation balloon still donning headphones. And he was in an observation aircraft that was attacked by an Italian fighter.

But for the most part the war meant interminable waiting accompanied by debilitating boredom. Hayek sought solace in reading, and after he was lent an economics book, he discovered the discipline that became his life's passion. "The first two books of economics [I encountered] . . . were so bad that I'm surprised they didn't put me permanently off,"[5] he said. Hayek became interested in how a peacetime economy transformed during war, when the free market gave way to the state's needs. He read the work of Walter Rathenau, an economist turned politician in charge of raw materials for the Austrian war effort. "I think his ideas about how to reorganize the economy were probably the beginning of my interest in economics," said Hayek. "And they were very definitely mildly socialist."[6]

"I never was a social democrat formally, but I would have been what in England would be described as a Fabian socialist,"[7] Hayek remembered. It placed him to the left of Keynes, a lifelong member of the Liberals, a progressive party that urged a middle way between social democracy, which aimed to democratically introduce public ownership of the main industries, and conservatism, a belief in the status quo and the free market. "I never was captured by Marxist socialism," Hayek said. "On the contrary, when I encountered socialism in its Marxist, frightfully doctrinaire form . . . it only repelled me. But of the mild kind, I think German Sozialpolitik, state socialism of the Rathenau type, was one of the inducements which led me to the study of economics."[8] While on leave, Hayek registered to study economics at the University of Vienna as soon as the war ended.

After the armistice on November 11, 1918, Hayek returned to a Vienna that had been transformed from the colorful, sophisticated, and confident city he once called home. The war also left Hayek in poor physical shape. In its final weeks he contracted malaria. In defeat, the Austro-Hungarian emperor Karl I, who had led an empire of fifty million, absolved himself from running the remnants of his former realm. As the war ended, separatist movements took advantage of the mayhem to set up independent states. The empire lost seven-tenths of its territory to new nations such as Czechoslovakia, Poland, and Jugoslavia. Hungary also detached itself from Austria and declared itself a Marxist Soviet republic. The revolutionary changes even affected the von Hayeks' patronym: by decree of the new republican government in Austria, the prefix "von" was removed from the surnames of once prominent families.

The Treaty of Saint-Germain-en-Laye was no less burdensome to Austria than the Treaty of Versailles was to Germany. "German Austria," the rump of land that, like a head without a torso, survived the dissolution of the Austro-Hungarian empire, was forbidden by the victors to call itself "German" and was prohibited from aligning itself with Germany without permission from the League of Nations. The depradations inflicted on the Austrian people during the war, as the Central Powers bankrupted themselves to pay for the conflict, became even more acute in peacetime. As Hayek remembered, "Vienna, which was one of the great cultural and political centers of Europe . . . became the capital of a republic of peasants and workers."[9] Stripped of its imperial supply routes, the city soon ran out of its meager stores of Hungarian wheat and Czech coal. Basic commodities such as bread and electricity were prohibitively expensive. Women and children begged on the streets.

It was into this hellish turmoil that Keynes's *Economic Consequences of the Peace* landed and was eagerly devoured by Hayek and his friends. Keynes was, as always, motivated by a desire to ameliorate suffering and described the beggaring of the Austrians as one of the most notable inequities of the postwar settlement. He accused the Allied leaders of cold-hearted indifference to the Austrians' plight. "Europe starving and disintegrating before their eyes was the one question in which it was impossible to arouse the interest of the Four [Allied leaders],"[10] he wrote. Members of the quartet were so obsessed with revenge that they seemed blind to consigning the defeated nations to chaos and revolution. "The danger confronting us," Keynes wrote, "is the rapid depression of the standard of life of the European populations to a point which will mean actual starvation for some (a point already reached in Russia and approximately reached in Austria.) . . . These in their distress may overturn the remnants of organisation, and submerge civilization itself."[11] The Austrians would not be able to afford the stinging reparations imposed on them, "for they have nothing," Keynes wrote.[12] In Austria, he wrote, "Famine, cold, disease, war, murder, and anarchy are an actual present experience."[13]

Keynes quoted the German government's view that reparation payments would turn the clock back half a century, to a preindustrial economy that could sustain only a fraction of Germany's current population. "Those who sign this Treaty will sign the death sentence of many millions of German men, women and children," he wrote. "The indictment is at least as true of the Austrian, as of the German, settlement." Keynes quoted an editorial published in *Arbeiter Zeiteng*, the Viennese newspaper: "Every provision [of the Treaty of Saint-Germain] is permeated with ruthlessness and pitilessness, in which no breath of human sympathy can be detected, which flies in the face of everything which binds man to man, which is a crime against humanity itself, against a suffering and tortured people." Keynes commented, "I am acquainted in detail with the Austrian Treaty and I was present when some of its terms were being drafted, but I do not find it easy to rebut the justice of this outburst."[14]

Keynes pointed out an insidious threat to civil society in Germany and Austria: a rapid rise in prices. Even Viennese families like the Hayeks, who were comfortably well-off before the war, were not immune to this galloping assault on their living standards. A pair of shoes that cost twelve marks in 1913 changed hands for thirty-two trillion marks a decade later. A glass of beer cost a billion marks. Million-mark notes were used to light stoves. While the price of essentials soared, the savings of families like the Hayeks became worthless and their possessions sharply diminished in value. The government bonds that loyal and patriotic Austrians bought to fund the war became valueless.

For Hayek, nineteen years old, the end of hostilities entailed a change of career path. Although he had enrolled at the University of Vienna to study economics, while still in uniform he made alternate plans lest the war go on "indefinitely."[15] He plotted what he considered to be an honorable escape from the dangers of the front line: the Austrian diplomatic corps. He applied for a transfer to the air force, whose lengthy training would grant him time to study for the diplomatic academy's entrance exam. "I didn't want to be a coward, so I decided, in the end, to volunteer for the air force in order to prove that I wasn't a coward," he said. "If I had lived through six months as an air fighter, I thought I would be entitled to clear out. Now, all that collapsed because of the end of the war. . . . Hungary collapsed, the diplomatic academy disappeared, and the motivation, which had been really to get honorably out of the fighting, lapsed."[16]

Hayek resumed his earlier plan and joined the University of Vienna law department, which taught economics. He began acquainting himself with the Austrian School of economics. When Hayek started studying economics, the Austrian School was not as distinct as it would become after confronting the Marxians who emerged after World War I, when it began to promulgate the virtues of leaving the free market alone, the laissez-faire approach to an economy. The Austrian School was particularly concerned with prices, in particular the "opportunity cost" of a product, that is, the alternatives that consumers choose between when buying competing goods. If a person buys a beer, he does so instead of buying wine; if a person invests money, she forgoes interest; if a person sells investments, he forgoes the price the investment may achieve later. And so on. It is the notion of opportunity costs that lies behind the capital theory of the various "stages of production" in which producers forgo making one good in order to provide a more valuable good later. Hayek started by reading the *Principles of Economics* and *Investigations into the Method of Social Sciences* by Carl Menger,[17] who first postulated the notion of marginal utility: that the greater the quantity of a good, the less it may be perceived to be of value. He was taught by Friedrich von Wieser,[18] who contended that prices were the key to understanding how the market works and that entrepreneurs play a key part in ensuring progress through developing new markets.

Postwar Vienna was a perfect place for Hayek to explore economics. He was not immune from the raging inflation (rising prices) around him. His father, who as a physician was able to adjust his fees upward, could fund his son's university fees, but there was no money to finance his travels to study elsewhere. When the University of Vienna closed in the winter of 1919–20 because of a shortage of heating fuel, Hayek spent eight weeks in Zurich, Switzerland, at the expense of botanist friends of his father, who, according to Hayek, "as part of the general efforts on behalf of the undernourished German and Austrian children, wanted to help the son of a friend who had recently returned from the war and not only needed some feeding up but was also suffering from malaria."[19]

"Zurich in 1919–20 gave me a first taste in the postwar period of what a 'normal' society could be like, Vienna still being in the throes of inflation and semi-starvation,"[20] said Hayek. He had hoped to take a second degree at the University of Munich as he was an admirer of the sociologist Max Weber,[21] who taught there. The plan collapsed, however, when in June 1920 Weber, at age fifty-six, died of influenza, though that was not the main reason for Hayek's change of mind. As he explained, "The later stages of the Austrian inflation would in any case have made it altogether impossible for my father to pay the costs of my studying for a year in Germany."[22] But some good was to come from the disappointment. Instead of spending a year in Bavaria, Hayek was compelled to find a job. In the process he met the man who would become the most important and long-lasting influence on his life and work, Ludwig von Mises, an economics lecturer at the University of Vienna with close contacts in the Austrian government who had studied the rising prices engulfing his country. The long-nosed Mises, a difficult, self-obsessed personality who sported a Charles Chaplin moustache, was to become the father of market economics, the author of a penetrating study of the inadequacies of socialism, and the inspiration for those who believed the amount of money in an economy was the key to understanding inflation.

Having spent as much time studying economics and psychology as law, which he deemed "a sideline," Hayek completed his degree within two years, graduating in November 1921. It was Wieser who commended Hayek to Mises for a job as a legal assistant to a government body set up to administer the settling of war debt between Austria and other nations. Hayek therefore began working in a field similar to that of Keynes. Hayek's first meeting with Mises was less than promising. In a letter of commendation, Wieser had described Hayek to Mises as "a promising economist," to which the egotistical Mises said to Hayek, "Promising economist? I've never seen you at my lectures."[23] Nonetheless, Mises offered him the position, which he took up in October 1921.

Hayek experienced Austria's runaway inflation with each salary check. His first month's pay was five thousand old kronen, but the following month he was paid fifteen thousand kronen to compensate for the fall in the value of the currency. By July 1922 Hayek was paid a million kronen to keep pace with the hyperinflation.[24] In just eight months Hayek was awarded two hundred pay rises. In January 1919 an America dollar bought 16.1 austrian crowns; by May 1923 it bought 70,800 crowns.[25] The Austro-Hungarian Bank printed bank notes night and day to keep up with demand.

In *The Economic Consequences of the Peace*, Keynes had raised the perils of inflation running out of control in language that would be hurled back at him by Hayek and his "sound money" followers. Keynes was aware that the fixed relationship between currencies before World War I, pegged to the price of gold, had been overtaken by events, because governments had printed money to pay for the war. Keynes reminded readers that the undermining of currencies was an invitation to revolution. "Lenin is said to have declared that the best way to destroy the Capitalist System was to debauch the currency," wrote Keynes. "By a continuing process of inflation, governments can confiscate, secretly and unobserved, an important part of the wealth of their citizens."[26] Keynes gave credit to the Bolshevik leader for his perspicacity. "Lenin was certainly right," he wrote. "There is no subtler, no surer means of overturning the existing basis of society than to debauch the currency."[27] In November 1918, by Keynes's reckoning, "in Russia and Austro-Hungary this process [of printing money] has reached a point where for the purposes of foreign trade the currency is practically useless." But Keynes cautioned that "the preservation of a spurious value for the currency, by the force of law expressed in the regulation of prices, contains in itself, however, the seeds of final economic decay."[28] For those, like Hayek, huddled in winter coats in their apartments because they could not afford fuel, Keynes's warning rang true.

Keynes directed his thoughts toward practical remedies for price inflation and sinking currency values. He was commissioned by the editor of the *Manchester Guardian*, C. P. Scott, to edit a series of supplements addressing the problems of European reconstruction. This new set of arguments from Keynes quickly proved a huge international success. Among other languages, the supplements were translated into German, and Hayek, Mises, and others keenly devoured each issue.

"We all read eagerly his famous contributions . . . and my admiration for him was only enhanced by the fact that he anticipated in the *Tract on Monetary Reform* [Keynes's 1923 book, largely drawn from his *Guardian* contributions] my first little discovery,"[29] Hayek recalled. The "little discovery" that Keynes had "anticipated" was that by fixing a currency's price to gold—"the gold standard"—domestic prices would fluctuate and could not be controlled. Governments were faced with a choice: to have a fixed-price currency or fixed domestic prices. As Keynes put it, "If the external price level is unstable, we cannot keep *both* our own price level and our exchanges stable. And we are compelled to choose."[30] At this moment, Keynes and Hayek were thinking along similar lines—simultaneous inspiration, perhaps— despite Mises's warning to Hayek that Keynes "was supporting a good cause with some very bad economic argument."[31]

Keynes received extravagant fees for the *Guardian* supplements. C. P. Scott often became frustrated with Keynes, calling him "a brilliant and original thinker" but also "the most obstinate and self-centered man I ever encountered."[32] Among those Keynes persuaded to contribute were H. H. Asquith, the British wartime prime minister; Ramsay MacDonald, the future British Labour prime minister; Léon Blum, who was to become prime minister of France three times; Sidney Webb, cofounder, with his wife Beatrice, of the Fabian social democratic movement in Britain and of the London School of Economics; Walter Lippmann,[33] the American journalist; Maxim Gorky, the Russian author; Harold Laski of the London School of Economics and Political Science; Oxford historians Richard Tawney and G. D. H. Cole; the chief German negotiator at the Paris peace talks, Carl Melchior; even the queen of Romania. To add a Bloomsbury twist, Keynes commissioned Duncan Grant and Vanessa Bell to illustrate the cover.

In the first supplement, published in April 1922, Keynes contributed three articles, including two that would form the first chapters of *A Tract on Monetary Reform*. The subject was of paramount interest to the former belligerent countries, whose currencies had almost without exception been steeply devalued since 1914. Keynes believed nations would pay a high price if they restored their currencies to prewar values, and proposed instead a new order fixing the currencies at their current prices, with sterling allowed to revalue upward by no more than 6 percent a year.[34] This was opposite to the line advocated by the British Treasury and the Bank of England, both of which wanted sterling to be restored to its prewar value.

The cost of returning currencies to the prewar parities was massive deflation (a continuing drop in prices) accompanied by high interest rates and selling as many goods abroad as goods imported. Or as Keynes put it, "to work and slave." Despite Mises's misgivings, Hayek found little in Keynes's analysis to disagree with. It was Keynes who advocated neither inflation (rising prices) nor deflation but steady prices to avert more injustice being visited on European families. Indeed, when he wrote, "He who neither spent nor 'speculated,' who made 'proper provision for his family' . . . has yet suffered her heaviest visitations,"[35] he might have been describing the Hayek family, brought to near penury by their patriotism.

Keynes introduced in the supplements the first step toward recommending that governments manage their economies, a line of thinking that would set him apart from Mises, Hayek, and other devotees of the free market. European governments were being obliged to choose between inflation and deflation. For Keynes, this was evidence that laissez-faire was no longer appropriate. He advocated instead that the government act to prevent prices from fluctuating.

Mises and, eventually, Hayek believed that the "natural forces" of the market that worked toward an "equilibrium" could restore order to a fluctuating economy. For Keynes, "sitting quietly by" and being buffeted by "chance causes deliberately removed from central control" was unnacceptable because such an approach would lead to mayhem, not to firm, unshakable price levels. Keynes concluded, "We must free ourselves from the deep distrust which exists against allowing the regulation of the standard of value to be the subject of *deliberate decision*."[36]

In a withering assault on the maintenance of the value of the American dollar by hoarding gold, a policy he dismissed as "burying in the vaults of Washington what the miners of the Rand have laboriously brought to the surface,"[37] Keynes added an observation that would inform his arguments about the relative virtues of the free market and those of a managed economy. By his reckoning, the gold standard—by which the price of a currency was fixed to the price of gold—was not a true free-market device because its exchange price was set by central bankers. "In the modern world of paper currency and bank credit there is no escape from a 'managed' currency, whether we wish it or not," he argued. "Convertibility into gold will not alter the fact that the value of gold itself depends on the policy of the Central Banks."[38] It was a line of thinking that Hayek, too, would come to adopt.

Keynes also began testing the logic behind the notion that over time an economy would come to rest at a point where everyone was employed, a "truth" taught to him by Alfred Marshall that was also a main tenet of the Austrian School. In diagnosing the relationship between money and prices over time, Keynes concluded that "in the long run" there must be a constant relationship between the quantity of money in a system and stable prices. However, "this long run is a misleading guide to current affairs,"[39] he argued, as what changed prices in relation to the quantity of money over time was the speed with which money is spent (the "velocity of circulation"), which could alter prices out of proportion to the quantity of money. While equilibrium depended on "the long run," he averred, in what was to become one of his most famous remarks, that "in the long run we are all dead."[40]

The observation was aimed at the relationship between money and prices, but Keynes was to discover that "in the long run we are all dead" held a wider truth for all attempts to assess the role equilibrium theory played in economics. Though it would be some years before Keynes came to abandon his belief in equilibrium theory, he had found a means of explaining why the promised state of equilibrium did not cure persistent high unemployment. Though equilibrium theory suggested that in the long run a state would be reached where everyone was employed, Keynes found that the long run was an elusive timescale that was always set at some indeterminate time in the future. Like a carrot on a stick to urge a donkey forward, the long run was forever out of reach. For those who were later to suggest that public spending remedies for unemployment would lead to inflation in the long run, he had provided himself with a ready riposte: "in the long run we are all dead."

Keynes's views on the role the exchange rate played in determining inflation were particularly pertinent to Hayek and others in the Austrian School. While most European governments had allowed their currencies to float free pending a broader decision about whether the continent should restore itself to the economic conditions of 1914, the Austrian government had decided to raise the value of the kronen without delay. A loan from the League of Nations to Austria was conditional up on public expenditure cuts, including the abolition of seventy thousand government jobs and ending food subsidies. In 1925 the kronen was linked to the price of gold at a high value.

While Keynes's *Guardian* articles addressed the principles involved in managing exchange rates, Hayek and his colleagues were witnessing at close quarters the painful consequences of measures to improve the value of the kronen.

Hayek soon became restless and decided to visit America to witness firsthand how unbridled capitalism operated. Thanks to his inflation-adjusted government salary, Hayek's income had kept pace with rising prices and he had even been able to save a little. In the spring of 1922, Mises introduced Hayek to Professor Jeremiah Whipple Jenks of New York University, who was visiting Vienna after he had served as part of a group of financial experts, including Keynes, who had been hired by the German government to advise it on how to stabilize the value of the mark.[41] Jenks, who was planning to write a book on the Central European nations' war-ravaged economies, invited Hayek to Manhattan to work as a researcher on the project.

Money was so tight that Hayek set off across the Atlantic with a one-way fare as he could not afford a round-trip. To save the price of a telegram, Hayek did not inform Jenks of his arrival date. Hayek disembarked at the passenger liner quay on Manhattan's West Side in March 1923 with just twenty-five dollars in his pocket and presented himself at Jenks's NYU office only to be told the professor could not be contacted. Hayek found himself in a strange land, penniless, without a friend. He decided to take a job until Jenks returned, and was offered one washing dishes in a Sixth Avenue restaurant. An hour before he was due to plunge his hands into the suds, he received a call from Jenks's office saying that the economist had returned. This was the nearest Hayek came to performing manual labor. Indeed, in all his ninety-two years, he never worked for the private sector.

Hayek set about his new American life with gusto. He began work on a Ph.D. at NYU under the supervision of J. D. Magee, a professor of economics; gate-crashed lectures by Wesley Clair Mitchell, an established authority of business cycles,[42] the phenomenon whereby economic booms (periods of fast economic growth) were followed by slumps (periods of contracting economic activity); and attended seminars by the German socialist J. B. Clark at Columbia. Hayek was intrigued by the secretive workings of the Federal Reserve Board, whose gold hoarding and money manipulation Keynes had addressed at length. Hayek went on to work briefly for Willard Thorp, an economic adviser to President Wilson at the Paris peace talks, during which time he mined information about fluctuations in the industrial performance of Germany, Austria, and Italy, which led him to consider the nature and predictability of the business cycle.

In May 1924, short of money and out of luck, Hayek set sail back across the Atlantic. At home he found a letter awarding him a Rockefeller fellowship that, had he received it earlier, would have funded his stay in America for another year. But the offer came too late. Hayek would not return to America for another twenty-five years.

THREE

The Battle Lines Are Drawn

Keynes Denies the "Natural" Order of Economics, 1923–29

On his return to Vienna in 1924, Hayek resumed his government job administering Austria's war debt. Mises took Hayek back under his wing and began acting as his mentor, even trying to find him a job in the Austrian chamber of industry. When Hayek began courting Helen Berta Maria von Fritsch, Mises helped cement the relationship by welcoming the couple home for dinner.

It was Mises who sowed doubts in Hayek's mind about the virtues of socialism. Mises's 1920 *Economic Calculation in the Socialist Commonwealth* and his landmark 1922 *Socialism: An Economic and Sociological Analysis* unsettled Hayek's social democratic beliefs and helped convince him that collectivism was a false god. As Hayek put it, "Socialism promised to fulfill our hopes for a more rational, more just world. And then came [Mises's *Socialism*]. Our hopes were dashed. *Socialism* told us that we had been looking for improvement in the wrong direction."[1]

Mises's principal objection to a communist or socialist society was that it ignored the price mechanism he believed essential for any economy to operate efficiently. He argued in *Economic Calculation* that because in a socialist society the government owned the main industries—"the means of production"—and therefore set the prices of goods, the key purpose of prices, to distribute scarce resources, was made redundant. He claimed that "every step that takes us away from private ownership of the means of production and from the use of money also takes us away from rational economics."[2] Mises's arguments went to the core of the debate that was to ensue between Keynes and Hayek, and they presaged one of Hayek's eventual contentions, that by ignoring market prices socialism deprives individuals of their unique contribution to society—to express, through their willingness to pay a price, their opinion of the worth of an object or service. Central planning, Hayek would argue, deprives individuals of a fundamental freedom.

While Mises tried to find Hayek a government-funded research post, Hayek began writing an account of what he had learned in America, reporting that cheap credit there was leading to a boom in capital goods industries that he believed would prove unsustainable. He extrapolated on the nature of the business cycle, what he called "industrial fluctuations," which would become essential to his contribution to economic theory and the battleground on which he would skirmish with Keynes. To become a paid university lecturer, Hayek had to publish a piece of original work. To this end he began assembling facts and arguments for what he hoped would be an important contribution to the theory of money. This, too, would bring him into conflict with Keynes.

While in America, Hayek concluded that the business cycle—in which an economy regularly switches between a period of high activity and prosperity to a period of business bankruptcies and unemployment—was a worthy subject for study. Having become familiar with the tools of empirical research that were in widespread use in America, though not yet taken up by European economists, such as time and motion studies of workers' behavior and recording the output of factories and machines, he hoped to establish an institute in which he could study the business cycle in detail. Hayek put the idea to Mises, who was skeptical to the point of being dismissive. Mises did not believe economics could be treated as a natural science, and he thought that attempts to record the elements of a business cycle would be misleading and pointless.

Meanwhile, in Britain, Keynes's mind was moving fast. He was preparing his *Guardian* pieces for publication as a book, and in the months before publication in December 1923 he began work on a new book about the role of money in society, *A Treatise on Money*. His forthright contributions to the economic debate were in great demand, from the establishment organ *The Times* to the populist *Daily Mail*. After he assumed the chairmanship of *The Nation and Athenaeum* in March 1923, he also wrote on current events in its columns.

The high unemployment rate that dogged Britain in the early 1920s began to preoccupy Keynes. His motivation was compassion for those without work and indignation that the economy was arranged in such a way that a large pool of unemployed—1.1 million, or over 11.4 percent of the workforce, by July 1923—was deemed necessary. It led him to question the key assumption that Alfred Marshall had taught him: that over time an economy would reach a stage of equilibrium at full employment. As the jobless figures continued to rise, Keynes became more vociferous in his view that the government should reduce interest rates by issuing government bonds. In addition, Keynes became persuaded that the government was duty-bound to directly employ workers in public works projects, such as building roads.

The exchange rate of the pound sterling was at the core of the economic debate. In late 1920, Keynes had proposed that the best way to restore Britain to economic health in the wake of World War I was to fix the pound at $3.60, the market level to which it had slipped from its prewar parity of $4.86, due to the vast government borrowing from American banks needed to fund the war. He believed that fixing the pound at $3.60 would keep prices steady with unemployment remaining at 6 to 7 percent. His proposal was ignored by officials at the Treasury and the Bank of England, who preferred to restore sterling to its prewar parity.

Between 1921 and 1922 the British economy suffered the simultaneous horrors of high interest rates, high wages, falling prices, a rising pound (which made exports too expensive, causing a trade imbalance), and high unemployment. In July 1923, despite Britain's wretched economic condition, the Bank of England, in its desire to lift the pound higher, raised the bank lending rate from 3 to 4 percent.[3] Keynes blasted the Bank's governors for introducing "one of the most misguided movements of that indicator that has ever occurred. . . . The Bank of England, acting under the influence of a narrow and obsolete doctrine, has made a great mistake."[4]

The following month, at the Liberal Summer School at Cambridge, he warned that capitalism itself was in danger from "attacks and criticism of Socialist and Communist innovators" unless the government, or the Bank of England, began managing the economy. He followed this critique in December, in an address at the National Liberal Club, Westminster, with a full-scale assault on the government's reliance on free-market ideas to solve its economic problems.

"It is obvious that an individualist society left to itself does not work well or even tolerably," he declared. "The more troublesome the times, the worse does a laissez-faire system work." As in *A Tract*, published the same month, which with typical Keynesian audacity was "humbly dedicated to the Governors and Court of the Bank of England," Keynes argued that the remedy to Britain's parlous economic condition was within the grasp of the Bank, which could, without recourse to new legislation, manage the British economy and the business cycle by cutting interest rates and issuing bonds. Again, Keynes issued a stern warning against inaction. "I prophesy that unless [the Bank governors] embrace wisdom in good time, the system upon which they live will work so very ill that they will be overwhelmed by irresistible things which they will hate much more than the mild and limited remedies offered them now."[5]

The year Hayek was in America, 1924, proved to be a key period for Keynes's fast-developing arguments against the operation of the free market. In January, Ramsay MacDonald became Britain's first Labour prime minister, albeit of a minority government, by depriving the Conservatives of a majority in the House of Commons. In April 1924, a correspondence in *The Nation* advocated a taxpayer-funded program of public works to put the country back to work. The proposal was a ploy by former Liberal prime minister Lloyd George to show his party as more protective of the working man than Labour, the party funded by trade unions that threatened to permanently displace the Liberals as Britain's natural alternative to the Conservatives. Keynes joined the debate the following month with an article headed "Does Unemployment Need a Drastic Remedy?" The answer, suggested Keynes, was a resounding yes.

"We must look for succour to the principle that prosperity is cumulative.[6] We have stuck in a rut. We need an impulse, a jolt, an acceleration," Keynes argued. He suggested as "the ultimate cure of unemployment" that £100 million be spent on public housing, better roads, and improvements to the electricity grid. He suggested that stimulating the economy would restore business confidence. "Let us experiment with boldness on such lines," he wrote, "even though some of the schemes may turn out to be failures, which is very likely."[7]

Keynes's carefree attitude to taxpayers' money was shocking, not least to the Labour chancellor, Philip Snowden, who outdid most Conservatives in his conservative views about how an economy should be administered. "It is no part of my job as Chancellor of the Exchequer to put before the House of Commons proposals for the expenditure of public money," he told his fellow members of Parliament. "The function of the Chancellor of the Exchequer, as I understand it, is to resist all demands for expenditure made by his colleagues and, when he can no longer resist, to limit the concession to the barest point of acceptance."[8] But Keynes was adamant that spending was essential and that waste was the lesser of evils. "With home investment, even if it be ill-advised or extravagantly carried out," he wrote, "at least the country has the improvement for what it is worth; the worst conceived and most extravagant housing scheme imaginable leaves us with some houses."[9]

Keynes returned to his radical theme in a second piece for *The Nation*. "In considering how to [stimulate investment at home]," he wrote, "we are brought to my heresy—if it is a heresy. I bring in the State; I abandon laissez-faire. . . . It entrusted the public weal to private enterprise unchecked and unaided. Private enterprise is no longer unchecked—it is checked and threatened in many different ways. . . . And if private enterprise is not unchecked, we cannot leave it unaided."[10]

Warming to his theme, Keynes was ready for the next step in his carefully moderated revolution in thinking: he suggested that laissez-faire was spurious, illogical, and had been overtaken by events. He floated this argument in his Sidney Ball Memorial Lecture at Oxford University, titled "The End of Laissez Faire," before taking it to the University of Berlin two years later, where he repeated it word for word for the benefit of the Germans—and German-speaking Austrians like Hayek. Keynes was in full Bloomsbury mode: smart, eloquent, sarcastic, radical, and debunking of the old order. By leading the intellectual assault on laissez-faire, Keynes moved far beyond the confines of economic theory, which was even less popularly understood then than it is today, to ideas about how to ensure that individuals enjoyed the maximum happiness.

Keynes began with a tour d'horizon of thinkers from the Age of Enlightenment to the present, taking in all those who had propounded laissez-faire as respectable, natural, just, and inevitable. He credited what he called "the Economists" for settling the competing arguments between "conservative individualists," such as John Locke,[11] David Hume,[12] and Edmund Burke,[13] and the "democratic egalitarians," Jean-Jacques Rousseau,[14] William Paley,[15] and Jeremy Bentham,[16] by contending that "by the working of natural laws individuals pursuing their own interests with enlightenment in conditions of freedom always tend to promote the general interest."[17] Or, put briefly, the public good was the sum of the individual self-interests of all individuals combined. It was the view expressed by the sociopath Bitzer in Charles Dickens's *Hard Times*: "I am sure you know that the whole social system is a question of self interest. What you must always appeal to is a person's self interest."[18] For Keynes, the result of relying on self-interest was the end of politics, for "the political philosopher could retire in favor of the business man—for the latter could attain the philosopher's summum bonum by just pursuing his own profit."

To these thinkers Keynes added Charles Darwin,[19] whose evolutionary theory of the survival of the fittest had been extended by some to explain economic behavior. While the Economists argued that free competition had built London, wrote Keynes, "the Darwinians could go one better than that—free competition had built Man." For those who claimed that the free market offered a just resolution of competing claims, Keynes spelled it out: "It is *not* true that individuals possess a prescriptive 'natural liberty' in their economic activities. There is *no* 'compact' conferring perpetual rights on those who Have or on those who Acquire. The world is *not* so governed from above that private and social interest always coincide. It is *not* so managed here below that in practice they coincide. It is *not* a correct deduction from the Principles of Economics that enlightened self interest always operates in the public interest. Nor is it true that self interest generally is enlightened; more often individuals acting separately to promote their own ends are too ignorant or too weak to attain even these. Experience does *not* show that individuals, when they make up a social unit, are always less clear sighted than when they act separately."[20]

Lest he be waylaid by accusations that he was a closet socialist,

Keynes took time to swipe at protectionism and Marxian socialism, the two major political traditions that opposed free-market solutions, and credited them with bolstering the very system they despised. While protectionism was plausible, though wrong, Keynes reserved most of his contempt for the Marxists. He wondered "how a doctrine so illogical and so dull can have exercised so powerful and enduring an influence over the minds of men."[21] Later he dismissed state socialism as "little better than a dusty survival of a plan to meet the problems of fifty years ago, based on a misunderstanding of what someone said a hundred years ago."[22] Keynes was at pains to make clear that, unlike Marxists and some socialists, he was not advocating that the state replace private enterprise. "The important thing for Government," he wrote, "is not to do things which individuals are doing already, and to do them a little better or a little worse, but to do those things which at present are not done at all."[23]

It is worth stressing, in the light of those who today persist in describing Keynes and the Keynesians as closet socialists, that while Hayek was for a time a social democrat, Keynes was never a socialist of any sort, nor did he even flirt with socialism, even in its anemic British version, Fabianism. Keynes was a long-standing member of the Liberals, who were in a battle for survival with Labour's social democrats. He believed in a "middle way" between capitalism and socialism, between conservatism and social democracy, and between what he believed to be the primitive dogmatisms of both sides. Inevitably, perhaps, he has been dismissed on one side as an apologist for capitalism who revived the fortunes of a failing system and on the other as a creeping socialist who behind his smooth talk quietly ushered Marxism in by the back door.

It is one of the less edifying aspects of the struggle of ideas between conservatives and liberals evoked by the controversy between Keynes and Hayek that political terms have often been wantonly misused to muddy the argument. For some, the dividing line between capitalism and socialism begins with government of any sort; for others, it starts with any social act, such as the kind deed of the Good Samaritan or even representative democracy. Keynes went out of his way in his Sidney Ball lecture to state that "for my part, I think that Capitalism, wisely managed, can probably be made more efficient for attaining economic ends than any alternative system yet in sight," although he conceded that "in itself [capitalism] is in many ways extremely objectionable." Or, as he wrote to Sir Charles Addis, a director of the Bank of England, "I seek to improve the machinery of society, not overturn it."[24]

In the lecture Keynes had, by his lights, slayed the dragon of laissez-faire, but he had not yet found a theoretical structure to put in its place. After a colorful diatribe, his conclusions were little more than thinking aloud. His alternative ideas were neither revolutionary nor alarming. He made the tentative suggestion that more should be done by non-state agencies that could provide more efficient and equitable results, such as universities and the Bank of England. For members of the Austrian School who read the Sidney Ball address, Keynes had defiled their guiding principle, that the free market was virtuous and that all attempts to tame it were either wicked or futile or both.

Although to some in government Keynes was little more than an irritating gadfly, ministers still turned to him for advice. When opinions were sought over whether the pound sterling should be fixed to the price of gold—"the gold standard"—at the prewar parity of $4.86, Keynes was in a small minority urging that it should not be fixed to gold at all. Then, when it became clear that that argument was lost, he suggested it be fixed at its current floating price of $4.44. In brief, amid a debate that saw Keynes duck and weave to find a compromise that would minimize the damage fixing the pound would inflict on the economy, he predicted that restoring the pound to its prewar parity would entail massive deflation (falling prices) and severely cutting the pay and living standards of key workers such as coal miners, whose product priced at the new level would not be internationally competitive.

In the general election of October 1924, the Conservatives brought to an end MacDonald's brief Labour government. In February 1925, the new Conservative chancellor, the former Liberal Winston Churchill, wrote a stinging memorandum to the financial controller at the Treasury, Otto Niemeyer. The maverick Churchill took pride in defying conventional views, and having read in *The Nation* Keynes's argument against a return to the prewar parity, he was persuaded that fixing the pound at $4.86 would further increase unemployment, which stood at over a million and rising. The corollary, the reduction of wages by between 10 and 12 percent to match the upward revaluation of the pound, was unlikely to occur, Keynes argued, because strong trade unions, such as the Miners' Federation, ensured that wage levels were "sticky," or slow to respond to other economic factors, and could not easily be cut.

"The Treasury have never, it seems to me, faced the profound significance of what Mister Keynes calls 'the paradox of unemployment amidst dearth,'" wrote Churchill to Niemeyer. "The Governor [of the Bank of England] allows himself to be perfectly happy in the spectacle of Britain possessing the finest credit in the world simultaneously with a million and a quarter unemployed."[25] The following month Churchill invited Keynes and leading lights of the financial world to dinner at his official residence at 11 Downing Street. Keynes and Reginald McKenna, the former wartime Liberal chancellor, argued that reducing wages by 10 percent would have to be imposed on the coal miners and that prolonged strikes and a contraction (slowing down of activity) in key industries would follow. Three days later, after persistent pressure from his more orthodox colleagues, Churchill abandoned his instinctive opposition to the Treasury view and agreed to restore fixing the pound sterling to the price of gold—"the gold standard"—at its prewar parity.

Churchill's decision led Keynes to write a series of articles for *The Nation* that were collected in a best-selling book, *The Economic Consequences of Mr. Churchill*, whose title echoed his *Economic*

Consequences of the Peace. Keynes argued that setting the value of the pound at 10 percent higher than the floating (or market) rate amounted to "a policy of reducing everyone's wages by two shillings [10 percent] in the pound."[26] As there was no mechanism to ensure that this would be imposed on workers across the board, those with weak bargaining power or timid trade unions would suffer disproportionately. The employers and government would find themselves "engaging in a struggle with each separate group in turn, with no prospect that the result will be fair, and no guarantee that the stronger groups will not gain at the expense of the weaker."[27]

Keynes suggested that raising the exchange rate was a brutal means of imposing deflation (a drop in prices). "Deflation does not reduce wages 'automatically,'" he wrote. "It reduces them by causing unemployment. The proper object of dear money is to check an incipient boom. Woe to those whose faith leads them to use it to aggravate a depression."[28] Keynes was solidly on the side of the miners, whom, he wrote, "are to be offered a choice between starvation and submission, the fruits of their submission to accrue to the benefit of other classes. . . . On grounds of social justice no case can be made out for reducing the wages of the miners. They are the victims of the economic juggernaut."[29] He warned that Churchill's decision would ignite revolutionary sentiments among workers.

Keynes predicted that to avoid the catastrophic social consequences of its decision to keep the pound at its prewar price, the government would have to borrow its way out of trouble, and he was soon proved right. When, in June, mine owners sent an ultimatum to the miners' union to accept a reduction in wages or face the consequences, and the union threatened a national strike, the prime minister, Stanley Baldwin, promptly offered the owners a loan of £10 million to continue paying their miners at the old and uncompetitive rate in the world market rather than face industrial mayhem.

Before long it became clear that the return to the gold standard was proving ruinous to the British economy. Few economic historians today consider the decision anything but disastrous. It was the first in a succession of events that would bring capitalism to the brink: the year 1926 saw Britain's first general strike; the Conservatives lost the general election of June 1929 and Labour was returned to power as the largest party in the House of Commons; the American stock market crash of October 1929 sparked a worldwide financial trauma; the financial crisis prompted the formation in August 1931 of an emergency coalition National Government in Britain; and the following month, after just six punishing years, the pound sterling was unhitched from the gold standard.

In 1926, Mises was offered a Rockefeller award to visit America and accepted. In the margins of a busy speaking schedule, he explored the methods used in the American empirical studies of the economy that had so intrigued Hayek. He returned to Vienna believing that so long as the methodology was carefully scrutinized and selectively applied, a quantitative study of the business cycle, the phenomenon whereby economic booms (periods of fast economic growth) were followed by slumps (periods of contracting economic activity), might prove worthwhile. Mises set about raising funds for the new Austrian Institute for Business Cycle Research and did not have to look beyond his own seminar room to find a director. The obvious person was Hayek, and on January 1, 1927, the new body began work, with Hayek at its head.

One of Hayek's first acts in his new role was to write to Keynes asking for a copy of Edgeworth's *Mathematical Psychics*. That Hayek should ask Keynes for a copy seems less an innocent inquiry than a purposeful attempt to snag Keynes's attention, an audacious act of homage rather than a challenge. Keynes's brief response on a postcard, albeit handwritten, must have seemed something of a disappointment. The layer of irony implicit in Keynes's reply—"I am sorry to say that my stock of 'Mathematical Psychics' is exhausted"—did not prove a deterrent to Hayek, though from his reply it is clear that Keynes had no idea who Hayek was. Hayek knew Keynes well from *The Economic*

Consequences of the Peace and had certainly read Keynes's *Tract on Monetary Reform* and found little with which to disagree. It is not known whether Mises and Hayek had read Keynes's assaults on the free market, such as his Sidney Ball lecture that directly contradicted their core beliefs. Keynes's repeated pleas for the British government to reduce interest rates and invest in public works, which ran directly counter to Austrian School economics, were conducted in English publications that seldom reached Vienna.

Hayek began to build on Mises's work and started to delineate the relationship between money, prices, and unemployment. In his exploration of the working of the American Federal Reserve,[30] Hayek noted that there were some in the Fed who hoped to iron out the recurring booms and busts of business cycles. He concluded that while there might be ways of reducing to a small extent the wildest fluctuations of the cycle, the goal of ridding America of the business cycle was a fool's errand.

In their effort to keep consumer prices stable, the Federal Reserve governors increased interest rates and sold government bonds, a remedy that Keynes had advocated in the *Tract*. But, Hayek argued, the consumer price index that inspired their actions was a blunt instrument that revealed little about the fluctuations of prices in individual commodities. It was therefore a misleading indicator by which to adjust general interest rates. He found that to pin interest rate and monetary policy on such a broad and inaccurate index would as likely exacerbate as cure the problem the Fed set out to solve. He concluded, "An index of the general price level cannot yield any relevant information as to the course of the cycle, nor more importantly can it do so at the right time."[31]

It was Keynes's contention that at the bottom of the economic cycle a chronic shortage of demand caused a slowing of economic activity, which resulted in unnecessary unemployment. He argued that in the absence of private enterprise ensuring adequate demand, governments should provide demand of their own through public works. (He had yet to concoct an intellectual justification for why this was so.) Mises, however, expanding theories postulated by the Swedish economist Knut Wicksell,[32] approached intervention in the business cycle in a different way. He contended that when a central bank reduced interest rates, it interfered with the natural equilibrium between individuals' savings and the investment in capital goods (machinery used to make products). More capital goods were bought with the cheaper money than could be sustained by the genuine level of saving, which led to a disequilibrium. Over time, the central bank was left with a dilemma: either continue reducing interest rates to provide even more investment, which again would pump too much money into a system chasing too few goods, provoking inflation; or increase interest rates, which caused investment to slow then shudder to a halt, bringing about a worse slump than the one the central bank was attempting to avoid in the first place.

Hayek took Mises's analysis one step further by examining what exactly happens when cheap money is used to invest in capital goods. He believed that by deliberately lowering interest rates and providing money for investment that was out of kilter with savings, the "period of production" (the length of time needed to produce goods) was unnaturally extended. The period of production was so long, in fact, that a good deal of the development of capital goods, in particular "goods of a higher order" (machinery making goods that are furthest away from goods that consumers buy) would have to be abandoned as there was no demand (desire by customers to buy them) by the time they were completed. For instance, a factory making the ice trays for commercial refrigerators might go out of business when there was a slump in demand for ice cream.

The nub of the issue, according to Hayek, was that by reducing interest rates, the central bank interfered in the relationship between savings and investment. He and the Austrian School believed that all markets over time, including the market in money, would reach a state of equilibrium where the supply of goods from manufacturers and demand came to be matched. Hayek suggested that the price mechanism reflected the tendency toward equilibrium and that any attempt to artificially alter prices would have dire consequences. In his view, to tamper with prices was merely to tinker with the symptoms of the shift toward equilibrium. To artificially reduce interest rates, or the price of borrowing money, merely led to price inflation, while raising interest rates artificially meant encouraging a contraction of business activity (a slump).

Behind these thoughts were Wicksell's postulations on the difference between the "natural interest rate," where personal savings equal investment, and the "market rate of interest," or the price of credit fixed by banks. For members of the Austrian School, the business cycle was thought to be set in motion by the difference between the natural and the market rate of interest. The problem for central bankers was that it was impossible to determine exactly what the natural interest rate was, so they inevitably set the market rate of interest at an inappropriate level, thereby setting off the booms and busts of the business cycle. Hayek believed that by staying true to the natural interest rate, money in an economy could be made "neutral" and that fluctuations of the business cycle in those circumstances would be caused by changes in other factors, such as the development of new products and new discoveries.

The battle lines between Keynes and Hayek were thus drawn. Keynes believed it was a government's duty to do what it could to make life easier, particularly for the unemployed. Hayek believed it was futile for governments to interfere with forces that were, in their own way, as immutable as natural forces. Keynes rejected adherence to the free market as an inappropriate application of Darwinism to economic activities and argued that a better understanding of the workings of an economy would allow responsible governments to make decisions that could iron out the worst effects of the bottom of the business cycle. Hayek eventually came to the conclusion that knowledge about how exactly an economy worked was difficult if not impossible to discover and that attempts to form economic policy based on such evidence were, like a barber practicing primitive surgery, likely to do more harm than good.

Keynes believed that man had been placed in charge of his own destiny, while Hayek, with some reluctance, believed that man was destined to live by the natural laws of economics as he was obliged to live by all other natural laws. Thus the two men came to represent two alternative views of life and government, Keynes adopting an optimistic view that life need not be as hard as it was if only those in positions of power made the right decisions, and Hayek subscribing to the pessimistic notion that there were strict limits placed on human endeavor and that attempts to alter the laws of nature, however well intended, were bound to lead at best to unintended consequences.

As the world headed toward the epochal year of 1929, the two men were well advanced toward honing their competing views. Thus far, Keynes's leaps of imagination had largely been met with incomprehension, but with little articulated opposition. Those who rejected his prescriptions did not mount an intellectual challenge to his ideas but instead clung to orthodox certainties and sheltered behind institutional inertia. Hayek largely worked with existing notions, and his contribution to refining the Austrian School theory of capital went mostly unnoticed outside of a small circle in Vienna. As in Aesop's moral fable of the hare and the tortoise, the energetic Keynes had set off at a sprint, with Hayek left at the starting line.

The American stock market crash of October 1929 was to change everything. As the world was hurled into financial turmoil, rulers and the governed alike demanded an explanation for what was happening and a fast route out of the mess. The hedonistic Roaring Twenties had careered into a slump and fallen headlong into what was to be a long decade of depression. The world was on the brink of ruin, with no end in sight to the twin afflictions of mass unemployment and grinding poverty. In the terrible new climate of hopelessness and despair, Keynes, the optimist, was at hand to offer a novel and clear way out of the mire, while Hayek, the pessimist, was to provide a rationale for why all attempts to fix the system were pointless.

Keynes found his ideas widely welcomed as he offered a glimmer of hope amid the gloom. Hayek would soon discover that his grim assessment, however accurate, would find few enthusiasts, for he brought a sobering message that excused unglamorous inaction. The Keynesian Revolution was about to take off amid the uncertainty and horror of the Age of Dictators, and no amount of pessimism, however logical, would dampen the clamor for politicians to find a way out of the economic morass. Before long the profound intellectual differences between Keynes and Hayek would become widely evident as the two men came to challenge each other at close quarters.

FOUR

Stanley and Livingstone

Keynes and Hayek Meet for the First Time, 1928–30

Hayek's brief journey to study economic thought in America confirmed that the home of unbridled capitalism wasn't where the future of economics was being debated. For that, Hayek found he would have to travel to Britain. Toward that end, in 1927 he wrote to Keynes, then set about finding a way to introduce himself in person. An opportunity arose in 1928[1] when Hayek was invited to a meeting of the London and Cambridge Economic Service,[2] founded five years earlier by Keynes as a joint venture between the London School of Economics (LSE) and Cambridge University. At the end of one of the sessions, the two men met for the first time.

The scene must have seemed comic to a bystander. Both men were over six feet tall, with Keynes having the slight edge, taking into account his stoop, which gave him a distinct advantage when browbeating an opponent. Both men sported full moustaches, with Hayek donning the sort of wire-framed spectacles that the British associated with middle-European intellectuals. Keynes wore dishevelled three-piece chalk-striped suits with a certain scruffy élan, his hands plunged into his coat pockets, while Hayek's stiff white collar and tweed jacket buttoned tightly down the front reflected his tidy, meticulous mind.

There were other clues to their contrasting personalities. Keynes disguised the sharpness of his tongue with a mellifluous voice that tended to first charm then hypnotize his rivals, while Hayek spoke English poorly, with a strong clipped Austrian accent that even Keynes, who as a child was brought up by a string of German governesses, must have found hard to decipher. Hayek's ultra-formality was immediately evident. "I can still see the door of my room opening to admit the tall, powerful, reserved figure which announced itself quietly and firmly as 'Hayek,'" recalled the young professor of economics at the London School of Economics Lionel Robbins,[3] of his first sight of Hayek.

Keynes and Hayek met as total strangers, though within seconds they had dispensed with formalities and were wrapped in heated debate. For Hayek the meeting was momentous, a fulfillment of a long-held ambition. For Keynes it was a routine scuffle, just another scrape with a misguided disciple of the free market. In terms of the history of economic ideas, however, it was as important as the meeting between Henry Stanley and David Livingstone. It was the first bout, albeit an exercise in shadow boxing, in a battle between titans that would last into the next century.

Hayek vividly recalled the encounter as a first taste of Keynes in unforgiving mode and as a fitting introduction to the intensity of the battle to come. "We at once had our first theoretical clash—on some issue of the effectiveness of changes in the rate of interest," he recalled. "Though in such debates Keynes would at first try ruthlessly to steamroller an objection in a manner somewhat intimidating to a younger man, if one stood up to him on such occasions he would develop a most friendly interest even if he strongly disagreed with one's views."[4] From the start of their prickly friendship, which lasted until Keynes died twenty years later, Hayek sensed that Keynes, though disagreeing with his Austrian School views, was interested in what he had to say. "The moment I stood up with serious arguments, he took me seriously and ever since respected me," remembered Hayek. "I know his general way of talking about me. 'Of course he is crazy, but his ideas are also rather interesting.'"[5]

Hayek found a friend in London: Robbins, who, rare among British economists of the time, read German and had explored the works of European economists, including Mises, the Swede Knut Wicksell, and the Austrian Eugen von Böhm-Bawerk.[6] Vigorous and ambitious, Robbins was elevated by the director of the LSE, William Beveridge,[7] to the chair of political economy in 1929 at the age of thirty-one, becoming "the youngest Professor in the country."[8] On his appointment, Robbins determined that the LSE should counter Cambridge, the home of Marshall and Keynes, as the fount of wisdom in British economic theory by presenting the full repertoire of European thinking. Hayek, too, had high hopes. He intended to work in London for a number of years as part of a grand plan that would lead to the top.

Hayek told his wife "half jokingly"[9] of his ambition to climb to the summit of Austrian society. He would first teach economics in London for a time before returning to teach in Vienna. Then, as his reputation grew, he hoped to be appointed president of the Nationalbank, the Austrian central bank. In his dotage he would return to London as Austria's ambassador. As he recalled, with the lack of modesty and self-awareness that was key to his personality, it was "by no means an unreasonable aspiration and would have given me that sort of life on the borderline of purely academic and public work which probably, in the later part of my life, I should have found most satisfactory."[10] By becoming known in London, Hayek took the first step of his elaborate life program.

Robbins, a former socialist labor organizer, was attracted to Hayek through his essay "The 'Paradox' of Saving,"[11] which sought to disprove the direct relationship between savings and demand, the amount saved by individuals and their desire to spend on goods, postulated by the American economists Waddill Catchings and William Trufant

Foster.[12] The pair had, like Keynes, proposed public works to promote demand in an economy during a recession, what Hayek called "the employment function," the direct correlation between employment and aggregate demand (the total amount of goods that customers want to buy in an economy). In their 1926 paper "The Dilemma of Thrift,"[13] Foster and Catchings contended that recessions were caused by a lack of demand for goods and services resulting from too much savings. They asserted that slumps came about when individuals chose to save rather than spend, leaving unbought the additional goods produced as a result of their savings being invested in capital goods. Hence, they argued, too much saving at the top of the business cycle led to a glut of unsold goods at the bottom.

They advocated a "Federal Budget Board" to invest in public works, on borrowed money if necessary, to provoke demand, thus providing consumers with money to buy the surfeit of goods produced in a slump. Hayek bemoaned the fact that the pair had persuaded Herbert Hoover,[14] President Warren G. Harding's conservative commerce secretary, to encourage federal agencies to spend taxpayers' money on creating jobs.[15]

Hayek's "'Paradox' of Saving" was an attempt to put Foster and Catchings straight. He argued that the pair's contention was based on a misconception: they had misunderstood the role capital plays in the productive process. In a real economy, savings are not available to invest in new production unless there are good reasons to believe that the new products made available by the new investment will find a ready sale. The circumstance in which consumers' savings were invested in making unwanted goods, rather than used to buy goods, therefore did not apply.

Hayek argued that production was not a single process with a single end product and price. There were likely to be economies of scale in any production spurred by new investment that would reduce the price of goods, making them affordable, so there would be no glut. Hayek recalled that Böhm-Bawerk had shown that the stages of capital production were many and of varying length, what Böhm-Bawerk had termed "roundabout" production. Beyond factories making goods were factories making elements that were assembled to make goods, and machine tool factories that made machines that made goods, or parts of goods. At each stage of the roundabout process investors were rewarded so that, contrary to Foster and Catchings's contention, they had enough money to pay for the goods resulting from the final stage of production.

Hayek conceded that "if administered with extraordinary caution and superhuman ability," the plan to have a government infuse money into the system to provoke demand "could . . . perhaps, be made to prevent crises."[16] But more likely, "in the long run" such manipulation of the economy "would bring about grave disturbances and the disorganization of the economic system as a whole."[17] He concluded that "the whole expediency of such attempts to alleviate unemployment by relief works and so on is in the light of this analysis highly questionable."[18]

At the time Hayek and Keynes first met and argued, "The 'Paradox' of Saving" was available in German only, in a small-run edition of a Viennese economics journal, and Keynes may be excused for not having read it. Even if Keynes had been given an English translation, it is not certain he would have gleaned too much from Hayek's counterargument. Closely reasoned in dense prose, with long Germanic sentences containing subsidiary clause upon subsidiary clause, "The 'Paradox'" is not an easy read. It contains numerous equations and charts to demonstrate that the stages of production involved in making a consumer good add incrementally to the final cost. Hayek takes for granted Böhm-Bawerk's lessons and chides those who have not made themselves familiar with the Austrian School master's works, even though, by Hayek's admission, only one, the first edition of Böhm-Bawerk's *Positive Theory of Capital*, was available in English, published in London forty years earlier.

Robbins had not only read Böhm-Bawerk in German but also

greatly enjoyed the skill with which Hayek had argued his corner in "The 'Paradox.'" On the strength of what he considered Hayek's convincing demolition of the "employment function," the concept that underpinned Keynes's thinking, Robbins invited Hayek to give four lectures at the LSE in February 1931. Hayek was aware of why he had been invited. "[Robbins] pounced on my subject: This is the thing we need at the moment, to fight Keynes,"[19] he recalled Robbins saying. "The 'Paradox'" was translated into English and published in the May 1931 edition of *Economica*,[20] the LSE journal that Robbins edited. By introducing Hayek into Britain, Robbins instigated the great debate between Hayek and Keynes.

The question arises why Robbins did not invite Mises to counter Keynes. Mises was more distinguished than Hayek and had already established a formidable body of work that challenged many of Keynes's contentions. Two factors appeared to have played their part. To be effective in countering Keynes, Robbins needed someone who could be readily understood. Mises's English was fractured and his Austrian accent was so heavy he found it hard to make himself understood. "He certainly was not at ease in French or English," explained his biographer Jörg Guido Hülsmann. "When he gave talks in foreign languages, his wit abandoned him."[21] In contrast, Hayek's short sojourn in New York had equipped him with rudimentary spoken English, albeit of a fractured nature.

Hayek's comparative youth was also a contributing factor. Robbins was young and perhaps felt more comfortable working with someone of a similar age. Mises was not only older but also set in his ways. He had a well-deserved reputation for being taciturn and ill-tempered. Even his wife, Margit, could not disguise her husband's recurring dark moods. "The one thing about [Mises] that was as astonishing as it was frightening was his temper," she recalled. "Occasionally he showed terrible outbursts of tantrums. . . . These terrible attacks were really a sign of depression."[22] Mises was also deeply impractical. According to Margit, "He did not even know how to boil an egg."[23] So Hayek, an even-tempered and rational individual as far as Robbins could judge, seemed the ideal choice. In "The 'Paradox,'" Hayek had a set of arguments that would immediately set him in opposition to the Keynesian infection Robbins saw spreading from Cambridge.

Between Hayek's first meeting with Keynes in London in 1928 and his arrival to deliver his four lectures in February 1931, a cataclysmic event took place that would completely change the stakes of their impending debate. The Wall Street stock market crash of October 1929 was an unprecedented economic disaster. The scale of the horror unleashed by the subsequent collapse of the American economy was to provoke a line of practical questions to economists. What caused the crash? What lessons can be learned to prevent it from happening again? And what can be done to alleviate the misery of unemployment unleashed by the catastrophe?

It was not at all obvious at the time how far the effects of the crash would spread to the rest of the world economy or what the political ramifications of the disaster would be. In the months and years ahead, however, Keynes would find himself well placed to advance his radical views, for not only was he concerned with promoting pro-employment policies through his journalistic and political activities, but his theories appeared to provide an intellectual justification for attempting to create jobs through public works. Hayek's rejection of Keynes's theories, and by association his rejection of the most common prescriptions for job creation, were to seem increasingly out of touch with public sentiment as the crash turned to depression and unemployment on both sides of the Atlantic began to mount.

Keynes perhaps knew better than Hayek the personal impact of the crash, for he was a daily speculator on the commodities and currency markets. Most mornings he remained in bed until noon, giving directions to his broker on the telephone. His financial acuity ensured that his Bloomsbury friends' meager trust funds earned enough for them to pursue their artistic endeavors without worrying about having to earn a living. Though Keynes owned no American shares, he was caught by the speed of the market collapse. The fortune he had amassed by market speculation was wiped out by the crash. (By playing the market he soon made a second fortune, as large as the first.) But if Keynes had failed to foresee the impending disaster, his theories seemed to snugly fit the new circumstances.

No sooner had he published his *Tract on Monetary Reform* in 1924 than he began writing *A Treatise on Money*. It was to be an epic venture. *The Economic Consequences of the Peace* took weeks to write; *A Treatise* took six years and two months, partly because he was distracted by British political controversies, such as his efforts on behalf of the Liberals in the general election of 1929, partly by his involvement in the affairs of King's College, and partly by the myriad other activities that claimed his attention. From 1925 on, his life became even more complicated when, after living half of his life as a homosexual, he married Lydia Lopokova, a boyish ballerina in Sergei Diaghilev's Ballets Russes, who was nine years his junior.

Keynes's marriage to Lydia upset the Bloomsburys, particularly the Woolfs, who thought her skittish mind and hilarious malaproprisms made her an unsuitable partner for their cerebral and homosexual friend. But Lydia was no beard; Keynes had fallen head over heels in love. He continued dividing his time between Cambridge, London, and his farmhouse at Tilton[24] in the Sussex Downs, where Lydia mostly lived. He wrote long letters to her most days, leaving a rich cache of intimate, unabashed, and sexually explicit correspondence[25] that was matched by the couple's passionate, adventurous, and uninhibited love life. The couple dearly hoped to have children, though after a while it became clear that Lydia was infertile. To save his wife embarrassment, Keynes held himself responsible and hid his disappointment behind black humor. Eventually ennobled as "Lord Keynes of Tilton," he used to refer to himself as "Barren Keynes."

Despite the many diversions, Keynes was determined to consolidate his most recent thoughts. But spreading the writing of *A Treatise* over nearly seven years took its toll on the coherence of the final work. He repeatedly revised the manuscript to account for his ever-changing thoughts, and more than once he abandoned whole chapters in the light of new inspiration. As late as August 1929, with publication set for the fall of 1930, Keynes wrote to his publisher, Daniel Macmillan, "I am ashamed to say that after I had got more than 440 pages into paged revise I had to come to the conclusion that certain chapters must be drastically rewritten, and the whole very considerably rearranged."[26]

As a result the book is a complex interweaving of disparate ideas into a not entirely convincing whole. "The book could not give a whole picture of his thought, but only a cross-section of it,"[27] observed Keynes's friend and biographer Roy Harrod. On the eve of publication, Keynes wrote to his parents, "Artistically it is a failure—I have changed my mind too much during the course of writing it for it to be a proper unity."[28] In the preface, Keynes acknowledged that "it represents a collection of material rather than a finished work."[29] Notwithstanding his reservations, *A Treatise* was published, in two large volumes, in December 1930.

One of the book's central themes, and one he believed added a novel dimension to the way an economy should be understood, was to draw a clear distinction between savings and investment (or capital outlay). Up to that point economists had assumed that over time savings and investment were of equal value. But Keynes suggested that because one group of people saved and quite another invested, an imbalance tended to occur. When the amount invested was larger than the amount saved, the result was a boom accompanied by price inflation. Conversely, when savings ran ahead of investment, a state of depression occurred, accompanied by deflation and unemployment. He reasoned that total income in an economy stemmed from the sale of both consumer goods and capital goods. If there were no savings and total income was instead spent on consumer goods, the price of those goods would sharply rise and there would be a boom. Conversely, if all income were saved, the price of consumer goods would fall and industries would fail.

The corollary of Keynes's argument had important implications for the attempt to manage the business cycle, for Keynes argued that if his contentions were correct, price inflation could be curtailed by increasing savings and a depression might be cured by increasing investment. Keynes suggested that the cause of the alternate booms and busts of the business cycle was the action of the banks, which also held the cure. "It is the machinery of banking which makes this [imbalance] possible,"[30] Keynes wrote, for banks created credit irrespective of a community's desire or ability to save. Banks did not base lending decisions on the level of savings they had in their coffers; "their main criterion of how much to lend is a totally different one,—namely the proportion of their cash reserves to their money liabilities."[31] The level of savings and investment could be brought into line if a central bank were to carefully control the amount of credit it offered. The result would be stable prices. Like Wicksell, Keynes differentiated between a "natural rate of interest," in which savings and investment were the same and prices remained stable, and a "market rate of interest," what the banks charged for their own ends.[32]

Throughout *A Treatise*, Keynes assumed that a state of equilibrium would be reached where savings and investment were equal and prices were stable, whatever the interest rate set by the central bank, and at that time there would be full employment. His view was that "monetary theory, when all is said and done, is little more than a vast elaboration of the truth that 'it all comes out in the wash.'"[33]

Keynes also returned to the thorny problem of fixed exchange rates and the role they played in promoting the booms and busts of the business cycle. He suggested that as long as the gold standard persisted, central banks would not be able to manage credit so that savings and investment were kept equal, as they would instead be using interest rate policy to maintain the currency at the fixed rate. He had fought fiercely to deter the British government from pegging the pound sterling at the prewar rate of $4.86. Once that battle was lost, however, Keynes readjusted his thoughts to accommodate the new conditions and concluded that there was some virtue in harnessing all currencies to a single common measure, such as gold, once the turbulence in the world economy caused by World War I had passed.

In *A Treatise* he went one stage further, proposing the formation of a new mechanism to link currencies together, a "Supra-national Central Bank," a notion that would come to fruition in the Bretton Woods fixed-currency exchange agreement of 1944. Instead of fixing currencies to the price of gold, which Keynes argued was in reality little more than fixing them to the dollar, he proposed in *A Treatise* that it would be more equitable if currencies were aligned to a basket of sixty key internationally traded commodities and allowed to float annually up to 2 percent either side of their pegged value. Even then he predicted that some countries would find it difficult to stick to their new fixed parity if their populations were suffering from "severe unemployment."[34] In this "special case," he argued, "it is not sufficient for the Central Authority to stand ready to lend. . . . [T]he Government must itself promote a programme of domestic investment [public works]."[35]

It was the ideas on display in *A Treatise* that Keynes channeled into Liberal policy ahead of the general election of June 1929. And it was in his political utterances at that time that the clearest picture of what would become the "Keynesian Revolution" can be seen taking shape. The Liberals had put their faith in the wily Welshman Lloyd George, whose cynical behavior at the Paris peace talks had appalled Keynes. But Keynes reluctantly concluded that Lloyd George was the Liberals' best hope, and he threw his weight behind formulating economic policies with which to entice the electorate, chief among them a pledge to put the country back to work. By the year of the election, 1929, unemployment in Britain had reached 1.34 million. At least one in ten Britons had been out of work for more than eight years, except for during a short period of recovery in 1924.

In March 1928, Keynes unveiled his new ideas at the National Liberal Federation. "Let us be up and doing, using our idle resources to increase our wealth. With men and plant unemployed, it is ridiculous to say that we cannot afford new developments. It is precisely with these plants and these men that we shall afford them,"[36] he said. In July, Keynes wrote a powerful plea for the job-creating policies he fashioned for Lloyd George. "When we have unemployed men and unemployed plant and more savings than we are using at home, it is utterly imbecile to say that we cannot afford these things. For it is with the unemployed men and the unemployed plant, and with nothing else, that these things are done,"[37] he wrote.

The following March, Keynes ridiculed the Treasury for suggesting that nothing could be done to cure unemployment. "They have believed that, if people can be induced to save as much as possible, and if steps are then taken to prevent anything being done with these savings, the rate of interest will fall," he wrote. "Indeed, if all forms of capital enterprise were to be rendered illegal, the rate of interest would sink towards zero—while the rate of unemployment would mount towards heaven."[38] As he would argue in *A Treatise*, by being tied to an inappropriate dollar/sterling price since 1925, Britain had become a "special case" where the full employment equilibrium remained elusive. Only public works, Keynes argued, could jolt the sluggish economy back to life. In the pamphlet "Can Lloyd George Do It?" Keynes put his contention simply: "There is work to do; there are men to do it. Why not bring them together?"[39]

Keynes costed his employment program in the face of Conservative jeers that the money would be wasted. He argued that, on the contrary, it was by not taking action that the nation's resources were wasted. Unemployment benefits were already costing taxpayers £50 million annually, not counting poor relief. In the previous eight years the unemployed had been paid a total of £500 million to do nothing. It was a staggering squandering of resources. Such a vast sum could have built a million new homes, or renewed a third of Britain's roads, or provided every third family with a free car, or could have set up a trust fund large enough to allow free entry to movie theaters for everyone in Britain until the end of time.[40] "But this is not nearly all the waste," he wrote. "There is the far greater loss to the unemployed themselves, represented by the differences between the dole and a full working wage, and by the loss of strength and morale. There is the loss in profits to employers and in taxation to the Chancellor of the Exchequer. There is the invaluable loss of retarding for a decade the economic progress of the whole country."[41]

The program he was proposing would cost £100 million a year. The Conservatives claimed this would produce only two thousand new jobs a year, but, Keynes argued, they were ignoring not only the savings in unemployment pay and foreign borrowing but also what he would come to term the "multiplier effect": every job created by the government would add a further job to supply that new worker with goods. "The greater trade activity would make for further trade activity; for the forces of prosperity, like those of a trade depression, work with a cumulative effect,"[42] he declared.

As election day approached, Keynes believed the Liberals would win. But it was not to be. Although the Conservatives won the most votes, taking 38 percent, winning 260 seats, the vagaries of the electoral system ensured that Labour won most seats in the new House of Commons, 287, with a slightly smaller proportion of the votes, 37 percent. The Liberals, winning 23 percent of the vote, could muster only 59 members. Although deprived of an overall majority, Ramsay MacDonald formed a minority government, depending for survival in a vote of confidence on Liberal support. Keynes was in great demand from the new government and was appointed, in the month following the Wall Street crash, to the Macmillan Committee on Finance and Industry to examine the relationship between the banking sector and the wider economy.

This marked the end of Keynes's long dalliance with the Liberals. Keynes, ever the pragmatist, now directed his energies toward persuading the new government to accept his prescriptions. MacDonald invited him to lunch three times between November and December 1929 to ask for advice, and appointed Keynes to his Economic Advisory Council. But it soon dawned on Keynes that the timorous MacDonald, for all his radical credentials, was no progressive and in many respects was far less "socialist" than he was.

Keynes provided the Macmillan Committee with a bravura performance at which he expostulated at length, and with extraordinary eloquence, his complex theories in language the layman could understand. The chairman, Lord Macmillan, a passionless judge, was so enamored with Keynes's hypnotic daily lectures that he told him, "We hardly notice the lapse of time when you are speaking."[43] For those who find the ideas in A Treatise hard to grasp, Keynes's exposition of them in plain language makes for hugely enjoyable reading, not least when he explains the effects of a disparity between savings and investment by invoking the workings of an imaginary banana republic.[44] Along with the principles established in A Treatise, Keynes described his views on a number of elements in the economy that would become important in advancing the Keynesian Revolution and would define the difference between his ideas and those of the Austrian School in the impending duel with Hayek.

His chief contribution to the hearings was to explain the role the bank rate, the interest rate fixed by the Bank of England, played in managing the economy. On the first day he described why the imposition of high interest rates leads to a contraction (reduction) in investment and a fall in prices, while a reduction in rates provides the circumstances for a boom. While this arrangement worked in the long term when there was a favorable trade balance and prices and costs could rise over time, it was catastrophic when a downward adjustment of costs was necessary. As Harrod explained, Keynes stressed that "it was important for [the committee] to understand that the mechanism on which we had come to place our exclusive reliance could only produce a downward adjustment through severe unemployment leading to cuts in money wages."[45]

Keynes declared that savings and investment were out of kilter, and acknowledged that monetary pressures, in the form of high interest rates leading to an increase in the cost of borrowing to businesses, could only put downward pressure on profits and costs, such as wages. The result was unemployment. One problem in Britain in the 1920s, however, was that because of collective bargaining by trade unions, wages were "sticky" and could not be easily cut. In fact, because of a reduction in the length of the working week and the maintenance of wages due to trade union demands, wages had actually increased. Keynes warned the committee that "there has never been in modern or ancient history a community that has been prepared to accept without immense struggle a reduction in the general level of money income."[46]

Though he denied to the committee that unemployment benefits had contributed to the "stickiness" in wage rates, likening the suggestion to those who blamed the provision of hospitals for encouraging ill health, in a radio broadcast he conceded that benefits for the unemployed had indeed added to the resistance of workers to countenance a reduction in wages. "The existence of the dole undoubtedly diminishes the pressure on the individual man to accept a rate of wages or a kind of employment which is not just what he wants or what he is used to,"[47] he said. Be that as it may, his suggested remedy for reducing wages to a level the country could afford was a government-administered incomes policy, what he called "an agreed reduction of the level of money incomes." He stressed that the reduction would have to apply to all sections of the community equally, not simply wage earners in the Industrial sector, and the result of the "social contract" would be a reduction in prices. Though it was "in some respects the ideal remedy,"[48] he conceded that such a policy was probably impossible to implement. To increase employment he urged public spending on roads and the telephone system. The Treasury's objection to increased government expenditure was shortsighted, he argued. "We get into a vicious circle. We do nothing because we have not the money. But it is precisely because we do not do anything that we have not the money."[49]

The Treasury spokesman who testified before the committee, Sir Richard Hopkins, whom Robbins described as "diminutive in stature, with a general appearance rather like that of an extremely intelligent monkey,"[50] did well to resist Keynes's argument for public works to create jobs. He believed that unprofitable investments would undermine the attraction of foreign investments in British companies, leading also to a drifting of British capital abroad; that directing funds into certain industries would dislocate the labor market, removing workers from more productive and profitable enterprises into comparatively worthless public projects; and that there was a limited amount of capital—if the government raised capital for its programs it would deprive private industry of the capital it needed. Keynes's response was that the reduction in unemployment payments and business losses resulting from a return to full employment would more than make up for such factors.

It was not only Keynes's persistent demands for government intervention that offended the Treasury, the Bank of England, and those who subscribed to the ideas of the Austrian School. Just as offensive was Keynes's assault on free trade and, after an anguished internal debate, his advocacy of import tariffs. In his Macmillan Committee evidence, Keynes rejected import duties as tantamount to taking drugs—once imposed they were hard to do without—yet, in his report to the prime minister's Economic Advisory Council, he advocated import levies—and export credits—as the only policy palatable to the general population. Keynes was adamant, however, that Britain and the world were in such dire straits that dire measures, such as imposing trade tariffs, had to be taken. "Free traders may, consistently with their faith, regard a revenue tariff as our iron ration, which can be used once only in an emergency," he wrote in March 1931. "The emergency has arrived."[51]

Keynes's change of heart over "revenue tariffs" was the main reason for his profound disagreement with the free-trader Robbins, whom he had personally appointed to the Economic Advisory

Council's Committee on Economic Outlook. Why Keynes offered Robbins such a position is hard to fathom as it was inevitable that they would soon disagree. Keynes's biographer Robert Skidelsky suggests that Robbins "alone had the intellectual conviction to resist Keynes's consensual embrace. Perhaps Keynes did not realise the strength of Robbins's free market convictions when he suggested him; or perhaps he simply overestimated his own powers of persuasion."[52]

Either way, the two men clashed in the Macmillan Committee in the most abrasive fashion. Both had quick tempers, and to the consternation of the other members, both were prepared to lose them. Until his encounter with Robbins, Keynes merely had to endure the hidebound conservatism and lack of imagination of the Treasury and Bank of England officials. With Robbins he was obliged to confront a form of nemesis, a young combatant with a brilliant mind who had ignored the radical ideas emanating from Cambridge in favor of the notions of the Austrian School. Robbins's answer to all of Keynes's putative remedies was to let the market run its course, however punishing it was to British industry, British employers, British enterprise, and British workers. If, as Keynes continually insisted, the British economy was in disequilibrium, then it should be allowed to right itself over time. All of Keynes's prescriptions would merely delay the inevitable, making matters worse and perpetuating the misery. As Harrod described it, Robbins "saw in [Keynes's tariff] proposals a turning away from the ancient traditions which made Britain great, and a devastating blow at the all-too-tender plant of internationalism. . . . He felt he must devote the whole of his strength to resisting it."[53]

Keynes, meanwhile, met Robbins's free-market solutions with ridicule: "A point may come . . . if we stick to laissez-faire [the free market] long enough, when we shall grow our own vines. Provided there is a residue of British exports (e.g. peers and old masters) which America is glad to have, and we can reduce our necessary imports plus our surplus savings to equality with this residue, equilibrium will be restored." He went on, "If you can't grin and bear it, and are prepared to have some abandonment of laissez-faire by tariffs, import prohibitions, subsidies, government investment and deterrents to foreign lending, then you can hope to get straight sooner. . . . You may, moreover, have avoided a social catastrophe."[54] Just as appalling, from Robbins's perspective, was that Keynes had come to the view that the best way to reduce wages was to allow prices to rise, thereby diminishing their real value.

Robbins wanted to call his friend Hayek as an expert witness to the committee, in the belief that Hayek would not buckle under the weight of Keynes's bombardment. But Keynes rejected the idea. Robbins accepted the dismissal of his star witness with surprising good grace, but his impatience with Keynes's lofty attitude soon came to a head. Unable to agree with the final report drawn up by Keynes and the others, Robbins demanded he be allowed to offer a dissenting minority opinion. As Robbins recalled, "Keynes, who, then as always, was capable of fits of almost ungovernable anger, was furious. . . . In his wrath he treated me very roughly."[55] Citing the opinion of the cabinet secretary, Keynes denied Robbins the right to distance himself from the rest of the committee. Precedents were summoned whereby it was deemed unconstitutional for a single individual to publish a minority report. The other members took turns to say it was bad form, not done, beyond the pale, and ungentlemanly to make such a fuss. It was not just that Robbins was creating an unnecessary precedent; "in order not to damage the chances of useful economic policies being adopted, they were prepared to minimize their disagreements."[56]

But Robbins stood firm. And Keynes was obliged to dismount from his high horse. Keynes reluctantly allowed a dissenting opinion, titled "Report by Professor L. Robbins," to be pinned to the main findings. But all of the heat and rancor of the row between Keynes and Robbins, an early skirmish in the war that Hayek was to wage, were wasted. In October 1930, MacDonald received the report, then sat on it, inertia being the better part of valor for a hidebound prime minister frozen in apprehension.

Keynes soon forgot the highly charged disagreement with Robbins. "It was not many weeks before Keynes and I were meeting again . . . as if there were nothing but intellectual differences between us," recalled Robbins. "I never felt that he was other than a great man and one whose stature was such that idiosyncrasies of personal behavior, such as those of which I had been the victim, sank into unimportance in the general perspective of his quality and character."[57]

Robbins, however, was determined to continue the debate. Now his intention of bringing Hayek from Vienna, like a western gunslinger, to target the troublesome Keynes became an urgent priority. What Robbins did not grasp was that the arrival of Hayek would play directly into the hands of William Beveridge, who held a low opinion of Keynes. Beatrice Webb, who co-founded the LSE with her husband, Sidney, had lunch with Beveridge and discovered that he "heartily dislikes Keynes and regards him as a quack in economics."[58] Like Robbins, Beveridge looked on Hayek's impending lectures as a means to put Keynes in his place.

The stage was now set for Hayek to mount a challenge to Keynes from the security of a staff post at the LSE, so long as he acquitted himself adequately when delivering an account of the Austrian School's theory of the business cycle in the quartet of lectures Robbins had invited him to deliver.

FIVE

The Man Who Shot
Liberty Valance

Hayek Arrives from Vienna, 1931

Lionel Robbins and William Beveridge appointed themselves seconds in the most telling duel in the history of economics. Friedrich Hayek arrived in London in January 1931 to take up Robbins's invitation to deliver four lectures based on his study of the business cycle and his attempt to prove, in "The 'Paradox' of Saving,"[1] that recessions were not caused by a lack of desire from customers to buy goods.

Hayek's first port of call, however, was not the London School of Economics, at Houghton Street off the Strand in London, but Cambridge, fifty miles north, where he was invited to deliver a lecture to the Marshall Society, an intense group of economists made up mostly of associates of John Maynard Keynes. The society, dedicated to the memory of the father of Anglo-Saxon economics, Alfred Marshall, was the spiritual home of Cambridge economics. It was a living reminder to Hayek that he had landed in alien territory, where the Austrian School's writ did not run. As Cambridge economists were wont to say, "Everything can be found in Marshall."[2] Hayek wanted to prove them wrong. With typical nerve, he strode into the lion's den.

It was in the nature of the ever-charming Keynes and the lure of his maverick ideas that he should gather about him a group of fiercely loyal disciples. Keynes had always enjoyed small clusters of intimates, from his early days as a member of the "Apostles" at Cambridge, a so-called secret society of like-minded young men devoted to the ideas of the English philosopher G. E. Moore, then as a core member of the Bloomsbury Group. As a charismatic teacher of economics at King's College, he offered a tight set of young men—Cambridge was in those days an overwhelmingly male bastion—generous and avuncular advice. He chose as his favored pupils those with original casts of mind who were capable of keeping him amused in lengthy conversations. The Marshall Society included a more exclusive band of followers who jokingly referred to themselves as the "Cambridge Circus."

One was Richard F. Kahn,[3] who remembered how he felt on first meeting the great man, slumped horizontally in an armchair with his long legs outstretched, in his sumptuous rooms in King's College decorated with murals by Vanessa Bell and Duncan Grant. "I actually trembled as I was about to enter Keynes's rooms in [King's] College for my first supervision [informal College teaching]," Kahn recalled. "But as soon as the three other students and I had settled down round the open fire, we found talking to us—and encouraging us to talk—a man who was friendly and genial, and anxious to build up our confidence." It was Keynes's ability to combine awe with accessibility that invested his closest admirers with a devotion that bordered on the spiritual. He was far more than a sublime teacher; he was worshipped as a guru and sage. Kahn recalled that "the publication of the 'Treatise' on 31 October 1930 led almost immediately to a group of younger Cambridge economists getting together to discuss the basic issues, stimulated by the knowledge that Keynes would shortly be embarking on a new book [*The General Theory of Employment, Interest and Money*]."[4]

Another important member of the circle, Austin Robinson, may have been the person to first dub the weekly informal seminar the "Cambridge Circus." "We were busily reading [*A Treatise on Money*] and digesting it," he wrote. "Inevitably some of us—Richard Kahn, Joan Robinson[5] [Austin's wife], Piero Sraffa,[6] James Meade,[7] and myself—found ourselves arguing together about it. What came to be called the 'Circus' first emerged by accident rather than design."[8] In addition to these five were C. H. P. Gifford, A. E. W. Plumptre, L. Tarshis, and a small number of undergraduates. Each new member was subjected to a searching interview by Kahn, Austin Robinson, and Sraffa. The group met regularly between January and May 1931 and enjoyed heated debate, though, in true Cambridge fashion, no offense was taken however sharp the disagreement or pointed the words. As Austin Robinson recalled, "It is only by argument, by conflict if you like, that economics makes progress."[9]

The Circus, which first met in Kahn's rooms in the Gibbs Building in King's and later in the Old Combination Room at Trinity College, provided Keynes with a sounding board, a group of trusted young economists with whom he could check galley proofs of *The General Theory*, and, important to his duel with Hayek, a loyal phalanx of disciples ready to defend their patriarch at every turn. Keynes did not attend Circus meetings. One of the regulars, James Meade, a fellow of Hertford College, Oxford, who was spending a year in Cambridge, recalled that "from the point of view of a humble mortal like myself, Keynes seemed to play the role of God in a morality play; he dominated the play but rarely appeared himself on the stage. Kahn was the Messenger Angel who brought messages and problems from Keynes to the 'Circus' and who went back to Heaven with the result of our deliberations."[10]

Kahn was an indifferent physicist turned inspired economist thanks to his mastery of mathematics, winning a first-class degree before being elected as a fellow of King's in 1930. Kahn's switch of subject led the Austrian School economist Joseph Schumpeter,[11] with a typical lack of sensitivity, to inform him that "many a failed race-horse makes quite a good hack."[12] Keynes thought Kahn had "as much natural aptitude for economics as anyone whom I have taught since the war."[13] Kahn was highly intelligent and meticulous in his logic, but he lacked the confidence to press his ideas on others. Soft spoken, impeccably mannered, and known to his peers as "Ferdinand," his middle name, he was perhaps the most important in a line of young men on whom Keynes bestowed the title "Favorite Pupil." An orthodox Jew, Keynes affectionately dubbed him the "Little Rabbi."

Despite a lifetime of studying economics, becoming a professor of economics at Cambridge from 1951 to 1972, Kahn published little and remains best known as the chief artisan in Keynes's atelier. Schumpeter was to make amends for his earlier tactlessness by crediting Kahn with a large portion of *The General Theory*, writing that Kahn's "share in the historic achievement cannot have fallen very far short of co-authorship."[14] Schumpeter cited Kahn's devotion to Keynes as an example of the generosity that typified Cambridge scholars. "They throw their ideas into a common pool. By critical and positive suggestion they help other people's ideas into definite existence. And they exert anonymous influence—influence as leaders—far beyond anything that can be definitely credited to them from their publications."[15]

Austin Robinson, a fellow of Sidney Sussex College, Cambridge, arrived from India in April 1919, having piloted flying boats during World War I, and was, like many of the generation of Cambridge undergraduates who survived the war, motivated by the prospect of making the world a better place. "We were determined that the problems of the world should never again have to be settled by war," he wrote. "Naïve we may have been, but we were nonetheless sincere."[16] He heard Keynes, fresh from the Paris peace talks, deliver a series of lectures that would become *The Economic Consequences of the Peace*. Robinson was smitten. After a spell doing good works in Liverpool, he returned to Cambridge to study economics. "My economics was concerned with improving the state of the world—with making it a somewhat better place for the poor as well as for the rich," he recalled.[17] His memory of the Circus was that he, Kahn, and others began meeting and that "Keynes knew of our meetings and asked Kahn what we were discussing, and Kahn conveyed to him our problems and difficulties."[18]

Austin Robinson's wife Joan, née Joan Violet Maurice, a graduate in economics from the women's college Girton, became, according to Keynes's biographer Skidelsky, "the only woman (so far) among the great economists."[19] Like her audacious major-general father, Sir Frederick Barton Maurice, who accused Prime Minister David Lloyd George during World War I of misleading Parliament over the number of British troops on the Western Front, Mrs. Robinson relished controversy and was a fierce advocate of the causes she supported. Her stock-in-trade was the ad hominem assault. As one contemporary recalled, "Hayek reproached her for assuming that, if people did not agree with her, they must be of extremely low intelligence, with their morals probably not the best either, so that argument back and forward with her was often difficult, to say the least."[20] She was to make a significant contribution to economics not only through her close collaboration with Kahn on Keynes's *General Theory* but also through her work on "imperfect competition" and for her pioneering work in salvaging the reputation of Karl Marx as an economist. She and Austin Robinson were ostensibly happily married with two daughters, but her close intellectual collaboration with Kahn led them to become lovers. The couple was once surprised by Keynes *in flagrante*, Keynes telling Lydia that the pair were "lovingly entangled on the floor of Kahn's study, though I expect the conversation was only on 'The Pure Theory of Monopoly.'"[21]

Hayek first encountered the Circus when he gave his talk to the Marshall Society as a prelude to his debut at the LSE. There were several factors working against his delivering a knockout blow in Keynes's backyard. He was suffering from a high temperature and, befuddled, rushed his preparation for the lecture, which entailed condensing the upcoming four dense, theoretical lectures written for the LSE into a single talk. This left him ill-equipped to anticipate the cool reception from a group that was at best skeptical of anything emerging from the Austrian School.

Hayek suffered from another significant inhibition. Notwithstanding the fourteen months he had spent in New York, his spoken English remained rudimentary. His Austrian accent was as thick as London smog and remained heavy for the rest of his life. When he came to address the Marshall Society, it did not help that he was often obliged to turn his back on his audience to draw on a blackboard a series of intricate, barely legible, and to the audience wholly incomprehensible diagrams. Keynes himself did not attend as he was in London, which may have encouraged his young followers to be even ruder to their guest than had he been present. In the circumstances, Hayek did well to last the distance.

It would be tempting to suggest that the Keynesians were so imbued with the lessons of their guru's recently published *Treatise* that they shunned Hayek on the grounds that he was proposing an opposing economic theory. Quite simply, however, they could make neither head nor tail of the concepts Hayek was trying to explain. Even had they been issued a prepared text beforehand, they may have been none the wiser, for Hayek's written English was in dire need of a good translator and editor and was even less comprehensible than his spoken English. As Hayek later admitted, the notions he referred to were taken for granted among Austrian School economists but were unfamiliar to the British economists, who treated continental economics with the deepest suspicion. Indeed, many of the arguments Hayek assumed his British audience would understand were not available in English.[22]

After spending more than an hour delivering his thesis and scribbling his spidery diagrams, detailing his explanation for why business cycles turn from boom to bust, Hayek invited questions from the floor. The young Keynesians gleaned that the main thrust of Hayek's talk was that, contrary to Keynes's assertion, he believed there was no direct link between aggregate demand (the total of goods that customers want to buy in an economy) and employment. Though always ready for a rough-and-tumble debate, not least when a misguided stranger dared enter their cosy world, the young Keynesians were for once quite lost for words. Hayek's request for questions was met with a chilling hush.

The well-mannered Kahn offered a more or less objective account of this notable assault on Marshallian orthodoxy and the new *Treatise* thinking. His record is harsh, even though, written more than fifty years after the event, it was softened by the passage of time. Try as he might, Kahn could not disguise the fact that the reception must have been devastating even to a character as robust and intellectually secure as Hayek, whose calm air of confidence combined with an almost aristocratic arrogance perfectly fitted him for his celebrated role as a master contrarian.

"The members of the audience—to a man—were completely bewildered," wrote Kahn. "Usually a Marshall Society talk is followed by a lively and protracted barrage of discussions and questions. On this occasion there was complete silence. I felt that I had to break the ice. So I got up and asked, 'Is it your view that if I went out tomorrow and bought a new overcoat, that would increase unemployment?' 'Yes,' said Hayek. 'But,' pointing to his triangles on the board, 'it would take a very long mathematical argument to explain why.'"[23]

Joan Robinson, who had a reputation for ruthlessly dispatching her opponents, was less forgiving. "I very well remember Hayek's visit to Cambridge on his way to the London School," she recalled nearly forty years later. "He expounded his theory and covered the blackboard with his triangles. The whole argument, as we could see later, consisted in confusing the current rate of investment with the total stock of capital goods, but we could not make it out at the time. The general tendency seemed to be to show that the Slump was caused by inflation." She cruelly summed up Hayek's unfortunate debut on the British stage as a "pitiful state of confusion."[24]

Hayek returned to London, somewhat chastened by his Cambridge experience but confident he would receive a warmer reception at the LSE. While acknowledging that the talks Hayek would give would be "at once difficult and exciting,"[25] Robbins had high hopes that the lectures would transform the British intellectual landscape. To ensure that Hayek did not again endure the chilly reception served to him in Cambridge, the largest lecture theater was reserved, and an audience handpicked by Robbins was primed to welcome Hayek's performance, come what may. Those who were not already familiar with Austrian School notions were urged to brush up their knowledge in advance so they could respond positively. Unlike at Cambridge, Hayek was given pride of place on the small elevated stage, with a dozen rows of wooden chairs set up below him and packed with about two hundred eager faculty and staff, and a further hundred or more crowding the gallery.

No one present doubted the importance of the event to the future of economic theory and the reputation of the LSE. The arguments Hayek was about to expound, on the key role the supply of money plays in the workings of an economy, were important first shots in the war against Keynes and Cambridge, and would indirectly provide the foundation for the monetarist counterrevolution that would eventually come to challenge Keynesianism. Hayek's first talk, "Theories of the Influence of Money on Prices," was an overview of the relationship between money, prices, and production.

He opened by acknowledging that the British Treasury's decision to return sterling to the gold standard at its pre–World War I parity had provided ample evidence that "the contraction of circulation"[26] of money (the reduction of money changing hands) leads to a reduction in industrial production. He bemoaned the fact that recent turbulent economic events, in Britain and Europe, had done little to help further the understanding of the key role that monetary forces played in the economy. He blamed this on "a certain change of attitude on the part of most economists in regard to the appropriate methodology of economics, a change which in many quarters is hailed as a great progress: I mean the attempt to substitute quantitative for qualitative methods of investigation."[27] He insisted that measuring elements of the economy was no substitute for understanding how an economy worked. He derided attempts "to establish *direct* causal connections between the *total* quantity of money, the general level of all prices and, perhaps, also the *total* amount of production"[28] in mathematical equations as if economics were a science no different from physics or chemistry. The true key to understanding economic activity, he argued, was the choices individuals made, which were so many and diverse they could not be easily measured. By the same token, he dismissed assumptions based on general price levels. Far more telling, he argued, were the myriad different prices agreed in the countless individual transactions that together made up the economy.

In a wide-ranging historical review of monetary theory, Hayek cited, with admiration, Richard Cantillon,[29] the Irish-French economist of the early eighteenth century who pioneered an understanding of monetary forces. Cantillon had traced how the new injection of money, in the form of gold and silver deposits discovered by seventeenth-century explorers in South America, increased the purchasing power of those who brought the precious metals back to Europe. Their new wealth led the explorers to spend more, which caused prices to rise, which in turn swelled the coffers of the sellers of goods, who in turn spent more, and so on. Cantillon, and later the Scots philosopher David Hume, observed that over time the general effect of the new supply of money helped only those who discovered and produced it, and that the rest of society ended up suffering as the new supplies of silver and gold raised prices. Although he considered it useful, Hayek said he had reservations about Cantillon's theory as "the effects may be quite opposite depending upon when the additional money comes first into the hands of traders and manufacturers."

Hayek then addressed an element missing from Cantillon and Hume, "the influence of the quantity of money on the rate of interest, and through it on the relative demand for consumers' goods on the one hand and producers' or capital goods on the other."[30] A glut of money tended to lower the price of borrowing, which caused consumer goods to increase in price while making saving less attractive. He traced how the relationship between money and interest rates had been explored by thinkers such as Henry Thornton,[31] David Richard,[32] and Thomas Tooke,[33] and how the link between money and capital, in the shape of "forced savings," was addressed by Jeremy Bentham, Thomas Malthus,[34] John Stuart Mill,[35] Léon Walras,[36] Knut Wicksell, and Eugen von Böhm-Bawerk. In drawing attention to what he perceived as a flaw in Wicksell's logic, Hayek took a swipe at the central assumption in Keynes's *Treatise on Money*,[37] that if the "natural rate" of interest and the "market rate" of interest were identical, prices would remain stable.[38] Exactly why he disagreed with Wicksell—and Keynes—Hayek promised to expand on in a later lecture.

But in his first lecture he did set forth a notion that cut to the heart of his difference with Keynes. "It seems obvious as soon as one once begins to think about it that almost any change in the amount of money, whether it does influence the price level or not, must always influence relative prices. And, as there can be no doubt that it is relative prices which determine the amount and the direction of production, almost any change in the amount of money must necessarily also influence production."[39] He believed he was on the verge of a breakthrough in the theory of money that would "no longer [be] a theory of the value of money in general, but a theory of the influence of money on the different ratios of exchange between goods of all kinds."[40]

Hayek then made a startling declaration: money has no intrinsic value. "There is . . . no need for money in this sense—the absolute amount of money in existence is of no consequence to the well-being of mankind—and there is, therefore, no objective value of money in the sense in which we speak of the objective value of goods. What we are interested in is only how the relative values of goods as sources of income or as means of satisfaction of wants are affected by money."[41]

For those in the audience, not least those who had read and digested with a skeptical eye Keynes's *Treatise*, published three months before, Hayek's lecture offered a new direction in which to start reassessing economic theory. In sharp contrast to the reception in Cambridge, Hayek's first lecture in London was met with warm applause. Importantly, the ever-competitive Robbins was delighted by what he heard and was convinced he had found the right man to challenge the potent new theories Keynes was propagating.

In his second lecture, given the following day and titled "The Conditions of Equilibrium between the Production of Consumers' Goods and the Production of Producers' Goods," Hayek addressed an important and, in light of the world slump, a highly topical subject: under what conditions do resources come to be left unused? He declared that to explain any economic phenomenon it was convenient to assume that over time an economy would reach a state of equilibrium in which all resources would be fully employed. But there would be times in the interim when all available resources were not used.

Of all the ways that production could be increased, Hayek suggested, the most effective was by employing capital to satisfy later demand in what—and here he borrowed from the Austrian economist Eugen von Böhm-Bawerk—he called "roundabout" methods of production. Hayek drew a diagram on the blackboard in the shape of a triangle, like the ones that had so baffled his Cambridge audience. He argued that to meet future demand, entrepreneurs over time invest in a succession of intermediate capital goods, such as tools and machinery, that are, in the main, sold to other producers of capital goods. In due course, the employment of these roundabout methods of production led to the provision of more consumer goods in the future. Entrepreneurs were prepared to delay making profit by investing in such intermediate production methods because it would allow them to produce more consumer goods in the future, thereby fulfilling the desires of consumers, who save today to have more tomorrow.

Which brought Hayek to the core question of his second lecture: how did methods of production needing less capital progress to methods needing more capital? The answer was simple: when people spent less on consumer goods and saved more, their savings were invested in capital goods. But there was another way: more capital goods might be produced when money was made available to producers by bank loans. This second method, he said, was not real saving but "forced saving" because the new investment had come about not because of an increase in savings but simply because it suited banks to lend. When the money lent to producers was reduced to its former level, the capital invested in equipment was lost. "We shall see in the next lecture," he said ominously, "that such a transition to less capitalistic methods of production necessarily takes the form of an economic crisis."[42]

Once again the audience was left on the edge of their seats. In his third lecture, the following day, Hayek invoked the work of his mentor Ludwig von Mises. Hayek opened the talk, titled "The Working of the Price Mechanism in the Course of the Credit Cycle," with a quote from Mises: "The first effect of the increase of productive activity, initiated by the policy of the banks to lend below the natural rate interest is . . . to raise the prices of producers' goods while the prices of consumers' goods rise only moderately. . . . But soon a reverse movement sets in: prices of consumers' goods rise and prices of producers' goods fall, i.e., the loan rate rises and approaches again the natural rate of interest."[43]

With his usual impeccably meticulous if forbiddingly desiccated approach, Hayek described how an unwarranted increase in borrowing led over time to a dislocation in the production process of capital goods, which in turn caused a collapse at the bottom of the business cycle. To help those without a remorselessly analytical bent, Hayek offered an example. "The situation would be similar to that of a people of an isolated island, if, after having partially constructed an enormous machine which was to provide them with all necessities, they found out that they had exhausted all their savings and available free capital before the new machine could turn out its product," he said. "They would then have no choice but to abandon temporarily the work on the new process and to devote all their labor to producing their daily food without any capital."[44]

In the real world, Hayek suggested, the result was persistent unemployment. He offered a simple if unpalatable truth to those, like Keynes, who advocated increasing the demand for consumer goods to increase employment: "The machinery of capitalistic production will function smoothly only so long as we are satisfied to consume no more than that part of our total wealth which under the existing organization of production is destined for current consumption. Every increase of consumption, if it is not to disturb production, requires previous new saving."

Hayek also confronted another Keynesian remedy, that if an idle plant was brought into use it would spur a depressed economy back to life and increase employment. "What [economists like Keynes] overlook is that . . . in order that the existing durable plants could be used to their full capacity it would be necessary to invest a great amount of other means of production in lengthy processes which would bear fruit only in a comparatively distant future."[45] He went on, "It should be fairly clear that the granting of credit to consumers, which has recently been so strongly advocated as a cure for depression, would in fact have quite the contrary effect." Such "artificial demand," he suggested, would merely postpone the day of reckoning. "The only way permanently to 'mobilize' all available resources is, therefore, not to use artificial stimulants—whether during a crisis or thereafter—but to leave it to time to effect a permanent cure."[46] In brief, there was no easy way out of a slump. In the long run the free market would restore an economy to an equilibrium where everyone was employed.

Once again Hayek scored a bull's-eye with his audience. Here at last was a cogent, convincing repudiation of Keynesian interventionist notions. Hayek showed that the remedies coming from Cambridge, which appeared so plausible, were riddled with logical flaws. Having the best of intentions was not enough. Addressing the symptoms of a depressed economy by investing with borrowed money only made matters worse. Instead Hayek offered a sober remedy of his own: forget about quick fixes, the uncomfortable truth is that only time will cure an economy in disbalance. Beware smooth-talking doctors, such as Keynes, who offered a quick cure, for they are charlatans, snake-oil salesmen, and quacks. Every short cut only leads back to the start. There are no soft options. Only the long haul will provide a true recovery. The market has its own logic and contains its own natural remedy. It was not Hayek's role to offer bromides as he, unlike Keynes, was no political agitator.

In his fourth lecture, the day after, Hayek ventured into the still largely unexplored territory of monetary theory, which would eventually underpin the main thrust of the theoretical opposition to Keynesian ideas. Hayek suggested that the amount of money in an economy, and the speed with which it passed from one to another, held the key to understanding how the system worked. "Under the existing conditions, money will always exert a determining influence on the course of economic events and . . . therefore, no analysis of actual economic phenomena is complete if the role played by money is neglected," he declared.[47] But he stressed that monetary theory, though an essential tool to a better understanding of the economic system, had severe limitations. It was good for normal times, but not perhaps for the times the world was currently enduring.

Hayek believed that for an economy to work most effectively it was essential that money operate as a neutral factor. "The increase or decrease of the quantity of money circulating within any one geographical area serves a function just as definite as the increase or decrease of the money incomes of particular individuals, namely the function of enabling the inhabitants to draw a larger or smaller share of the total product of the world," he said.[48] To increase the supply of money inflicted unnecessary burdens on certain sectors of society.

"The increase of the amount of money only means that somebody has to give up part of his additional product to the producers of the new money."[49] He was at pains to stress that the creation of additional money entailed money as measured not only by bank notes but also by bank loans, "book credits," and forms of credit not connected to banks. "The characteristic peculiarity of these forms of credit is that they spring up without being subject to any central control, but once they have come into existence their convertibility into other forms of money must be possible if a collapse of credit is to be avoided," he said.[50]

To avoid the most extravagant swings of a business cycle, he argued, banks should keep their lending in close check. "Bankers need not be afraid to harm production by overcaution," he said. The judicious action of banks was perhaps all that could be achieved in terms of keeping monetary policy under control. "Under existing conditions, to go beyond this is out of the question. In any case, it could be attempted only by a central monetary authority for the whole world: action on the part of a single country would be doomed to disaster."[51]

Although the removal of money as a source of disequilibrium was important, he warned that a strict monetary policy was no cure-all. "It is probably an illusion to suppose that we shall ever be able entirely to eliminate industrial fluctuations by means of monetary policy," he said. But those, like Keynes, who believed an economy worked best when there was a certain amount of inflation were misguided. "The most we may hope for is that the growing information of the public may make it easier for central banks both to follow a cautious policy during the upward swing of the cycle, and so to mitigate the following depression, and to resist the well-meaning but dangerous proposals to fight depression by 'a little inflation.'"[52]

So Hayek came to the end of his quartet of lectures. "In the event the lectures were a sensation," recalled Robbins, "partly for their revelations of an aspect of classical monetary theory which for many years had been forgotten."[53] There was a sense, according to Joseph Schumpeter, that Hayek was saying something new and startling.

Although Hayek's lectures raised as many questions as they answered, Robbins was particularly pleased, for they had achieved exactly his intended purpose, to introduce British economists to "this great tradition [the Austrian School], [that] will do something to persuade English readers that here is a school of thought which can only be neglected at the cost of losing contact with what may prove to be one of the most fruitful scientific developments of our age."[54]

The talks served as an extended job interview for Hayek, who dearly wished to join the LSE faculty. It was with delight, then, that on the strength of the lectures Beveridge offered Hayek a visiting professorship, and the following year awarded him the Tooke Chair in Economic Science and Statistics.[55] According to Robbins, "There was a unanimous vote in favor."[56] Hayek accepted the post without reservation.

SIX

Pistols at Dawn

Hayek Harshly Reviews Keynes's *Treatise*, 1931

The month Hayek arrived in London, Keynes was urging the housewives of London in a radio broadcast to spend, spend, spend. The cheapness of goods meant that British shoppers had never had it so good. But while those employed were doing well, millions stood idle. "Many millions of pounds' worth of goods could be produced each day by the workers and the plants which stand idle," said Keynes.[1]

The answer, said Keynes, was simple, if counterintuitive. "There are today many . . . who believe that the most useful thing which they and their neighbors can do to mend the situation is to *save* more than usual. If they refrain from spending . . . they believe that they will have helped employment. . . . In present circumstances . . . it is quite wrong." In the reductio ad absurdum that was his stock-in-trade, Keynes warned what would happen if everyone saved too much. "Suppose we were to stop spending our incomes altogether, and were to save the lot. Why, everyone would be out of work. And before long we should have no incomes to spend. No one would be a penny the richer, and the end would be that we should all starve to death."

"Whenever you save five shillings, you put a man out of work for a day," he told his audience. "On the other hand, when you buy goods you increase employment. . . . For if you do not buy goods, the shops will not clear their stocks, they will not give repeat orders, and someone will be thrown out of work," he said. "Therefore, oh patriotic housewives, sally out tomorrow early into the streets and go to the wonderful sales. . . . And have the added joy that you are increasing employment, adding to the wealth of the country."[2] At least one woman took Keynes's advice, his wife Lydia, who did her bit to lick unemployment by buying blankets at a London store.

Keynes urged local councils to invest in public works programs to create jobs. "For example, why not pull down the whole of South London from Westminster to Greenwich. . . . Would that employ men? Why, of course it would! Is it better that the men should stand idle and miserable, drawing the dole? Of course it is not."[3]

The broadcast caused an enormous stir, setting off editorial writers in at least forty newspapers to weigh in on Keynes's argument. "Never such publicity in my life,"[4] Keynes wrote to Lydia. But Ramsay MacDonald's ailing government took no notice. The chancellor, Philip Snowden, thought Keynes's idea highly irresponsible. He despairingly told the cabinet that the country's finances were "grim. . . . As each month passes with no sign of a lifting of the world economic crisis, the financial prospects constantly and steadily deteriorate."[5]

A Treasury memorandum echoed Snowden's nervousness about curing unemployment by public works, predicting that "continued state borrowing on the present scale without provision for repayment . . . would quickly call into question the stability of the British financial system."[6] Keynes conceded that his ideas might frighten world markets into believing the government would renege on its debts, prompting a run on sterling, and suggested temporary import duties. The about-face sparked a fresh round of jokes about Keynes's habit of altering his opinion. The most common was, "If you put two economists in a room, you get two opinions, unless one of them is

Lord Keynes, in which case you get three,"[7] a remark often attributed to Winston Churchill. Keynes's apocryphal response was, "When the facts change, I change my mind. What do you do, sir?"[8]

Keynes's proposal for import duties was met with opposition from political friends and foes alike. Both Snowden and Lloyd George were adamant free traders, while the Conservatives, who might have welcomed Keynes's endorsement of a policy they had long advocated, had no need to welcome him to their cause. They were awaiting the fall of MacDonald's second Labour government, which would herald their return to power.

The weight of work that Keynes took on was beginning to take its toll. In early 1931, the ill health that would dog him for the rest of his life became evident for the first time. A severe toothache degenerated into influenza accompanied by tonsillitis. Six years later he was found to be suffering from bacterial endocarditis, a debilitating infection of the heart valves that was incurable until penicillin became available. But Keynes kept to his punishing schedule. By the end of May he had recovered enough to undertake a lecture tour of America. It was his first trip to the United States for more than a decade. It was hardly a vacation.

Keynes was in demand on both sides of the Atlantic. The collapse of the Credit-Ansalt Bank in Vienna on May 11, 1931, after it was revealed that five-sixths of its capital had been lost to bad loans used to shore up failing Austrian businesses, heralded a general European economic emergency. In Britain, MacDonald's Labour government was at breaking point, and America, too, was in economic turmoil. Keynes was eager to see for himself the calamitous effects on the American economy brought about by the stock market crash of 1929. He was invited by the University of Chicago to speak on unemployment in America, the rate of which had reached 16.3 percent, but it wasn't long before other Americans solicited his views on how to cure the worldwide economic catastrophe.

Though he held no official British government position, nor was he sent to America as an informal ambassador, Keynes's renown offered him celebrity status that opened access to the most influential Americans. No sooner had the SS *Adriatic* arrived in New York than he and Lydia were whisked off to the Long Island country retreat of the chairman of the Federal Reserve, Eugene Meyer, who immediately took Keynes into his confidence. "[Meyer] was constantly on the telephone with the President [Hoover], Morgan's, etc. I was alone with him and he talked to me with astonishing freedom," Keynes wrote to his former pupil, the former editor of *The Nation*, Hubert Henderson.[9]

Meyer was wrestling with what to do about the collapse of the German economy in light of the crippling World War I reparations, a subject dear to Keynes's heart. Exactly what Keynes recommended to Meyer is not recorded, though his views on the insanity of demanding that Germany pay reparations it could not afford were so well known that perhaps it was not necessary for him to say anything at all. Whatever he said appeared to do the trick. Meyer immediately suggested to Hoover that the reparations be cut in half; three days later Hoover went a step further, declaring a moratorium on all debt payments for a year. Keynes declared the decision "a first step of the greatest possible value."[10]

Keynes reported back to his friend O. T. Falk[11] in London a parlous state of affairs in America that uncannily presaged the symptoms of the banking crisis that would overtake America half a century later, in September 2008. "[The banks] have purchased great quantities of second-grade bonds which have depreciated in value and their advances to farmers and against real estate are inadequately secured,"[12] Falk recorded.

In a lecture to the New School in New York Keynes rejected the free-market prescriptions "of the so-called 'economists' attached to leading New York banks,"[13] and advocated a rise in prices and a loosening of credit to put the economy back on track. Addressing economists and foreign-policy wonks in Chicago, he told his audience they were in "the greatest catastrophe due almost entirely to economic causes—

of the modern world,"[14] and suggested that the Great Depression had been provoked by the "extraordinary imbecility" of the Federal Reserve's high-interest-rate policy. In the most coherent intellectual justification thus far for the need to enlist government to invest when economic conditions became stagnant, he went on, "Nothing, obviously, can restore employment which does not first restore business profits. Yet nothing, in my judgment, can restore business profits which does not first restore the volume of investment."[15] He advocated raising investment by "programs under the direct auspices of the government or other public authorities" and "a reduction in the long-term rate of interest." Keynes was surprised to discover that in a city that was home to American entrepreneurs and a focal point of American business, the Chicago economists, led by Quincy Wright,[16] seemed as keen on increasing public expenditure as he was.[17]

Keynes arrived home to a Britain suffering a profound crisis in confidence in the government's ability to pay its debts, combined with a run on sterling, which was still pegged to the gold standard. The German elections of 1930, which left Adolf Hitler's extreme Nazi Party victorious, prompted visions of a civil war in Germany, leading to a flight of capital from the country and heavy withdrawals of gold and foreign exchange. In early 1931, the German Reichsbank was unable to honor its commitments, setting off a banking crisis that led in turn to an intense round of speculation against the pound sterling, causing the British Treasury to seek an American loan. To meet the terms of the loan, Snowden, the Labour chancellor, proposed a package of severe public-expenditure cuts drawn up by a former official of Prudential Assurance, Sir George May. These included a 20 percent reduction in unemployment pay. Keynes condemned May's measures as self-defeating and estimated that another 250,000 to 400,000 would be thrown out of work as a result, costing the exchequer far more than it hoped to save from cutting unemployment relief.

Asked by MacDonald his view of May's plan, Keynes replied that he was so angry that his thoughts were unprintable. Keynes strongly urged the prime minister to ignore May's advice. He predicted, rightly, that the maintenance of the value of the pound at its current level was unsustainable. Keynes condemned the May report in the *Daily Herald* as "the most foolish document I have ever had the misfortune to read," and Snowden's budget proposals to implement May's cuts as "replete with folly and injustice."[18]

At this stage of the slump, Keynes argued, it was better for Britain to live with the consequences of a large deficit than to try to pay it off quickly by cutting spending. As he explained, "At the present time all Governments have large deficits. For Government borrowing of one kind or another is nature's remedy, so to speak, for preventing business losses from being, in so severe a slump as the present one, so great as to bring production altogether to a standstill."[19] MacDonald's cabinet was overwhelmingly in favor of Keynes's import duties to help correct the balance of payments, but Snowden vetoed the idea. When MacDonald found he could not muster the requisite majority in the House of Commons to implement May's cuts, he resigned, only to have the monarch, King George V, urge him to try to form a coalition with the Conservatives, which he succeeded in doing. At a hurriedly called general election in October 1931, the National Government swept the polls with 552 seats in the new Commons, defeating MacDonald's own Labour Party, which had declined to follow its leader into the coalition and was left with just 46 members. The Liberals were reduced to a small group split into three competing factions. The trouncing of both Labour and the Liberals marked the ebb tide of Keynes's influence on British economic policy.

MacDonald took the helm of a new overwhelmingly Conservative administration devoted to a policy of deeply cutting public expenditures. On September 15, 1931, MacDonald abandoned the gold standard. As Keynes's biographer R. F. Harrod was to observe, "All these years of travail had been in vain. If only they had taken [Keynes's] advice in 1925!"[20] Keynes may have felt vindicated by the decision, but it was no time to celebrate. The damage to the economy in the intervening six years had devastated British industry. Hundreds of thousands of British workers had been unnecessarily thrown out of work because of the unsustainable value placed on sterling by those who clung to orthodox thinking. As the decade proceeded with no end in sight to the widespread economic misery, Keynes became alarmed that the young undergraduates around him at Cambridge were turning to communism. In the early 1930s, the Apostles, the largely homosexual Cambridge society Keynes belonged to, recruited Guy Burgess and Anthony Blunt, who became Soviet agents. It was to head off such extremism that Keynes redoubled his efforts to find a means of ameliorating capitalism's suicidal excesses.

In May 1931, while Keynes was crossing the Atlantic, Hayek was putting the finishing touches to a vituperative assault on Keynes's *Treatise,* for publication in the August issue of the LSE journal *Economica.* No sooner had Hayek joined the LSE faculty than Robbins, in his role as editor of *Economica*, put him to work subjecting the work of Keynes to close scrutiny. Robbins intended to rush the review into print in full confidence that Hayek would not mince his words. Hayek took avidly to his task. Here was a chance to counter the growing attraction of Keynesian ideas at the heart of the current debate about the world recession and to evaluate and answer the most recent theoretical work of the world's most influential economist.

Hayek set out to ensure that his critique would cause a stir. While he had made an impression of sorts on the Keynesians in the Circus, he had thus far failed to attract the attention of the great man himself. The quartet of talks at the LSE that had won him his appointment had failed to cause much of a ripple beyond Houghton Street. There was no evidence that Keynes had noticed Hayek's private triumph, but he would not be able to ignore a closely argued evaluation of his thinking in *Economica*. Hayek urgently sought fame in his new land and was convinced, as was Robbins, that a gently expressed, well-mannered, totally reasonable appraisal of Keynes would not do the trick. His contribution had to be a sharp assault written for maximum effect.

Hayek often told colleagues that he liked in particular those thinkers, like Schumpeter and Keynes, who tweaked the noses of the great and the good and liked to shock respectable opinion. Now he was about to offer Keynes a dose of his own medicine.

In the opening sentence of the review, Hayek was impeccably polite about Keynes and his many achievements, as befitted an Austrian gentleman who was very much Keynes's junior and a newcomer on the English academic scene. "The appearance of any work by Mr. J. M. Keynes must always be a matter of importance: and the publication of the *Treatise on Money* has long been awaited with intense interest by all economists," he wrote. Then he slipped a stiletto between Keynes's ribs. "Nonetheless, in the event, the *Treatise* proves to be so obviously—and, I think, admittedly—the expression of a transitory phase in a process of rapid intellectual development that its appearance cannot be said to have that definitive significance which at one time was expected of it."[21]

Hayek adopted the lofty air that would inform the rest of his appraisal, suggesting that Keynes was an ignorant, insular figure trapped in the provincial Anglo-Saxon thinking of his teacher and mentor Alfred Marshall, and that his belated attempt to catch up with Austrian thinking was too large a task for him. "So strongly does [*A Treatise*] bear the marks of the effect of recent discovery of certain lines of thought hitherto unfamiliar to the school to which Mr. Keynes belongs, that it would be decidedly unfair to regard it as anything else but experimental—a first attempt to amalgamate those new ideas with the monetary teaching traditional in Cambridge,"[22] he wrote.

Hayek continued to damn with faint praise. "If, to a Continental economist, this way of approach does not seem so novel as it does to the author, it must be admitted that he has made a more ambitious attempt to carry the analysis into the details and the complications of the problem than any that has been attempted hitherto."[23] But having offered some encouragement for Keynes's attempt to grasp continental economics, Hayek added a patronizing sting. "Whether he has been successful here, whether he has not been seriously hampered by the fact that he has not devoted the same amount of effort to understanding those fundamental theorems of 'real' economics on which alone any monetary explanation can be successfully built, as he has to subsidiary embellishments, are questions which will have to be examined later."[24]

What plainly aggravated Hayek was not so much the nature of the work at hand but the lessons Keynes drew from his adapted and often misapplied account of some Austrian School ideas in furthering his interventionist policy proposals in the real world: the urging on governments of public works programs to create employment. "That such a book is theoretically stimulating goes without saying," Hayek wrote. "At the same time, it is difficult to suppress some concern as regards the immediate effect which its publication in its present form may have on the development of monetary theory. It was, no doubt, the urgency which he attributes to the practical proposals which he holds to be justified to his theoretical reasoning, which led Mr. Keynes to publish the work in what is avowedly an unfinished state."[25]

Hayek then adopted the oratorical device a bloodstained Marc Antony employed when extolling the virtues of the newly assassinated Julius Caesar. "The proposals are indeed revolutionary, and cannot fail to attract the widest attention: They come from a writer who has established an almost unique and well-deserved reputation for courage and practical insight; they are expounded in passages in which the author displays all his astonishing qualities of learning, erudition and realistic knowledge."[26] Then comes the condemnation: Keynes's theories may seem to be plausible, even convincing, to the ignorant, but they were little more than mumbo-jumbo to anyone who knew anything about economics. The work was "so highly technical and complicated that it must forever remain entirely unintelligible to those who are not experts."[27] Hayek made little attempt to disguise his contempt for the key terms and equations on which Keynes built his theory. Keynes's exposition was so "difficult, unsystematic, and obscure" and "extremely difficult," with "a degree of obscurity which . . . is almost unbelievable," that "one can never be sure whether one has understood Mr. Keynes aright."[28]

Having in his opening remarks excoriated Keynes for his intellectual inadequacies and his lack of knowledge of basic Austrian economic theories, Hayek sets off on a long, complex, and often barely comprehensible explanation for why Keynes's ignorance of Austrian capital theory, including Hayek's own contribution, which had not yet been published in English and therefore Keynes could not have read, ensured that *A Treatise* was of little use in explaining the fluctuations of the business cycle.

Throughout, Hayek adopted an ill-tempered tone of indignation, as if Keynes had deliberately set out to offend him personally. "I have no fundamental objection to this somewhat irritating distinction [between entrepreneurs' profits and money income],"[29] he writes, before listing what he seems to imagine are a succession of personal slights. "I cannot agree with his explanation of why profits arise,"[30] he writes. "I must confess that I am absolutely unable to attach any useful meaning to his concept."[31] And "I shall repeatedly have occasion to point out"[32] another of Keynes's perceived misapprehensions. While Keynes, who was not without a large ego himself, was so confident he often changed his mind and admitted his faults, Hayek's stance was based on absolute certainty that he was right in every particular. Keynes reveled in controversy and debate and welcomed those who disagreed with him, while Hayek, in Robbins's assessment, "was no proselytizer. He had strong convictions himself. But in discussion his focus was always directed not to persuade but rather to pursue implications."[33]

Rather than confine himself to explaining his differences with Keynes's reasoning and conclusions, Hayek's tetchy remarks are littered with ad hominem snipes, such as "he seems to think . . ." and "in spite of some clearly contradictory statements of Mr. Keynes," whom he accuses of "very mischievous peculiarities." He condemns Keynes's obscurity of language while compounding his rival's error, as in: "Most of the difficulties which arise here are a consequence of the peculiar method of approach adopted by Mr. Keynes, who, from the outset, analyses complex dynamic processes without laying the necessary foundations by adequate static analysis of the fundamental process."[34]

As for substance, Hayek tangles with Keynes over definitions, preferring established Austrian terms for such basic concepts as "savings" and "investment" to those either already in use at Cambridge or newly minted by Keynes to describe what he believed to be freshly observed phenomena. Hayek's main objection to Keynes's treatise, however, is his ignoring Austrian notions of capital theory, in particular the implications to prices and demand of "roundabout" means of production of capital goods that he had so singularly failed to explain adequately in his lecture to the Marshall Society. Hayek drew attention to two notions at the heart of their conflicting views of how an economy works: Hayek could not agree with Keynes's rejection of the need for an equilibrium between savings and investment; nor could he accept Keynes's assertion that the importance of the divergence between investment and savings was that it adversely affected the stability of prices.

On other matters of disagreement, Hayek found unforgivable Keynes's decision to adopt some but not all of the notions of Knut Wicksell and not to integrate the further work on capital theory developed by Eugen von Böhm-Bawerk. "It is a priori unlikely," he wrote, "that an attempt to utilise the conclusions drawn from a certain theory without accepting that theory itself should be successful. But in the case of an author of Mr. Keynes's intellectual caliber, the attempt produces results which are truly remarkable. Mr. Keynes ignores completely the general theoretical basis of Wicksell's theory. But, nonetheless, he seems to have felt that such a theoretical basis is wanting, and accordingly he has sat down to work one out for himself."[35] In scolding Keynes for not having taken into account the work of Frank Taussig,[36] the economic theorist known as the "American

Marshall," Hayek asked snarkily, "Would not Mr. Keynes have made his task easier if he had not only accepted one of the descendants of Böhm-Bawerk's theory, but had also made himself acquainted with the substance of that theory itself?"[37]

At the very end of his diatribe, Hayek pulled back from his hostile mode and returned to flattering Keynes, the more to upbraid him for his errors of omission and of judgment. It is as if he had been advised, perhaps by Robbins, that it was important to leave on a less sour note, the better to impale Keynes on his hook. "There is just one word more I feel I should add at this point," he wrote. "It is very likely that in the preceding pages I have quite often clothed my comments in the form of a criticism where I should simply have asked for further explanation and that I have dwelt too much on minor inaccuracies of expression. I hope it will not be considered a sign of inadequate appreciation of what is undeniably in so many ways a magnificent performance that what I have had so far to say was almost exclusively critical."

He continued, somewhat disingenuously, "My aim has been throughout to contribute to the understanding of this unusually difficult and important book, and I hope that my endeavor in this direction will be the best proof of how important I consider it."[38] An extraordinary arrogance informed his next statement, that if only Keynes had been able to explain himself better in *A Treatise* he might have discovered that he agreed with Hayek's way of seeing things. "It is even possible that in the end it will turn out that there exists less difference between Mr. Keynes's views and my own than I am at present inclined to assume," he opined. "The difficulty may be only that Mr. Keynes has made it so extraordinarily hard really to follow his reasoning. I hope that the reviewer will be excused if, in a conscientious attempt to understand it, he may sometimes have been betrayed into impatience with the countless obstacles which the author has put in the way of a full understanding of his ideas."

Hayek's concluding remarks proved to be a false coda. His review was merely the first blow in what was to be a double whammy. He used a postscript footnote to send a warning salvo toward Keynes in Cambridge that more of the same was to come when he resumed the second part of his review in the following month's *Economica*, because, he confessed, "it is sometimes extremely difficult to find out exactly what the meaning of Mr. Keynes's concepts is," and "I am by no means certain whether I have understood Mr. Keynes correctly."

Hayek made a direct appeal for Keynes to provide a quick rejoinder to his criticisms to clarify some of the points he found muddled or unclear. "There have accumulated so many questions of this kind which Mr. Keynes could certainly clear up that it is probably wiser to stop for the moment in the hope that further elucidations will in the meanwhile provide a firmer basis on which discussion may proceed."[39] And with that Hayek's guns fell silent, for now. He did not know for certain whether Keynes would take the bait, but from his knowledge of the man, he—and Robbins—had little doubt that they would soon be on the receiving end of heavy pounding emanating from Keynes's rooms in King's.

Experimental, a first attempt, unfinished, entirely unintelligible, weakness of the argument, so difficult, unsystematic, obscure, extremely difficult, inconsistent, obscurity, unbelievable, extreme caution, greatest reserve. With these harsh words and dismissive phrases Hayek opened his salvo against the mighty Keynes. His intention was clear: to challenge him at every turn, to give no quarter, to draw attention to himself by crying out that the emperor has no clothes. It is telling, perhaps, that Robbins did not commission himself to review *A Treatise* in such terms, for he would have been inhibited by established academic convention and plain good manners, and would have laid himself open to accusations of vindictiveness following his scrap with Keynes when they served on the Macmillan Committee.

But Robbins was inextricably implicated in the attack. As the editor of *Economica*, he not only assigned Hayek to the task but also approved and amended the text. Indeed, it is almost certain that Robbins helped Hayek write the assault, for the use of English throughout "Reflections on the Pure Theory of Money of Mr. J. M. Keynes" is without fault, even though Hayek at the time struggled with written English. When Hayek's four lectures to the LSE were published in book form as *Prices and Production*, Hayek acknowledged the contribution Robbins made to cleaning up his English, or, as he put it, "the considerable labour of putting the manuscript into a form fit for publication."[40] At the very least, Robbins did nothing to help Hayek avoid the offensive tone and language that he used throughout the Keynes review.

As the summer of 1931 turned to fall, Hayek's most pressing, indeed almost sole concern was whether Keynes would deign to respond. Keynes would have been within his rights to have ignored Hayek's ill-tempered critique on the grounds that he had far bigger fish to fry. For Keynes, responding to Hayek's assault was just one of a number of tasks he was juggling, both national and international, public and private. Had he been a less generous character he might have argued that there was little point in engaging with the obscure Hayek, whose conservative approach to economics was a given, when Keynes was busy trying to save the world from economic oblivion.

The announcement that Britain was, at last, to abandon the gold standard might have allowed Keynes a brief moment of Schadenfreude, but he was probably in little mood for celebration. For all his explaining, cajoling, campaigning, and urging successive governments over more than a decade to cure unemployment by increasing public spending, he had precious little to show for his efforts. He dismissed his failure to win support among those in power as "the croakings of a Cassandra who could never influence the course of events in time."[41] He was already developing ideas beyond *A Treatise*, with the aid of his small coterie of disciples. He was working toward what came to be known as the "General Theory." So, the moment he scanned Hayek's spikey review in *Economica*, he might well have shrugged his shoulders and thrown it in the waste basket. Instead he turned and faced his foe.

SEVEN

Return Fire

Keynes and Hayek Lock Horns, 1931

It was always Keynes's instinct to meet criticism head-on, however absurd he might think the competing analysis. The governing ethos at Cambridge was to profit from argument. When Keynes himself became involved, a debate was invariably conducted in colorful language. A natural and gifted polemicist, he could not help himself from dramatizing his differences with opponents. Even the mighty mind of the British philosopher Bertrand Russell[1] could be intimidated by Keynes's dazzling intelligence. "Keynes's intellect was the sharpest and clearest that I have ever known," he wrote. "When I argued with him, I felt that I took my life in my hands, and I seldom emerged without feeling something of a fool. I was sometimes inclined to feel that so much cleverness must be incompatible with depth, but I do not think this feeling was justified."[2] The art historian Kenneth Clark[3] concurred, reporting, "He never dimmed his headlights."[4] Roy Harrod agreed: "No one in our age was cleverer than Keynes nor made less attempt to conceal it."[5]

It is a mark of Hayek's sublime confidence, tinged perhaps with the fearlessness that can accompany ignorance, that he was willing to take on Keynes on Keynes's home territory. Keynes's response was to meet fire with fire. The result was Keynes unplugged, an almost visceral response to an opponent he felt was so hardwired in the narrowness of Austrian School thinking that he was incapable of understanding a point of view that demanded a daring leap of imagination. Hayek's harsh review of Keynes's *Treatise on Money* invoked howls of rage from Keynes, who was offended at his opponent's failure to take into account that he was publishing ideas he had been assembling for nearly seven years and that he deemed a work in progress. Indeed, as Hayek's principal intellectual goal was to counter Keynes, he must have been aware that Keynes was already moving well beyond the ideas expressed in *A Treatise*.

In the preface to *A Treatise*, Keynes admitted that he was dissatisfied with his efforts. "There is a good deal in this book which represents the process of getting rid of the ideas which I used to have and of finding my way to those which I now have," he wrote. "There are many skins which I have sloughed still littering these pages. . . . I feel like someone who has been forcing his way through a confused jungle."[6]

It was an extraordinary confession for such a conspicuously public figure and offered an insight into the paradoxical relationship he enjoyed with his followers and the public at large. Keynes was humble enough to admit his inadequacies while supremely confident that his intellectual journey, however incomplete, was worth making public. Besides, with *A Treatise* he was reluctant to abandon his labor. He might have done better to follow the advice Sir Arthur Quiller-Couch proffered writers,[7] that an author should be ruthless and "murder his darlings."[8] Instead, Keynes offered up a ready hostage to a meticulous, dogged, and unforgiving rival set on making a reputation at his expense.

That Hayek's review made no concession to Keynes's admission of inadequacy ensured that the subsequent debate, between Keynes, with the support of his followers in Cambridge, and Hayek, backed by his band of Austrian School devotees at the LSE, quickly descended into blunt and often brutal personal assaults that would long outlive both Keynes and Hayek. In the fall of 1931, Keynes found himself in the uncomfortable position of having to defend thoughts he no longer believed in, though his response in the November issue of *Economica* revealed that he was somewhat intrigued by the thrust of Hayek's argument. Which is why, perhaps, he was prepared to expend so much energy defending himself from Hayek's assault.

Keynes read Hayek's twenty-six-page review, the first of two parts, with pencil in hand and became increasingly furious, scribbling thirty-four rejoinders in the margin. By the end he was exasperated by Hayek's approach not only to *A Treatise* but to academic debate in general. "Hayek has not read my book with that measure of 'good will' which an author is entitled to expect of a reader," he wrote. "Until he can do so, he will not see what I mean or know whether I am right. He evidently has a passion which leads him to pick on me, but I am left wondering what this passion is."[9] Keynes conceded in his "Reply to Dr. Hayek" that Hayek's contributions to the current economic debate had aroused his curiosity. He began by brutally assessing the arguments Hayek had presented in *Prices and Production*. "The book, as it stands, seems to me to be one of the most frightful muddles I have ever read, with scarcely a sound proposition in it beginning with page 45," he wrote, "and yet it remains a book of some interest, which is likely to leave its mark on the mind of the reader." In the next sentence he granted that the book had some virtue. "It is an extraordinary example of how, starting with a mistake, a remorseless logician can end up in Bedlam," he wrote. "Yet Dr. Hayek has seen a vision, and though when he woke up he has made nonsense of his story by giving the wrong names to the objects which occur in it, his Khubla Khan is not without inspiration and must set the reader thinking with the germs of an idea in his head."[10]

In fact the ideas Keynes advanced in *A Treatise* were not too distant from the notions Hayek had expressed in *Prices and Production*. What was to be an important similarity, but not for long, was that both assumed that in a closed economy total output was fixed and an equilibrium would arise where everyone was employed. The main difference was that in establishing the reasons for—and the results of—savings and investment being unequal, Hayek, unlike Keynes, resorted to the Austrian School theory of capital and concluded that during such times the level of credit in an economy was out of kilter with true demand.

Cooler heads than Hayek and Keynes may have spotted the many similarities between their arguments and concentrated on the interesting differences. Instead, in their sharp exchanges in *Economica* and in their subsequent private correspondence, Keynes and Hayek became deeply entangled in efforts to determine the meaning of the terms they used in an attempt to decipher what the other was saying. Even for a trained economist with the benefit of decades of hindsight, the differences between the two men are often erudite to the point of impenetrability.[11] At one point, Keynes even appeals to Robbins to mediate. For Hayek and Keynes, unprepared as much as incapable of seeing each other's point of view, it was as if two ships had passed in the night.

Keynes's irritation with Hayek over the inability to find common ground even in the use of terms is evident from the start of his *Economica* article. "Dr. Hayek has invited me to clear up some ambiguities of terminology which he finds in my *Treatise on Money*, and also other matters. As he frankly says, he has found his difference with me difficult to explain. He is sure that my conclusions are wrong (though he does not clearly state which conclusions), but he finds it 'extremely difficult to demonstrate the exact point of disagreement and to state his objections.' He feels that my analysis leaves out essential things, but he declares that 'it is not at all easy to detect the flaw in the argument.' What he has done, therefore, is to pick over the precise words I have used with a view to discovering some verbal contradiction or insidious ambiguity."[12] Keynes was happy to elucidate the meaning of the terms he used, but diminished the importance he assigned to the differences by relegating his clarification to an appendix at the end of the article. Despite Hayek's attempt to refocus the argument on technical terms and to exploit the difference between Anglo-Saxon Marshallian economics and Austrian capital economics, Keynes was unprepared to abandon the broader picture he accused Hayek of missing.

He was not willing to accept that Hayek's reluctance to confront the novelty of his ideas was merely a matter of obtuseness. "Dr. Hayek has seriously misapprehended the character of my conclusions," he wrote. "He thinks that my central contention is something different from what it really is." He accused Hayek not only of misrepresenting his views but of putting words into his mouth. "No wonder that he finds many of my conclusions inconsistent," he wrote. He accused Hayek of hiding behind an argument over terminology when in fact he was simply "looking for trouble" and, to that end, had represented "molehills in the pathway as mountains."

Keynes blamed himself for some of the misapprehensions about the arguments in *A Treatise*, as others, too, had been confused as to his exact meaning. He admitted that during the years it had taken to write *A Treatise*, he had changed his mind on a number of key elements and that perhaps he had not totally purged the finished work of his earlier reasoning. "Traces of old trains of thought are not easily obliterated, and certain passages which I wrote some time ago may have been unconsciously cast into a mould less obviously inconsistent with my own former views than they would be if I were writing now."[13] But that was all Keynes was prepared to concede. In Hayek's case, he suggested, devotion to the Austrian School's way of thinking was enough to ensure that the original and sophisticated thoughts expressed in *A Treatise* were too great a leap for hidebound scholars like Hayek to grasp. "Those who are sufficiently steeped in the old point of view simply cannot bring themselves to believe that I am asking them to step into a new pair of trousers, and will insist on regarding it as nothing but an embroidered version of the old pair which they have been wearing for years."[14]

Keynes doubted that "a competent economist" could misunderstand and misstate his point of view, but he suggested Hayek was incapable of seeing beyond the notions he had learned in Vienna. "Any denial of his own doctrine has seemed to him so unthinkable, that even thousands of words of mine directed to its refutation have been water off a duck's back, and whilst he notices that I hold conclusions inconsistent with it, he seems still unaware that I have disputed it from the outset."[15]

Keynes spelled out where he believed he differed from Hayek. Hayek asserted that when savings and investment were not equal, it was the result of banks offering inappropriate or "unnatural" levels of credit, which resulted, over time, in a change in the price of goods. Keynes, however, was concerned with the times when the "natural" rate of interest and the "market" rates did not coincide. Hayek and he were therefore occupying "different terrains." Keynes offered Hayek an olive branch. The solution, he suggested, was for more work to be done on the theories of capital and interest, building on the works of Böhm-Bawerk and Wicksell, whom he agreed had been ignored for too long by English economists. It was work he said he was to some extent prepared to do himself, the results of which would be forthcoming in the book he was even then in the process of writing. And after offering his definition of various terms, and remarking that a "thick . . . bank of fog still separates his mind from mine," Keynes abruptly concluded his riposte.

The sharp tone of Keynes's response raised eyebrows throughout the academic community. It was well known that Keynes did not suffer fools and relished dispatching his critics with quotable vigor. According to one who knew him, "He must have been responsible for more inferiority complexes among those with whom he came in contact than anyone else in his generation."[16] But the to-and-fro between Keynes and Hayek was unusually personal and poisonous even for the viper-tongued Keynes. By abandoning the usual courtesies, Keynes, as the senior of the two men, laid himself open to the charge that he was unfairly pillorying a less accomplished scholar who had lived in the country only a short time.

While the grumbles about Keynes's behavior were mostly confined to senior common rooms, the discomfort at the spirit of the argument felt by many academics surfaced when Marshall's successor as professor of political economy at Cambridge, Arthur Pigou,[17] lamented the decline in standards of civility that Keynes's riposte represented. "Are we, in our secret hearts, wholly satisfied with the manner, or manners, in which some of our controversies are carried on?" he asked during a lecture at the LSE in 1935. "A year or two ago, after the publication of an important book, there appeared an elaborate and careful critique of a number of particular passages in it. The author's answer was, not to rebut the criticisms, but to attack with violence another book, which the critic had himself written several years before! Body-line bowling![18] The method of the duello! That kind of thing is surely a mistake."[19] He dismissed the squabbling between Keynes and Hayek as a scrap "conducted in the manner of Kilkenny cats."[20]

While the tenor of the Keynes-Hayek duel offended many, Robbins for one was delighted with the controversy and eager to keep it boiling, not least because of the attention it drew to *Economica* and the LSE. He asked Hayek to immediately answer Keynes's riposte in the same issue. Both Robbins and Hayek were grateful to Keynes for taking the bait, and happy that the great man was prepared to engage in a detailed discussion that would pit new Keynesian ideas against those of the Austrian School. At this stage of the argument, little separated them. Both had assimilated ideas from the "classical school," which based its reasoning on the cost of a product, such as its scarcity, and the cost of land and wages, as well as the "neoclassical school," which took into account the value of a good dependent on its usefulness, and the idea of "marginal utility," which suggested that the more there was of a good, the less value it held in the eyes of a buyer. Keynes, however, was already exploring how demand, supply, and prices could be manipulated, while Austrian School thinking led Hayek to believe that interfering with the free market would lead to unforeseen consequences.

Hayek broke off from writing the second part of his critique of *A Treatise* to hurriedly compile a response to Keynes's reply. "Unfortunately," Hayek wrote in his codicil to Keynes's retort, "Mr. Keynes's answer does not seem to me to clear up many of the difficulties I have pointed out, or indeed to improve the basis for further discussion."[21] If Keynes had been offended by Hayek's initial assault, Hayek was similarly taken aback by the fury implicit in Keynes's reply. In particular, he was wounded by Keynes's dismissal of his *Prices and Production*. "I am bound to say," wrote Hayek, "that while I am very ready and indeed eager seriously to consider any definite criticism which Mr. Keynes may care to make, I cannot see what possible end is served by an unproved condemnation of my views in general. I cannot believe Mr. Keynes wishes to give the impression that he is trying to distract the attention of the reader from the objections which have been raised against his analysis by abusing his opponent, and I can only hope that after my critical article has appeared in its entirety he will not only try to refute my objection somewhat more specifically, but also to substantiate his counter-criticism."[22]

Again Hayek listed the differences in terminology he believed to be at the heart of their disagreement. "He has failed to elucidate his concept of investment. I am as much at a loss as ever to see what it means exactly. . . . The same thing is true of his concept of profits. Indeed, until he has elucidated the concept of investment I do not see how he can be clear in his use of the term profit."[23] Hayek expresses the hurt of an eager pupil who finds himself condemned simply for asking for elucidation. "I should have expected that an author who has shown that almost all his fundamental concepts are ambiguous, and that some are even defined in several flatly contradictory ways, would have been more anxious to make clear in exactly what sense he wants them to be understood. Is it not the least we can ask from him that at any rate at this stage he should commit himself to a definite and unequivocal definition of his concepts?"[24]

Hayek said that in the absence of clear definitions he was obliged to speculate on Keynes's meaning. Again he slipped into the tone of hurt indignation that peppered the first part of his critique. "I have been compelled to [assume that this is what Keynes means] because I have been unable, and indeed still am unable, to detect in his *Treatise* or his subsequent eludications any other tenable explanation of this phenomenon, and because I refused to believe, as I am afraid I must now believe, that Mr. Keynes could possibly consider his analysis of the relation between profits and investment an independent and sufficient explanation of how his discrepancy arises."[25]

After offering his explanation for the flaws in Keynes's argument, Hayek returned to the charge that by ignoring European capital theory Keynes had revealed his ignorance of economics. As to Keynes's suggestion that capital theory should be looked at afresh, he wrote, "Even if we have no quite satisfactory theory, we do at least possess a far better one than that on which [Keynes] is content to rely, namely that of Böhm-Bawerk and Wicksell. That he neglects this theory, not because he thinks it is wrong, but simply because he has never bothered to make himself acquainted with it, is amply proved by the fact that he finds unintelligible my attempt to develop certain corollaries of this theory."[26]

Although Keynes had hoped to bring the skirmish to a swift end, on reading in *Economica* Hayek's scolding rejoinder to his riposte, he wrote a short personal note to his critic on a point of information that would lead to a series of barely penetrable exchanges that Keynes was to share with select members of the Circus, in particular Piero Sraffa. In true Cambridge debating style, Keynes's queries were on the face of it simple, an innocent academic grasping toward a better understanding of his opponent's objections, though it is plain that he intended to trip up Hayek by eliciting a reckless or flawed response. Addressing Hayek as plain "Hayek," as was the English public school way, Keynes wrote, "If you could elucidate for me a little further the definition of saving . . . I should find this clearer if you could give me a formula which shows how saving is *measured*. Also, what is the difference between 'voluntary saving' and 'forced saving' in *your* terminology?"[27] He signed it formally, "J. M. Keynes."

Hayek replied within the week, in a letter opening "Dear Keynes," with a complex algebraic definition of "saving" that he believed took into account Keynes's contention that part of "saving" was to do with replenishing worn-out plant. Hayek believed he now had Keynes on the end of his line, and he was anxious not to allow him to slip off. Hayek narrowed in on what he believed to be the outstanding terminological difference between them. "I entirely agree with you that it would be better not to use the word saving in connection with what I have called 'forced saving' but only to speak of investment in excess of saving," he wrote. "While it is essential for an equilibrium that saving and investing in my sense should correspond, there seems to me to exist no reason whatever why saving and investment in your sense should correspond."[28]

The day Hayek's answer arrived, Keynes wrote back. "Many thanks for your letter, which makes things a good deal clearer to me," he wrote. "There are, however, two expressions as to which I should like still further explanation."[29] He was puzzled over Hayek's use of "velocity," "since I reckon that there are now nine senses in which contemporary economists use this term, some of them differing but slightly and subtly from one another," and he added a new query about Hayek's use of the term "existing capital."[30]

Three days later, Hayek obliged, explaining that by "velocity" he meant "total effective circulation," though "I do not normally work with this concept at all." He directed Keynes toward Pigou's *Economics of Welfare*, "which on the whole agrees with my views."[31] After four days, Keynes hit the ball back over the net. "I am sorry to be tiresome," wrote Keynes, "but what I really wanted to get at was the exact significance you attach to 'effective circulation.'"[32]

Even the arrival of Christmas did not slow the to-and-fro. On Christmas morning Hayek wrote to Keynes, "I am sorry I have misunderstood your question." The "total effective circulation" was "simply the total of all money payments effected (in cash, bank deposits, or whatever form) during any arbitrary period of time."[33] That afternoon—in those days the Royal Mail delivered twice daily, even on Christmas Day—Keynes replied, "That is what I thought you meant," though he quickly added, "and that is just my difficulty." Hayek may have felt that despite Keynes's reservation about terms, he was moving closer to his rival the better to refute his ideas: after three letters signed "J. M. Keynes," Keynes this time signed off his Christmas letter with the marginally less formal "J. M. K."

After a short hiatus, because Hayek spent some days over Christmas out of London, the correspondence continued. Again Hayek's tone was one of barely concealed irritation. "If I had thought that you had any difficulties about [the replacement of capital from savings] I should have long ago tried to make it clearer,"[34] he protested. But Hayek did not find it easy to be clear. His answer to Keynes's apparently simple query involved a single sentence of subsidiary clauses and ellipses, amounting to a barely digestible two hundred words. Even Hayek, by this stage, was conscious that he was finding it far from easy to express his thoughts simply, adding in parentheses, "I apologize for this terrible 'German' sentence." Again, in attempting to address the question of replacing worn-out plant, he directed Keynes toward the Austrian notion of "roundabout" stages of production that had so baffled the Marshall Society.

Keynes wrote back within the week. If Hayek imagined he was moving closer to answering Keynes, he was mistaken. "The point you go into was not really the one that bothered me," he wrote. "I quite follow the point as to the proportion of income required to make good depreciation [by replacing worn-out plant]." But he continued to press Hayek on his definition of saving and tempted him to address the world as it really is, not as a mere conceptual construct. "What would happen in a progressive society or in a society where, e.g. new inventions are liable to cause obsolescence of existing plant (as distinct from depreciation) and where there is no stable relationship between cash turnover [the amount of money changing hands] and the national income [the total of wealth generated] (e.g., 1931 the relationship between the two, here or in America, was widely different from what it was in 1929.)"[35]

On January 23, 1932, after a hiatus of nearly two weeks, during which Hayek suffered "a slight attack of influenza," he responded at length. Again he clung to the stages of production, while attempting to answer Keynes's objections. He remained in the conceptual realm of Austrian School economics and resisted being drawn into speculating on real-life conditions, conceding that "it is, of course, one of the most difficult tasks of monetary theory to determine what monetary changes become necessary to offset changes in the organization of business." He attempted to address Keynes's main thrust about the raising of capital to replace outdated plant and promised to return to the question. "I am dealing with this aspect of the problem in the second part of my 'Reflections' of which I have just read the proofs."[36]

Keynes was tiring of the correspondence. Sharing Hayek's latest salvo with Sraffa, he wrote, "What is the next move? I feel that the abyss yawns—and so do I. Yet I can't help feeling that there is something interesting in it."[37]

It was three weeks before Keynes replied to Hayek's letter of January 23. He raised a white flag, if not of surrender then of truce. As he had told Sraffa, he was weary of digging further into a field that was not his current concern, which was the practical application of his fast-developing theories, and his patience was running out. "Your letter helps me very much towards getting at what is in your mind," he wrote. "I think you have now told me all that I am entitled to ask by way of correspondence. The matter could not be carried further except by an extension of your argument to a more actual case than the simplified one we have been discussing. And that is obviously a matter for a book rather than for correspondence." He explained to Hayek that he had hoped to discern in their exchange a clear line of thinking that would be of use to him in his current explorations of how best to address the chronic economic conditions that surrounded them, but that he had made insufficient progress to warrant any more of his time and energy.

"Going back to the point at which our correspondence started, I am left where I began," Keynes wrote, "namely in doubt as to just what you mean by voluntary saving and forced saving as applied to the actual world we live in; though I think I understand now what you mean by them in certain special cases, and this of course gives me some sort of general idea as to the sort of thing you have in mind. Many thanks for answering me so fully."[38]

Keynes was eager to put a quick end to his disagreement with Hayek as he had so much else to do, not least of which was writing what was to become *The General Theory*. He concluded that there was little chance he could persuade Hayek of the errors in his thinking. As he put it, "In economics you cannot convict your opponent of error; you can only convince him of it. And, even if you are right, you cannot convince him, if there is a defect in your own powers of persuasion and exposition or if his head is already so filled with contrary notions that he cannot catch the clues to your thought which you are trying to throw to him."[39] Keynes was happy, however, for the duel to proceed by other means. Keynes and Hayek may have sheathed their swords for a while, but the debate about their differences continued to rage between their disciples.

Ben Higgins, an LSE student between 1933 and 1935, remembered the intensity of the rivalry. "We in London regarded the strange things going on in Cambridge as nonsense, and very dangerous nonsense," he recalled. "Moreover, we could see that a man with such grace and wit and charm [meaning Keynes] added to his brilliance might just possibly succeed in persuading some people that he was right. That was a frightening prospect indeed. It wasn't that there was a keen debate between London and Cambridge, because there was hardly any point of contact at all. We were very much under the influence of Hayek. He was our god."[40]

Robert Bryce, a Canadian-born Cambridge economist whose devotion to Keynesian ideas was akin to a religious experience, penetrated Hayek's seminars at the LSE and felt much the same as Higgins, but from the other side of the barricade. "I went in the spring of 1935 down to the London School of Economics a day or two a week as a missionary," he recalled. "There I attended von Hayek's seminar. . . . This was the nearest concentration of heathen available from Cambridge and I was encouraged to go and tell them about [Keynes's ideas]. . . . Hayek very courteously gave me several sessions of his seminar to expose this thing to his students. I must say it was an exciting experience and I found a lot of people quite prepared to give the paper serious attention."[41]

Abba Lerner, a Hayekian graduate student at the LSE spending a term at Cambridge, approached Richard Kahn and other Circus members "to suggest that the young generation on each side should get together and settle the debate amongst themselves."[42] The Cambridge contingent agreed, and both sides decided that an account of the debates should be logged in a new journal, *Review of Economic Studies*. There were also face-to-face meetings between the two sides at a public house in Newport, Essex. The location was significant. Newport was in an intellectual no-man's-land about halfway between Cambridge and London. At the first meeting, in August 1933, in the Cambridge corner were Kahn, Joan and Austin Robinson, and James Meade; on the LSE team were Lerner, Sol Adler, Ralph Arakie, and Aaron Emanuel.[43] Typical of the tone of the discussion was Kahn's remark, "If Hayek believes that the spending of newly printed currency on employment and consumption will worsen our current terrible depression, then Hayek is a nut."[44]

Joint seminars were also held one Sunday each month in either

Cambridge, Oxford, or London, with young economists such as Hugh Gaitskell[44] from University College London joining. The Cambridge group's more aggressive stance gave them the upper hand. Ludwig Lachmann, who studied under Hayek at the LSE, confessed to feeling like a junior officer in a war that was fast being lost. Sometimes Hayek, Keynes, Robbins, and Dennis Robertson attended, much to the excitement and consternation of the younger members. Paul Rosenstein-Rodan, who in 1931 was an economics lecturer at University College, recalled one meeting in which Robertson gave a talk on the role of money and accused both Hayek and Keynes, who were present, of failing to take into account the passage of time. Faced for once with a common enemy, Hayek responded with a "lengthy diatribe," followed by Keynes, "who rose to say he entirely agreed [with Hayek]."[46]

Alongside the antics of the Circus, Keynes had another more vicious means of assaulting Hayek by proxy. In response to reprimands by opponents and his peers for swiping at Hayek's *Prices and Production* in his defense of *A Treatise*, Keynes decided to set matters right. Unprepared to return to the scene of the crime, he decided to field a surrogate to review *Prices and Production* at length in the next available issue of *Economic Journal*. His choice was Sraffa, who, outside of Joan Robinson, was the most aggressive and articulate of his disciples. It would result in perhaps the most brutal assault on Hayek since his arrival in Britain.

EIGHT

The Italian Job

Keynes Asks Piero Sraffa to Continue the Debate, 1932

It was in eager anticipation of Keynes's response that Hayek and Robbins published the second installment of Hayek's "Reflections on the Pure Theory of Money of Mr. J. M. Keynes" in the February 1932 issue of *Economica*. Hayek's argument was again delivered in a voice of indignant incomprehension. Sentences such as "The point in question concerns a statement so extraordinary that, if it were not clearly in his book in black and white, one would not believe Mr. Keynes to be capable of making it" were typical of his stance of faux disbelief. The tenor of the second part of his critique was little different from the uncompromising language in the first that had prompted Keynes's even more intemperate reply.

Hayek again scolded Keynes for his imprecise use of economic terms, but the main thrust of his argument cut to the heart of his disagreement with Keynes. Hayek confronted the central theme of Keynes's repeated public pronouncements: the means whereby a government might with intellectual justification interfere in the market to counter high unemployment at the bottom of the business cycle.

"Like so many others who hold a purely monetary theory of the trade cycle," wrote Hayek, "[Keynes] seems to believe that, if the existing monetary organisation did not make it impossible, the boom could be perpetuated by indefinite inflation. . . . Hence he was quite consistent when, despairing of a revival of investment brought about by cheap money, he advocated, in his well known broadcast address, the direct stimulation of the expenditure of the consumers . . . for, on this theory, the effects of cheap money and increased buying of consumers are equivalent."

The radio broadcast to which Hayek was referring was the one in which Keynes urged "patriotic housewives" to "sally out tomorrow early into the streets and go to the wonderful sales."[1] The broadcast echoed his familiar refrain, that "in the chief industrial countries of the world, Great Britain, Germany, and the United States, I estimate that probably 12,000,000 industrial workers stand idle. . . . Many million pounds' worth of goods could be produced each day by the workers and the plants which stand idle."[2] In the second part of his "Reflections," Hayek took Keynes at his word and attempted to put a price on what Keynes did not quantify when he proposed curing unemployment "at all costs." Hayek concluded that the price was roaring inflation, and having witnessed hyperinflation destroy civil order in Vienna and undermine his family's savings, he believed it a price too high to pay.

Hayek summarized Keynes's explanation of the business cycle. "Since, according to [Keynes's] theory, it is the excess of the demand for consumers' goods over the costs of the available supply which constitutes the boom, this boom will last only so long as demand keeps ahead of supply and will end either when the demand ceases to increase or when the supply, stimulated by the abnormal profits, catches up with demand. Then the prices of consumers' goods will fall back to costs and the boom will be at an end, though it need not necessarily be followed by a depression; yet, in practice, deflationary tendencies [falling prices] are usually set up which will reverse the process."[3]

Hayek denied there was anything much new about this account of a boom. "In essence [Keynes's explanation] is not only relatively simple, but also much less different from the current explanations than its author seems to think."[4]

Hayek addressed why he believed Keynes's idea of increasing investment by reducing interest rates, thereby boosting production, was shortsighted and, after a while, ineffective. "He considers what I have called changes in the structure of production (i.e. the lengthening or shortening of the average period of production) to be a long-run phenomenon which may, therefore, be neglected in the analysis of a short-period phenomenon, such as the trade cycle," wrote Hayek. "I am afraid that this contention merely proves that Mr. Keynes has not yet fully realized that *any* change in the amount of capital per head of working population is equivalent to a change in the average length of the roundabout process of production and that, therefore, all his demonstrations of the change in the amount of capital during the cycle prove my point."

Furthermore, "If the increase of investment is not the consequence of a voluntary decision to reduce the possible level of consumption for this purpose, there is no reason why it should be permanent and the very increase in the demand for consumer goods which Mr. Keynes has described will put an end to it as soon as the banking system ceases to provide additional cheap means for investment."[5] He concluded, "It is not difficult to understand, in the light of these considerations, why the easy-money policy which was adopted immediately after the crash of 1929 was of no effect."[6]

Hayek specifically addressed the implications of Keynes's repeated assertion that in the absence of private investment, where savings and investment were out of step, demand could be maintained at a high rate and jobs restored by government-funded public works. Hayek was so sure he had refuted what he believed to be one of Keynes's central contentions that he emphasized the importance of the passage by highlighting it in italics. "Any attempt to bring about an increase in investment to correspond to this 'saving' which is already required to maintain the old capital would have exactly the same effect as any other attempt to raise investment above net saving; inflation, forced saving, misdirection of production and, finally, a crisis."[7]

It was a forceful rebuttal of Keynes's ideas. But Hayek was too late; Keynes's caravan had moved on. After the initial flurry of counterargument in his response to the first part of Hayek's critique, Keynes had decided to ignore Hayek's continuing criticism. He was now fully occupied with developing an intellectually watertight explanation, which had long eluded him, for why raising public investment in place of absent private investment at a time of recession would put the jobless to work without prompting the crisis Hayek believed to be inevitable. The result would be his monumental *General Theory of Employment, Interest and Money.*

Keynes's decision not to respond was a significant setback for Hayek. By splitting Hayek's review into two parts, Robbins and Hayek had failed to gain Keynes's full attention. Having exploded at the tone of the first part, and having accused Hayek of deliberately misunderstanding his argument, Keynes had no intention of returning to the debate. Thus the first and perhaps best chance to nip Keynesianism in the bud was lost. Had Hayek first published the second part of his "Reflections," which addressed the nub of Keynes's interventionist thoughts, or published the whole of his critique in a single pass, he may have held Keynes's wandering attention long enough to stop him in his tracks. Instead, perhaps because neither Hayek nor Robbins had expected Keynes to respond so quickly to the first part, the more substantial and persuasive line of Hayek's argument was left unanswered by Keynes.

Instead, Keynes set a hound onto Hayek in the shape of the young Circus member Piero Sraffa. The decision to assign Sraffa to the task was an act of outright hostility. Of all Keynes's disciples, Sraffa, a formidable figure with short dark hair, a high forehead, and a small black moustache, who had written a searching analysis of inflation in

Italy during World War I, was the perfect person to take on Hayek. He was a brawler, forensic when taking apart an argument and caustic when articulating criticisms. Even the formidable Joan Robinson, an eager warrior in the Cambridge–London School of Economics skirmishes, considered Sraffa, ostensibly a shy and well-mannered soul, the only person she genuinely feared.

Sraffa's close friend the philosopher Ludwig Wittgenstein was so in awe of the Italian's argumentative skill that after an encounter with Sraffa he said he felt like the bare trunk of a tree that had been stripped of its branches.[8] "The tree, freed of its old wood, could sprout powerfully from the new,"[9] he wrote. Another student of Sraffa's modus operandi reported that it "would be a frontal attack on carefully chosen strategic points in the theoretical structure. No time would be wasted in offering all possible, subsidiary and peripheral criticism."[10] It was an ideal technique for use against the meticulous, almost mechanical mind of Hayek. The result, according to one Austria School devotee, was "an onslaught conducted with unusual ferocity."[11]

Sraffa owed his mentor Keynes a particular debt. Born in Turin to a law professor and his wife, he studied from 1921 to 1922 at the LSE and while in London was introduced to Keynes by Mary Berenson,[12] wife of Bernard Berenson,[13] the American art critic and dealer based in Florence. Returning to Italy to become a political economy professor in Perugia, Sraffa found himself a marked man. He was a friend of the Italian communist leader Antonio Gramsci and his socialist counterpart Filippo Turati, which was enough to make Sraffa an enemy of the state according to Mussolini's fascist party, which rose to power in 1922. Leftists were being removed from state jobs and replaced by fascists, and violence by fascist gangs was becoming increasingly commonplace.

It was Sraffa's reputation as an economist with an original cast of mind that led Keynes to commission him to write an article for the "Reconstruction in Europe" series, a piece that was sharply critical of the three largest Italian banks. The piece was so damning of Italian banking practices that it drew the attention of Mussolini himself, who was, coincidentally, in the midst of trying to solve a banking crisis by using state funds to rescue the ailing Banco di Roma. Sraffa's piece was perfectly timed to cause the maximum mischief, and Keynes was delighted. Mussolini, however, was not. He decried Sraffa's article as a "slander against Italy,"[14] the unpatriotic act of a radical agent paid by foreigners. In threatening telegrams to Sraffa's father Angelo, Mussolini demanded that a retraction and apology be published. Sraffa told his father that his article was wholly based on verifiable facts and that he stood by his words.

While Sraffa remained in Italy as the banks prepared to file a libel lawsuit, Keynes moved fast. He offered Sraffa safety in the shape of a Cambridge economics lectureship. Sraffa, who had to step down from a state job in Milan because of the banking furor, set off for England, only to be detained by customs officials at Dover after the British Home Office received a tip from Italian authorities that he was a dangerous revolutionary. Sraffa was sent back to Calais in northern France, and when the crisis subsided,[15] he took up the post Keynes had created for him.

Although Sraffa joined the Circus, his age—he was just over thirty, so a little older than the others—and his reputation for exposing errors in the work of classical theorists set him apart from the others. One of the first tasks Keynes gave him was to translate his *Tract on Monetary Reform* into Italian. Then Keynes asked Sraffa to review Hayek's *Prices and Production* in the *Economic Journal* of March 1932. He could not have chosen a more formidable champion.

Like the LSE lectures on which it was based, *Prices and Production* is not an easy work to fathom. As John Hicks, an LSE lecturer sympathetic to the Austrian School who would later soar to prominence for translating Keynes's notions into a simplified mathematical model,[16] wrote, "*Prices and Production* was in English, but it was not English economics. It needed further translation before it could be properly assessed."[17] Nor are the arguments Sraffa employed against Hayek easy to follow. Even Chicago School economist Frank Knight,[18] steeped in Austrian School thinking, found the whole matter too obtuse. As he wrote to Oskar Morgenstern, "I wish [Hayek] or someone would try to tell me in a plain grammatical sentence what the controversy between Sraffa and Hayek is about. I haven't been able to find anyone on this side who has the least idea."[19]

What could not be missed, however, was the personal, sarcastic, and unforgiving tone of Sraffa's assault. Sraffa opened his critique by describing Hayek's LSE lectures as "a feat of endurance on behalf of the audience as much as of the lecturer. . . . There is one respect in which the lectures. . . . fully uphold the tradition which modern writers on money are rapidly establishing," writes Sraffa, "that of unintelligibility." While Sraffa complimented Hayek on concentrating on the way the amount of money in the system affected commodity prices, rather than looking at prices in general, "in every other respect the inescapable conclusion is that [Hayek's thoughts] can only add to the prevailing confusion of thought on the subject."[20]

In *Prices and Production*, Hayek had sought to prove that if money is lent at a rate that is out of step with the sum of savings, it is invested in production that cannot sustain itself. When further funding dries up, factory owners find they do not attract customers and some lines of production are brought to an abrupt halt. In other words, when the price of borrowing money is out of kilter, it corrupts the ordered stages of production of goods until, after a period of crisis, the economy finds a new equilibrium. Hayek suggested that there was an ideal rate at which money should be lent, a rate that sustained production at all stages without waste and provided goods at prices consumers could meet. That was the "natural rate of interest" that effectively left money with a "neutral" role, because it had no bearing on the "natural" operation of the productive system.

Sraffa's approach to his task was clear. He had been commissioned to assess *Prices and Production* and to direct attention to Hayek's errors. He was not concerned with defending Keynes's theories. Sraffa first takes Hayek to task for considering that money could ever be neutral, "that is to say, a kind of money which leaves production and the relative prices of goods, including the rate of interest, 'undisturbed,' exactly as they would be if there were no money at all." Sraffa accuses Hayek of a rudimentary error by reminding him that his notion of neutral money is confounded by "the beginning of every textbook on money. That is to say, that money is not only the medium of exchange, but also a store of value." Sraffa describes Hayek's theories as "a maze of contradictions [that] makes the reader so completely dizzy that when he reaches the discussion of money he may out of despair be prepared to believe anything." As for the elaborate theory of the stages of productions that Hayek liked to explain with triangular diagrams, Sraffa dismisses it as "a terrific steamhammer in order to crack a nut— and then he does not crack it. Since we are primarily concerned in this review with the nut that is not cracked, we need not spend time criticising the hammer."

As for Hayek's central contention, that "there can be no doubt" that, if producers employ credit that is larger than the amount of saving, that inflation and collapse will ensue, Sraffa throws Hayek's words back at him. "As a moment's reflection will show, 'there can be no doubt' that nothing of the sort will happen. One class has, for a time, robbed another class of part of their incomes; and has saved the plunder. When the robbery comes to an end, it is clear that the victim cannot possibly consume the capital which is now well out of their reach." While Hayek contended that when easy credit was cut off manufacturers were left with redundant machinery, Sraffa suggests that the factory owners got to keep their plant, which could be brought into use when the market picked up. All this was paid for by their customers. Hayek predicted disaster for factory owners if banks lent at too low a rate. Sraffa counterargued that during the period when additional capital unbacked by savings was available, manufacturers would earn enough to put aside cash to pay the interest on the additional capital when its provision came to an end. In the meantime, producers would have gained the means to make a greater number of goods at a lower price. Thus, far from being inflationary, reducing interest rates to bolster production tended in the long run to reduce prices.

After concluding with the uncompromising judgment that "Dr. Hayek's discussion is utterly irrelevant to money and to inflation," Sraffa accuses Hayek of "running away from his problem of neutral money" and inadvertently landing "right in the middle of Mr. Keynes's theory." According to Sraffa, Hayek was not an opponent of Keynes but an unwitting admirer and supporter. "And here this review must stop," Sraffa declares, adding the teasing line, "Space does not allow of an adequate criticism of the new and rather unexpected position taken up by Dr. Hayek."[21]

Hayek lost no time in penning a reply to Sraffa's review for the next edition of *Economic Journal*. In his usual sarcastic style, he feigned compassion for Sraffa's plight "at having spent so much time on a work from which he has obviously derived no profit and which appears to him merely to add to the prevailing confusion of thought on the subject." He confronted Sraffa's criticism of what Hayek claimed to be his novel contribution to economics, that "capital accumulated by 'forced saving' [would] be, at least partly, dissipated as soon as the cause of 'forced saving' disappears." Hayek agreed with Sraffa, that "it is upon the truth of this point that my theory stands or falls."

In repeating his explanation for what pertains when new capital unbacked by savings is injected into an economy, Hayek put emphasis on the fact that those employed would eventually be paid more, as the additional money hosed into the system would prompt wage inflation. The incremental spending on wages rather than capital would, he suggested, over time slow up the growth in producers' goods and a new equilibrium would be reached where interest rates would be "the same rate as before the forced saving took place, and [producers'] capital worn down to something approaching its former state." The fact that producers may be left with idle equipment did not mean that the value of their plant had not diminished, for it had. Unused machinery was less valuable than productive plant, and in the meantime producers had to pay interest on their borrowing.

Challenging Sraffa to justify his "surprisingly superficial objection to this analysis," Hayek switched gears, asking, "Does he belong to the sect which believes in [employing idle plant] by stimulating consumption" as Keynes believed? As for Sraffa taunting Hayek by saying he appeared to be in agreement with Keynes on a number of matters, Hayek was having none of it. "I venture to believe that Mr. Keynes would fully agree with me in refuting Mr. Sraffa's suggestion," he wrote. "That Mr. Sraffa should have made such a suggestion, indeed, seems to me only to indicate the new and rather unexpected fact that he has understood Mr. Keynes's theory even less than he has my own." To which Keynes appended a mischievous footnote: "With Mr. Hayek's permission I should like to say that, to the best of my comprehension, Mr. Sraffa has understood my theory accurately."[22]

Sraffa instantly wrote "A Rejoinder" that appeared in the same issue of the *Economic Journal* as Hayek's response. First came the ritual baiting of his subject. "This specimen of Dr. Hayek's manner of arguing is by itself such an eloquent illustration of my review that I am reluctant to spoil it by comments," he wrote. What Hayek called "forced saving," which would lead to catastrophe, Sraffa preferred to call "spoilation," in which "those who had gained by the inflation chose to save the spoils" and "those on whom forced saving had been inflicted would have no say in the matter." Sraffa contended that far from ending in catastrophe, as Hayek suggested, "forced saving"— which may perhaps better be described as "inappropriate lending"— ended happily. From the moment that inflation ends as "the newly started processes of production begin to yield consumable products, . . . entrepreneurs will be able to meet their outgoings for current production and for maintenance of the increased capital entirely out of their receipts from sales, without need of any additional inflationary money." This could only happen, Sraffa agreed with Hayek, if wages did not rise to meet the new costs. "I contend that this will not happen," Sraffa declares, for the reason Hayek gives in a footnote to his previous article: "Except for such amounts as may be absorbed in cash holdings in any additional stages of production." "Exactly," Sraffa exclaims. "If Dr. Hayek had taken as much pains in writing his book as his reviewer has taken in reading it he would remember that under his assumptions such cash holdings will absorb not merely certain exceptional amounts, but the whole of the additional money issued during the inflation; that consequently incomes cannot rise at all, and there will be no occasion for any dissipation of capital."

In his article Hayek challenged Sraffa to reveal what he really believed, as the intellectual basis of his thought had been left unstated. Now Sraffa responded with the deepest ridicule. "After [Sraffa's exposition of the flaw in Hayek's logic], Dr. Hayek will allow me not to take seriously his questions as to what I 'really believe.' Nobody could believe that anything that logically follows from such fantastic assumptions is true in reality. But I admit the abstract possibility that conclusions deduced from them by faulty reasoning may, by lucky accident, prove quite plausible." Sraffa had intended the sentence to be a knockout blow.

There was one last piece of tidying up for Sraffa. In his arguments about the natural rate of interest, which at a time of equilibrium left money effectively neutral, what Hayek called the "money rate," Hayek had conceded, on Sraffa's prompting, that there was no single overall natural rate but a succession of different natural rates that were appropriate for different commodities. Having considered the matter further, Sraffa was ready to pounce. The Austrian School economist Knut Wicksell, who had developed the notion of the natural rate and money rate of interest, had acknowledged that there was no single natural rate but a number of different natural rates for each commodity. There was, for instance, a natural rate for apples and a different natural rate for wool. Sraffa's solution was to notionally weight each of the natural rates so that there emerged a composite natural rate that equalled the aggregate money rate for the whole of the economy at a time of equilibrium. "This way of escape was not open to Dr. Hayek," crowed Sraffa, "for he had emphatically repudiated the use of averages."[23] And on that sour note the to-and-fro between Hayek and Sraffa came to an abrupt end.

This side duel in the great Keynes-Hayek debate was technical, obtuse, difficult to follow, and ill-tempered. Much of it amounted to little except an exercise in logistical sparring between two heavyweight thinkers. Hayek was convinced that the economy as a whole was an elusive subject that could only be understood, and even then only partially, by considering the interaction of individuals in the marketplace. Keynes, however, was in the process of making a breakthrough in thinking that would emerge only on publication of *The General Theory*. He believed an economy could best be understood by grasping the big picture, looking from the top down at aggregates of such elements of the economy as supply, demand, and interest rates. Hayek was stuck in what came to be known as "microeconomic" thinking, looking at the different elements such as costs and value that made up an economy, while Keynes was making the leap to a new way of considering the working of the economy: macroeconomics, which appraised the economy as a whole. It is little wonder that the arguments between Keynes and Hayek before *The General Theory* was published settled so little, for they were attempting to explore by wholly microeconomic means the profound difference that was emerging between Hayek's microeconomic approach and Keynes's nascent macroeconomic notions.

There was no meeting of minds. As Frank Knight sighed, "I should like to see some headway which I do not see towards establishing terms and concepts in which economists could talk to each other and when they argue, argue issues rather than disputing about the meaning of each other's assertions." As for the Hayek-Sraffa sideshow, he wrote, "I haven't seen anyone who could tell what Sraffa and Hayek were arguing about."[24]

It was far from clear at the time that the debate between Hayek and Sraffa would be of any importance to the history of economics. Some suggested it amounted to nothing but letting off steam, "the almost juvenile sparring of two young Turks."[25] However, Ludwig M. Lachmann, Hayek's graduate assistant at the time of the Sraffa exchange, recalled that "the more perceptive sensed that they were witnessing a clash of two irreconcilable views of the economic world. The less perceptive were just puzzled by what the two contestants were after. But nobody liked what he saw. . . . That these were the opening shots in a battle between two rival schools of economic thought was not one that would readily occur to the average Anglo-Saxon economist of the 1930s."[26]

NINE

Toward *The General Theory*

The Cost-Free Cure for Unemployment, 1932–33

The next few years saw a distinct shift in strategy from Keynes. He was a brilliant popular polemicist, but for all his phrase making and eloquence urging governments to instigate public works to cure unemployment, he felt that he was making little progress. In the aftermath of *A Treatise on Money*, Keynes was suffering from a distinct lack of influence in high places. Ramsay MacDonald's "National" administration was a Conservative government by any other name. The Conservatives thought Keynes antibusiness, and he was declared persona non grata in Whitehall. The Labour Party, in defeat, had swung leftward, and members had little time for Keynes's prescriptions for what they were sure was a doomed capitalist system. For their part the Liberals, the party Keynes felt was his spiritual home, were beaten, down and out.

Keynes was now barely tolerated in the corridors of power. It is true he could still be found having lunch from time to time with MacDonald at the establishment watering hole, the Athenaeum Club in Pall Mall, but this was but a lingering ghost of the sway he once enjoyed with those who operated the levers of power. He retained a position on the Committee on Economic Information, a subset of the prime minister's Economic Advisory Council, but when yet another new committee of top economists was set up in February 1932 to advise on policy, Keynes was left out, while his orthodox rival Lionel Robbins was awarded a place.

Keynes determined that the new book he was setting out on would be aimed not at the general public, nor at politicians, nor civil servants in the Treasury, nor the masters of finance in the banks, but at his fellow economists. Having failed to instigate change via a more direct route, he now embarked on a long march to finesse his theories so that economists would take up the campaign on his behalf. To that end he decided that the arguments in *The General Theory*, as the name immodestly suggested,[1] should be soberly presented, comprehensive in their range, and logically tight. He began sifting his thoughts, sharing the burden by accepting criticism from members of the Circus, and consulting close colleagues whose keen intellects he believed would help *The General Theory* be wholly convincing to those prepared to be persuaded. It would take more than five years to complete the work.

Keynes's combative encounters with Hayek had proved so irritating, and so fruitless, that he deemed further debate with the classical economists to be futile. He was attempting to reach beyond the constraints of orthodox market economics and believed Hayek to be so trapped in the old thinking as to be incapable of grasping the brave new concepts he was now configuring. He scrawled over a copy of Hayek's essay "Capital Consumption," published in English in 1932, "The wildest farrago of nonsense yet."[2] They crossed each other's paths now and then and had glancing conversations about their differences, but Keynes felt no urge to try to persuade Hayek of the errors in his thinking. "Hayek has been here for the weekend," Keynes wrote to Lydia from King's College in early 1933. "I sat by him in hall last night and lunched with him at Piero's [Sraffa] today. We get on very well in private life. But what rubbish his theory is—I felt today that even he was beginning to disbelieve it himself."[3] Keynes was an eager progressive, keen to help advance the world toward a more humane future; Hayek, though he claimed throughout his life that he was not a conservative, was deeply skeptical of the new. Hayek was aware that his contribution to the debate with Keynes was little more than repeating the pessimistic logic inherent in Austrian School thinking. As he was later to confess, "What I had done had often seemed to me more to point out barriers to further advance on the path chosen by others than to supply new ideas which opened the path to further development."[4]

A person with whom Keynes kept in regular contact during this important period of brainstorming was the Oxford economist Roy Harrod, who had studied economics under Keynes in the fall of 1922 and whose official biography of Keynes, published six years after Keynes's death, "must be credited as a major element in the rapid dissemination of Keynes' ideas in the 1950s."[5] Harrod was periodically sent sets of galley proofs of *The General Theory* to solicit his observations and criticisms. He recalled that his comments on each successive draft "were composed with fervour, in a strain of ardent admiration and with a sense of his mighty achievement, but also with a persistent and implacable zeal to convert him on certain points."[6]

As the features of *The General Theory* slowly began to emerge, it became plain that Keynes, in his usual controversial style, felt he needed to fully refute the thoughts of Hayek and his kind if he was to overcome the unthinking adherence to classical economics that stalked the corridors of the Treasury. While members of the Circus were in the trenches in the battle against orthodoxy and were eager to egg him on, Harrod remained a rare voice of moderation. "My main endeavour was to mitigate his attack on the 'classical school,'" recalled Harrod. "I agreed with him that there was a woeful gap in the traditional theory of unemployment and that the root of the matter was an incorrect theory of interest; where I disagreed was in regard to his allegation that the traditional theory of interest did not make sense. It seemed to me that this was pushing his criticism too far, would make too much dust, and would give rise to irrelevant controversies."[7] Keynes was not worried about making dust and declined to remove a barely veiled ad hominem attack on Hayek in the final draft of *The General Theory*. If the old ways of thinking were obstructing a wider appreciation of his radical new approach to understanding economics, and thereby increased unnecessary misery in the world, Keynes felt Hayek's ideas must be addressed, dissected, and convincingly dispatched.

The most important influence on Keynes's thinking in the early 1930s, however, remained the Circus. And none was more significant than Richard Kahn in allowing Keynes to square the circle and show that increased investment would raise demand without causing a catastrophic increase in prices. The Circus proper met in earnest during the academic year 1930–31, disbanding its formal meetings before the Cambridge examinations of May 1931, many months before Keynes began to gather his thoughts to write *The General Theory*. Richard Kahn, Joan and Austin Robinson, Piero Saffra, James Meade, and others, however, continued to tease and dissect every twist and turn in Keynes's thinking and made a substantial contribution to his internal debate. Keynes wrote in his preface to *The General Theory*, "The writer of a book such as this, treading along unfamiliar paths, is extremely dependent on criticism and conversation if he is to avoid an undue proportion of mistakes. It is astonishing what foolish things one can temporarily believe if one thinks too long alone."[8]

Some doubt has been cast on the contribution the Circus made to *The General Theory*,[9] but Circus members themselves were certain that their often tart criticisms, funneled through Kahn to Keynes, made a considerable difference to Keynes's thinking and the final work. "To anybody who did not know Keynes, it is astonishing that he was willing, week after week, to discuss with me, acting as the group's spokesman, the problems which had arisen and their implications,"[10] recalled Kahn. It was a sentiment endorsed by Austin Robinson, who offered an important insight into why Keynes felt he needed to vanquish the ideas of orthodox economists such as Hayek.

"At no moment in his life, I think, did Keynes's greatness of character appear more strongly than at this time," he recalled. "Keynes never even appeared to hesitate. He was off with the rest of us in pursuit of truth with as enthusiastic a zest as if he were demolishing the work of his worst enemy."[11] Which, when it came to the work of Hayek and Robbins, he was.

The Circus certainly left its mark. Members were instrumental in persuading Keynes that he was in error in *A Treatise* when he invoked "the widow's cruse," a typically colorful Keynesian analogy that suggested that when entrepreneurs spent part of their profit on buying goods, they raised prices to a similar degree, thereby restoring their profits to their former level and leaving them as rich as before, much like the pitcher of oil in the biblical story of the "widow's cruse" (1 Kings 17:8-16) that remained full however much the widow poured from it. By the same token, they disabused him of his fondness for the obverse notion to the widow's cruse, which he termed "the Danaid jar," after the Greek myth that told of the daughters of Danaus in the Underworld who were sentenced to perpetually replenish a leaky jar. Keynes's Danaid jar theory suggested that when entrepreneurs sought to curtail their losses by cutting their consumption and increasing savings, the law of diminishing returns meant they could never recover their former wealth.[12] Both Kahn and Joan Robinson drew Keynes's attention to his error in thinking that, in describing the closed economy necessary to establish his conclusions, he deemed the output of consumption goods to be fixed and finite. Kahn exposed the fallacy thus: "If entrepreneurs responded to the abnormal profits by increasing the output of consumption goods, the price level of consumption goods would progressively fall, and abnormal profits would fall, until either entrepreneurs earned no more than normal remuneration or some barrier was encountered—full capacity utilisation or full employment of labour."[13]

In his defense, in an anguished letter to Joan Robinson, Keynes pointed out that in parts of *A Treatise*, "I have long discussions [on] the effects of changes in output; it is only at a particular point in the preliminary theoretical argument that I have assumed constant output."[14] But the objection of Circus members to both fallacies suggested to Keynes what was to become a pivotal element of *The General Theory*, that overall output was not fixed and could be raised through increased investment to a point where everyone in an economy was employed.[15] It was this first slender thread of thought that led to Keynes's wholesale contradiction of the claim of classical economists like Hayek that an economy, left to its own devices, in the long run inevitably came to rest at a state of equilibrium where there was full employment. Keynes was to argue in *The General Theory* that in the short and medium terms an economy could reach equilibrium with considerable unemployment and that the full employment equilibrium predicted by classical economists too often proved to be elusive. Keynes believed that the chronic unemployment endured in Britain and America in the 1920s and 1930s was evidence that the full employment equilibrium was a fallacy.

During the writing of *The General Theory*, Kahn proved to be far more than Keynes's favorite and most devoted pupil; he acquired something of the status of a missing son. He alone was invited to take part in the intense long hours of conversation Keynes needed to define and refine his thoughts. From an early date Kahn was admitted into Keynes's lonely ivory tower and allowed to act as a patient and clearheaded creative partner. Kahn explained how he was used as a sounding board to monitor Keynes's far-flung ruminations. "It was in the course of the year 1930 that I began to spend part of most vacations staying with Keynes and Lydia at [Keynes's Sussex farmhouse] Tilton,"[16] Kahn recalled. "I relieved the solitude and provided, by being on the spot, a more rapid method of discussion than correspondence by post."[17] Kahn also amended Keynes's text. "My written—as opposed to oral—contributions were made in the margins of galley proofs," he wrote. "Such a note would take the form either of minor redrafting; or of an indication that Keynes and I should discuss the passage indicated, or of the correction of a misprint."[18]

It was Kahn, too, who provided perhaps the most important single new element to Keynes's thinking by providing a cogent explanation for why public investment, even on borrowed money, could soon recoup its cost while drastically reducing unemployment: what Kahn at first termed "the ratio" and Keynes famously renamed "the multiplier." Keynes had intuitively concluded that public investment would soon pay for itself while putting the jobless to work in his 1929 Liberal Party general-election pamphlet, "Can Lloyd George Do It?" coauthored with Hubert Henderson. The Liberals promised to invest £100 million a year in public works for three years to create jobs, a policy the Treasury dismissed as a waste of money.

Keynes argued that, on the contrary, the new jobs would cost little, that they would if anything boost business confidence because entrepreneurs would invest to take advantage of the new demand from those newly employed, and that the jobs directly created by the government would be accompanied by new private sector jobs for those who provided goods and services to the newly employed. "The fact that many workpeople who are now unemployed would be receiving wages instead of unemployment pay would mean an increase in effective purchasing power which would give a general stimulus to trade," Keynes and Henderson argued. "Moreover, the greater trade activity would make for further trade activity; for the forces of prosperity, like those of a trade depression, work with a cumulative effect."[19] It was common sense that this was so, Keynes argued, while conceding that "it is not possible to measure effects of this character with any sort of precision."[20] In his article "The Relation of Home Investment to Unemployment," published in the June 1931 issue of *Economic Journal*, Richard Kahn set himself the task of statistically proving that what Keynes surmised about the multiplier was true.

Kahn recalled how his work toward solving the riddle of the

multiplier came about. "I began work on my so-called 'multiplier' article in the Austrian Tyrol in August 1930," he wrote. "I was inspired by 'Can Lloyd George Do It?' partly because this marked a milestone in the development of thought, but also because of certain arithmetical and logical problems which it raised."[21] The more Kahn explored the problem of how to assess how many would be indirectly employed as a result of the government employing workers, the more he was amazed by how accurate Keynes and Henderson's guesswork had been. Kahn set aside the problem of attempting to quantify the additional jobs deriving from the added investment stemming from the growth in business confidence that an injection of a substantial sum of public funds into the marketplace would provoke because "the state of confidence about the near future . . . is a difficult subject to assess, still more to quantify."[22] He was certain there would be additional employment from improved business confidence, but left such tricky calculations about exactly how many new jobs it would create for later.

Kahn concentrated instead on the central contention in Keynes and Henderson's claim, that for every million pounds spent on the construction of new roads, five thousand new jobs would be created, about half directly and half indirectly. Keynes and Henderson had estimated that "nearly half of the capital cost would be recovered at the time," with a full one-fourth saved by not having to pay out money in unemployment relief. Kahn, too, concluded that government savings from not having to pay unemployment insurance, plus savings from spending on poor relief, amounted to half the cost. He also agreed with the pair's estimate that the new employment would generate taxation revenue amounting to a further eighth of the cost. Kahn was astounded that Keynes and Henderson's estimates should be so similar to the results of his own more demanding mathematical analysis. He wrote, "It is remarkable that the inspired guesses of Keynes and Henderson turned out to be so accurate, although, so far as is known, they made no estimate of the 'multiplier'—the ratio of the total additional employment (primary and secondary) to the primary employment."[23] Kahn concluded that the multiplier might vary from country to country, depending on how much benefit from the public investment leaked abroad, as it would with major trading nations like Britain. He estimated that in Britain the figure lay between 0.56 and 0.94 "and I suggested that the adoption of $3/4$ would be 'erring in the direction of under-statement.'"[24]

"My main concern—from the start," recalled Kahn, "was to prove that the various offsets—the increase in the yield of taxation, savings of various kinds to the Exchequer . . . the increase in the excess of imports over exports"—as the newly employed would likely spend on imported goods but would not contribute to exports—"the increase in private savings (mainly out of profits), and the change in the rate of saving due to the rise in prices—added up to the cost of the investment."[25] Kahn anticipated two objections to public works funded by government that would soon be raised by the classical school, that such measures would increase inflation and, from Dennis Robertson,[26] that they would achieve little more than add to the quantity of money in circulation. Kahn dismissed the predicted rise in the cost of living as an "extraordinary fatuity," because "the rise in prices, if it occurs at all, is a natural concomitant of increased output, to a degree indicated by the slope of the supply curve."[27] That is, whenever demand was increased, by whatever means, it tended to raise prices. There was nothing special about inflation caused by artificially raising demand. He concluded that the objection against increasing output, or supply, because it was prompted by the use of public funds, or borrowing, rather than private funding of employment, was therefore a red herring. As for the objection to the government printing money rather than raising it from lenders, Kahn argued that "there was no reason why additional expenditure on public works needed to be financed by the creation of additional money as against borrowing from the public (though if a heavy programme was started off suddenly, some temporary help from the banking system would be useful for pump-priming purposes)."[28]

While Keynes's thinking toward *The General Theory* was not known outside of his small band of intimates, those who were opposed to his developing ideas, such as Hayek and Robbins at the LSE, could hardly avoid hearing that Keynes was making considerable headway toward his magnum opus. Then, in the summer of 1932, all started to come clear. Keynes began expounding on his post-*Treatise* thoughts in a series of Monday-morning lectures to his Cambridge students, titled "The Pure Theory of Money," which were widely attended by members of the faculty, by undergraduates from other disciplines, and even by a number of interested invited visitors. In the autumn term, after a long summer of heavy rumination at Tilton, Keynes resumed his lecture series with a significant announcement to his assembled pupils, that the new title of his subsequent lectures would be "The Monetary Theory of Production." "With these words in October 1932," recalled Lorie Tarshis, a visiting postgraduate student from Toronto University who attended all four of the series, "Keynes . . . in effect announced the beginning of the Keynesian Revolution."[29]

Lecture by lecture, reading from successive sets of galley proofs amended in his own hand, Keynes presented the latest iterations of his thinking. It was clear to those who attended that they were witnessing something out of the ordinary. As Tarshis recalled, "As the weeks passed, only a stone would not have responded to the growing excitement [the lectures] generated."[30] Michael Straight, an American undergraduate, recalled, "It was as if we were listening to Charles Darwin or Isaac Newton. The audience was hushed as Keynes spoke."[31] By the end of the series, Keynes had worked through his ideas to his own satisfaction and was ready to consign to his publisher, Macmillan, the final set of corrected proofs of a work that many would view as the most influential body of economic theory written in the twentieth century.

Although Keynes largely confined himself to academic life during the gestation of *The General Theory*, he did allow himself one significant sally into the public realm. When it was announced that an international summit, the World Economic Conference, was to be held in London in June 1933, Keynes could not resist a chance to contribute. He wanted to ensure that his most recent thinking would be available to policy makers. He proposed to the editor of *The Times*, Geoffrey Dawson, a series of articles suggesting a way to solve the worldwide economic trough through international cooperation. The articles offered a sneak preview of a revolutionary theory that would soon alter the world.

After appearing in *The Times*, the articles were collected as a pamphlet, *The Means to Prosperity*, a document that proved to be the base camp to *The General Theory*'s peak. For once, Keynes, now aged fifty, abandoned the easy phrase making and colorful sarcasm that had become his stock-in-trade and instead set out clearly and without sensation an argument he felt would attract the attention of the economists and finance ministers heading to London. He challenged them to either agree with his prescription for creating millions of new jobs at a minimum of cost to the taxpayer or point out where he was mistaken. It was the most cogent, disciplined, persuasive account of his imaginative ideas yet expressed, and contained all the elements that would come to be known as "Keynesianism." Far more than *The General Theory*, which was intended to influence academic economists, *The Means to Prosperity* was made deliberately accessible for those, like many of the world's finance ministers, who had little knowledge of economics. For the Hayekians, *The Means to Prosperity* was the clearest signal yet of the scale of the impending Keynesian challenge to their philosophy. It gave them fair warning of what was to come in *The General Theory* and suggested to them that it was time to prepare counterarguments.

In *The Means to Prosperity*, Keynes was blunt about those who suggested that the world economy would recover if traditional remedies were employed. "There are still people who believe that the way out can only be found by hard work, endurance, frugality, improved business methods, more cautious banking, and, above all, the avoidance of devices,"[32] he wrote. Armed with Kahn's paper, Keynes for the first time publicly integrated the multiplier into his proposal that governments should spend to raise overall demand in the economy. And he confronted head-on the assertion by Hayekians that government spending would only spur inflation.

"If the new expenditure is additional and not merely in substitution for other expenditure, the increase of employment does not stop there," he wrote. "The additional wages and other incomes paid out are spent on additional purchases, which in turn lead to further employment. If the resources of the country were already fully employed, these additional purchases would be mainly reflected in higher prices and increased imports. But in present circumstances this would be true of only a small proportion of the additional consumption, since the greater part of it could be provided without much change of price by home resources which are at present unemployed."[33]

For those who were coming to terms for the first time with how the multiplier worked, Keynes spelled it out. "The newly employed who supply the increased purchases of those employed on the new capital works will, in their turn, spend more, thus adding to the employment of others; and so on." He suggested that the multiplier figure in Britain was 2, but he did not want to overpromise lest his arguments appear fantastic, so he suggested that every pound the government spent on creating new jobs was worth one and a half pounds to the total economy. "Additional loan-expenditure of £200 on materials, transport, and direct employment puts, not one man to work for a year, but—taking account of the whole series of repercussions— one and a half men,"[34] he wrote. He stressed that employment was not the only benefit of the multiplier. "Half of what [the chancellor of the exchequer] remits will in fact return to him from the saving on the dole and the higher yield of a given level of taxation."[35] This was to become a key element of *The General Theory*, that economists and financial ministers should scrutinize not whether the income and outflow of national expenditures were in balance but the scale of the overall income of the nation, what Keynes would call a nation's "aggregate demand."

In an argument familiar to the one that would reemerge after the banking crisis of 2008, when plans for a stimulus from government borrowing were immediately countered by anxiety about the budget deficit, Keynes asserted that "it is a complete mistake to believe that there is a dilemma between schemes for increasing employment and schemes for balancing the Budget—that we must go slowly and cautiously with the former for fear of injuring the latter. Quite the contrary. There is no possibility of balancing the Budget except by increasing the national income, which is much the same thing as increasing employment."[36] Again, a pivotal element of *The General Theory* was on display: that national income was equal to the sum of the incomes of those employed.

Keynes estimated it would cost £100 million a year to put 1 million people to work, of which £50 million might come from a reduction in taxation. This was Keynes's first suggestion that tax breaks could be used to stimulate the economy, a policy that became a hallmark first of Keynesians and Keynesian finance ministers but then a talisman of their conservative opponents. He cautioned that for such a reduction in taxes to have the desired effect on the job market, it "does not apply to a relief of taxation balanced by an equal reduction of Government expenditure (by reducing school teachers' salaries, for example); for this represents a redistribution, not a net increase, of national spending power."[37] As Harrod observed, "We begin here to get the first inkling of an idea, more radical than any recommended so far, that the Chancellor of the Exchequer should pump in additional purchasing power, not only by financing public works through loans, but also by remitting taxation without reducing current expenditure. This is almost 'deficit finance' in the full sense."[38]

On top of this, Keynes made a broader appeal for concerted action to increase demand worldwide and, in the face of widespread deflation (falling prices) that deterred business activity, to deliberately raise prices as an incentive to entrepreneurs and private industry. "There is no effective means of raising world prices except by increasing loan-expenditure throughout the world," he asserted. "It was, indeed, the collapse of expenditure financed out of loans advanced by the United States, for use both at home and abroad, which was the chief agency in starting the slump."[39]

Keynes then ventured into territory that would guide the thinking of the victorious Allies attempting to restore the worldwide economy after the devastation inflicted by World War II. He had often expressed his contempt for gold as an arbitrary measure of wealth. What he now proposed was that the world's finance ministers should print money in concert, as if it were backed by gold. For Keynes, "notional gold" was every bit as useful as real gold ingots. Individual nations had long abandoned tying their supply of banknotes to the actual amount of gold stored in their treasuries; why not apply the same financial logic to a worldwide system of credit, where each nation would be provided with "gold notes" that had all the benefits of a cache of gold but without that cache actually existing. It was, Keynes urged, a means of restoring confidence in a world market that had frozen in the face of economic failure. But if it was an instrument to reinstate confidence, it was more than a mere confidence trick. As Roy Harrod would explain, "No one would think it a confidence trick if all these nations discovered an equivalent amount of gold in local mines and were encouraged to go forward by the reserves thereby acquired. Why should not gold certificates play a similar role?"[40]

Keynes then ventured an idea that would come into its own when the Allies contemplated how to ensure that the postwar world would avoid repeating the errors of the Versailles Treaty: the establishment of a world banking body, an idea that would become manifest in the World Bank. He proposed $5 billion in "gold-notes" distributed to each country according to "some such formula as the amount of gold which it held in reserve at some recent normal date, e.g., at the end of 1928."[41] To ensure currency stability, Keynes, who had long dismissed gold as a useful standard against which to peg currencies, was, perhaps reluctantly, convinced that the notional-gold standard should continue to rule his new world financial regime. "The notes would be gold-notes," he wrote, "and the participants would agree to accept them as the equivalent of gold. This implies that the national currencies of each participant would stand in some defined relationship to gold."[42]

There was a deeply ominous note in one of Keynes's parting observations. In *The Economic Consequences of the Peace* he had predicted that reparations imposed on the defeated nations would foster ideal conditions for the flowering of extreme political movements, whether of the Right or the Left. While he did not in *The Means to Prosperity* allude to events that had taken place in Germany, just two months before his pieces appeared—namely, the rise of the Nazis headed by Adolf Hitler, appointed chancellor in January 1933—he did hint at another set of circumstances that would also display his prescient understanding of how the world span.

"Some cynics, who have followed the argument thus far, conclude that nothing except a war can bring a major slump to its conclusion," he wrote. "For hitherto war has been the only object of governmental loan-expenditure on a large scale which governments have considered respectable. In all the issues of peace they are timid, over-cautious, half-hearted, without perseverance or determination, thinking of a loan as a liability and not as a link in the transformation of the community's surplus resources, which will otherwise be wasted, into useful capital assets. I hope that our Government will show that this country can be energetic even in the tasks of peace."[43]

TEN

Hayek Blinks

The General Theory Invites a Response, 1932–36

Through the early 1930s, Friedrich Hayek also watched events unfolding in Germany with a growing sense of foreboding. Before long the rise of the Nazis would long lead to the absorption of Austria into the Third Reich in the Anschluss Österreichs of 1938. Hitler's public works program of road building and the manufacture of war materiel, backed by the full terror of the Nazi state, was a cruel parody of what Keynes was proposing. But Hitler's direction of the German economy would prompt Hayek to think beyond economics to consider the importance of the free market In ensuring a free society. Just as his experience of rampant inflation had underpinned his belief in the Austrian School theory of capital, so too did his sympathy with the plight of those under Nazi tyranny, including his close family, lead to a broader philosophical understanding of how denial of the free market could lead to totalitarianism. But as the 1930s slowly began to unfold, Hayek's mind was still on convincing the insular British of the merits of continental economic ideas.

His exchange with Keynes had reached a stalemate, with Keynes politely hinting that he had become bored. "I doubt if I shall return to the charge in *Economica*," Keynes wrote to him in March 1932. "I am trying to re-shape and improve my central position, and that is probably a better way to spend one's time than in controversy."[1] The new direction Keynes was moving in was clear for all to see, in his open lectures at Cambridge and in his articles for *The Times*. Hayek's principal concern, however, was to bring British economists up-to-date with his own writing, for, as his sparring with Keynes had revealed, few except for Robbins had ever looked outside of theory published in English.

Keynes admitted in *A Treatise on Money* that "in German, I can only clearly understand what I already know—so that new ideas are apt to be veiled from me by the difficulties of the language."[2] Hayek therefore commissioned Nicholas Kaldor and H. M. Croome to translate his 1929 work *Monetary Theory and the Trade Cycle*, to be published by Harcourt, Brace in 1933. The London School of Economics lectures that had secured him a professorship were revised and published by Routledge as *Prices and Production* in 1931, and he took pains to revise his ideas in a second edition in 1935. He began collecting a series of essays, published as *Profits, Interest and Investment* in 1939. And in response to Keynes's intention to address the inadequacy of existing capital theories, Hayek began writing for Routledge his own thoughts on the subject, in *The Pure Theory of Capital*, which he hoped would become the counterpart to Keynes's *General Theory*.

Hayek meanwhile settled himself, his wife Helen, daughter Christine Maria Felicitas, born in 1929, three years after their marriage, and son Laurence Joseph Heinrich, born in 1934, in a comfortable red-brick home in Hampstead Garden Suburb, a planned ideal "garden city" of Edwardian housing and communal amenities that had become a redoubt for North London's left-leaning intelligentsia. Among his academic neighbors was Robbins, who had become a close friend. Hayek followed Karl Marx's example by frequenting the circular reading room of the British Library. He joined the Reform

Club in Pall Mall, founded to mark the 1832 Reform Act that extended the voting franchise to the populations of the newly expanded cities of the Industrial Revolution. As London's principal gentlemen's club not populated by Conservatives, the Reform's dazzling clubhouse, based on the Farnese Palace in Rome by the architect of the Palace of Westminster, Charles Barry, was adorned with portraits of British history's most radical figures. Hayek felt at home among the memorials not only to those, such as Lord Grey, who had passed the Reform Act in the face of Conservative opposition, but also to the regicide Oliver Cromwell.

One of Hayek's LSE duties was to teach graduate students. P. M. Toms, who attended Hayek's seminars between 1934 and 1935, left a vivid picture of the incongruous figure Hayek presented to his British charges. He "looked to me at least fifty, though much later on I discovered [he was in his mid-thirties]. It may have been partly due to his old-fashioned way of dressing, in a thick tweed suit with a waistcoat and high cut jacket. I nicknamed him 'Mr Fluctooations' as he so often used that word and pronounced it that way."[3] John Hicks, an Oxford economist turned LSE lecturer, also attended. "We seemed, at the start, to share a common viewpoint, or even a common faith. The faith in question was a belief in the free market, or 'price-mechanism'—that a competitive system, free of all 'interferences,' by government or monopolistic combinations, of capital or of labour, would easily find an 'equilibrium.' Hayek, when he joined us, was to introduce into this doctrine an important qualification—that money (somehow) must be kept 'neutral,' in order that the mechanism should work smoothly."[4]

Teaching gave Hayek pleasure, though his difficulty with English hampered his ability to transmit his message. "All of us were excited to hear that Hayek had arrived," recalled Theodore Draimin, an LSE undergraduate in 1932. "When we arrived for the first lecture he commenced to talk in English. After a few minutes, it became apparent that none of us could understand a word he said. Some suggested he speak in German. This he did, and those of us unable to understand had to leave the course."[5] It was a common experience. "Read a new book yesterday," student Ralph Arakie wrote to a friend. "It is by old Hayek or *von* Hayek as he is called here. This year he is giving twenty lectures in bad English (God help us) and has recommended us to read [a] book in Dutch!; besides thirty other weighty volumes. But he is a very clever chap."[6] Aubrey Jones,[7] an LSE undergraduate, recalled that Hayek "wore a perpetually benevolent smile, a trait which did not belie his nature. But his accent in English was thick and his thoughts appeared tangled. One had to sit near the front in order to follow."[8] It is tantalizing to consider how the debate with Keynes might have turned out had Hayek been as fluent in English as his eloquent rival.

But if Hayek found speaking English a trial, he was more at home when, unhurried, he could collect his thoughts in written English, especially when aided by Robbins, Kaldor, and Croome, among others. The republication in English of his University of Vienna dissertation on monetary theory and the trade cycle in 1932 gave him the chance to offer his explanation of the 1929 stock market crash and the Depression.[9] He considered the book "not only a justification of the monetary approach but also a refutation of some oversimplified monetary explanations that are widely accepted." While Keynes was spurred by a desire to confront real-life dilemmas, Hayek's works were usually pure theory. But in his preface to the English edition of *Monetary Theory and the Trade Cycle*, Hayek addressed recent catastrophic events.

Hayek's reasons for the slump, posited clearly in English for the first time, represented a passing rebuke to Keynes, who believed that the financial mayhem had been exacerbated by the deflation of prices through the Federal Reserve's raising of interest rates. Hayek conceded that Keynes's criticism had some merit, but he thought his remedy, to reinflate the American economy, was wrongheaded. "There can, of course, be little doubt that, at the present time, a deflationary process [falling prices] is going on and that an indefinite continuation of that deflation would do inestimable harm," wrote Hayek. "But this does not, by any means, necessarily mean that the deflation is the original cause of our difficulties or that we could overcome these difficulties by compensating for the deflationary tendencies . . . by forcing more money into circulation." His preferred solution, however, was based on a false premise. "There is no reason to assume that the crisis was started by a deliberate deflationary action on the part of the monetary authorities,[10] or that the deflation itself is anything but a secondary phenomenon, a process induced by the maladjustments of industry left over from the boom," he wrote. "If, however, the deflation is not a cause but an effect of the unprofitableness of industry, then it is surely vain to hope that by reversing the deflationary process, we can regain lasting prosperity."[11]

He concluded that the business cycle had been thrown out of kilter by tinkering and that the "stages of production" would need to be restored for the economy to return to the status quo ante. He suggested that Keynes's remedy was already being applied in America and had only made matters far worse. "Far from following a deflationary policy, central banks, particularly in the United States, have been making earlier and more far-reaching efforts than have ever been undertaken before to combat the depression by a policy of credit expansion—with the result that the depression has lasted longer and has become more severe than any preceding one," Hayek wrote.

Hayek continued to press his point, that government intervention only aggravated the problem. "To combat the depression by a forced credit expansion is to attempt to cure the evil by the very means which brought it about." In conclusion, he feared there was no easy way for the economy to be restored to health, but he was certain that government intervention would only prolong the crisis. "For the last six or eight years, monetary policy all over the world has followed the advice of the stabilizers. It is high time that their influence, which has already done harm enough, should be overthrown," he wrote. "The opponents of the stabilization program [such as himself] still labor . . .

under the disadvantage that they have no equally simple and clear-cut rule to propose; perhaps no rule at all that will satisfy the eagerness of those who hope to cure all evils by authoritative action. But . . . the one thing of which we must be painfully aware . . . is how little we really know of the forces that we are trying to influence by deliberate management; so little indeed that it must remain an open question whether we would try if we knew more."[12]

At the end of 1932, Keynes and others, including Arthur Pigou, sparked a correspondence in *The Times* about the need to spend, not save. Their letter to the editor, which reads as if Keynes had drafted it, argued that when there was a lack of business confidence and a sharp reduction in spending, individual savings did not automatically translate into productive investment. "Instead of enabling labour-power to be turned to a different and more important use," Keynes and his colleagues argued, "[saving] throws them into idleness." They concluded that "the public interest in present conditions does not point towards private economy; to spend less money than we should like to do is not patriotic." And in words that unmistakably suggest Keynes's pen, the economists suggested that "if citizens of a town wish to build a swimming-bath, or a library, or a museum, they will not, by refraining from doing this, promote a wider national interest. They will be 'martyrs by mistake,' and, in their martydom, will be injuring others as well as themselves. Through their misdirected good will the mounting wave of unemployment will be lifted still higher."[13]

Two days later, *The Times* published a response from Hayek, Robbins, and other LSE colleagues. While they agreed that "hoarding money, whether in cash or in idle balances, is deflationary" and that "no one thinks that deflation is in itself desirable," they could not agree that it did not matter whether money was spent or invested. "We regard it as little short of a disaster if the public should infer from what has been said that the purchase of existing securities and the placing of deposits in building societies, &c., were at the present time contrary to public interest or that the sale of securities or the withdrawal of such deposits would assist the coming of recovery," they wrote. "We are of the opinion that many of the troubles of the world at the present time are due to imprudent borrowing and spending on the part of public authorities," they wrote. "[Such practices] mortgage the Budgets of the future, and they tend to drive up the rate of interest. . . . The depression has abundantly shown that the existence of public debt on a large scale imposes frictions and obstacles to readjustment very much greater than the frictions and obstacles imposed by the existence of private debt." Their advice to the government was "not to revert to their old habits of lavish expenditure, but to abolish those restrictions on trade and the free movement of capital (including restrictions on new issues) which are at present impeding even the beginning of recovery."[14]

• In 1933, Hayek moved away from economic theory when he discovered that "people were seriously believing that National Socialism was a capitalist reaction against socialism. . . . The main exponent whom I came across was Lord Beveridge. He was actually convinced that these National Socialists and capitalists were reacting against socialism. So I wrote a memorandum[15] for Beveridge on this subject."[16] Socialism and Nazism were not diametric opposites, he argued, they were near identical in their removal of the free market, thereby curtailing the liberties essential to a free society.

To promote his line of thinking, Hayek moved to ensure that key works published in German and other languages that explained the importance of prices in determining a free society should be made available in English. It was his belief that prices reflected the innumerable economic judgments made by individuals. As he would explain, "I am convinced that if [the price mechanism] were the result of deliberate human design, and if the people guided by the price changes understood that their decisions have significance far beyond their immediate aim, this mechanism would have been acclaimed as one of the greatest triumphs of the human mind."[17] In 1935 he brought together key texts, *Collectivist Economic Planning: Critical Studies on the Possibilities of Socialism*, which featured as its centerpiece Mises's caustic critique of the shortcomings of socialist planning, "Economic Calculation in the Socialist Commonwealth," originally published in Austria in 1920. Hayek's concluding essay took to task "market socialists" who believed they could combine prices freely arrived at by individuals with prices fixed according to demands laid down by socialist planners.

As the 1930s progressed, Hayek found the news from Austria and Germany increasingly alarming. His travels to Vienna and the graphic reports of Nazi brutality in what remained of the German free press confirmed his belief that Nazism had to be defeated. Hitler's informal pact with anticommunist business leaders, who wished to avoid a repeat of the Spartacist coup in Berlin in 1919, amounted to the establishment of a corporatist state with all business decisions dependent on Nazi patronage.

As the news from Austria and Germany grew darker, Hayek began to shun his Austrian roots. In his early years in London, the Hayeks spoke English in public and German at home. As the decade progressed and a second world war began to seem likely, he decided to speak English at all times and quietly abandoned any thoughts of returning to live in Austria. "I became in a sense British, because that was a natural attitude for me," he recalled. "It was like stepping into a warm bath where the atmosphere is the same temperature as your body."[18]

Meanwhile, Keynes became increasingly confident that *The General Theory* would profoundly alter the traditional political divide between capitalism and socialism. Socialist theorists, like Marxists, assumed a crisis in capitalism was unavoidable. Fabian socialists like George Bernard Shaw believed that their brand of mixed-economy socialism could save the troubled system from outright socialism or communism. Keynes believed that by providing an intellectual justification for intervening in the economy to cure mass unemployment, he could ameliorate conditions so effectively that the predicted collapse of capitalism would be postponed indefinitely. It was therefore with a typical sense of mischief that on New Year's Day 1935 Keynes wrote to Bernard Shaw, announcing that, thanks to his upcoming book, a Fabian future would no longer be in the cards.

"I believe myself to be writing a book on economic theory, which will largely revolutionise—not, I suppose, at once but in the course of the next ten years—the way the world thinks about economic problems," he wrote Bernard Shaw. "I can't expect you, or anyone else, to believe this at the present stage. But for myself I don't merely hope what I say,—in my own mind I'm quite sure."[19] Keynes spent the rest of 1935 revising and refining his *General Theory* and amending the waves of page proofs from the publisher.

The General Theory of Employment, Interest and Money was published on February 4, 1936. Keynes had done such a good job of drumming up interest that the book was pounced on, particularly by young economists eager to boast an early familiarity with the new ideas in its four hundred pages. To maximize the book's sales and impact, Keynes set a low cover price, just five shillings. *The General Theory* was far from an easy read. To head off Hayek's criticism of *A Treatise*, Keynes attempted to merge his often idiosyncratic economic terms with those used by traditional economists. He accommodated counterarguments posed by friends and collaborators, and attempted to anticipate objections from classical economists. As simple as he tried to make his case, however, much of his reasoning remained beyond the reach of the lay reader. As he explained, "I cannot achieve my object of persuading economists to re-examine critically certain of their basic assumptions except by a highly abstract argument."[20]

Paul Samuelson,[21] the Massachusetts Institute of Technology economist who was to become Keynes's greatest evangelizer, summed up the accomplishment of *The General Theory*: "It is a badly written book, poorly organized," he wrote. "It is arrogant, bad-tempered, polemical, and not overly generous in its acknowledgements. It abounds with mares' nests and confusions. . . . Flashes of insight and intuition intersperse tedious algebra. An awkward definition suddenly gives way to an unforgettable cadenza. When it is finally mastered, we find its analysis to be obvious and at the same time new. In short, it is a work of genius."[22] John Kenneth Galbraith,[23] who was to appoint himself Keynes's high priest, agreed. "Unlike nearly all of Keynes's other writing, this volume is deeply obscure," he wrote. "Perhaps had it been otherwise and had economists not been called upon to debate his meaning and intentions, it would not have been so influential. Economists respond well to obscurity and associated puzzlement."[24]

Keynes was in combative mode from the opening paragraph, declaring that the target of his general theory was traditional economics. He had in his sights everyone who had gone before, not only his close Cambridge colleague Arthur Pigou but even his generous mentor, the founder of Cambridge economics, Alfred Marshall. But above all Keynes relished mounting an unforgiving assault on his archrivals in the Austrian School, Mises, Robbins, and Hayek. Indeed, on first reading the final draft, Roy Harrod, who had repeatedly urged Keynes to make the attack less personal, was taken aback by the severity of the onslaught against Hayek and his kind.

"He went out of his way to stress differences from and find weaknesses in traditional economic theory," Harrod recalled. "Would it not have been wiser to stress his own contribution and leave it to others to decide how much scrapping of established doctrine was entailed? To some he seemed to take a mischievous pleasure—perhaps he did—in criticizing revered names. In fact this was done of set purpose. It was his deliberate reaction to the frustrations he had felt, and was still feeling, as the result of the persistent tendency to ignore what was novel in his contribution. He felt he would get nowhere if he did not raise the dust."[25]

Keynes appeared to relish pointing out the Austrian School's errors and magnified the abuse not only by singling out those like Hayek and Robbins who failed to understand the shortsightedness and lack of vision in their adherence to the "classical school" but also by dismissing their obduracy not in the main text but in a footnote, as if he were not vanquishing dragons but swatting flies. Orthodox economists like Hayek were simply out of touch with reality, he contended. "It may well be that the classical theory represents the way in which we should like our Economy to behave," he wrote. "But to assume that it actually does so is to assume our difficulties away."[26]

"The characteristics of the special case assumed by the classical theory happen not to be those of the economic society in which we actually live," he wrote, "with the result that its teaching is misleading and disastrous if we attempt to apply it to the facts of experience."[27] Keynes argued that classical economists had tacitly blamed the unemployed for their plight. "A classical economist may sympathise with labor in refusing to accept a cut in its money-wage, and he will admit that it may not be wise to make [such a cut] to meet conditions which are temporary; but scientific integrity forces him to declare that his refusal is, nevertheless, at the bottom of the trouble."[28] Keynes demonstrated why he believed that while demands for increases in pay may be a factor in joblessness, they were by no means the principal reason for unemployment, as classical economists had long insisted.

Keynes denied one of the most commonly accepted laws governing economics, Say's Law, which says that supply creates its own demand.[29] The notion "still underlies the whole classical theory, which would collapse without it. . . . Contemporary thought is still deeply steeped in the notion that if people do not spend their money in one way they will spend it in another,"[30] which leads, he suggested, to another misconception of the classical school, that "an act of individual saving inevitably leads to a parallel act of investment."[31]

Denying Say's Law was central to the fresh thinking in *The General Theory*, leading to the notion of "liquidity preference," Keynes's explanation for why savings did not automatically translate into investment. Keynes had concluded that the way classical school economists came to assess what contributed to the cost of money, or rate of interest, was inadequate. Though he had once subscribed to similar views, it was, as he put it, "a nonsense theory."[32] For classical economists, interest rates depended on the relationship between savings and investment: if too many people saved, interest rates fell, encouraging them to invest in businesses to maximize their yield; if too few saved, interest rates rose to attract more savers.

Keynes explored the motivation of savers and came to a quite different conclusion. He believed that rather than lodge money in a bank or invest in stocks and shares, savers often preferred to keep their savings in "liquid" form (i.e., cash), so that they could take advantage of rapidly changing circumstances. The notion of liquidity preference upset the traditional understanding of the relationship between savings and investment, for if a saver believed he would get a better deal by waiting, he would keep his savings in cash, or jewelry, or gold. The implication was clear to Keynes. Because of liquidity preference, interest rates were kept higher than necessary because banks had to offer savers a premium to part with their money.

Keynes believed that liquidity preference negated the "common-sense" notions about the virtue of saving over spending that underpinned classical economics. "The absurd, though almost universal, idea that an act of individual saving is just as good for effective demand as an act of individual consumption" is a fallacy, he wrote. "It is of this fallacy that it is most difficult to disabuse men's minds. It comes from believing that the owner of wealth desires a capital asset as such, whereas what he really desires is its prospective yield."[33]

Keynes introduced other novel concepts, among them the multiplier. Each pound spent was worth far more than a single pound, as the money was spent again and again as it worked its way through the system. To persuade the noneconomists who thought public works financed by borrowing to be profligate, irresponsible, and wasteful, he departed from the otherwise sober approach to conjure up a suitably absurd project to demonstrate that even apparently "wasteful" schemes could cure chronic unemployment and pay for themselves.

"If the Treasury were to fill old bottles with banknotes, bury them at suitable depths in disused coalmines which are then filled up to the surface with town rubbish, and leave it to private enterprise on well-tried principles of laissez-faire to dig the notes up again," he wrote, "there need be no more unemployment and, with the help of the repercussions, the real income of the community, and its capital wealth also, would probably become a good deal greater than it actually is. It would, indeed, be more sensible to build houses and the like; but if there are political and practical difficulties in the way of this, the above would be better than nothing."[34] To emphasize how a commonsense grasp of economics differed from how economics worked in real life, he repeated his ominous conclusion that "just as wars have been the only form of large-scale loan expenditure which statesmen have thought justifiable, so gold-mining is the only pretext for digging holes in the ground which has recommended itself to bankers as sound finance."[35]

Importantly in the light of Hayek's subsequent writings about the threat to liberty of the state intervening in the economy, Keynes raised a key issue about the problems posed for individual freedoms when governments assumed an expanded role to achieve full employment. "The central controls necessary to ensure full employment will, of course, involve a large extension of the traditional functions of government," he wrote. "Furthermore, the modern classical theory has itself called attention to various conditions in which the free play of economic forces may need to be curbed or guided."[36] He later conceded that "the theory of output as a whole, which is what [*The General Theory*] purports to provide, is much more easily adapted to the conditions of a totalitarian state than is the theory of the production and distribution of a given output produced under conditions of free competition and a large measure of laissez-faire."[37] But Keynes was optimistic about human nature and did not believe that authoritarianism was a necessary corollary to his theory, nor that his reforms would lead to a creeping tyranny, what Hayek would call "serfdom."

Keynes believed that a prosperous society in which everyone is employed was the surest way of maintaining the independence of thought and action he considered the guarantor of true democracy. "There will still remain a wide field for the exercise of private initiative and responsibility," he wrote. "Within this field the traditional advantages of individualism will still hold good."[38] Furthermore, he thought that "individualism, if it can be purged of its defects and its abuses, is the best safeguard of personal liberty in the sense that, compared with any other system, it greatly widens the field for the exercise of personal choice."[39] Keynes had no intention of ushering in a grim gray future in which individual liberties were lost under a welter of state regulations. His prescription was a light hand on the tiller and a prosperous and contented crew. As his biographer Robert Skidelsky put it, "He gave people hope that unemployment could be cured without concentration camps."[40]

Keynes further anticipated Hayek's pessimistic assessment of the effects of departing from a free market when he offered an olive branch to the classical school by suggesting that classical theory still had an important part to play. "Our criticism of the accepted classical theory of economics has consisted not so much in finding logical flaws in its analysis as in pointing out that its tacit assumptions are seldom or never satisfied, with the result that it cannot solve the economic problems of the actual world," he wrote. The means to bring about full employment did not imply a socialist, or semi-socialist, or social democratic society. "If [government-inspired investments in public works succeed] in establishing an aggregate volume of output corresponding to full employment as nearly as is practicable, the classical theory comes into its own again from this point onwards," he wrote. "Apart from the necessity of central controls to bring about an adjustment between the propensity to consume and the inducement to invest, there is no more reason to socialise economic life than there was before."[41] Keynes argued that when full employment was reached, many of the certainties of the classical school would come into their own.

The General Theory was an implicit invitation to Hayek and his kind to respond. Indeed, Keynes specifically taunted Hayek at a number of turns. "When Professor Hayek infers that the concepts of saving and investment suffer from a corresponding vagueness," he wrote, "he is only right if he means *net saving* and *net investment*."[42] He dismissed Hayek's account of the doctrine of "forced saving" as "interesting"[43]—that damning term when employed by an Englishman. But for the most part, to avoid a repetition of the nitpicking debate over definitions that had occupied Hayek when criticizing *A Treatise*, Keynes devoted whole chapters of *The General Theory* to defining economic concepts, such as "saving," "forced saving," and "investment," so that those who wished to take issue with his central argument—that increasing aggregate demand was the key to full employment—should not become waylaid by semantics.

Similarly, Keynes addressed arguments Hayek had raised concerning the replacement of redundant plant that had formed a central part of their meandering correspondence following Hayek's review of *A Treatise*. He also specifically questioned the usefulness of elements of Hayek's celebrated LSE lectures on the "stages of production" and "roundabout" methods of production. It was with Hayek clearly in his sights that Keynes wrote, "It is true that some lengthy or roundabout processes are physically efficient. But so are some short processes. Lengthy processes are not physically efficient because they are long. Some, probably most, lengthy processes would be physically very inefficient, for there are such things as spoiling or wasting with time. With a given labour force there is a definite limit to the quantity of labour embodied in roundabout processes which can be used to advantage."[44]

Keynes's principal aim in writing *The General Theory* was to alter the way economists thought about the operation of the economy and through them to persuade decision makers to adopt measures to increase aggregate demand. An important secondary purpose, however, was to challenge Hayek and others to counter the ideas in his magnum opus.

Keynes's ideas could take firm root only if classical economics was shown to be wrong, so Keynes, ever confident that he had anticipated all objections, was eager to hear the classical economists' rejoinder. Hayek, who had set himself the formidable task of contradicting the steady stream of arguments emanating from Keynes's prodigious pen, now seemed honor bound to respond.

Why was the raising of aggregate demand an inappropriate way to increase employment? In what way did the multiplier not operate as Keynes and Kahn suggested? Why did the notion of liquidity preference not undermine the classical explanation of how interest rates were set? If *The General Theory* was riven from top to bottom with misapprehensions, misleading assumptions, false logic, and inappropriate and deluded leaps of imagination, this was surely the time for Hayek to dismantle Keynes's arguments before they took hold.

But answer came there none. Hayek remained hushed. Faced with confronting Keynes at full flow, Hayek blinked. Weeks passed, but his expected counter-blast was not forthcoming. Hayek's life purpose, the very reason Robbins summoned him from Vienna to the LSE, a key reason Beveridge had leapt at the chance to appoint him to the LSE staff, appeared to have come to nothing. Keynes's great work was met with neither a bang nor a whimper. Hayek's response, so keenly awaited by classical economists throughout Britain and the continent, was a yawning silence.

ELEVEN

Keynes Takes America

Roosevelt and the Young New Deal Economists, 1936

With publication of *The General Theory* in February 1936, Keynes fired the starting pistol for what came to be known as the Keynesian Revolution. In the opening sentence, he declared, "This book is chiefly addressed to my fellow economists," an admission that a decade spent trying to persuade politicians and public servants to heed his call to reduce unemployment via publicly funded works had made little headway. In America, however, the administrations of first Herbert Hoover, then Franklin Roosevelt, had been quietly installing piecemeal small-scale public works programs to alleviate the Depression's massive jobless toll.

The two presidents arrived at a similar conclusion: that something should be done, that electors expected something to be done, and that it was better to be seen trying to do something than to be accused of doing nothing. "[Roosevelt] sought to provide jobs on a great scale because men were jobless, and endeavoured to meet as much of the cost as possible by taxation," explained Harrod. "If there was a deficit, that was just too bad; it could be remedied later."[1] Keynes directed his *General Theory* arguments toward providing an intellectual justification for such action. His target audience, therefore, was the generation of young idealistically driven economists in British and American universities who were eager to help the Depression's victims.

From the 1920s, Keynes was known in America as an economist who, rather than bury himself in abstruse theories, channeled his energies toward practical remedies. As in Britain, he burst onto the American scene at the end of World War I with *The Economic Consequences of the Peace*, whose publication coincided with President Woodrow Wilson's desperate campaign to persuade the Senate to pass the Treaty of Versailles. The treaty was contentious because for the first time it would tie America to a world government, the League of Nations, Wilson's brainchild. While Keynes was sympathetic to Wilson's peaceful aims in Paris, he could not resist lambasting the president for his regal demeanor and his endorsement of the severe reparations imposed on the defeated nations. Keynes's colorful description of the pious Wilson in *The Economic Consequences* was eagerly picked up by the American press, who relished an excuse to traduce their beleaguered president with the sharply chiseled words of a seasoned master of invective.

Keynes set Wilson on a lofty pedestal the further to topple him. "When President Wilson left Washington he enjoyed a prestige and a moral influence throughout the world," he reported. "How the crowds of the European capitals pressed about the carriage of the President! With what curiosity, anxiety, and hope we sought a glimpse of the features and bearing of the man of destiny who, coming from the West, was to bring healing to the wounds of the ancient parent of his civilization."[2] However, the peacemaker Wilson, stiff, clerical, and frozen in moral rectitude, succumbed to the Allied clamor for vengeance. "The disillusion was so complete," wrote Keynes, "that some of those who had trusted most hardly dared speak of it. . . . What had happened to the President? What weakness or what misfortune had led to so extraordinary, so unlooked-for a betrayal?"[3] Keynes explained what many Americans had discovered for themselves, that the president was "solitary and aloof" and "strong-willed and obstinate." Above all, he "was not a hero or a prophet; he was not even a philosopher; but a generously intentioned man, with many of the weaknesses of other human beings."[4]

Keynes magnified the effect of his meticulous demolition of Wilson by describing the impression of the president he formed at close quarters. "His head and features were finely cut and exactly like his photographs, and the muscles of his neck and the carriage of his head were distinguished," Keynes wrote. But it was soon evident that "he was not only insensitive to his surroundings in the external sense, he was not sensitive to his environment at all." Witnessing Wilson surrounded by wily statesmen like Britain's Prime Minister Lloyd George and France's Prime Minister Clemenceau was like watching the president "playing blind man's buff." "Never could a man have stepped into the parlor a more perfect and predestined victim," wrote Keynes, whose grasp of what had taken place at Paris played to American sentiments about the treacherous nature of "Old Europe," confirming that America had done well to keep out of the war for so long and would do well to maintain a safe distance from the nascent League. Wilson, "this blind and deaf Don Quixote," Keynes wrote, "was entering a cavern where the swift and glittering blade was in the hands of the adversary."[5]

Far from being a white knight, Keynes judged that Wilson, by failing to halt the crippling reparations imposed on the vanquished nations, threatened the noble bid to bring a just end to "the war to end all wars" and made more likely another catastrophic war before long. The prophecy was soon fulfilled. By the time *The General Theory* was published, Hitler was ensconced in the chancellory in Berlin and his fellow fascist Benito Mussolini was strutting his stuff in Rome, both extremist beneficiaries of the miserable economic conditions that the punitive Versailles settlement had brought about. To many

Americans, Keynes was a clearheaded seer whose sharpened pen had sketched a nightmare vision of how the world really span.

While his views on Wilson may have first brought Keynes to the attention of Americans, they soon found his unorthodox economic thinking similarly uncompromising. The welcome Keynes received from political leaders and academics during his short American visit in 1931 showed that news of his radical economic remedies had reached way beyond Britain. By syndicating in America articles written for London papers he had become a celebrity economist, writing in such unlikely organs as *Vanity Fair*,[6] with an entertaining line of argument that sparked a lively debate.

The 1929 stock market crash and the subsequent Depression offered fertile ground for Keynesian ideas. From the moment Roosevelt arrived in the White House, he encouraged his staff to try different ways to alleviate the miseries of the Depression in a program he dubbed the "New Deal."[7] The collapse of investment, down 90 percent since the crash, left 13 million Americans unemployed, or one in four of the adult population. The situation was even more dire than the figures suggested, as poor measuring methods severely underestimated the extent of the catastrophe. If farm workers were excluded, unemployment was thought to be more than 37 percent. In Toledo, Ohio, four out of five were out of work.[8] The new administration was overwhelmed by the task it confronted. As Arthur M. Schlesinger Jr.[9] put it, "The machinery for sheltering and feeding the unemployed was breaking down everywhere under the growing burden. . . . It was a matter of staving off violence, even (at least some thought) revolution."[10]

It was into this maelstrom that Keynes proffered his advice to the new president, first by sending Roosevelt in early 1933 a copy of *The Means to Prosperity*, which sketched out ideas he would later expound more fully in *The General Theory*, then by addressing him in an open letter, published in *The New York Times* on December

31, 1933. Keynes wrote at the suggestion of Felix Frankfurter,[11] professor of administrative law at Harvard University and, as leader of the president's "brain trust," one of Roosevelt's closest political friends. Keynes first met Frankfurter at the Paris peace talks, where the American was promoting the Zionist movement. Frankfurter, a visiting scholar at All Souls College, Oxford, in the fall and winter of 1933–34, suggested to Keynes that if he were to urge Roosevelt to spend more public money to alleviate unemployment, he would be pushing at an open door. "You might like to know that . . . I have had American news indicating that there will be considerable sentiment in the Senate for heavy increases in public works," Frankfurter wrote. "The President is, I believe, receptive. I write because I think that a letter from you with your independent arguments and indications would greatly accelerate the momentum of forces now at work."[12] To ensure that Keynes's newspaper contribution did not appear impertinent by coming out of the blue, Frankfurter sent an advance copy to the president.[13]

Keynes began by flattering Roosevelt. "You have made yourself the Trustee for those in every country who seek to mend the evils of our condition by reasoned experiment," he wrote. "If you fail, rational change will be gravely prejudiced throughout the world, leaving orthodoxy and revolution to fight it out. But if you succeed, new and bolder methods will be tried everywhere." Having paid his obeisance, Keynes described the president's landmark National Industrial Recovery Act (NIRA), passed into law in June 1933, which allowed among other things private monopolies, the fixing of prices, and the setting up of the Public Works Administration to implement a public works program, as a mixed blessing. The NIRA, "which is essentially Reform and probably impedes Recovery," wrote Keynes, "has been put across too hastily, in the false guise of being part of the technique of Recovery."

While he praised the president's policy of deliberately raising prices to fill farmers' and other producers' pockets, he warned that "there is much less to be said in favor of rising prices, if they are brought about at the expense of rising output." Keynes wrote that "the stimulation of output by increasing aggregate purchasing power is the right way to get prices up; and not the other way round." He reiterated his belief that borrowing to pay for public works was good policy. "I lay overwhelming emphasis on the increase of national purchasing power resulting from governmental expenditure which is financed by Loans and not by taxing present incomes," he wrote. "In a boom, inflation can be caused by allowing unlimited credit to support the excited enthusiasm of business speculators. But in a slump, governmental Loan expenditure is the only sure means of securing quickly a rising output at rising prices." In an observation that was to prove horribly portentous, he wrote, "That is why a war has always caused intense industrial activity. In the past, orthodox finance has regarded a war as the only legitimate excuse for creating employment by governmental expenditure."

In urging more state spending on public works, Keynes sympathized with the president's plight. As the British had found, it was not always easy to find shovel-ready projects in which public money could be usefully invested. The spending on hydroelectric dams, new highways, and national parks that Roosevelt favored was a slow business, funneling money into the economy many months, even years ahead. "I am not surprised that so little has been spent up-to-date," Keynes wrote. "Our own experience has shown how difficult it is to improvise useful Loan-expenditures at short notice. There are many obstacles to be patiently overcome, if waste, inefficiency and corruption are to be avoided." But he urged on the president large-scale public spending as a sure way to increase demand and return the country to prosperity. He dismissed those who urged an increase in the money supply rather than in spending to increase demand as "like trying to get fat by buying a larger belt. In the United States today your belt is plenty big enough for your belly."

Having sympathized with Roosevelt for slipping the dollar off the gold standard, leading to a gradual devaluation of the currency, Keynes returned to flattery lest he seem too harsh. "You remain for me the ruler whose general outlook and attitude to the tasks of government are the most sympathetic in the world," he wrote. Keynes concluded with direct, practical advice. He advocated "cheap and abundant credit and in particular the reduction of the long-term rates of interest." And he again urged more public spending, more swiftly. "Preference should be given to those [public works projects] which can be made to mature quickly on a large scale. . . . The United States is ready to roll towards prosperity, if a good hard shove can be given in the next six months."[14]

Roosevelt did not directly respond to Keynes's contribution to the economic debate, but he wrote to Frankfurter, "You can tell the professor[15] [Keynes] that in regard to public works we shall spend in the fiscal [financial] year nearly twice the amount we are spending in this fiscal year, but there is a practical limit to what the Government can borrow—especially because the banks are offering passive resistance in most of the large centers."[16] The following year, at Frankfurter's suggestion, the president agreed to meet Keynes. "He is really devoted to your efforts and perhaps the single most powerful supporter of the New Deal in England," Frankfurter wrote to the president. "Not only does he wield a trenchant economic pen. As the head of an important insurance company,[17] he exercises considerable influence in the City [the financial district of London]. . . . Therefore I believe it to be doubly important that he hear about the Administration's efforts and purposes at first hand, because during his stay in New York every effort will be made to fill him with poison."[18] Roosevelt was happy to meet Keynes and wrote to his private secretary, "I want to see him and get him in some time at tea alone." But economics was not the only thing on Roosevelt's mind. He added, "When you get hold of Keynes, ask him to bring his wife."[19]

In May 1934, Keynes traveled to New York, without Lydia, to accept an honorary degree from Columbia University and acted on

Frankfurter's letters of introduction to meet a wide array of New Dealers, business leaders, and members of the president's brain trust. Keynes was eager to know from the inside what was going on in the American economy, but, ever the controversialist, he could not resist arguing against the primitive and ignorant attitudes of the bankers and businessmen he met. It was, however, a strain on him. He told Lydia he found it "awful hard work trying to be at the top of one's form, to put oneself over the blighters all day."[20]

On Monday, May 28, Keynes left the Mayflower Hotel in Washington for the White House, and at 5:15 P.M. he strode into the Oval Office and shook hands with the seated president. They talked for about an hour. As he had when he assessed Woodrow Wilson's character, Keynes believed he could tell a great deal by looking at the president's hands. "Naturally my concentrated attention was on his hands," he recalled. "Firm and fairly strong, but not clever or with finesse, shortish round nails like those at the end of a businessman's fingers. I cannot draw them right, yet while not distinguished (to my eye) they are not of a common type. All the same they were oddly familiar. Where had I seen them before? I spent ten minutes at least searching my memory as for a forgotten name, hardly knowing what I was saying about silver and balanced budgets and public works. At last it came to me. [Former British foreign secretary] Sir Edward Grey."[21]

Keynes credited Roosevelt with a more sophisticated knowledge of economics than the spotty grasp of the dismal art the president had acquired from a Harvard history degree. Roosevelt had announced on his election that he was in favor of "sound money," but when pressed to explain what he meant, he responded, "I don't intend to write a book about it."[22] At their meeting, Keynes launched into a technical explanation for how Kahn's multiplier ensured that borrowing to pay for public works should be considered investment, not expenditure, and that public works would soon pay for themselves through taxation revenue of those newly re-employed. But most of what Keynes told Roosevelt sailed over his head.

On leaving the White House, Keynes dropped in on Frances Perkins, FDR's labor secretary. "Keynes repeated his admiration for the actions Roosevelt had taken," she recalled, "but said cautiously that he had 'supposed the President was more literate, economically speaking.'"[23] According to Perkins, Keynes had "talked lofty economic theory" to Roosevelt, whereas when Keynes explained the multiplier to her, he abandoned high-flown theory in favor of a more everyday example, explaining that "a dollar spent on relief by the government was a dollar given to the grocer, by the grocer to the wholesaler, and by the wholesaler to the farmer, in payment of supplies. With one dollar paid out for relief or public works or anything else, you have created four dollars' worth of national income."[24] For Perkins, who was constantly pressing the president to be bolder, the meeting seemed a missed opportunity. "I wish he had been as concrete when he talked to Roosevelt, instead of treating him as though he belonged to the higher echelons of economic knowledge,"[25] she wrote. Not long after, Roosevelt confirmed to Perkins that he remained oblivious of much of what Keynes had told him. "I saw your friend Keynes," he said. "He left a whole rigamarole of figures. He must be a mathematician rather than a political economist."[26] Still, Keynes confessed he found his encounter with the president "fascinating and illuminating,"[27] while Roosevelt reported back to Frankfurter, "I had a grand talk with Keynes and liked him immensely."[28]

Roosevelt may not have grasped the full thrust of Keynes's remarks, but the very fact that he had welcomed the world's most vocal opponent of laissez-faire, free-market ideas to the heart of the New Deal was not lost on the legions of young economists who were flocking to Washington to put the world to rights. Nor was the significance of Keynes being ushered into the president's presence lost on the regiments of Roosevelt's conservative opponents, who suggested that the president was in the thrall of a dangerous foreigner whose approach to the free market was, by definition, un-American.

It is by no means certain that the brief encounter between

Keynes and Roosevelt directly bore fruit. Nevertheless, Keynes's recommendations to Roosevelt were soon credited with promoting more government intervention in the economy. "I do not know whether you realize how great an effect that letter [in *The New York Times*] had," the columnist Walter Lippmann wrote to Keynes, "but I am told that it was chiefly responsible for the policy which the Treasury is now quietly but effectively pursuing of purchasing long-term government bonds with a view to making a strong bond market and to reducing the long-term rate of interest."[29] Lippmann, a recent convert to Keynesian thinking, told an audience of Harvard academics in 1934 that "laissez-faire is dead and the modern state has become responsible for the modern economy as a whole."[30]

Although Keynesianism was not official policy in Roosevelt's first term, large amounts of taxpayer money were spent on schemes to get the jobless back to work. Typical of the president's ambiguous management style, he charged two of his closest aides with the same task. Harold Ickes, the interior secretary, presided over a variety of public works programs, including the Public Works Administration and the Civilian Conservation Corps, that enrolled over a quarter of a million in "socially productive work." Meanwhile, FDR's close friend Harry Hopkins, who was critical of the pace of Ickes's programs, was put in charge of the Civil Works Administration, an emergency relief program that oversaw the creation of four million new jobs. "Let me see," Roosevelt said to Hopkins. "Four million people—that means roughly four hundred million dollars."[31] Partly as a result of such measures, the public sector budget deficit soared, reaching $6 billion within a year of Roosevelt's election. The figure so alarmed the administration's budget director, Lewis Douglas, that he resigned rather than preside over such an apparently disastrous set of accounts. Even Roosevelt took fright at the extent of the deficit, and in April 1934 he instructed Hopkins to abruptly end the Civilian Works Administration's most ambitious endeavors, building bridges and public buildings.

Keynes was skeptical of much of what was being done in the New Deal and was keen to put his ardent admirers straight on his thinking. For those prepared to listen, while in America he reiterated his belief that government-funded aid to alleviate unemployment was appropriate only at the bottom of a cycle, or during a recession, and that it was not appropriate to continue pumping money into the system when an economy had recovered. "Only in the event of a transition into Socialism would anyone expect government expenditure to play a predominant part year in year out,"[32] he told Victor von Szeliski, a top statistician in the National Recovery Administration, the vanguard of New Deal activism. On his return to New York, Keynes was at pains to point out the consequences that loomed if the state continued to finance demand when the economy had reached a state of full employment. "When a point has been reached at which the whole of labour and capital equipment of the community are employed, further increases in effective demand would have no effect whatever except to raise prices without limit."[33]

It was clear to Keynes from his short visit to America that the economic old guard in the nation's capital was fast being replaced by young, ambitious economists committed to radical change. As Keynes told Frankfurter, "Here, not in Moscow, is the economic laboratory of the world. The young men who are running it are splendid. I am astonished by their competence, intelligence and wisdom. One meets a classical economist here and there who ought to be thrown out of [the] window—but they mostly have been."[34] The inspiration that Keynes offered young American economists was summed up by perhaps the best-known young Keynesian, John Kenneth Galbraith. "Though young and unimportant, by following the master we could feel superior to the great men of Morgan's Chase, National City and the New York Federal Reserve Bank,"[35] he declared. Galbraith was so enamored of Keynes that on his honeymoon in 1937 he took his young bride Kitty from Cambridge, Massachusetts, to Cambridge, England, to seek out an audience with the great man.[36] There was a quasi-religious aspect to Galbraith's journey that reflected the deification of Keynes among the young. "I had resolved to go to the temple,"[37] Galbraith recalled.

Not all of the architects of Roosevelt's New Deal were young. And many had come to a conclusion similar to Keynes's from their own experience in business. No one would dare suggest that Marriner Eccles,[38] a multimillionaire Mormon banker from Utah, was a soft touch or a naïve idealist. He was a hard-nosed former Republican who owned the First Security Corporation, which ran twenty-six banks, as well as one of the largest beet sugar producers in America, a vast dairy chain, and lumber companies, among other businesses. He came to the conclusion from his own understanding of businesses that a boost in demand was what the country needed. "There is not cause nor reason for the unemployment with its resultant destitution and suffering of fully one-third of our entire population," he told a Senate committee hearing in 1933. A return to full employment could be brought about, he said, only "by providing purchasing power sufficiently adequate to enable the people to obtain the consumption goods which we, as a nation, are able to produce."[39]

He went on, "The nineteenth century economics will no longer serve our purpose—an economic age 150 years old has come to an end. The orthodox capitalistic system of uncontrolled individualism, with its free competition, will no longer serve our purpose."[40] Eccles advocated public works financed by federal government borrowing. "There are times to borrow and times to pay," he declared. "You have got to take care of the unemployed or you are going to have revolution in this country."[41] If some of the senators raised an eyebrow at Eccles's radical posture, the significance of his remarks was not lost on the White House. In 1935, Roosevelt appointed Eccles the first chairman of the board of the Federal Reserve, a position he was to hold for the next fourteen years.

The man Eccles chose as his assistant at the Fed was Lauchlin Currie, an LSE- and Harvard-educated economist who also believed that the only way out of the Great Depression was to stimulate demand, if necessary through public works financed by borrowing. Eccles and Currie were instrumental in hiring a slew of like-minded young economists at the Fed and other government agencies, particularly after the near failure to pass the 1935 Banking Act, which regulated banks more tightly. (Such was Keynes's fame by this time that opponents of the act described it as "Curried Keynes.") According to Galbraith's biographer Richard Parker, "Currie realized how woefully understaffed the Keynesian camp was in the administration compared to the trust-busting and national-planning camps. Serious recruitment and careful placement of sympathetic allies in key Washington offices became an imperative."[42] Inspired by a common creed, the young Keynesians sought each other out in the corridors of power and began meeting at the National Planning Association, set up in 1934.

Keynesian ideas also took root in America thanks to the work of econometricians and statisticians like Simon Kuznets, professor of economics and statistics at the University of Pennsylvania, and his followers at the National Bureau of Economic Research and the U.S. Department of Commerce, whose work logging the workings of the economy warranted Kuznets an honorable mention in *The General Theory*. Although Kuznets never became a Keynesian, his pioneering work on compiling statistics about national income and gross national product were called in evidence to fuel Keynes's argument that bolstering aggregate demand would boost economic growth.

Kuznets and his followers provided the means of measuring economic activity that proved, by and large, that Keynesian remedies did indeed perform as Keynes predicted. As Galbraith explained, armed with Keynes's theories and Kuznets's means of measuring, the small army of young economists in the federal government "knew not only what needed to be done but how much. And many who would never have been persuaded by the Keynesian abstractions were compelled to belief by the concrete figures from Kuznets and his inventive colleagues."[43]

There were few more eager to take up the Keynesian cause than the young economists at Harvard. The old guard in Cambridge, Massachusetts, were by no means convinced by the waves of disturbing ideas spilling out from the other Cambridge across the sea. As the future Nobel economics laureate James Tobin, an ardent young Keynesian, recalled, "The senior faculty was mostly hostile. A group of them had not long before published a book quite critical of Roosevelt's recovery program."[44] But for the young it was different. Like Tobin, they were devoted to the idealism expressed by Roosevelt in the New Deal. "Keynes's uprising against encrusted error was an appealing crusade for youth," remembered Tobin. "The truth would make us free, and fully employed too."[45] Such was the sense of excitement and expectation in the winter of 1935 when *The General Theory* was about to be published in Britain that Harvard undergraduates arranged for special consignments to be dispatched across the Atlantic the minute it was available. As soon as the boxes of books arrived, they pounced on them to be among the first to read the revolutionary ideas revealed in the text. As Tobin recalled, "Harvard was becoming the beachhead for the Keynesian invasion of the New World."[46]

Paul Samuelson, described by Galbraith as "almost from the outset . . . the acknowledged leader of the younger Keynesian community,"[47] recorded the spirit of feverish exhilaration that surrounded the arrival of Keynes's masterwork in Harvard in February 1936. "*The General Theory* caught most economists under the age of thirty-five with the unexpected virulence of a disease first attacking and decimating an isolated tribe of South Sea islanders," he recalled. "Economists beyond fifty turned out to be quite immune to the ailment."[48] Galbraith also recalled the generational divide that Keynes's work revealed. "The old economics was still taught by day," he wrote. "But in the evening, and almost every evening from 1936 on, almost everyone discussed Keynes."[49] According to Samuelson, *The General Theory* acquired an almost mystical significance, and he compared it to the shock of the new the romantic poet John Keats expressed in his sonnet "On First Looking into Chapman's Homer."

Galbraith jokingly observed, "Some will wonder if economists are capable of such refined emotion."[50]

One young Harvard economics graduate student, Robert Bryce,[51] a Canadian, enjoyed the added allure of having just arrived from Cambridge, England, where he had been taught by Keynes himself and had attended Hayek's seminar at the LSE with the attitude of a Christian minister witnessing a cannibal ceremony. Bryce took full advantage of his links to the master, so much so that Joseph Schumpeter was prompted to remark, "Keynes is Allah and Bryce is his prophet."[52]

Just as not all of those in Washington who fell under the spell of Keynes were young, some older economics professors at Harvard also underwent an unlikely epiphany. Alvin H. Hansen, who before long came to be known as the "American Keynes," was a fifty-year-old classical economist when recruited by Harvard from the University of Minnesota in 1937. Hansen had heavily criticized Keynes's *Treatise* on its publication, and at first he was skeptical of the ideas expressed in *The General Theory*. Then he changed his mind. Before long he became the most vociferous, articulate, prodigious, and persuasive proselytizer on behalf of Keynes's ideas. He led the charge against economists who believed that deficit spending would lead to national ruin. As Galbraith recalled, "Without ever seeking to do so or being quite aware of the fact, [Hansen] became the leader of a crusade."[53] Samuelson and Tobin, who were among the first of Hansen's young charges, found themselves having to jostle with policy makers from Washington to find a place at Hansen's overcrowded lecture series in the new Graduate School of Public Administration. "Often the students overflowed into the hall," Galbraith remembered. "One felt that it was the most important thing currently happening in the country. . . . The officials took Hansen's ideas, and perhaps even more, his sense of conviction, back to Washington."[54]

Joining with John Hicks, who in 1930 was one of the first to be influenced by Hayek at the LSE, Hansen described in graphical form the complex interrelationship Keynes suggested between interest rates, liquidity-money supply, investment-savings, and the national income that became famous among economists as the IS-LM (Investment Saving / Liquidity preference Money supply) model. By putting the core of Keynes's ideas into simplified algebraic form, they spread the new creed. Hansen's 1941 book, *Fiscal Policy and Business Cycles*, where fiscal policy was the amount governments taxed and levied, was the first American work to support Keynes's analysis of the causes of the Great Depression. Hansen's 1953 tome, *A Guide to Keynes*, became the first Keynesian Revolution textbook and inspired generations of young economists.

One of Hansen's close colleagues, Seymour E. Harris, was another late convert to Keynes and rivalled Hansen in his prodigious output of books, as both author and editor, spreading the new Keynesian credo. He used to open his lectures with, "I am Seymour Harris, Professor of Economics at Harvard University and author of 33 books," all of which were about Keynes. But for all Hansen and Harris's industry on behalf of the Keynesian cause, they did not trump Paul Samuelson's best-selling Keynesian primer, *Economics: An Introductory Analysis*, published in 1948, which was instantly to become the most influential economic textbook since *Principles of Economics*, Alfred Marshall's definitive exposition of the classical economic case.

Thus in the course of just a few years, Keynes captured the hearts and minds of many young American economists. The spectacular rise in his influence on the thinking of American academic economists can clearly be seen by the number of mentions he received in learned journals. In 1934, his theories inspired just 20 articles; between 1936 and 1940 the number had soared to 269.[55]

The speed with which the Keynesian Revolution took hold in America's many departments of economics and then scaled the high ground of the federal government in Washington, D.C., was dazzling. An idea appeared to have found its time, and it soon spread across the nation. Some dissenters expressed doubts about the motives of those who responded to Keynes's ideas as if they were written on tablets of stone, and were happy when, among the thousands of Keynesians, some, including Currie, turned out to be Soviet agents. But the Keynesian Revolution was less a pernicious plot than a spontaneous movement of individuals, who reached Keynes by their own routes. "Those who nurture thoughts of conspiracy and clandestine plots will be saddened to know that this was a revolution without organisation," recalled Galbraith, who through writing over a thousand newspaper and magazine articles became the chief popularizer of Keynesian ideas. "All who participated felt a deep sense of personal responsibility for ideas; there was a varying but deep urge to persuade. But no one ever responded to plans, orders, instructions, or any force apart from his own convictions. That perhaps was the most interesting single feature of the Keynesian Revolution."[56]

Roosevelt may not have understood Keynesianism or knowingly applied its remedies, but the young people in his administration most certainly did. They believed that while the amount of money provided to them fell far short of what was needed, the implementation of Keynesianism even at a reduced rate was paying off. Unemployment was not cured quickly, but year by year it began to fall. In 1933 it had reached its peak at 25 percent; by the following year it had fallen to 17 percent, and in 1935 it reached a still intolerable but encouraging 14.3 percent. By 1936 national production had recovered to its 1929 levels.

But seeing the figures moving in the right direction only emboldened the rump of classical economists who still clung to many of the levers of power in Washington. What transpired next proved that, however successful the Keynesian Revolution might have been in bringing interventionist ideas to the Roosevelt administration, it was all too easy to sabotage the American economy's fragile recovery.

TWELVE

Hopelessly Stuck in Chapter 6

Hayek Writes His Own "General Theory," 1936–41

Why did Friedrich Hayek not instantly confront what he believed to be the missteps of logic in Keynes's *General Theory*? Had he volunteered his counterarguments at the time of publication, he might have nipped the Keynesian Revolution in the bud. For the remainder of his life, Hayek was coy about the missed opportunity. As he confessed nearly forty years later, "I have to the present day not quite got over a feeling that I had then shirked what should have been a plain duty."[1]

Keynes went out of his way to invite Hayek's criticism. He sent Hayek advance copies so that his nemesis could compile his critique in time for publication day. Among his talents, Keynes was a master publicist and knew the value of courting controversy. A heated debate with Hayek would have boosted sales.

It was not just a keen commercial sense that drove Keynes. He had long targeted Hayek and his classical school colleagues and genuinely wanted to debate them. His ambition was not merely to out-argue his opponents but to supercede them. And that could be achieved only if they were willing to engage in argument. He was limbered up, ready for a fight. Indeed, he must have been disappointed that Hayek declined to enter the ring. To drown the classical economists in the rip tide of enthusiasm that accompanied *The General Theory*'s debut was not enough. The book repeatedly challenged Hayek and his colleagues to defend their position. Hayek, however, was a no-show. He thought Keynes was taking economics in a dangerous direction, but he remained a reluctant combatant.

Lionel Robbins may have been partly responsible for Hayek's atypical silence. Always conscious of the potential for controversy, Robbins was eager to use the arrival of *The General Theory* to bolster the reputation of the London School of Economics and his own place in the national economic debate. On his first reading of the book, Robbins considered Keynes's pointed assault on his Cambridge colleague Arthur Pigou to be the most newsworthy line. A response by Pigou in *Economica* would more likely gain attention than a contribution from Hayek. He would also avoid a repeat of the persnickety and testy stalemate with Keynes that emerged after Hayek's review of *A Treatise on Money*.

Robbins was aware of the personal friction that existed between Keynes and Pigou. Once, when he and Keynes were out walking in Cambridge, in Robbins's words, "a not very lively Pigou returning with upright strides from a conscientiously self-imposed routine daily walk" came into view. The ever-sarcastic Keynes whispered to Robbins, "Here comes a man who has ruined his health with manly sport."[2] Pigou had severely reprimanded Keynes for using inappropriately personal language in his response to Hayek's critique of *A Treatise*, describing it as "the method of the duello!"[3] So it was that Pigou, not Hayek, was given first chance to tilt at Keynes in the May 1936 issue of *Economica*.

Pigou took full advantage of the invitation to defend himself, delivering a carefully worded and often personally pained complaint at the tone of Keynes's dismissal of his orthodox views. He honed his darts to match the verbal dexterity of Keynes's assault. Pigou ridiculed

Keynes's arrogant presumption, that what "Einstein actually did for Physics . . . Mr. Keynes believes himself to have done for Economics," and pointed out that Einstein "did not, in announcing his discovery, insinuate, through carefully barbed sentences, that Newton and those who had hitherto followed his lead were a gang of incompetent bunglers." Pigou's schoolmasterly reprimand continued, "The general *de haut en bas* and the patronage extended to his old master Marshall are particularly to be regretted."

Pigou's vanity was piqued by having his work bundled with that of other classical economists, not least because the criticism became general rather than particular and thereby difficult to counter. "When a man goes on a sniping expedition in a large village, nobody will have the patience to track down the course of his every bullet," complained Pigou. When it came to assessing the substance of *The General Theory*, Pigou affected despair. "His argument is in places so obscure that the reader cannot be certain what precisely it is that he is intending to convey," he wrote. "How is it that an author, whose powers of exposition . . . not to say one whose vividness of phrase has made him a valued contributor to the 'Daily Mail' . . . is barely intelligible to . . . his own professional colleagues?" Like Hayek, Pigou blamed Keynes's incoherence on his "inconsistent use of terms."[4] Then Pigou went on to meticulously dismantle the many original concepts, such as liquidity preference, that Keynes had forged. The article was a tour de force. Pigou had plainly relished bringing Keynes down to size.

But Pigou's harsh review was hardly enough to halt the stampede toward Keynesian thought that *The General Theory* sparked. It soon became clear to Robbins that the scale of Keynes's achievement, in setting off a firestorm of enthusiasm among younger economists, might deserve a prolonged debate in the pages of *Economica*. But after Pigou's rejoinder, which made barely a ripple among economists, Robbins inexplicably brought the debate to an end, not even assigning a supplementary salvo from the pen of Hayek.

But Robbins's *Economica* was not the only academic forum in which Hayek might have volunteered to counter the latest iteration of Keynes's ideas. Why did he not express himself elsewhere? When sent an early copy of *The General Theory*, Hayek wrote to Keynes that he had scanned the work with interest and had identified a number of arguments with which he disagreed. He said he was "puzzled" in particular by two issues, Keynes's account of the relationship between savings and investment, and the notion of liquidity preference. Hayek informed Keynes that as soon as he had given proper attention to the text, he would beg space in Keynes's *Economic Journal* to respond. "If my present doubts remain I shall probably ask for your hospitality for some notes on particular points in the E.J.,"[5] he wrote. Those "notes" were never forthcoming.

In later life, Hayek was repeatedly pressed to explain why he did not meet Keynes head-on after publication of *The General Theory*. He never came up with a convincing reply. It is hard to give credence to Hayek's suggestion that "one of the reasons why I did not return to the attack" was that "I feared that before I had completed my analysis he would again have changed his mind,"[6] as Keynes had done even after publishing *A Treatise*. Why not enumerate the many flaws in what was being widely hailed as Keynes's masterwork? Hayek's dismissal of *The General Theory* with the remark, thirty years later, that "it was too obviously another tract for the times, conditioned by what he thought were the momentary needs of policy,"[7] does not wash.

Hayek's reticence is hardly explained, either, by his assertion that it was the very nature of Keynes's reasoning that made him shun the challenge. He admitted to a feeling, "then only dimly felt,"[8] that Keynes's new work was hard to confront because it was a macroeconomic, rather than a microeconomic, account of the working of the economy. It was Hayek's belief that an economy's operation could be explained only through an understanding of the innumerable individual choices that together contributed to the whole economy. He suggested that it was too difficult to adequately express objections to Keynes's top-down approach to economics when his counterarguments assumed that the key to understanding economics was bottom-up. While it may have been a profound inhibition to contradict the assumptions of *The General Theory* when Keynes was talking apples and Hayek was talking oranges, it was hardly beyond Hayek's ability. That, too, appears a lame excuse for failing to take a clear shot on goal.

Hayek attempted many years later to answer those who found his failure to confront Keynes not merely a sin of omission but a culpable act, for with the right intervention he might have slowed, if not altogether halted, a theory that classical economists believed unleashed a raft of destructive economic policies. "I ought to explain why I failed to return to the charge after I had devoted much time to a careful analysis of his writings—a failure for which I have reproached myself ever since,"[9] he wrote in a 1983 piece to mark the centenary of Keynes's birth. "It was not merely . . . the inevitable disappointment of a young man when told by the famous author that his objections did not matter since Keynes no longer believed in his own arguments. Nor was it really that I became aware that an effective refutation of Keynes's conclusions would have to deal with the whole macroeconomic approach. It was rather that his disregard of what seemed to me the crucial problems made me recognize that a proper critique would have to deal more with what Keynes had not gone into than with what he had discussed, and that in consequence an elaboration of the still inadequately developed theory of capital was a prerequisite for a thorough disposal of Keynes's argument."[10]

So it was that after nearly fifty years of obfuscation, Hayek volunteered a plausible explanation for his echoing silence. What Hayek did not explain in his belated mea culpa was that when *The General Theory* burst upon the world, he thought he was on the verge of publishing his own mammoth work that would provide a new twist on the Austrian theory of capital and, he hoped, would offer a comprehensive contradiction to Keynesianism. By 1936, he was well advanced in writing such a thesis. Three years earlier, he had applied to the LSE's Rockefeller Research Fund Committee for money to hire an assistant.[11] "During the next eighteen months (or two years at the outside) I hope to finish what, I am afraid, is going to be a rather voluminous volume on the theory of capital," he wrote. "In the further course of preparation of this volume, about one-fourth of which is already completed, I shall badly need the continuous assistance of a really good mathematician, who would not only be able to work out with greater exactness the rather elaborate diagrammatical apparatus which I have developed, but also to help me in the analytical exposition which, although I hope to confine it to appendices, is unfortunately indispensable."[12] A suitable mathematician who spoke English, German, and French was found and assigned to help Hayek through 1934 and 1935.

Work on the project got off to a sticky start. Hayek had already put the book aside for a while in 1935, but in 1936, just two weeks after Keynes sent him an early copy of *The General Theory*, he told his friend Gottfried Haberler,[13] a fellow Austrian and Austrian School adherent, that work on his magnum opus was crowding out everything else, including his ability to get a handle on Keynes's latest offering. "I try to concentrate exclusively on the work on my book and must leave everything else," he wrote. "Even though it would be exaggerating to speak of an early appearance, I still hope to complete the first draft in the Easter holidays." As for *The General Theory*, he wrote, "I should like temporarily to say nothing about it, since I am hopelessly stuck in chapter 6."[14]

By March, Hayek informed Haberler that he had all but completed his book, barring a couple of chapters based on lectures he had given. Haberler had by this time read *The General Theory* and sent Hayek a piece intended for *Economica* pointing out perceived flaws in Richard Kahn's multiplier theory. Hayek returned the article, quoting unexplained "difficulties" at the journal. In his covering note Hayek wrote, "In the May number appears Pigou's article on Keynes, which in the meantime has also come in first and is immensely sharp, or will be (I have not yet seen it myself). You will understand that in these circumstances we want to avoid anything which could create the impression that we are conducting a planned campaign against Keynes. I myself have for that reason determined to submit a note . . . to the *Economic Journal*, where Keynes cannot well refuse. . . . I believe you should try first of all the same. In the event he refuses, one can then talk about other possibilities."[15]

While Robbins and Hayek may have been anxious not to appear to be waging a campaign against *The General Theory*, it is plain from Hayek's letter that there was indeed a plot afoot involving Hayek, Robbins, Pigou, John Hicks, and others, to deflate the soaring Keynes. "The chance exists just now to isolate Keynes and to bring to a stand a common front of other Cambridge and London [economists]," Hayek confided to Haberler. "These possibilities we would not [want to] jeopardize by putting *Economica* in the forefront of the attack. Pigou's article will cause enough sensation."[16]

In May, Hayek offered Harbeler his verdict on *The General Theory*. He said he was "of course awfully annoyed" by the work, not least because "through his formulation [Keynes] discredits many important ideas, which now lie in the air, among many people, and it will make it hard to try to persuade them without tackling all the other nonsense."[17] But that brief aside proved to be the sum of Hayek's contemporaneous critical assessment of *The General Theory*. Rather than expand on his "annoyance" and confront Keynes's "nonsense," Hayek concentrated his efforts on completing the first part of *The Pure Theory of Capital*, a two-volume work he hoped would directly compete with *The General Theory*.

While Hayek was confident he would soon finish his tour de force, and suggested that being "hopelessly stuck in chapter 6" was a temporary setback, before long he found himself bogged down in *The Pure Theory* and unable to make progress. His ambition for the work was to expand on his "stages of production" notions. But for the next four years he struggled to explain to his own satisfaction the key role that capital and money played in an economy. The more he worked at it, the more the scale of his task appeared to grow. His mind was racing far ahead of his ability to capture his thoughts and express them on paper.[18]

Before long, *The Pure Theory* became a grinding chore. He put the work aside for a second time in 1937. In 1938 he was in such disarray that he discovered he had lost part of the manuscript and had to ask his fellow Viennese economist friend, Fritz Machlup,[19] who had been reading the work in progress and suggesting changes, for his copy of the missing pages. Hayek became distracted by broader aspects of economics that would take him far from the dense territory of capital theory toward original insights into the impulses behind the economic behavior of individuals. While British economists, particularly those at the LSE and Cambridge, waited eagerly for Hayek to challenge *The General Theory*, his mind was drifting elsewhere.

The first result of the new direction in Hayek's thinking became evident in "Economics and Knowledge," his presidential address to the London Economic Club on November 10, 1936. The lecture was a startling reassessment of the notion of an economic equilibrium that had proved such a bone of contention in his arguments with Keynes. Even more important, Hayek for the first time, when discussing the importance of prices, hit on a novel approach that not only set him further apart from Keynes but also established him as an original thinker rather than a mere follower of the Austrian School.

The notion of an economy reaching a state of equilibrium is commonplace in economic theory, the best-known example in the debate between Hayek and Keynes being the assumption, held by classical economists, that over time, when savings and investment became perfectly aligned, an economy would come to rest at a state of full employment. Keynes challenged the existence of such an equilibrium because the facts of the real economy in Britain and America during the 1920s and 1930s were demonstrably at odds with the notion. In as much as the economy in either America or Britain had come to rest, it was at a state of mass unemployment, not full employment. The cries of classical economists that the equilibrium had not yet been reached sounded unconvincing when the economy was stuck in a prolonged slump.

Hayek looked afresh at the notion of an equilibrium and, contrary to his former belief, became convinced that there is rarely if ever a time when an economy comes to rest. To make his argument easier to follow, in "Economics and Knowledge" Hayek offered the example of a group working on a building project. "Brickmakers, plumbers, and others will all be producing materials which in each case will correspond to a certain quantity of houses for which just this quantity of the particular material will be required," he told his audience. "Similarly, we may conceive of prospective buyers as accumulating savings which will enable them at certain dates to buy a certain number of houses. . . . We can say that there is equilibrium between them."[20]

But Hayek was quick to point out that this need not be so, "because other circumstances which are not part of their plan of action may turn out to be different from what they expected. Part of the materials may be destroyed by an accident, weather conditions may make building impossible, or an invention may alter the proportions in which the different factors are wanted. This is what we call a change in the (external) data, which disturbs the equilibrium which has existed. But if the different plans were from the beginning incompatible, it is inevitable, whatever happens, that somebody's plans will be upset and have to be altered and that in consequence the whole complex of actions over the period will not show those characteristics which apply if all the actions of each individual can be understood as part of a single individual plan."[21]

If an equilibrium was invariably elusive in the real world, Hayek argued, then the a priori assumptions that theoretical economists make about the operation of an economy, or a market, tending toward an equilibrium would always fall short. An equilibrium can be predicted only if the intentions of each of the participants is known, and that is impossible both in theory and in practice. This may seem a slight point, as he readily admitted, but by denying the existence of a predictable equilibrium and denying the validity of a priori assumptions about the many accurate and inaccurate human choices that make up even the simplest decisions in a market, Hayek broke new ground. In the process he distanced himself from Mises and his Viennese colleagues, as well as other gods of the Austrian School universe for whom equilibrium was a central assumption.

Although Hayek did not at this time quite make the final leap of logic by which he was to become famous, in "Economics and Knowledge" he reached the threshold of an important breakthrough. A priori assumptions about mass economic behavior depend on an ideal set of conditions in which each individual possesses perfect knowledge of both existing and future conditions needed to make a decision in a perfect market. But, Hayek reminded his audience, the perfect market does not exist. Economic decisions in real life are made by individuals based on partial knowledge of current conditions coupled with their best guess of what may happen. Each individual comes to a different (and often contrary) judgment about what those conditions might be. Some get the decisions right, some wrong. But together their decisions combine to form a moving picture of the market in operation.

From this line of reasoning he came to two important conclusions, neither of which he made explicit in the lecture but both of which were to pave the way for a new direction in his thought: that it is through prices that the communal wisdom of what is going on in a market is reflected, and that when outside forces such as governments interfere in the setting of prices, it is tantamount to trying to regulate the speed of a car by holding the needle of the speedometer in place; and that no single person, not even an "omniscient dictator," as he put it, can know the minds, desires, and hopes of all the individuals that make up an economy. If a totalitarian ruler, or even apparently benign apolitical "planners," were to interfere in the economy on the assumption that they knew best or thought they knew the minds of others, they would inevitably frustrate the wishes and curtail the happiness and liberties of the individuals in whose interest they claimed to act. It was Hayek's eureka moment. He was to describe this pivotal notion as "the one enlightening idea which made me see the whole character of economic theory in what to me was an entirely new light."[22]

Hayek had introduced a new notion, the division of knowledge, that he believed was as important as the economic notion of the division of labor, the stage of industrial development where instead of individuals making a whole product, workers specialize in single tasks that together make a whole product. He maintained that it was impossible to understand or measure the full weight of the countless individual economic decisions made by the vast number of individuals that made up an economy, but that their intentions were reflected in ever-fluctuating prices. The price of an object was the point at which at least two individuals agreed. Because prices are essentially organic, like the people whose combined will contributes to their determination, any attempt to alter or interfere with prices was ultimately futile, for human behavior will always circumvent the presumptions on which a price is fixed. By the same token, price inflation, whether deliberately or unintentionally stoked by government action, was a means whereby those in command of an economy could flout the wishes of those obliged to pay the price, thereby denying their citizens' will.

Such was the hubbub surrounding Keynes's *General Theory* that Hayek's lecture was little noticed. As Hayek biographer Alan Ebenstein testified, "After Keynes published *The General Theory* . . . Hayek was virtually forgotten as a technical economist. . . . By the end of the decade, there was little interest in him."[23] To be ignored was a terrible fate, but it was not the worst thing to happen to Hayek around this time. There was a change, too, in the attitude of those attending his LSE seminars. Where once they were in awe of Hayek's reputation and magisterial pronouncements, over time familiarity had bred a form of contempt that was exacerbated by the swift ascendancy of his glamorous rival Keynes. Keynesian economists lined up at Hayek's LSE seminars to poke fun at a man they considered a fossil and flat-earther. In 1937, one of the scoffing participants, John Kenneth Galbraith, witnessed Hayek's fast-dwindling authority firsthand. "The urge to participate (and correct Hayek) was ruthlessly competitive,"[24] he recalled. "So competitive was the effort to be heard that Professor Hayek, a gentle man of comprehensively archaic views . . . was only rarely able to speak. . . . On one memorable evening he arrived, took his seat, bowed and in his polished accent said, 'Now gentlemen, as I proposed to you at our last meeting, we will on this evening discuss the rate of interest.' Nicholas Kaldor saw the opportunity and said, 'Professor Hayek, I really must beg to disagree.'"[25]

Kaldor, his Hungarian-born amanuensis on *Prices and Production* and his English-language adviser for much of the correspondence with Keynes, was one of the most prominent of Hayek's acolytes to treat him with disrespect. Kaldor recalled that over time Hayek became "frightfully annoyed with me. At first he was terribly *for* me, but then I discovered he was so silly I sort of teased him, made him look ridiculous, contradicted him in seminars. I remember one occasion when I had an argument with Hayek. I said, 'Professor Hayek, this is intermediate economics.' And Hayek got redder and redder, and afterwards in the tea room Hayek came in [and said], 'You know what Kaldor said? What Nicky said? He said, "Professor Hayek, this is intermediate economics and you ought to know it."' I said, 'I protest. I never said you ought to know it.' Everyone burst out laughing."[26]

Kaldor, who went on to coauthor William Beveridge's 1944 Keynesian call to action, *Full Employment in a Free Society*, set a trend among the Hayek disciples who steadily began to desert him for Keynes. Indeed, Kaldor later departed the LSE faculty for a post at Cambridge to preach unadulterated Keynesianism. Two more of Hayek's brightest pupils, John Hicks and Abba Lerner, who fronted the LSE team that countered the Circus at their lively joint seminars, followed suit, publicly recanting their allegiance to Hayek and proclaiming loyalty to Keynes. After Lerner spent the academic year 1934–35 at Cambridge, consuming Keynesianism from its source, he returned to the LSE to teach the Keynesian gospel. Not long after, even Pigou, on rereading *The General Theory*, retracted his objections and fell in behind the long line of distinguished economists who came to applaud the work.

The cumulative effect of the quick defection to Keynes of so many close colleagues and intimate friends hardly gave Hayek the confidence to concentrate on completing *The Pure Theory of Capital*. And when the book was eventually completed in June 1940 and published the following year, it landed with a resounding thud, its Germanic sentences and leaden prose adding impenetrability to its seeming irrelevance. Samuelson recalled that "Hayek's *The Pure Theory of Capital* was not stillborn. But it was a pebble thrown into the pool of economic science that seemingly left nary a ripple."[27] The diagram-laden convolutions of *Prices and Production* seemed like a beach read in comparison. As Milton Friedman,[28] a disciple of Hayekian thinking, put it, "I am an enormous admirer of Hayek, but not for his economics. I think *Prices and Production* was a very flawed book. I think his capital theory book is unreadable."[29]

Hayek acknowledges at the start of *The Pure Theory of Capital* that he approached his subject with a heavy heart. He writes of his "great reluctance" to embark on the task and expresses sympathy with those, like Keynes, who had tired of abstractions and turned to addressing how economics works in the real world. The very scale of the subject daunted and depressed him. "My reluctance to undertake this work would have been even greater if from the beginning I had been aware of the magnitude of the task,"[30] he wrote. The whole tone of the book is one of apology and despair. "The present book with all its shortcomings is the outcome of work over a period so prolonged that I doubt whether further effort on my part would be repaid by the results."[31] Later he was to confess that "it very gradually dawned on me"[32] that "the thing's become so damned complicated it's almost impossible to follow it."[33]

Notwithstanding the opacity of the text, the remaining Hayekians who hoped that here at last their hero would confront the growing cult of Keynesianism were to be disappointed. It was, however, the closest Hayek would come to enumerating his disagreement with *The General Theory*, though it is performed with the minimum of vim. "I have generally found it inadvisable to interrupt the main argument by explicit references to particular views,"[34] he wrote. He did, however, address some aspects of Keynes's analysis, but often merely to continue the arcane argument about economic terms that had distracted him from trying to disprove Keynes's calls to increase employment by public works. He writes that his main objection to Keynes's suggestion, that during a recession there are unused resources that could be productively brought into use to create jobs, is that "it is certainly not a normal position on which a theory claiming general applicability could be based."[35]

Hayek diminishes the main thrust of *The General Theory* as a piece of casuistry that denies the abiding concern of economists, to confront the problems of scarcity. "What [Keynes] has given us is really that economics of abundance for which they have been clamouring so long," he wrote. By denying the operation of the free market, Keynes had redefined scarcity as an "artificial" state of affairs "created by the determination of people not to sell their services and products below certain arbitrarily fixed prices." Keynes had ignored market prices and suggested that they came into play only "at rare intervals when 'full employment' is approached and the different goods begin successively to become scarce and to rise in price."[36]

Hayek dismisses Keyne's notion of what prices represent as a profound misunderstanding of how prices are truly determined. Hayek's belief that prices are the key to understanding the process of production— indeed, are the basis for understanding the working of an economy as a whole—and that prices are based on the scarcity of goods, rather than the relationship between what Keynes described as the imbalance between savings and investment and the "real cost" of production, causes him to disregard without explanation the whole of Keynes's complex counterargument.

In a telling footnote, Hayek condemns *The General Theory* not for its inappropriate novelty, but, surprisingly perhaps, for its being the product of outmoded thinking. Hayek mockingly describes as "one of the major advances of modern economics" Keynes's dismissal of the notion of the scarcity of resources and marvels that Keynes should nonetheless acknowledge the existence of "bottlenecks" to explain why goods become scarce toward the end of a boom. Hayek thought "bottlenecks" a misnomer; the term assumed that the market was failing to match supply with demand. "Bottlenecks" was therefore "a concept which seems to me to belong essentially to a naïve early stage of economic thinking and the introduction of which into economic theory can hardly be regarded as an improvement."[37]

Remarking that "this critical excursion [from the central thread of his book] was unfortunately made necessary by the confusion which has reigned on this subject since the appearance of Mr. Keynes' *General Theory*,"[38] Hayek resumed his Saharan dry investigation of capital and interest rates. There is a glancing reference to "liquidity," a notion at the core of Keynes's *General Theory*, but only to allow Hayek to remark that his own work was not the place to dig as deeply as he would like on the subject and that "little could be gained by scratching on the surface of this problem."[39] Again, with Keynes clearly in his sights, Hayek could not bring himself to pull the trigger.

In the concluding part of his *Pure Theory*, Hayek takes Keynes to task for concentrating on the short-term effects of economic problems and remedies, "not only as a serious and dangerous intellectual error, but as a betrayal of the main duty of the economist and a grave menace to our civilisation." "It used . . . to be regarded as the duty and the privilege of the economist to study and to stress the long effects which are apt to be hidden to the untrained eye, and to leave the concern about the more immediate effects to the practical man," he wrote. "It is alarming to see that after we have once gone through the process of developing a systematic account of those forces which in the long run determine prices and production, we are now called upon to scrap it, in order to replace it by the short-sighted philosophy of the business man raised to the dignity of a science."[40]

He ended on an ominous note by misappropriating one of Keynes's most famous quotes. "Are we not even told that, 'since in the long run we are all dead', policy should be guided entirely by short-run considerations?" he asks. "I fear that these believers in the principle of *après nous le déluge* may get what they have bargained for sooner than they wish."[41]

As Hayek must have been all too aware, such arch, pained sideswipes at Keynes were hardly enough to slow, let alone halt the mass baptism of young economists caught in the Keynesian thrall. There were, however, in passages of *The Pure Theory* arguments that, intended primarily as a warning to Keynesians, were to hint at a way forward—and also offer a warning—to those, such as Milton Friedman, who would follow Hayek into the anti-Keynesian camp.

"There is little ground for believing that a system with the modern complex credit structure will ever work smoothly without some deliberate control of the monetary mechanism," Hayek wrote, "since money by its very nature constitutes a kind of loose joint in the self-equilibrating apparatus of the price mechanism which is bound to impede its working. The aim of any successful monetary policy must be to reduce as far as possible this slack in the self-correcting forces of the price mechanism, and to make adaptation more prompt so as to reduce the necessity for a later, more violent, reaction."[42] But, in a warning to those like Friedman who would come to resort to quantitative monetary theory as a cure-all, Hayek suggested there were strict limits to this means of managing the economy. "We are certainly entitled to conclude . . . that the extent to which we can hope to shape events at will by controlling money are much more limited, that the scope of monetary policy is much more restricted, than is today widely believed," he wrote. "We cannot, as some writers seem to think, do more or less what we please with the economic system by playing on the monetary instrument."[43]

Hayek intended *The Pure Theory of Capital* to be succeeded by a complementary work, *The Pure Theory of Money*, but he never completed the second half of his schema. Ironically, perhaps, a parallel can be drawn between the failure to complete both parts of his grand opus and the consequences of a breakdown in the stages of production of capital goods during a credit-fueled slump that was his original inspiration. He had been hoist with his own petard.

In *The General Theory* Keynes concluded that the demand for commodities was equivalent to the demand for labor, and so had urged that aggregate demand be increased to provide full employment. Hayek profoundly disagreed with Keynes's analysis, believing it was not supported by empirical evidence. There were perhaps other ways of reading the figures. As Hayek later put it, "The correlation between aggregate demand and total employment . . . may only be approximate, but as it is the only one on which we have quantitative data, it is accepted as the only causal connection that counts."[44] The final sentence of *The Pure Theory* suggested that Keynes had fallen for a false hypothesis. "More than ever it seems to me to be true that the complete apprehension of the doctrine that 'demand of commodities is not demand for labour'—and of its limitations—is 'the best test of an economist.'"[45]

And on that emphatic note Hayek offered his final words on economic theory and fired his last purely economic salvo against Keynes. Hayek turned instead to the political philosophical themes he had first raised in "Economics and Knowledge" and in so doing opened a second and arguably more persuasive front against Keynes and the Keynesians.

THIRTEEN

The Road to Nowhere

Hayek Links Keynes's Remedies to Tyranny, 1937–46

The success of the Keynesian Revolution in America seemed assured after publication of *The General Theory*, yet the application of Keynesian ideas by the Roosevelt administration was patchy. Franklin Roosevelt may have welcomed Keynes to the White House, but he was nervous about funding public works on the scale the new doctrine demanded. And when, in the spring of 1937, production, profits, and wages returned to their 1929 levels, suggesting that the recovery was on its way, the president signaled a change in direction. Unemployment was at 14.3 percent, down from 16.9 percent the previous year, persuading some of Roosevelt's advisers, including the Federal Reserve chairman Marriner Eccles,[1] that the New Deal job schemes had worked their magic.

In June 1937, Roosevelt re-embraced orthodoxy with spending cuts, a credit squeeze, and an increase in taxes.[2] The work of federal job-creating agencies was slowed. Soon after, America was heading back into recession. The "Roosevelt Recession" lasted throughout 1938 and caused industrial production to slump by a third, prices to fall about 3.5 percent, and unemployment to climb to 19 percent.[3] Roosevelt tried to avoid blame by attacking big business. In January 1938, with a fall election looming, the president switched course, sending Congress a $3.75 billion spending bill and a further $1.25 billion in April, to fund fresh job-creating initiatives.

In a "fireside chat" on April 14, FDR adopted Keynesian logic. "We suffer primarily from a failure of consumer demand," he said. "It is up to us to create an economic upturn." He announced $300 million for slum clearance, $100 million for highways, and millions more for "public improvements." Roosevelt justified his reversal by claiming that putting the jobless back to work would protect America from the extremism rampant in Germany and Italy. "The very soundness of our democratic institutions depends on the determination of our Government to give employment to idle men," he declared.[4]

In February, Keynes wrote to Roosevelt. Dismissing the Roosevelt Recession as "an 'error of optimism,'" he urged the president on, recommending he focus on house building as "by far the best aid to recovery." And he urged Roosevelt to curb his rhetoric against business people, who were "perplexed, bemused, indeed terrified," he wrote. "If you work them into the surly, obstinate, terrified mood . . . the nation's burdens will not get carried to market."[5]

Fast-moving events in Germany obliged Roosevelt to spend on the vast scale Keynes prescribed. Hitler assumed power in January 1933 and set off on a massive rearmament program, in direct defiance of the Versailles treaty. Within a year, Germany, dogged by mass joblessness since World War I, was enjoying full employment.[6] Rearmament by the anxious European democracies gave American war industries a boost. In Britain, Neville Chamberlain's government was quietly rearming. Unemployment in Britain began to fall, though it remained at a record high until war was declared against Germany on September 3, 1939,[7] the day Wall Street stock prices returned to their pre-1929 crash levels.[8] Europe was not alone in fearing the Axis powers. Despite Roosevelt's assurances during the 1940 presidential campaign—"I have said this before, but I shall say it again and again and again: Your boys are not going to be sent into foreign wars"[9]— he ordered a gargantuan rearmament program: in 1940, the annual defense expenditure was $2.2 billion; the following year it reached a sizzling $13.7 billion.

"If expenditure on armaments really does cure unemployment, a grand experiment has begun," Keynes declared in 1939. "We may learn a trick or two which will come in useful when the day of peace comes."[10] The multiplier effect of so much public money being pumped into the American economy caused the gross domestic product (GDP) to jump by about $25 billion, with arms and other defense spending accounting for 46 percent of the increase.[11] Even so, employment was not restored to the pre–Roosevelt Recession level until 1941, the year America was attacked by the Japanese at Pearl Harbor. "We saw the war as a justification of the Keynesian theory, the Keynesian doctrine, and the Keynesian recommendation,"[12] John Kenneth Galbraith recalled.[13]

The German occupation of Austria in March 1938 coincided with Hayek becoming a British citizen, and he made one last trip to the old country before the outbreak of war. Unable to serve in the British armed forces because of his former nationality, in September 1939 he wrote to the Ministry of Information, suggesting that his "exceptional experience and somewhat special position might enable me to be of considerable help in connection with the organization of propaganda in Germany."[14] Hayek's offer was ignored.

Hayek could have been treated far worse. Piero Sraffa was interned on the Isle of Man merely for being Italian, a cruel fate in light of his having escaped Italy after Mussolini had threatened him. He was released after Keynes petitioned the home secretary. Hayek was aware of his good fortune. "I was still the ex-alien, enemy alien. I had a very privileged position," he recalled. "I was not used for any war purposes, but I was not molested. It couldn't have been a more ideal position."[15]

Keynes, at fifty-six, was too old for active service, far from healthy, and too out of favor with Chamberlain's government to be welcome at the Treasury. As his biographer Skidelsky explained, "He was too eminent to be made an ordinary civil servant, and too stimulating to be let loose in Whitehall."[16] But standing idly by was not his way. Unasked, he directed his thoughts toward solving how to pay for the war. He rejected the inflationary approach used in World War I, nor was he in favor of rationing. "The abolition of consumers' choice in favor of universal rationing is a typical product of that onslaught, sometimes called Bolshevism,"[17] he wrote in April 1940.

Chamberlain's chancellor, Sir John Simon,[18] had, inadvertently, been behaving like a model Keynesian, financing rearmament by public borrowing rather than raising taxation. He increased defense spending by £600 million, while imposing taxes of only £107 million. The Treasury concluded that there was little risk of inflation so long as unemployment remained at 9 percent.[19] Keynes, however, believed the huge spending on arms combined with the recruitment of armed forces would employ the whole of the workforce, stoking a massive increase in demand. Not only would this starve the government of essential supplies with which to fight the war, but inflation would follow as too much money chased too few goods. The choice was between high taxes, or inflation, or rationing, or a combination of all three.

In "War Potential and War Finance," a lecture to the Marshall Society on October 20, 1940, Keynes unveiled his plan. Instead of a straight income tax, earnings would be subject to a levy that combined progressive taxation with compulsory savings, "deferred pay" credited to interest-bearing accounts to be cashed once the war was won. Keynes believed the accumulated money spent after the war would counter what he believed would be a slump once war expenditures came to an end. Hayek described Keynes's approach as "ingenious." Hayek also welcomed Keynes's opposition to rationing, believing the removal of prices would result in injustices. Because he disliked the notion of countering a postwar slump with a contrived surge in spending, Hayek suggested instead that the deferred pay should be invested in shares. He also, surprisingly, floated the idea of paying down war debt with a "capital levy on old wealth"[20] to be placed in "a kind of giant holding company, [that] would in turn issue shares to the holders of the blocked balances."[21]

In reviewing Keynes's plan, Hayek described Keynes as having "the most fertile mind among living economists"[22] and concluded that "Mr. Keynes's proposal . . . appears to be the only real solution."[23] While remarking that it was "doubtful whether such a wholesale increase of expenditure is really a safe cure for slumps," he welcomed Keynes back to the fold. "The difference which had so long separated him from the more 'orthodox' economists had disappeared."[24] "During the war I was fighting on Keynes's side against his critics, because Keynes was very much against inflation," Hayek said later, telling only part of the story when he suggested that it was "to strengthen his influence against the inflationists" that he did not complete the second volume of *The Pure Theory of Money*.[25]

After the London School of Economics was evacuated from London in 1940 because of the Blitz, it moved to Peterhouse College, Cambridge, where Keynes's sternest critics, Hayek and Pigou, shared teaching duties. The move completed Hayek's assimilation into English life. "Life at Cambridge during those war years was to me particularly congenial," he recalled. "Somehow the whole mood and intellectual atmosphere of the country had at once proved extraordinarily attractive to me, and the conditions of a war in which all my sympathies were with the English greatly speeded up the process of becoming thoroughly at home."[26]

Hayek was due to move into Peterhouse when Keynes, in a typically humane gesture, insisted that his old rival be found rooms near his own at King's College. The two men met from time to time at King's and took part in faculty duties. And so it was that the surreal scene took place when Keynes and Hayek, armed with shovels and brooms, found themselves patrolling the Gothic roof of King's Chapel, scouring the night sky for German bombers. It was a truce of convenience. Neither had given ground, but in the face of a vicious common enemy each agreed to become affable acquaintances. "We shared so many other interests, historical and outside economics," Hayek recalled. "On the whole when we met we stopped talking economics. . . . So we became personally very great friends, including Lydia Lopokova."[27]

In August 1940, Keynes was given an unpaid Treasury job that allowed him to rove across all areas of economic policy. In particular, he was asked to negotiate war loans from America. He developed plans for a postwar economic order to replace the unbridled competition between nations that had fomented the war, and he invented a more orderly system of currency trading fixed around a revived gold standard, what became the Bretton Woods agreement. He was also instrumental in conceiving two other pivotal organizations, the International Monetary Fund and the World Bank.

Hayek, meanwhile, set out on his pessimistic masterwork, *The Road to Serfdom*.[28] As his biographer Alan Ebenstein observed, "'The Road to Serfdom' revolutionized Hayek's life. Before its publication, he was an unknown professor of economics. A year after it was published, he was famous around the world."[29] Not bad for a book that Hayek, with rare modesty, believed only a few hundred would read.[30]

Hayek had written to Walter Lippmann in 1937, "I wish I could make my 'progressive' friends here understand that democracy is possible only under capitalism and that collectivist experiments lead inevitably to fascism."[31] Originally titled "The Nemesis of the Planned Society," the book drew on ideas Hayek had explored in two essays in 1938 and 1939, that those who advocate a planned economy in place of a free market are, however well intentioned, treading a path that could lead to tyranny. "Once the free working of the market is impeded beyond a certain degree," he declared, "the planner will be forced to extend his controls until they become all-comprehensive."[32]

The Road to Serfdom was published in Britain on March 10, 1944, in an edition of 2,000. Within days, however, Routledge ordered 2,500 more and thereafter struggled to keep up with demand. In America, the University of Chicago Press published the book on September 18, 1944, after a number of mainstream publishers declined.

The principal targets of *The Road to Serfdom* are what Hayek deemed the twin evils of socialism and fascism, though because at the time of writing Stalin's Soviet Union was allied to Britain and America, he felt obliged to soften his criticisms of communism and allude more to the dangers of Nazism and fascism. He asserted that the common perception that the extremes of Left and Right were polar opposites was a misapprehension, for both, by replacing market forces with comprehensive state planning, assaulted individual liberties. He reiterated his belief that as economic planners cannot know the will of others, they end up acting like despots.

Hayek feared that when World War II was won, the Allied victors might conclude that wartime economic management would speed a more prosperous, more just postwar society. Such policies, he warned, invited the preconditions for totalitarianism and might cause history to repeat itself. "We have progressively abandoned that freedom in economic affairs without which personal and political freedom has never existed in the past,"[33] he wrote. "It is Germany whose fate we are in some danger of repeating."[34]

Little of Hayek's argument in *The Road to Serfdom* is directed toward Keynes, who is mentioned by name only twice,[35] though it seems it is Keynes and other newfound colleagues at Cambridge whom Hayek had in mind when he wrote that the book "is certain to offend many people with whom I wish to live on friendly terms."[36] Threaded between the lines of his central thesis can be found a belated, if slender, response to *The General Theory*. Yet gone was his usual shrill tone. Time at Cambridge, and proximity to Keynes, appear to have softened his zeal to prove his old adversary wrong.

The Road to Serfdom is hardly a rebuttal of *The General Theory*. Hayek acknowledges the motive behind Keynes's grand scheme: the dangers of prolonged widespread unemployment and that "combating general fluctuations of economic activity and recurrent waves of large-scale unemployment which accompany them" presented a "supremely important problem" and "one of the gravest and most pressing problems of our time."[37] His solution, however, rejects government intervention. "Though [the] solution [to chronic unemployment] will require much planning in the good sense," he wrote, "it does not— or at least need not—require that special kind of planning which according to its advocates is to replace the market."[38]

Hayek conjures up a Keynesian world where economic activity is directed by the state. "This might lead to much more serious restrictions of the competitive sphere," he wrote, "and, in experimenting in this direction, we shall have carefully to watch our step if we are to avoid making all economic activity progressively more dependent on the direction and volume of government expenditure." "We shall have carefully to watch our step" is hardly the robust demolition of Keynes's *General Theory* that Hayek had long promised.

Hayek's next two sentences are ambiguous. "[The remedy of large-scale public works to cure unemployment] is neither the only nor, in my opinion, the most promising way of meeting the gravest threat to economic security," he writes. "In any case, the very necessary efforts to secure protection against these fluctuations do not lead to the kind of planning which constitutes such a threat to our freedom." Did he mean to suggest that his ominous warnings about the dangers to freedom of state intervention did not include the "very large-scale" public works programs proposed by Keynes? It is hardly likely that he would exclude them, yet it is far from clear that he did. Once again, with Keynes clearly in the crosshairs, Hayek failed to discharge a fusillade.

Yet if Hayek was accepting that Keynesian planning would not necessarily lead to a diminution of freedom, he was clear that in his view Keynes's program came at too high a price: creeping inflation. "If we are determined not to allow unemployment at any price, and are not willing to use coercion [compel people to work], we shall be driven to all sorts of desperate experiments, none of which can bring any lasting relief and all of which will seriously interfere with the most productive use of our resources,"[39] he wrote.

In terms of his belated response to Keynes, there is a second significant omission in *The Road to Serfdom*. In *The General Theory*, Keynes not only provided an intellectual justification for government intervention but inadvertently invented a whole new branch of economics: macroeconomics, which offered a top-down perspective on economic activity the better to allow planners to understand, then manage a national economy. Until then economics had been understood solely in "microeconomic" terms, that is, looking at each element of economic activity in turn. Keynes was so far ahead of his time that the terms "macroeconomic" and "microeconomic" were not even coined until after his death. "Econometrics," too, was Keynes's unintended and much disparaged invention, the measurement of economic activity that came into its own as soon as planners came to assess the dimensions of an economy and set goals. Hayek and the Austrians thought such methods inappropriate. Yet Hayek omits any reference to the new disciplines, as well as the switch from the philosophical to the social scientific approach that Keynes's masterwork heralded.

Hayek later conceded that the Keynesians did not set out to do harm. "It has frequently been alleged that I have contended that any movement in the direction of socialism is bound to lead to totalitarianism," he wrote in 1976. "Even though this danger exists, this is not what [*The Road to Serfdom*] says. What it contains is a warning that unless we mend the principles of our policy, some very unpleasant consequences will follow which most of those who advocate these policies do not want."[40] Hayek suggested that moderate, "middle way" thinkers like Keynes who advocated ameliorative measures, although not themselves socialists, had gone some way toward adopting socialist ideas, imagining them to be a step toward enlightened progress. "The supreme tragedy is still not seen that in Germany it was largely people of good will . . . who prepared the way for, if they did not actually create, the forces which now stand for everything they detest," Hayek wrote. "If we take the people whose views influence developments, they are now in the democracies in some measure all socialists."[41]

Although not a critique of representative democracy per se, which Hayek supported, *The Road to Serfdom* is nonetheless an indictment of all who aspire to do good through the offices of the state as well as of politicians of all stripes who struggle—and, by his lights, inevitably fail—to understand the true will of the people. He recognized that the existence of a democratically elected government ensured that the size of the state would continue to grow. "The fault is neither with the individual representatives nor with the parliamentary institutions as such but with the contradictions inherent in the task with which they are charged,"[42] he wrote.

Classical economists and conservatives do not fare much better than socialists and communists in Hayek's stark analysis. He condemns the "wooden" advocates of free-market solutions, while rejecting conservatism, a devotion to existing institutions. "Though a necessary element in any stable society, [conservatism] is not a social program," he wrote. "In its paternalistic, nationalistic, and power-adoring tendencies it is often closer to socialism than true liberalism; and with its traditionalistic, anti-intellectual, and often mystical propensities it will never . . . appeal to the young and all those others who believe that some changes are desirable if this world is to become a better place."[43]

In a coda, Hayek takes a swing at the idealistic notions of a new world order that preoccupied Keynes in the final year of the war. While conceding that "the need is for an international political authority which, without power to direct the different people what they must do, must be able to restrain them from action which will damage others," he casts doubt on the prospect of achieving an international system of economic management that would not entail a drift toward authoritarianism. "The problems raised by a conscious direction of economic affairs on a national scale inevitably assume even greater dimensions when the same is attempted internationally," he wrote.

By coincidence, Keynes read *The Road to Serfdom* in June 1944 while he was sailing across the Atlantic en route to the Bretton Woods hotel in New Hampshire to preside over the negotiations for the international currency mechanism that took the hotel's name, the sort of supra-national body that made Hayek nervous. Hayek had in April sent *The Road to Serfdom* to Keynes, who had responded that the book "looks fascinating. It looks to me in the nature of medicine with which I shall disagree, but which may agree with me in the sense of doing me good. . . . Something to be kept at the back of one's head rather than at the front of it."[44] Plainly relaxed after his sea crossing, Keynes dropped a line to his old rival from the Claridge Hotel in Atlantic City, New Jersey. "The voyage has given me the chance to read your book properly," he wrote. "In my opinion it is a grand book. We all have the greatest reason to be grateful to you for saying so well what needs so much to be said. You will not expect me to accept quite all the economic dicta in it. But morally and philosophically I find myself in agreement with virtually the whole of it; and not only in agreement with it, but in a deeply moved agreement."

If Hayek's spirits were lifted by such warm praise, he was in for a shock. Keynes was soon on the counterattack. "I should say that what we want is not no planning, or even less planning, indeed I should say that we almost certainly want more," Keynes continued. "But the planning should take place in a community in which as many people as possible, both leaders and followers, wholly share your own moral position. . . . Moderate planning will be safe if those carrying it out are rightly orientated in their own minds and hearts to the moral issue. This is in fact already true of some of them. But the curse is that there is also an important section who could almost be said to want planning not in order to enjoy its fruits but because morally they hold ideas exactly the opposite of yours, and wish to serve not God but the devil." Keynes conceded that some British socialists were closet totalitarians.

He went on, "What we need, therefore, in my opinion, is not a change in our economic programmes, which would only lead in practice to disillusion with the results of your philosophy; but perhaps even the contrary, namely, an enlargement of them." Keynes reminded Hayek that Hitler's rise was facilitated not by big government but by the failure of capitalism and mass unemployment. "Your greatest danger ahead is the probable practical failure of the application of your philosophy in the U.S. in a fairly extreme form," Keynes continued, suggesting that if in peacetime America returned to the unemployment rates of the 1930s it might provoke the political extremism that had drawn the world into war.

"No," Keynes continued, "what we need is the restoration of right moral thinking—a return to proper moral values in our social philosophy. If only you could turn your crusade in that direction you would not look or feel quite so much like Don Quixote. I accuse you of perhaps confusing a little bit the moral and the material issues. Dangerous acts can be done safely in a community which thinks and feels rightly, which would be the way to hell if they were executed by those who think and feel wrongly."[45] This was an acute observation: that Hayek's analysis rested on an understanding of economics or sociology rather than of people. While Hayek was wary of the relationship between government intervention and tyranny, Keynes believed that the tendency toward totalitarianism stemmed from individual moral choices.

Hayek conceded in *The Road to Serfdom* that in the case of tackling chronic unemployment, planning might play its part and that the right form of planning might not lead to oppression. As he later expressed it, "So far as government plans for competition or steps in where competition cannot possibly do the job, there is no objection."[46] He also believed that the state may have a moral duty to step in and that was admissible so long as the spirit of free enterprise was not compromised. "There can be no doubt that some minimum of food, shelter, and clothing, sufficient to preserve health and the capacity to work, can be assured to everybody," he wrote. "Where, as in the case of sickness and accident, neither the desire to avoid such calamities nor the efforts to overcome their consequences are as a rule weakened by the provision of assistance—where, in short, we deal with genuinely insurable risks—the case for the state's helping to organize a comprehensive system of social insurance is very strong."[47]

Keynes pounced on this rare glimmer of moderation. There may be a slippery slope from planning to totalitarianism, but Hayek was on a slippery slope too. "I come to what is really my only serious criticism," Keynes wrote. "You admit here and there that it is a question of knowing where to draw the line. You agree that the line has to be drawn somewhere; and that the logical extreme is not possible. But you give us no guidance whatever as to where to draw it. It is true that you and I would probably draw it in different places. I should guess that according to my ideas you greatly underestimate the practicability of the middle course. But as soon as you admit that the extreme is not possible, and that a line has to be drawn, you are, on your own argument, done for, since you are trying to persuade us that so soon as one moves an inch in the planned direction you are necessarily launched on the slippery path which will lead you in due course over the precipice."[48]

Hayek did not attempt to answer the points raised in Keynes's letter, grateful, perhaps, for the general benevolence of his rival's appraisal. He did, after a time, counter Keynes's suggestion that planning would not invite tyranny in a country, like Britain, that held freedom dear. "I'm afraid many of my British friends still believe, as Keynes believed, that the existing moral convictions of the English would protect them against such a fate. This is nonsense," he declared. "You cannot rely on an inherent 'British character' saving the British people from their fate."[49]

Hayek's failure to respond to Keynes was perhaps because he imagined he had in *The Road to Serfdom* already dealt at some length with Keynes's specific objection—that it was a matter of drawing the line between state intervention and the free market. The key to the state's role was whether the rule of law was applied in every case. The law should be impartial, which meant ensuring that it did not skew in favor of a particular section of a community. "The state controlling weights and measures (or preventing fraud and deception in any other way) is certainly acting, while the state permitting the use of violence, for example, by strike pickets, is inactive," he wrote. "Yet it is in the first case that the state observes liberal principles and in the second that it does not."[50]

Government policies such as subsidies for certain industries or individuals, the granting of commercial monopolies, or discriminatory policies, even to right an injustice, confounded the rule of law. But welfare state provision, such as alleviating poverty and ill health, were legitimate state activities so long as they treated all citizens equally. "There is no reason why, in a society which has reached the general level of wealth which ours has attained, [this] kind of security should not be guaranteed to all without endangering general freedom," he wrote, though "whether those who rely on the community should indefinitely enjoy all the same liberties as the rest . . . might well cause serious and perhaps even dangerous political problems."[51]

When the University of Chicago Press asked Frank Knight, who might have been expected to approve the book's warnings, to advise on whether the press should publish the book, he said that Hayek had overstated his case. "The work is essentially negative," Knight wrote. "It hardly considers the problems of alternatives, and inadequately recognizes the necessity, as well as political inevitability, of a wide range of governmental activity in relation to economic life in future. It deals only with the simpler fallacies, unreasonable demands and romantic prejudices which underlie the popular clamor for governmental control in place of free enterprise." He concluded, "I doubt whether it would have a very wide market in this country, or would change the position of many readers."[52]

In that Knight was plainly wrong. Over time the *The Road to Serfdom* established itself as a key work in challenging the legitimacy and usefulness of economic planning. Starting with a print run of two thousand in America, the book received a prominent review in *The New York Times* describing it as "one of the most important books of our generation."[53] A second run of five thousand was followed quickly by a third, of ten thousand. Then Max Eastman,[54] a former leftist firebrand who had turned against socialism, arranged for an abridged version in *Reader's Digest* that coincided with the death of Franklin Roosevelt on April 12, 1945, when the New Deal and the future of economic policy became a hot topic. Before long a million copies had been ordered. *Look* magazine even printed a cartoon version.

In Britain, Hayek's arguments were treated mostly with fairness. Typical was a review by the author of *Nineteen Eighty-Four*, George Orwell,[55] no slouch when it came to recognizing creeping authoritarianism. "In the negative part of Professor Hayek's thesis there is a great deal of truth," he wrote. "Collectivism is not inherently democratic, but, on the contrary, gives to a tyrannical minority such powers as the Spanish Inquisitors never dreamed of." But he added, "Professor Hayek . . . does not see, or will not admit, that a return to 'free' competition means for the great mass of people a tyranny probably worse, because more irresponsible, than that of the State. The trouble with competitions is that somebody wins them. Professor Hayek denies that free capitalism necessarily leads to monopoly, but in practice that is where it has led, and since the vast majority of people would far rather have State regimentation than slumps and unemployment, the drift towards collectivism is bound to continue if popular opinion has any say in the matter."[56]

Others on the Left, such as the formidable public intellectual Barbara Wootton,[57] found Hayek's analysis on target but recoiled from its propagandist tone. "I wanted to point out some of these problems," she wrote Hayek, "but now that you have so exaggerated it I must turn against you."[58] She took his views seriously enough, however, to publish a riposte, *Freedom under Planning*."[59]

The Road to Serfdom was given an unexpected fillip in Britain in June 1945 when Winston Churchill simplified its theme in a radio broadcast opening the 1945 Conservative election campaign.[60] Hayek's warning that socialist planning could lead to tyranny chimed with Churchill's belief that Labour under his wartime coalition deputy Clement Attlee[61] put at risk the freedom just won. "[The Labour Party] would have to fall back on some form of Gestapo," he declared. "It would gather all the power to the supreme Party and the Party leaders, rising like stately pinnacles above their vast bureaucracies of Civil Servants, no longer servants and no longer civil."[62] The prime minister's biblical sense of foreboding, so apt in wartime, suddenly seemed extreme, alarmist, even undemocratic. The broadcast was, according to Churchill biographer Roy Jenkins,[63] "the most ill-judged of all his famous wireless addresses."[64]

Churchill's adoption of Hayek's critique did little to enhance Hayek's reputation. Pointing out that the prime minister was inspired by a "second-hand version of the academic views of an Austrian professor," the mild-mannered Attlee declared, "When I listened to the Prime Minister's speech last night . . . I realized at once what was his object. He wanted the electors to understand how great was the difference between Winston Churchill, the great leader in war of a united nation, and Mr. Churchill, the party Leader of the Conservatives. He feared that those who had accepted his leadership in war might be tempted out of gratitude to follow him further. I thank him for having disillusioned them so thoroughly."[65] Much to the surprise of Churchill—and Attlee—Labour was returned with a landslide, not least because voters feared a return of the prewar high unemployment presided over by the Conservatives. As the Labour politician Tony Benn recalled, "All these soldiers said, 'Never again. We're never going back to unemployment, the Great Depression.'"[66]

In America, Hayek recalled, "[The book] was treated even by

the academic community very largely as a malicious effort by a reactionary to destroy high ideals."[67] Harvard's leading Keynesian, Alvin Hansen, in his article "The New Crusade against Planning,"[68] joined Keynes in noting that Hayek had made a distinction between good and bad intervention, and asked, like Keynes, where exactly would Hayek draw the line.

Professor T. V. Smith[69] of the University of Chicago turned up the heat, calling Hayek's argument "hysterical," "alarmist," and "overstrident." "No country has yet wittingly or . . . unwittingly slipped into serfdom whose presuppositions are democratic,"[70] he wrote. The point, wrote Smith, was "to distinguish harmful from helpful planning rather than to damn all planning. . . . The author is not opposed to planning. Like the rest of us, he is opposed only to planning which subverts freedom."[71] "The preparation for an electrocution and for an electrocardiograph is the same, up to a point,"[72] Smith suggested. The difficulty was telling one from the other.

Smith discerned a further flaw in Hayek's reasoning: that it was hardly undemocratic to plan if democratically elected governments followed the electorate's wishes that planning occur. "The greatest success of the Constitution . . . is that in a century and a half it has won the people from an ancient distrust of government to an acceptance of it as their friend," wrote Smith. "A democratic government is the people themselves incorporated."[73]

Another University of Chicago professor, Herman Finer,[74] responded with *The Road to Reaction,* in which he dismissed Hayek's "jungle of fallacies." He went on, "Hayek's apparatus of learning is deficient, his reading incomplete, . . . his understanding of the economic process is bigoted, his account of history false, . . . his political science is almost nonexistent, his terminology misleading, his comprehension of British and American political procedure and mentality gravely defective; and . . . his attitude to average men and women is truculently authoritarian."[75] He described the work as "the most sinister offensive against democracy to emerge from a democratic country for many decades."[76]

It soon became clear that, though hugely popular, *The Road to Serfdom* was a defining work that not only divided the Left from the Right but also the Right from the Ultra-Right. The quarrelsome libertarian Ayn Rand,[77] who rarely met Hayek in person, and when she did dismissed him as a "compromiser,"[78] was enraged by the book. In the margins of her copy she scribbled abusive comments, calling Hayek a "God damn fool," an "abysmal fool," an "ass," and a "total, complete, vicious bastard."[79]

Hayek was taken aback that in the United States he found himself caught in a caustic ideological battle. In America, he remembered, "The great enthusiasm about the New Deal was still at its height. And here there were two groups: people who were enthusiastic about the book but never read it—they just heard there was a book which supported capitalism—and the American intelligentsia, who had just been bitten by the collectivist bug and who felt that this was a betrayal of the highest ideals which intellectuals ought to defend. So I was exposed to incredible abuse, something I never experienced in Britain at the time. It went so far as to completely discredit me professionally."[80]

In January 1946, Hayek and Keynes met in Cambridge. Hayek turned the conversation from Elizabethan books to the way, it seemed to him, that Keynes's followers—it is thought Joan Robinson and Richard Kahn were mentioned—appeared to be adapting Keynes's ideas for their own ends. Did this not trouble Keynes? What could he do about it? "After a not very complimentary remark about the persons concerned," Hayek recalled, "he proceeded to reassure me by explaining that those ideas had been badly needed at the time he had launched them. He continued by indicating that I need not be alarmed; if they should ever become dangerous I could rely upon him again quickly to swing round public opinion—and he indicated by a quick movement of his hand how rapidly that would be done."[81] "Keynes had a supreme conceit of his power of playing with public opinion," recalled Hayek. "He believed he could play with public opinion as though it were an instrument. And for that reason, he wasn't at all alarmed by the fact that his ideas were misinterpreted. 'Oh, I can correct this any time.' That was his feeling about it."[82] Three months later, Keynes was dead.

On Easter Sunday morning, April 30, 1946, the strain of living several hectic lives in parallel took its toll on the frail body of John Maynard Keynes. He died in his bed in his farmhouse in Tilton, East Sussex, of the heart disease[83] that had plagued his middle age. Lydia and his mother were by his side. He was just sixty-two. His onetime opponent Lionel Robbins, who had accompanied him to America to negotiate Britain's war debt, wrote to Lydia that Keynes "has given his life for his country, as surely as if he had fallen on the field of battle."[84] Hayek, too, wrote to Lydia, describing Keynes as "the one really great man I ever knew, and for whom I had unbounded admiration. The world will be a very much poorer place without him."[85]

Hayek told his wife that with Keynes dead he was now "probably the best known economist living," a remark he was to "bitterly regret." "Ten days later it was probably no longer true," he remembered. "At that very moment Keynes became the great figure and I was gradually forgotten as an economist."[86] As he put it some forty years later, "In the middle 1940s—I suppose I sound very conceited—I think I was known as one of the two main disputing economists: there was Keynes and there was I. Now, Keynes died and became a saint; and I discredited myself by publishing 'The Road to Serfdom,' which completely changed the situation."[87]

FOURTEEN

The Wilderness Years

Mont-Pèlerin and Hayek's Move to Chicago, 1944–69

Hayek did little to build on the popular success of *The Road to Serf-dom* in America. He was a reluctant public figure and found that the acclamation he received on his book tour disturbed his decorum. "I was asked to come over to give five series of lectures at five universities," he recalled. "I imagined very sedate academic lectures, which I had written out very carefully. . . . While I was on the high seas, the condensation of *The Road to Serfdom* in the *Reader's Digest* appeared. So when I arrived I was told . . . I was to go on a public lecture tour around the country. I said, 'My God, I have never done this. I can't possibly do it. I have no experience in public speaking.' [They said], 'Oh, it can't be helped now.'"[1]

Hayek found the vast audiences alarming. "I rather imagined a little group of old ladies like the Hokinson[2] women in the *New Yorker*," he remembered. "I asked, 'What sort of audience do you expect?' They said, 'The hall holds 3,000, but there's an overflow meeting.' Dear God, I hadn't an idea what I was going to say." For the next five weeks he crisscrossed America, speaking to attentive crowds. He had become an instant hero. Over time he came to take pleasure in playing the role of seer and sage, but the actor's life did not come naturally. "What I did in America was a very corrupting experience," he recalled. "You become an actor, and I didn't know I had it in me. But given the opportunity to play with an audience, I began enjoying it."[3]

It is worth speculating how the battle with Keynesian ideas would have turned out had Hayek been more of a showman. Keynes knew how to sell his ideas. He was a master of the op-ed article and enjoyed being the center of attention. Had Hayek possessed Keynes's self-confidence, his commercial nous, and his love of performance, he might have been able to persuade more people that managing an economy was not desirable. He had self-confidence, but perhaps his heavy accent and his introverted nature worked not only against him but also against his ideas. One colleague described Hayek at this time as "very correct and rather serious, portly, gracious, slow, rather ponderous-speaking, sometimes thinking what his next sentence is going to be."[4] Hardly the qualities of a media star. Whatever the merits of the argument between Keynes and Hayek, Keynes held the advantage, even after his death.

Hayek was admired, but he was not widely liked, except by those who knew him well. He was known as a contrarian, which attracted him to mavericks but did not endear him to those who liked to belong. Keynes offered a hopeful view of the future, with everyone employed, based on an optimistic view of human nature. Hayek was a doubter and pessimist: those who strived to make the world better would likely end up inviting unintended consequences. The free market worked best according to rational decisions based on self-interest, and failed to work when tempered by idealism. Thus, optimists and idealists tended to follow Keynes; pessimists found in Hayek a sober guide to the disappointments of the real world.

After his American book tour, Hayek returned to England with a thud. "Keynes was disputed as long as he was alive—very much so. After his death, he was raised to sainthood. Partly because Keynes himself was very willing to change his opinions, his pupils developed an orthodoxy: you were either allowed to belong to the orthodoxy or not. At about the same time, I discredited myself with most of my fellow economists by writing *The Road to Serfdom*, which is disliked so much. So not only did my theoretical influence decline, most of the departments [at the London School of Economics] came to dislike me."[5]

In a lecture in early 1944, Hayek exposed the protracted hurt he had endured by arguing against progressive ideas. "I have every reason to wish that I were able to believe that a planned socialist society can achieve what its advocates promise," he said. "If I could convince myself that they are right, this would suddenly remove all the clouds which to me blacken all the prospects of the future." Had he bent with the socialistic wind, he said, "I might rise to be a trusted leader instead of a hated obstructionist." "Whatever else you may think of the classical economists, you must admit that they never feared being unpopular," he said.

Hayek had been taken aback by the hostility to *The Road to Serfdom*. Nor would such forcefully expressed antipathy soon abate. As the journalist Ralph Harris[6] recalled, "Hayek went through a period in the Fifties and Sixties [when] he was hated, execrated. Academics on the Left, who were by no means unpleasant individuals, would not meet him. I had occasions when a professor of philosophy at Oxford didn't want to meet 'That Man.' . . . It was a deep hatred."[7]

Over time, the aversion to Hayek's ideas was transferred to all those who offered a free-market alternative to Keynesianism. "There was something of a religious war about it, that to criticize this noble ideal of socialism, of fairness, of equality, was to desecrate something that was fine," explained Harris. "It was a glint in the eye with many quite ordinary people who thought that socialism not merely was bound to come, but was the ultimate fulfillment of a civilized society."[8] In turn, free-market ideas acquired a quasi-religious dimension that would lead some adherents to appear disciples of a secret sect rather than seekers after truth.

Shunned in his adopted country, Hayek contemplated moving to America, but having migrated to a new land once, he was reluctant to endure a second change of culture. The experience of his mentor Ludwig von Mises, who had fled Nazism to New York and had struggled to find work in American academe, did not suggest Hayek would be made welcome. Besides, Hayek enjoyed living among the English. When he first visited America in the 1920s, he recalled, "I still was too much a European and didn't the least feel that I belonged. But at the moment I arrived in England, I belonged to it."[9] Two profound disruptions to his life would change his mind.

But first he was to address a phenomenon he had encountered when touring around America: the feeling of stark insularity among those, like him, who continued to believe in orthodox economics despite the widespread conversion to Keynesianism. "Everywhere I went I met someone who told me that he fully agreed with me, but that at the same time he felt totally isolated in his views and had nobody with whom he could even talk about them," he said. "This gave me the idea of bringing these people, each of whom was living in great solitude, together in one place."[10]

Hayek wanted to lead the opposition to Keynesianism, with himself at its head. All of his collaborators would be "economic liberals," though by no means would they all be adherents to the Austrian School. "Liberal economists" believed that the economy and markets should be free from interference. They were not to be confused with the "liberals" in America who advocated freedom for individuals to behave as they liked in their private lives, without inhibition from constricting social mores, and who were often anything but liberal in their economics. The conflicting use of the word "liberal" was to become a constant source of confusion.

Hayek had taken the first step on the counterrevolutionary trail in April 1938. The distinguished American journalist and commentator Walter Lippmann became the subject of a colloquium in Paris to boost his book *The Good Society*, which highlighted the threat to liberty inherent in planned societies such as Soviet Russia and Nazi Germany. Hayek, Mises, and Robbins were invited, along with the anti-Marxist French sociologist Raymond Aron,[11] the Manchester University economist Michael Polanyi,[12] the free-market thinker from Freiburg Wilhelm Röpke,[13] and twenty or so others to discuss "the crisis of liberalism." Their arguments did little more than lay the foundation for further debate, but an ambitious agenda for action after the war began to form in Hayek's mind. As soon as the war was won, Hayek contacted the "Colloque Walter Lippmann" attendees and other like-minded thinkers.

Hayek proposed a summit in the most literal sense, a ten-day conference in April 1947 at the vertiginous Hôtel du Parc,[14] which sat atop Mont Pèlerin, looking down over Lake Geneva, near Vevey in Switzerland. A top manager of the Schweirzerische Kreditanstalt underwrote 93 percent of the 18,000 Swiss francs the symposium cost to stage. Albert Hunold,[15] a Zurich businessman who headed the Swiss watch manufacturers, diverted money intended for a liberal journal. There were grants from the free-market Foundation for Economic Education in Irvington-on-Hudson, New York, and from the libertarian William Volcker Charities Fund of Kansas City, Missouri, that funded Americans making the trip.[16]

Hayek invited about sixty, promising that all expenses would be paid, and thirty-seven from ten countries accepted, about half from America. To subsequent generations of libertarians, those who attended the first Mont-Pèlerin meeting came to be treated with the awe that well-born New Englanders reserve for those who sailed on the *Mayflower*. It did not escape notice that the French word *pèlerin* meant pilgrim. The Pèlerinos who ascended the funicular railway to the Hôtel du Parc, a resort more used to hikers than intellectuals, were a disparate group brought together by a shared sense of righteous isolation and noble persecution. As the historian George H. Nash[17] put it, "The participants, high in the Swiss Alps, were only too conscious that they were outnumbered and without apparent influence on policymakers in the Western world."[18]

Among those present were Mises; Robbins; Frank Knight; George Stigler,[19] the Chicago School economist; Fritz Machlup, the Austrian School economist who fled to America in 1933; John Jewkes,[20] the British antiplanning economist; Karl Popper,[21] the LSE scientific philosopher; Henry Hazlitt, whose laudatory review of *The Road to Serfdom* in the *The New York Times* helped ensure the book's success in America; William Rappard, head of the École des Hautes Études in Geneva; Wilhelm Röpke, of Geneva, who was to reform the German currency; and Veronica Wedgwood,[22] the Oxford-educated English Civil War historian who wrote pieces for *Time and Tide*. Stigler joked—but only half-joked—that the list was little more than "The Friends of F. A. Hayek."

Of all those who attended that first meeting, perhaps the most important for the practical advancement of Hayek's ideas was Milton Friedman, a thirty-five-year-old Chicago economist enjoying his first trip outside the United States. Friedman, who had briefly met Hayek in Chicago during the *The Road to Serfdom* publicity tour, was invited at the suggestion of his wife's brother Aaron Director,[23] a member of the University of Chicago Law School. Director had met Hayek at the LSE and was instrumental in having the University of Chicago Press publish *The Road to Serfdom*. The trio from Chicago—Director, Stigler, and Friedman—jokingly referred to the trip as "a junket to Switzerland . . . to save liberalism"[24] and were not expecting to do much more than play cards. Stigler asked Friedman to "train Aaron on bridge, and let's find a fourth liberal and teach him."[25] As Friedman recalled, "Here I was, a young, naïve provincial American, meeting people from all over the world, all dedicated to the same liberal principles as we were; all beleaguered in their own countries, yet among them scholars, some already internationally famous, others destined to be; making friendships which have enriched our lives, and participating in founding a society that has played a role in preserving and strengthening liberal ideas."[26]

Hayek's opening address reflected the long road he had traveled and the even longer journey that stretched ahead before he invited his charges to discuss "the relation between 'free enterprise' and a really competitive order," the problem of "the inflationary high-pressure economy which . . . [is] the main tool by which a collectivist development is forced on the majority of countries," the teaching of history, the relationship between liberal economic thought and Christianity, the future of Germany, prospects for a European federation, and the rule of law.

"The place is unbelievably wonderful," Friedman gushed in a postcard home to his wife Rose. "We've been meeting three times a day. . . . It's pretty wearing, but also very stimulating."[27] The discussions were intense and often too lively for comfort. "Our sessions were marked by vigorous controversy,"[28] recalled Friedman. There were, inevitably, heated rows and disagreements. During one dispute between Mises, Robbins, Friedman, Stigler, and Knight on the redistribution of income, Mises stormed out of the room shouting, "You're all a bunch of socialists!" Another time Mises accused Harbeler of being a communist.[29] As Friedman explained, "Mises was a person of very strong views and rather intolerant about any differences of opinion."[30] To literally cool things down, walks were arranged to explore the surrounding mountainside. The combative atmosphere of the first meeting set the tone for subsequent meetings, leading to repeated rows and resignations as the contrarians argued over differences imperceptible to an outsider. As Samuelson drily noted, "The number of Mont Pelerin resignations never quite reached the number of its new members."[31]

After more than a week of debates, Robbins wrote a mission statement. Declaring that "the central values of civilization are in danger," Robbins asserted that the threat to freedom had been "fostered by the growth of a view of history which denies all absolute moral standards and by the growth of theories which question the desirability of the rule of law. It holds further that they have been fostered by a decline of belief in private property and the competitive market." He concluded, "The group does not aspire to conduct propaganda. It seeks to establish no meticulous and hampering orthodoxy. It aligns itself with no particular party. Its object is solely . . . to contribute to the preservation and improvement of the free society."[32]

Hayek was confident that the conference would mark "the rebirth of a liberal movement in Europe."[33] Friedman considered it "an attempt to offset *The Road to Serfdom*, to start a movement, a road to freedom as it were."[34] It took more than a year to arrange the second meeting, in 1949 in Seelisberg, Switzerland, but the society met annually from then on.

Inasmuch as the Keynesians noticed the Mont-Pèlerin meeting, it was to diminish those they liked to deride as fossils. Typical was John Kenneth Galbraith's dismissal: "The small remaining band of free market economists met on an Alpine peak to form a society which, however, soon foundered over a division within its ranks on the question [of] whether the British Navy should be owned by the government or leased from the private sector."[35]

Energized by his new quest, Hayek returned to Britain to a more painful chore. He had married Helen Berta Maria von Fritsch, known as "Hella," in Vienna in 1926. For the next twenty years, to friends such as Robbins, the marriage seemed a happy one, blessed with two children. But Hayek had married Hella on the rebound. As a young man in Vienna he had first fallen in love with his cousin, Helene, but when he traveled to New York in 1923 the distance proved too much, and "through some misunderstanding of intentions,"[36] Helene tired of waiting and married another.

Hayek married Hella soon after, because, he explained, she looked somewhat like Helene. Hella became "a very good wife to me,"[37] he recalled. After the war, in 1946, when Hayek was visiting Vienna, alone, to discover how his relations had fared under the Nazis, he met Helene, who told him she was free to marry him. Despite the years of Hella's devotion and the existence of a daughter, Christine, aged seventeen, and a son, Laurence, aged twelve, and contrary to his lapsed Roman Catholic faith, Hayek decided to divorce Hella and marry Helene. Hurt and angry, Hella refused to grant Hayek a separation and the divorce negotiations became acrimonious.

Hayek celebrated Christmas Day 1949 with Hella and the children in their snug family home in Hampstead. Two days later he left them for good, traveling to New York to attend the American Economic Association convention. Hayek's finances were more on his mind than economics. To avoid the expense of a contested divorce, he slipped a note under the hotel room door of Harold Dulan, chairman of the economics and business department at the University of Arkansas, Fayetteville, asking for a teaching post. Hayek's plan was to establish residency in Arkansas, a state whose permissive marriage laws would allow him to wrest a cheap divorce from Hella. Dulan duly obliged, as did the chancery division of the Arkansas high court. Hayek's divorce became absolute in July 1950. "Finally I enforced it," Hayek recalled. "I'm sure that was wrong, and yet I have done it," he said. "It was just an inner need to do it."[38]

The divorce scandalized Hayek's LSE colleagues, none more so than Robbins, who was dumbfounded when Hayek resigned his LSE post in February 1950. Robbins wrote that he felt Hayek had "behaved in such a way . . . I find impossible to reconcile with the conception of his character and his standards which I have cherished through twenty years of friendship. As far as I am concerned, the man I knew is dead." In the following ten years, such was Robbins's disgust that he resigned from the Mont Pelerin Society in protest at Hella's treatment and made no contact with Hayek. The two men were reconciled only after Hella's death, when Robbins attended the wedding in 1961 of Hayek's son, Laurence, his godson.

Hayek needed to make himself scarce. In the light of his personal dramas, his move to America can be seen as a financially driven decision rather than an attempt to exploit his newfound fame as a paragon of liberty. He needed to earn a larger salary than he received from the LSE to support Hella and the children while maintaining himself and Helene. He eventually landed a post at the University of Chicago, though that proved far from easy.

Chicago had been a home away from home during his *Road to Serfdom* publicity tour. The University of Chicago Press was his American publisher, and he enjoyed being billeted in the university's congenial Quadrangle Club. (By contrast, Columbia University parked him in a vast empty dormitory, which he took as a personal and political slight.)

Nothing would have pleased Hayek more than to join the University of Chicago School of Economics. But after delivering a lecture at the Economic Club in Detroit, Hayek was approached by Harold W. Luhnow, president of the libertarian William Volcker Charities Fund, who invited him to write an edition of *The Road* tailored toward Americans. Luhnow was prepared to pay Hayek's asking price of $10,000 a year for three years. "I didn't take him very seriously,"[39] recalled Hayek, who was wary of being paid by a conservative think tank rather than becoming an independent academic at an established university.

Hayek tried to obtain a teaching post at the Institute for Advanced Studies at Princeton University, which was not happy for a salary to be designated by a private concern. Hayek then approached the University of Chicago, hoping for a position in the School of Economics, where he felt he would be welcomed by scholars such as Frank Knight and Jacob Viner.[40] Hayek's request was taken up with enthusiasm by the university's president, Robert Maynard Hutchins, an educational reformer who, in his effort to make Chicago a more serious institution, had abolished fraternities and the football program, reforms that made him unpopular with the faculty, not least the conservative-minded professors at the School of Economics. Hutchins's suggestion that Hayek join the school was therefore hampered from the start, though antipathy to Hutchins was not the only reason Hayek was rejected.

"He was not a person they would have chosen to add," explained Friedman. "They didn't agree with his economics. . . . If they had been looking round the world for an economist to add to their staff, their prescription would not have been the author of *Prices and Production*"[41] Hayek's Austrian School economics was considered abstruse and outdated. The difference between Hayek's thinking and Chicago School notions is significant. Friedman's championing of Hayek's libertarian approach to the economy and politics ignored the Austrian "stages of production" notions in favor of government regulation of the supply of money, a process that the Austrians thought anathema. And while Hayek believed that the free market held a monopoly of virtue, Chicago scholars such as Frank Knight believed it could be equally as inefficient as government intervention. However, the fact that both the Austrian and the Chicago School believe that prices hold the key to understanding the economy, and that the free market is preferable to intervention, has meant that the competing traditions are commonly deemed to be synonymous.

Friedman's breakthrough in economics, determining the link between unnecessary constrictions in the money supply and recessions that follow, showed how profoundly Chicago's economists could differ. Unlike Hayek and Mises, who thought economic activity too complex to quantify and that averages were misleading indicators of how individuals set prices, Friedman's research took as a given the Keynesian notion of observing the economy as a whole and using averages to determine the cause and effect of economic changes. While careful never to criticize Hayek's Austrian School notions too harshly, Friedman remained unconvinced of their merit.

Hayek's venture into doomsday prognostication in *The Road to Serfdom* was also cited as evidence that he lacked the intellectual rigor expected at the Chicago School. According to John Nef, chairman of Chicago's Committee on Social Thought, some Chicago economists believed *The Road to Serfdom* "too popular a work for a respectable scholar to perpetrate. It was all right to have him at Chicago so long as he was not associated with the economists."[42] In the fall of 1950, at the suggestion of Nef, Hayek became professor of social and moral science in the Committee on Social Thought, a chair funded in part by the Volcker fund. Despite the rebuff, Hayek accepted the post.

Hayek wanted to kick-start his counterrevolution by writing a work that would be as popularly received as *The Road to Serfdom*. As his biographer Alan Ebenstein explained, "He hoped *The Constitution of Liberty* would be [Adam Smith's] *The Wealth of Nations* of the twentieth century."[43] Over the next nine years he worked on and off on a work that would explain why the rule of law is the best way to safeguard individual liberties from governments. He began with a brief history of the notion of liberty and an elaboration on the concept of the rule of law first expressed two hundred years earlier by "the father of liberalism," the English philosopher John Locke, whose work inspired both the French Revolution and America's Founding Fathers. Locke declared all people to be equal and denied the logic of a monarch's claim to rule by divine right. He defined the "social contract" between men who live peaceably in society, and suggested that consent is a prerequisite for obeying laws and government. The aspect of Locke's thinking that particularly engaged Hayek was his assertion that only if everyone is considered equal under the law can a society be considered truly free.

Hayek took Locke's idea of the rule of law and ran with it, claiming that only the existence of the rule of law can ensure that a free market works fairly for all and, to the contrary, that when the rule of law is absent, tyranny reigns. Chastened somewhat by the charge that sensationalism informed *The Road to Serfdom*, in *The Constitution of Liberty* his approach was deliberately understated. "I have endeavored to conduct the discussion in as sober a spirit as possible,"[44] he wrote.

The Constitution of Liberty's first general conclusion is that for individuals to be free of coercion by others, the state must coerce some into not coercing others. The second is that both democracy and capitalism, with its ideas of private property and enforceable contracts operating within a free market, demand the rule of law. "There is probably no single factor which has contributed more to the prosperity of the West than the relative certainty of the law,"[45] Hayek declares. The rule of law allows citizens the certainty to make decisions about the future, which is a prerequisite for making investments, and provides the ordered conditions in which societies can become wealthy. Hayek presupposes limits on the intrusion of laws into a person's private life, allowing an individual to enjoy what he called "some assured private sphere."[46] It was Locke for the modern age.

Hayek then ventured into more treacherous territory concerning key elements of the American dream: that all men are created equal and that to ensure the fair treatment of all of its citizens an administration should pursue policies that make its citizens equal in esteem. Hayek dissects the word "equal" and, en passant, dismisses Locke's contention that the mind acquires wisdom through experience not inheritance. "It has been the fashion in modern times to minimize the importance of congenital differences," he wrote. "We must not overlook the fact that individuals are very different from the outset. As a statement of fact, it just is not true that 'all men are born equal.'"[47] Little wonder, perhaps, that Hayek had warned in the preface, "I cannot claim to write as an American."[48]

While Hayek accepted that everyone should be considered of equal worth, and treated equally under the law, he thought it ridiculous for governments to attempt to make everyone equal, or even to treat everyone the same by providing them with identical resources. It was the very differences between people that he thought essential for the maintenance of progress and prosperity. "The rapid economic advance that we have come to expect seems in a large measure to be the result of inequality and to be impossible without it," he wrote.[49]

He argued that it was inevitable for the progress of civilization that some nations draw ahead of others. "If today some nations can in a few decades acquire a level of material comfort that took the West hundreds of thousands of years to achieve, is it not evident that their path has been made easier by the fact that the West was not forced to share its material achievements with the rest?"[50] he argued.

Controversial views kept coming. Conservatives who read *The Road to Serfdom* may have been excused for concluding that Hayek was one of their number; the book was such a challenge to socialists and communists and an endorsement of the free market that conservatives widely considered it a manifesto. In *The Constitution of Liberty*, however, Hayek disabused them with a postscript titled, "Why I Am Not a Conservative."[51] Hayek declared that he was a "liberal." "One of the fundamental traits of the conservative attitude is a fear of change, a timid distrust of the new," he wrote, "while the liberal position is based on courage and confidence, on a preparedness to let change run its course even if we cannot predict where it will lead."[52] He went on, "The conservative position rests on the belief that in any society there are recognizably superior persons whose inherited standards and values and position ought to be protected and who should have a greater influence on public affairs than others. The liberal, of course, does not deny that there are some superior people—he is not an egalitarian— but he denies that anyone has authority to decide who these superior people are."[53]

Hayek declared that conservatives were like socialists, and that both held detestable, undemocratic views. "The conservative does not object to coercion or arbitrary power so long as it is used for what he regards as the right purposes. He believes that if government is in the hands of decent men, it ought not to be too much restricted by rigid rules. . . . [L]ike the socialist, he regards himself as entitled to force the value he holds on other people,"[54] he wrote. "It is not democracy but unlimited government that is objectionable, and I do not see why the people should not learn to limit the scope of majority rule as well as that of any other form of government."[55]

He argued that conservatives were cursed by nationalism. "It is this nationalistic bias which frequently provides the bridge from conservatism to collectivism: to think in terms of 'our' industry or resource is only a short step away from demanding that these national assets be directed in the national interest,"[56] he declared. "Nationalism of this sort is something very different from patriotism and . . . an aversion to nationalism is fully compatible with a deep attachment to national traditions."[57] Writing in the shadow of the anticommunist show trials conducted by the House Un-American Activities Committee and Senator Joseph McCarthy, Hayek let slip that he had little patience with such sinister developments: "It is no real argument to say that an idea is un-American, or un-German, nor is a mistaken or vicious ideal better for having been conceived by one of our compatriots."[58]

Hayek finished writing *The Constitution of Liberty* on May 8, 1959, his sixtieth birthday, and it was published in February 1960. He sent signed copies to Richard Nixon, Herbert Hoover, Walter Lippmann, John Davenport, Henry Hazlitt, to the publisher of *Time,* Henry Luce, and to a top editor at *Reader's Digest*, hoping the magazine might publish a short edition, as it had with *The Road to Serfdom*. Not only was his project of reviving liberalism at stake, but Hayek needed income. With two wives and two children to support, and retirement looming but no pension, he dearly hoped the book would become a best seller.

It fell flat. While it received encouraging words from the usual suspects, it failed to take off in the public mind. Compared to *The Road to Serfdom*, it was long-winded and heavy going. As Robbins put it, "It cannot be said to be easy reading; the arguments, although clear and well marshaled, demand frequent pauses for reflection."[59] For a work intended to prompt intellectuals to reconsider basic concepts about freedom, it received little notice even in learned journals, and the few who did review it found fault, even those who might be expected to agree with its conclusions.

Typical was Jacob Viner from Princeton, who, with Frank Knight, had from the 1930s onward guided the University of Chicago School of Economics in a pro-market direction. Viner complained of Hayek's oversimplicity, self-contradiction, and poor academic method, of "the conspicuous absence in Hayek's argument of ifs and buts and of painful wrestling with the task of weighing pros and cons."[60] He reiterated George Orwell's criticism of *The Road to Serfdom*, that Hayek had solely concentrated his objections to coercion in the public sector, when identical arguments could be made about private corporations. Viner derided Hayek for excusing private cartels while objecting to unions who monopolized the supply of labor.[61] He ridiculed Hayek's plea for a "flat tax" in which the same was paid by all: "Even in its most extreme manifestations, progressive taxation [taxing the rich proportionately more than the poor] has never been carried so far that 'survival' has become more difficult for the pre-taxation rich than for the poor."[62]

Viner rejected Hayek's "social Darwinism," a belief that over time those best fitted to the demands of society became better off, saying it conflicted with his dismissal of "historicism,"[63] that history is determined by immutable laws rather than efforts by individuals, and said Hayek's advocacy of a limited welfare state, with universal health care and the state provision of basic housing, ran contrary to his central concern at state "coercion." These contradictions would "destroy any claims Hayek may have to the laissez faire label" and would be "enough to trouble many of the 'libertarians' with whom he is commonly associated."[64] Above all, Viner berated Hayek for lauding economic growth and income maximization above all other values, such as religion or democracy.[65]

In Robbins's review in *Economica*, the estrangement between the two men became evident. Robbins faulted Hayek's definition of liberty based primarily on the lack of coercion. Surely, claimed Robbins, there were important positive acts, such as democracy and the right to vote, "especially where women or coloured people have been concerned," that were also signs of true liberty. "That [democracy] carries with it liberty to destroy other liberty is undeniable; and we may agree with . . . Professor Hayek that, for this reason, popular government carries with it very grave dangers. But this is just one of those paradoxes of life."[66]

When it came to Hayek's objections to state intervention, Robbins found his former friend's approach unreasonably extreme. "Any absolute skepticism regarding the stability of all mixed economies seems to me to have little basis in either logic or history,"[67] he averred. Robbins argued, like Keynes, that state intervention in aid of the public good is only as bad as the society in which it takes place. In the hands of a benign population, state aid could be worthwhile. "When I look at social conditions in contemporary Britain, with its well fed, healthy and essentially decent and humane citizens and their children, and draw the contrast with what, as a young man, I knew 40 years ago, I do perceive a most solid and substantial improvement,"[68] Robbins wrote. "Hayek is somewhat too apt . . . to assume that deviations from his norm lead cumulatively to disaster. . . . Why should he argue as if these were at all likely to lead us to social disintegration and the concentration camp?"

The disappointing reviews, and sales, of *The Constitution of Liberty* coincided with a crisis in the Mont Pelerin Society, which, after years of dwindling membership and attendance, became riven by factionalism, personal animosity, and infighting whose details were so embarrassingly petty they have not been made public. The internecine troubles of an institution Hayek considered very much his own had proven so troubling to him that at the 1960 meeting he stepped down as president and declined to attend the 1961 gathering.

There was another upsetting development. In 1960, Hayek suffered his first bout of clinical depression. The following year he experienced a mild heart attack that was not diagnosed properly, and he fell further into gloom. In 1962, still anxious about his failure to make adequate financial arrangements for his old age, and concerned he might leave Helene in penury, he accepted a post with a pension at the University of Freiburg in Germany, about a hundred miles from the Austrian border. In some ways, the move represented a homecoming; in another, it marked a retreat, a form of home exile. After more than twenty years of living without the honorific prefix "von," in Freiburg he began calling himself "von Hayek" again. Although in 1964 Hayek was made honorary president of the Mont Pelerin Society, the turmoil in the organization added to his sense of failure. He felt isolated and, worse, ignored. As he recalled in 1978, "Most of the [university] departments came to dislike me, so much so that I can feel it to the present day. Economists very largely tend to treat me as an outsider."[69]

What seemed like a final blow to Hayek's confidence came when his erstwhile close family friend and fiercest champion, Lionel Robbins, tempered his belief in free-market ideas and embraced aspects of Keynesianism. For Robbins, the breaking point came when Hayek and Mises blamed the Great Depression in America on businessmen borrowing too much money at too low an interest rate and investing it in loss-making businesses. Robbins, in his English understated way, described this explanation as "misleading" and described Hayek's remedy for the Depression—letting the market find its own level by writing down mistaken investments and raising interest rates to encourage more saving and to deter consumer spending—"as unsuitable as denying blankets and stimulants to a drunk who has fallen into an icy pond, on the ground that his original trouble was overheating."[70]

Robbins had at first swallowed the Hayckian diagnosis whole and written a book, *The Great Depression,* hewing closely to Hayek's argument that a tough-love policy toward the broken economy and its victims was the only way to purge the capital imbalance and restore the economy to health. But he came to describe the volume as "something which I would willingly see forgotten" and "the greatest mistake of my professional career." He was filled with remorse, not only for his adherence to Hayek's beliefs, but also for his slowness in embracing Keynesianism. As he put it, "It will always be a matter of deep regret to me that, although I was acting in good faith and with a strong sense of social obligation, I should have so opposed policies which might have mitigated the economic distress of those days."[71]

In 1969, Hayek moved back to Austria for financial reasons. The University of Salzburg, a minor college with a tiny economics department, bought his library for a decent sum, and by moving there Hayek was able to draw upon his books and continue to write. The same year he suffered a second heart attack, which was again not diagnosed correctly. For the next five years he endured long periods of ill health, pain, and acute depression, preventing him from working for any length of time. The debilitating condition lasted for the rest of the decade and he resorted to antidepressant drugs.

According to Ralph Harris, "When Hayek moved back to his native Austria, he was depressed. The success of mixed economies made his free market theories, and Hayek himself, seem more irrelevant than ever."[72] "The world was very much a socialist world," remembered his son, Laurence. "His ideas were not fashionable. Nobody seemed to listen to him. Nobody seemed to agree with him. He was alone."[73] Hayek was at his lowest ebb. "My impression was, 'I'm finished,'"[74] he recalled.

FIFTEEN

The Age of Keynes

Three Decades of Unrivalled American Prosperity, 1946–80

On his death in 1946, Keynes was celebrated with services befitting a hero. His ashes were scattered on the Sussex Downs near his country home.[1] At a memorial service in Westminster Abbey, the prime minister, Clement Attlee, led mourners, who included Lydia, Keynes's aged parents, most of the cabinet, the American ambassador John Winant, as well as a clutch of Bloomsburys, Duncan Grant, Vanessa Bell, Clive Bell, and Leonard Woolf. America gave him a regal send-off at the National Cathedral in Washington, D.C.

The death of Keynes did little to slow the onward march of the revolution that took his name. His initial motivation for studying the business cycle was to reduce the mass unemployment of the Great Depression, and *The General Theory* offered governments a means to avoid joblessness. The absence of Keynes, however, placed the revolution in the hands of Keynesians. No longer would they be tempered by his wisdom. The gap between what Keynes intended and what the Keynesians did in his name became larger. For some, like Hayek, Keynes had unleashed a generation of reckless economists. As

Alan Peacock, a young economist at the London School of Economics, put it, Keynes was the "Kerensky[2] of the Keynesian Revolution,"[3] a moderate leader pushed aside by more aggressive revolutionaries.

In Britain, Keynesian reforms were given a boost by Attlee, who as deputy prime minister in wartime was given more or less a free hand to administer domestic policy while Winston Churchill ran the war. According to Churchill biographer Martin Gilbert, the wartime coalition's 1942 "budget speech was thoroughly Keynesian . . . the use of national income and expenditure estimates in relation to the formulation of the budget was a major event in the history of the application of economics to policy formation."[4] The key measures were a taxpayer-funded welfare state and full employment as a national goal. Both were the work of William Beveridge, Hayek's erstwhile employer at the LSE who believed that "the ultimate responsibility . . . to set up a demand for all the labour seeking employment, must be taken by the State."[5]

That Keynesianism was championed by one of his earliest benefactors was not lost on Hayek, who had always had a low opinion of Beveridge. "I have never known a man who was known as an economist and who understood so little economics," Hayek recalled.[6] The problem with Beveridge was that he lacked any enduring principles. "He was the type of a barrister who would prepare, given a brief, and would speak splendidly to it, and five minutes later would forget what it was all about,"[7] said Hayek.

More distressing to Hayek, perhaps, was that Beveridge's aman-uensis both for the *Beveridge Report*, presaging nationalized social security and the National Health Service, and for full employment as national policy was Hayek's star pupil, Nicholas Kaldor. Hayek conceded, with irritation, that "Kaldor, through the Beveridge Report, has done more to spread Keynesian thinking than almost anybody else."[8]

The notion of full employment as a government's prime responsibility was not restricted to Britain. The Australian Labor premier John Curtin, who attended Keynes's London memorial, in 1945 introduced

"Full Employment in Australia," mandating the government to find a job for everyone capable of working. The same year, drafters of the Charter of the United Nations included a pledge that all governments should strive for "higher standards of living, full employment, and conditions of economic and social progress."[9] The UN took a further step in 1948 when it declared, "Everyone has the right to work, to free choice of employment, to just and favourable conditions of work and to protection against unemployment."[10]

War-torn Europe became a laboratory for Keynesianism. With the Russians on Western Europe's threshold, America deemed that the lessons of Keynes's *Economic Consequences of the Peace* should be taken to heart: the preconditions for extremism should not be allowed to develop. Instead of punishing the defeated with poverty, American taxpayers helped them become prosperous through the Marshall Plan. That Germany, Japan, and Italy should simply be handed back to the free market was hardly given a thought. In 1946, the Keynesian high priest John Kenneth Galbraith was made State Department adviser on economic policy in the occupied countries.

In America, too, Keynesianism was on the march. In 1943, the New Deal–era National Resources Planning Board had floated a "New Bill of Rights" to "promote and maintain a high level of national production and consumption by all appropriate measures."[11] Roosevelt announced in the 1944 State of the Union "a second Bill of Rights" that would guarantee "the right to adequate protection from the economic fears of old age, sickness, accident, and unemployment."[12] In January 1945, Senator James Murray,[13] a Democrat from Montana, introduced a Full Employment Bill drafted with the help of Alvin Hansen, the "American Keynes," and based on the ideas of New Deal economist Leon H. Keyserling[14] in his 1944 essay "The American Economic Goal."[15]

The bill was Keynes 101. It declared that "private enterprise, left to its own devices, cannot provide full employment and cannot eliminate periodic mass unemployment and economic depressions,"[16] that "all Americans able to work and desiring to work are entitled to an opportunity for useful, remunerative, regular, and full-time employment," and that the federal government should "provide such volume of Federal investment and expenditure as may be needed . . . to assure continuing full employment."[17] The short, folksy, self-assured, piano-playing senator from Missouri, Harry S. Truman,[18] who succeeded Roosevelt as president on April 12, 1945, was not trusted to obey Congress's instruction, so the executive branch was directed to submit an annual budget to forecast the output needed to generate full employment, as well as estimate the output the economy would have attained were there no federal stimulus. The president then had to propose "compensatory finance" legislation that would either stimulate the economy through deficit spending or, in the event of labor shortage, reduce spending to choke off excess demand. The management of the American economy was to be overseen by the newly created Council of Economic Advisers matched by the Joint Economic Committee of Congress. Like the UN, the bill deemed full employment a basic human right.[19]

Keynesians were delighted. "The unhappy memory of a decade of about 10 million unemployed has not yet been erased," MIT economist Seymour E. Harris wrote, "and the effects of a reduction, already begun, of $75 billion annually of federal government war expenditures concerns all of us." He predicted a loss in the following decade of up to 62 million jobs. "Is an unguided economy likely to yield at least 50 per cent more consumption and perhaps five times as much investment as in the Thirties, and that despite the heavy burden of taxation?"[20] he asked.

The Keynesians were not without their critics. Hayek's friend at Harvard, Gottfried Haberler, pointed out a central flaw in the bill. "The danger is . . . that policies in terms of aggregate expenditure will be overdone," he wrote. "If the unemployed are concentrated in certain 'depressed' areas and industries, while there is full employment elsewhere, a general increase in expenditure would serve only to drive prices up in the full employment area, without having much effect on the depressed industries. Then the paradox of depression and unemployment in the midst of inflation would be experienced."[21] It would take thirty years before Harberler was proved right.

Opponents of the bill had the challenge of halting a popular piece of legislation, and they employed arguments that closely followed Hayek's perennial objections to Keynes's remedies. Business cycles and the slumps they contained were natural phenomena that reflected legitimate business activity and should therefore not be legislated against. Full employment was a fantasy because some unemployment was essential as workers moved from one employer to the next. Tampering with the jobs market would end in corrupting dislocations. Opponents further argued that there were no accurate economic measurements to correctly estimate future levels of employment and stimulate the economy appropriately. They also objected to making a job a human right: it would lead to disillusionment as Americans came to expect something no administration could deliver.

Conservatives in Congress ensured that the bill was considerably softened by the time Truman signed it into law in February 1946. The title was changed from the "Full Employment Act" to simply the "Employment Act." The "right" and "entitlement" to a job became the "responsibility of the Federal Government . . . to promote maximum employment." The demand that "the President shall transmit to Congress . . . a general program . . . for assuring continuing full employment" became a vague intention to maintain full employment. And the annual job-creating budget was demoted to the less prescriptive "Economic Report of the President."[22]

Despite the compromises and defeats, Keynesians believed the new law would serve their purpose. It made the executive branch take responsibility for the economy. For the first time the administration would assume the right to manage the economy, extending executive powers way beyond the existing constitutional duties to control money and trade. For the next thirty years administrations of both stripes pushed their new powers to the limit, manipulating the economy by taxation and similar measures in an attempt to maximize prosperity and win reelection. Macroeconomics, the new branch of the dismal science inadvertently founded by Keynes, became an official instrument of the U.S. government. It was at this time that the terms "microeconomics" and "macroeconomics" were first used: microeconomics was the study of an economy's individual elements; macroeconomics studied the economy as a whole.

Truman had little interest in economics and little time for economists. He joked that he would like to meet a one-armed economist so he could not be told, "On the one hand, on the other." He was oblivious of the fork in the road that the competing theories of Keynes and Hayek represented. He did not grasp the importance of the Employment Act, nor the new bodies it set up. When he came to appoint the first chairman of the Council of Economic Advisers, he ignored the obvious claim of the Keynesian Alvin Hansen in favor of Edwin Nourse,[23] a conservative economist at the Brookings Institute. "Truman was a formal supporter of the Murray Full Employment Act, and of the Council, and he wrote a letter of genuine endorsement when the act was passed, but he didn't know what it was all about," Nourse recalled. "That was beyond his intellectual ken."[24] Still, the president was happy to take credit for the fact that every American had a job. In the 1947 State of the Union message he boasted about "virtually full employment."[25]

Nourse's reign did not last long. His successor in 1949 was Leon Keyserling, an architect of the Employment Act and key elements of the New Deal who fervently believed in planning to maintain high growth and full employment. Truman went with the Keynesian flow, though he favored a balanced budget and set in train a series of deep defense cuts to pay for domestic programs. "Leon, you are the greatest persuader I ever knew," he told Keyserling, "but nobody can ever convince me that the Government can spend a dollar that it's not got. I'm just a country boy."[26] The Korean War, in which the

Chinese-backed North Koreans attempted to take the southern part of the country by force, was to change the debate. When renewed military spending led to a sharp rise in inflation, Keyserling opposed the Federal Reserve's remedy of defense cuts and higher interest rates to choke off soaring prices, and instead advocated manipulating the economy to lift economic growth. The Korean War provided a good pretext for the Keynesians to resume high public spending through the Defense Department—a trend that was to continue for decades.

Keynesian thinking was given a boost in 1948 with the publication by Paul Samuelson, a student of Hansen at Harvard and a professor at MIT, of *Economics: An Introductory Analysis*, which was to become the Keynesians' bible. In the early editions Samuelson ignored orthodox economics; he described only two alternatives: "socialism" and Keynesianism. Neither Mises nor Hayek nor the Austrian School warranted a mention. In the next sixty years, 40 million copies were sold in more than forty languages, ensuring that Keynesianism became the new orthodoxy in the noncommunist world. Where Keynes read Alfred Marshall, the Keynesians read, then taught, Samuelson. "I don't care who writes a nation's laws," Samuelson said, "if I can write its economics textbooks."[27]

Truman's Republican successor, the leader of the Allied forces who defeated Hitler, Dwight D. "Ike" Eisenhower,[28] was a conservative who doubted the wisdom of many of Keynes's prescriptions. Like Hayek, he feared inflation more than unemployment. But there was no turning back to the old days of allowing the economy to manage itself. According to Houston political science professor John W. Sloan, former five-star general Ike "was the most significant player in determining his administration's macroeconomic policy" and was "constantly attentive and often assertive in this policy area."[29] Eisenhower depended on Arthur Burns,[30] the Austrian-born expert on business cycles and chairman of his Council of Economic Advisers, who substantially revised the conservative position on Keynesian macroeconomic management. "Only a generation ago it was the typical view of economists and other citizens that storms of business depression must be allowed to blow themselves out, with little or no interference on the part of government," he said. "Today there is substantial agreement among Americans that the Federal government cannot remain aloof from what goes on in the private economy, that the government must strive to foster an expanding economy, and that the government has a definite responsibility to do all it can to prevent depressions."[31] True to his word, in the first Eisenhower recession of 1954, as the Korean War ended, tax cuts of $7 billion were allowed to go ahead, despite widespread wailing from conservatives, driving the federal budget into deficit. Galbraith's biographer Richard Parker suggests that "Ike may have been the first Keynesian Republican President."[32]

As Eisenhower's administration came to its close, *Life* magazine described his economic policy as "virtually a textbook model of how to befriend and stimulate a free-market system."[33] Keynesianism was built into government in an approach tagged "Business Keynesianism," ensuring that the three brief Eisenhower recessions, of 1953–54 and 1957–58 and 1958–59, were minimized by the use of "automatic fiscal stabilizers," instruments such as unemployment and welfare payments that boosted government spending when the economy faltered, and as a result of a reduction in income and corporation tax revenues that fell as the economy shrank, the raising of expenditure and reduction of revenue to maintain the size of the economy. If not entirely happy about creeping Keynesianism, Ike was prepared to plunge into deficit spending during times of recession.

Eisenhower spent taxpayers' money like no peacetime president before him, though he overcame conservative objections by passing off the expenditures as essential for national security. The vast network of interstate highways that started construction in 1956—the perfect example of a Keynesian infrastructure project—was billed the "National Defense Highway" program and sold to conservatives as a means of transporting supplies in the event of a military emergency.

234 / KEYNES HAYEK

The escalation of the Cold War was also a spur to defense spending,[34] not least when the Russians sent a satellite, *Sputnik*, into space in October 1957. The ensuing space race over the next fifty years would lift the NASA annual budget to a truly astronomic $18.7 billion, with a further $20-plus billion[35] spent on Pentagon satellites and rockets. "We are living under a curious kind of military Keynesianism in which Mars has rushed in to fill the gap left by the market economy,"[36] wrote historian Richard Hofstadter in 1950. By the end of his presidency, Ike had spent more on defense than Roosevelt spent on winning World War II.

For all that, there was a trace of Hayekian thinking in Eisenhower's farewell address that warned against corporatism, or private companies conspiring with government. Eisenhower's remorse was that his administration's vast spending on arms had led to "the military-industrial complex."[37] "We must never let the weight of this combination endanger our liberties or democratic processes,"[38] he warned.

What was best remembered of the 1950s, however, was the endless prosperity that spread across America. It was a perfect reward for "the greatest generation" for winning the war against fascism. Consumerism was rampant, with household appliances like refrigerators and washing machines filling newly built ideal homes, with a car in every driveway. The era is still looked back on with fondness as a time of peace and plenty. In Britain, Harold Macmillan, a Keynesian, won the 1959 election on the slogan, "You've never had it so good."

Eisenhower was the first president to fully understand that manipulating the economy by Keynesian measures gave the incumbent an electoral advantage, though there was to be a twist in this tale when it came to the 1960 presidential election. Against a $13 billion deficit run up in financial year 1958–59, the result of a mini-recession that spiked welfare spending and cut tax revenues, Ike fought the 1958 midterms urging voters, with an irony that was not missed on Keynesians and conservatives alike, not to send "people that I would class among the spenders"[39] to Washington.

The electorate ignored Ike's warning and returned a Democratic majority to both Houses. In his last year in office, anxious not to leave a huge budget deficit as his legacy, Eisenhower attempted to cut public spending. "I want to get [expenditures] down to the last cent," he said. But the Democrats, mindful perhaps that cuts would dampen the economy in the runup to the presidential contest that pitted Eisenhower's brooding, jowly vice president, Richard Nixon,[40] against their young champion, John F. Kennedy,[41] cut expenditures further, leading to a surprise surplus of $269 million. At the same time, the Federal Reserve made borrowing more expensive by sharply increasing the interest rate.

A new recession duly began in April 1960 and voters blamed the Republicans. They had the wherewithal to put people back to work, to cut interest rates, to reduce taxes, to keep the economy buoyant, and they had chosen not to act. The fact that inflation had been kept to 1.4 percent between 1952 and 1960 counted for little. Kennedy campaigned with the slogan "Let's get the country moving again," and he won—by a whisker. One-tenth of 1 percent divided the tallies of the two opposing candidates. Had Eisenhower eased up a fraction, Nixon might have sailed to victory. Nixon complained long and hard in the coming years that Eisenhower had stymied his chances of winning the White House the first time round. It was a hard lesson that all subsequent presidents learned: success at the ballot box comes from managing the economy to bring the business cycle into line with the four-year electoral cycle. Those who dared to "do the right thing" by the budget deficit would be doomed.

In John F. Kennedy, the young glamorously handsome scion of the Boston Kennedy clan, America elected a president who for the first time openly acknowledged he would employ Keynesian countermeasures not merely at the bottom of the cycle but as a general policy tool to boost the nation's productivity. He knew little about economics, despite being taught at Harvard by Galbraith. Kennedy once confessed to not being able to remember the difference between fiscal and monetary policy—that is, between taxation and spending set by the administration and the regulation of the supply of money and interest rates laid down by the Federal Reserve—and that he could recall that the Federal Reserve was in charge of monetary policy only because the Fed chairman's surname began, like "money," with an "M."[42] Kennedy surrounded himself with Keynesians, chief among them Galbraith, who wrote JFK's stump speech on economics. When Kennedy took office, Galbraith was installed in the Executive Office Building with a roaming brief from JFK to "tell me not what I should do but what I should tell others to do."[43]

Kennedy named as Treasury secretary a Republican, C. Douglas Dillon, a Wall Street banker, and as Federal Reserve chairman the cautious William McChesney Martin Jr.,[44] whose role he defined as "to take away the punch bowl just as the party gets going"—that is, to curb the inflation that accompanied high public spending by raising interest rates.[45] Otherwise Kennedy surrounded himself with Keynesians. At first he approached Samuelson to chair the Council of Economic Advisers, then sounded out Galbraith, who opted to become ambassador to India, before picking Walter Heller,[46] who dubbed the administration's Keynesian approach the "New Economics." Heller, joined on the council by Kermit Gordon[47] and James Tobin, was convinced they could deliver full employment—which they defined as a 4 percent unemployment rate—without inflation.

Kennedy's economic aim was to bridge the "growth gap," the difference between what the American economy produced when left to private enterprise and the fully productive economy he believed possible if the administration intervened. It was little more than the "missing growth" theory of the Full Employment Bill in new clothes. In his first speech to Congress, JFK bemoaned the fact that "more than a million and a half unemployed—over one-third of all unemployed—could have had jobs. Twenty billion dollars more personal income could have been earned in 1960. Corporate profits could have been $5 billion higher. All this could have been accomplished with readily available manpower, materials and machines—without straining productive capacity and without igniting inflation." He sounded like Keynes during the Depression.

Kennedy continued, "An unbalanced economy does not produce a balanced budget. Lower incomes earned by households and corporations are reflected in lower Federal tax receipts. Assistance to unemployed workers and the costs of other measures for alleviation of economic distress are certain to rise as business declines." With the economy working at full tilt, increased tax revenues would pay down the national debt. "Debt retirement at high employment contributes to economic growth by releasing savings for productive investment by private enterprise,"[48] he declared. Calling Heller that evening, Kennedy confided, "I gave them straight Heller and Keynes and they loved it."[49] Little wonder that Arthur M. Schlesinger Jr., JFK's Boswell, described Kennedy as "unquestionably the first Keynesian President."[50]

Despite the Keynesian rhetoric, Kennedy was made cautious by his narrow win over Nixon. He feared the Democrats' conservative wing, led by Senator Harry F. Byrd Sr. of Virginia, chairman of the Senate Finance Committee, who remained staunchly opposed to deficits. For two years Kennedy did little to stimulate the economy beyond the huge sums spent on defense and space, both of which, like Eisenhower, he claimed were essential to national security, an argument that took on added weight after the Cuban Missile Crisis of October 1962. Military and space expenditures accounted for three-fourths of all spending increases during Kennedy's presidency, and space funding rose even more dramatically, from $1 billion in 1960 to $6.8 billion four years later.[51] Yet despite this massive injection of public money, joblessness continued to rise. In 1961 and 1962, the unemployment rate remained at over 5 percent. When Keyserling was called before Congress, he declared, much to the president's fury, "They're sending up a pygmy's program to do a giant's job."[52]

When Kennedy finally acted to create full employment, he did it in a most unexpected way. Addressing Wall Street types in December

1962, he announced his counterintuitive plan. It was Keynesianism, with a twist. "There is no need for us to be satisfied with a rate of growth that keeps good men out of work and good capacity out of use. . . . To increase demand and lift the economy, the Federal Government's most useful role is not to rush into a program of excessive increases in public expenditures, but to expand the incentives and opportunities for private expenditures," he said. "It is a paradoxical truth that tax rates are too high today and tax revenues are too low and the soundest way to raise the revenues in the long run is to cut the rates now."[53]

He urged Congress to cut income taxes by $10 billion, despite the budget deficit. When Heller and Samuelson first proposed the cuts, Kennedy was taken aback. "I've just campaigned on a platform of fiscal responsibility and balanced budgets and here you are telling me that the first thing I should do in office is to cut taxes?"[54] he asked. As Heller and Samuelson knew, the initiative followed Keynes's proposal in *The Means to Prosperity* in 1933 that tax cuts could pump money into an economy to bolster demand just as effectively as public spending.

Some Keynesians—and almost all conservatives—contested the wisdom of the plan. Keynesians argued that more federal spending was the surest way to give the economy a boost, and conservatives reasoned that to cut taxes when there was a budget deficit was a reckless gamble. Galbraith complained that cutting taxes amounted to a "reactionary" form of Keynesianism that did not address public ills as readily as targeted spending.[55] Besides, tax cuts were inflationary. Heller, however, was no gambler. He was operating according to the latest neo-Keynesian notions that intended to offer a more predictable means of managing the economy. Keynes's protégé Roy Harrod and Harvard's Evsey Domar[56] had, in their "Harrod-Domar model," built on Kahn's multiplier theory to predict how tax cuts could lead to economic growth. And Heller himself, working with his colleague Robert Solow,[57] took account of the work in 1958 of an LSE economics professor, the New Zealander William Phillips,[58] who postulated in a graph dubbed the "Phillips curve" a trade-off between reducing unemployment and rising inflation. By formulating policy according to the Phillips curve, Heller believed he had found a way to provide full employment without provoking higher prices.

JFK's proposal for tax cuts languished in the Senate, but after his assassination in November 1963, the accidental president Lyndon Johnson vowed to continue his predecessor's legacy in every particular. Johnson was no economist, though he took a keen interest in the advice Heller and others offered. "He was particularly fascinated, for example, with the state of the economy and his capacity to remember key indicators and to query his economic advisers on various indicators,"[59] recalled LBJ's special assistant Douglass Cater.[60] Johnson used all of the horse trading tricks he had learned from his decades in Congress and his capacious natural wile to counter conservatives in both parties to push through in 1964 Kennedy's tax-cutting "gamble," decreasing general income tax rates and reducing the top level from 91 percent to 65 percent. Within four years critics of the tax cuts from both Left and Right were proved wrong. Federal tax revenue rose by $40 billion,[61] while economic growth increased from 5.8 percent in 1964 to 6.4 percent in 1965 and 6.6 percent in 1966. The unemployment rate fell from 5.2 percent in 1964 to 4.5 percent in 1965 and 2.9 percent in 1966.[62] Inflation remained under 2 percent in 1964 and 1965, sliding up to 3.01 percent in 1966. Kennedy's gamble had paid off spectacularly. Like penicillin, Keynesianism was the new wonder drug.

In December 1965 *Time* gave its "Man of the Year" accolade to John Maynard Keynes. Keynes was the top, the Tower of Pisa, the smile on the Mona Lisa. "Today, some 20 years after his death, his theories are a prime influence on the world's free economies," *Time* trumpeted. "In Washington the men who formulate the nation's economic policies have used Keynesian principles not only to avoid the violent cycles of pre-war days but to produce a phenomenal economic growth and to achieve remarkably stable prices."

How had Washington's economists done it? "By their adherence to Keynes's central theme: the modern capitalist economy does not automatically work at top efficiency, but can be raised to that level by the intervention and influence of the government." Hayek's hated "planners" were in control. "Economists . . . sit confidently at the elbow of almost every important leader in Government and business, where they are increasingly called upon to forecast, plan and decide," *Time* chirruped. Keynesianism had even won over hard-nosed businessmen. "They have begun to take for granted that the Government will intervene to head off recession or choke off inflation, [and] no longer think that deficit spending is immoral. . . . Nor, in perhaps the greatest change of all, do they believe that Government will ever fully pay off its debt, any more than General Motors or IBM find it advisable to pay off their long-term obligations.[63] For those with a nose for hubris, the extravagant claims made for Keynes's theories suggested that the Keynesian ascendancy had reached its high tide.

Bolstered by a booming economy and burgeoning tax revenues, Johnson set about building his legacy. In May 1964, at the University of Michigan in Ann Arbor, he declared, "We have the opportunity to move not only toward the rich society and the powerful society, but upward to the Great Society."[64] He vowed to end poverty and racial inequality, to protect the countryside, to educate every child, and to "rebuild the entire urban United States." Armed with a landslide victory over the ultra-conservative Barry Goldwater[65] in the 1964 election, Johnson, an avid New Dealer in the 1930s, embarked on a vast public spending spree. As Arkansas representative Wilbur Mills[66] recalled, "Johnson always was a spender, in a sense, different from Kennedy. He thought that you could always stimulate the economy better through public spending than you could through private spending."[67] Johnson's program was as radical as anything Franklin Roosevelt had attempted. He extended civil rights to African-Americans, embarked on a "war on poverty" through federal entitlements, and instituted Medicare to give health care to everyone over age sixty-five and Medicaid for those who could not afford health insurance.

The 1960s was a decade of unparalleled wealth. Whereas the 1950s had been years of widespread affluence, the 1960s made the average worker comfortably well-off. Luxuries such as color televisions, airplane travel, and a second car in the driveway became commonplace. Hard work gave way to increasing leisure. Far from introducing creeping authoritarianism, as Hayek had predicted, the new wealth that Keynesian planning produced offered new freedoms. Women, African-Americans, and teenagers began to flex their newfound liberty. The Keynesian Revolution was accompanied by a cultural revolution that questioned the traditional mores of a poorer, quainter society.

The Keynesian miracle continued to work for Johnson. Productivity increased, real take-home pay doubled compared to that during the Eisenhower years, and joblessness was down from 4.5 percent in 1965 to an average of 3.9 percent in the subsequent four years. Johnson increased the proportion of the federal budget spent on antipoverty programs from 4.7 percent in 1961 to 7.9 percent in 1969. On top of his domestic overhaul, Johnson escalated the war against communist insurgents in South Vietnam. With eventually half a million Americans posted to Vietnam, defense spending leapt from $49.5 billion in 1965 to a mammoth $81.2 billion in 1969. The budget remained in surplus, but it was dwindling fast, and inflation began to take off, hitting 4.2 percent in 1968. An income tax surcharge in 1968 to arrest the rise in prices did little to keep the economy in balance. But it was the war, not the economy, that felled Johnson, and his departure spelled the beginning of the end of the "Great Society."

Richard Nixon arrived in the White House in January 1969 suggesting he was ready to turn back the Keynesian tide. "In the decade of the Sixties the federal government spent $57 billion more than it took in in taxes," Nixon said in his 1970 State of the Union address. "Millions of Americans are forced to go into debt today because the federal government decided to go into debt yesterday. We must balance our federal budget."[68] He concluded that full employment fueled by the deficit had caused a scarcity of labor that was pushing up wages and prices. To counter inflation, Nixon directed his conservatively inclined economic team, among them Paul McCracken,[69] head of the Council of Economic Advisers; Herbert Stein,[70] a Council member soon to be McCracken's successor; and George Shultz,[71] director of the Office of Management and Budget, to balance the budget by sharply cutting spending.

The cuts, however, coincided with a mild recession in which unemployment rose from 3.9 percent in January 1970 to 6.1 percent at the end of the year.[72] In line with Nixon's belief that unemployment led him to lose the presidential race in 1960,[73] Nixon switched tracks, saying he wanted "a full employment budget, a budget designed to be in balance if the economy were operating at its peak potential. By spending as if we were at full employment, we will help to bring about full employment." He proposed an expansionary budget to "stimulate the economy and thereby open up new job opportunities for millions."[74] It was pure Keynesianism, prompting Nixon in January 1971 to declare, "Now I am a Keynesian in economics."[75] As Stein recalled, "Calling himself a Keynesian won him no praise from Keynesian economists, but it did rouse complaints from outraged Republicans."[76]

A candid line in Nixon's 1970 State of the Union address betrayed the calculation behind his change of mind. "I recognize the political popularity of spending programs," he said, "and particularly in an election year." The most overtly opportunistic postwar president, Nixon let his ambition steer the economy less in the nation's best interest than in his own, to guarantee his reelection. His Keynesian tactics would ensure that he would, in Stein's words, be "disdained by liberals and conservatives alike."[77] Milton Friedman, Nixon's economic adviser during the 1968 campaign, concluded, "Nixon was the most socialist of the presidents of the United States in the twentieth century."[78]

The agent of Nixon's rush toward Keynesianism was the former

Democratic governor of Texas, John Connally,[79] once a close Johnson confidant, whom Nixon appointed Treasury secretary in December 1970. Amid clamor from voters and legislators for the administration to "do something" about the sluggish economy, with Federal Reserve chairman Arthur Burns taking the lead, Nixon called a summit of advisers at Camp David in June 1971 to discuss the way forward. He found them in disarray. Stein urged "a more stimulative fiscal policy—a tax cut or expenditure increase or both,"[80] while Shultz urged spending cuts and austerity. Nixon agreed to do nothing, a policy known as "the Four Noes: no expenditure increase, no tax cut, no prices and wage controls, and no devaluation of the dollar."[81]

Within months, however, Nixon performed a perfect backward somersault. In line with what he called his "New Economic Policy," he approved the devaluation of the dollar followed by the removal of the dollar from the gold standard; a financial stimulus of lower taxes and increased spending that plunged the federal budget into a $40 billion deficit; cheap federal loans to prevent aircraft company Lockheed from going broke; and in August 1971, a legal ban on the raising of prices and wages. Later, free trade was abandoned and a 10 percent import levy imposed. It was an about-face that caused even Keynesians to flinch. One key part of Keynes's legacy, the Bretton Woods system of currencies fixed to the dollar, and through the dollar to gold, was gone in an instant. But the rest was Keynesian to a fault. William Safire, the conservative columnist and Nixon's speechwriter in 1960 and 1968, invoked the ghost of Karl Marx: "Laissez-fairies of the world unite! You have nothing to lose but your Keynes."[82] Nixon set the phone tappers on him.

Nixon endorsed a raft of intervention measures to conjure the prosperity he felt essential for reelection. When an angry Republican congressman complained, "I'm going to have to burn up a lot of old speeches denouncing deficit spending," the president replied, "I'm in the same boat."[83] "There was always this notion that somehow if you just had [price and income controls] for a little while it would get things under control and then you could go back [to allowing prices and incomes to find their market price]," recalled Shultz. "But it turns out it's always much easier to get into something like that than to get out of it."[84] Any chance that Nixon would be the master of his economic destiny was delivered a mortal blow by a fourfold increase in oil prices imposed by the Arab oil cartel, the Organization of Petroleum Exporting Countries (OPEC), in 1973–74 to punish America for rearming Israel during the Yom Kippur War. The result was higher prices and the brakes being slammed on economic growth. Traditional tools such as the Phillips curve seemed no longer to apply. Low or no economic growth was accompanied by inflation in a combination hitherto thought impossible, dubbed "stagflation."[85] The Age of Keynes was in its death throes. The Age of Stagflation had arrived.

Up against a weak opponent, George McGovern, Nixon walked to a landslide in the 1972 election. It was ultimately the burgling of Democratic headquarters in the Watergate Hotel in Washington, D.C., not his somersaults on the economy, that triggered Nixon's hasty departure from the Oval Office in 1974. But stagflation certainly led to the demise of his hapless successor, the former University of Michigan football star Gerald Ford,[86] who presided over rates of inflation and unemployment not experienced since the Great Depression. One of Nixon's final acts was to appoint the ultra-conservative Alan Greenspan[87] head of his Council of Economic Advisers.[88] Greenspan had resisted Nixon's blandishments for years and was grateful not to have been implicated in the policy U-turn that introduced price and income controls. But he could do little to save Ford. He watched from the sidelines as the amiable president was pressed by a gaggle of conflicting advisers to flip-flop from one putative panacea to the next.

Ford achieved a brief compromise when a Democratic Congress agreed to curb spending and cut taxation by $9 billion; the economic data began moving in the right direction. Inflation dropped from 9.2 percent in 1975 to 4.88 percent in the presidential election month of

November 1976.[89] Joblessness fell too, from a peak of 9 percent in May 1975 to 7.8 percent in November 1976. But the turnaround came too late to save Ford. Stagflation had claimed its first scalp.

The Keynesians' belief that it was impossible for unemployment and inflation to rise simultaneously was shown to be false and undermined confidence in much of the rest of their theories. The certainty that Keynes brought to the management of the economy was shattered. "Stagflation was the end of naïve Keynesianism,"[90] observed Milton Friedman. Economists, once omniscient, were left scrabbling for explanations. "A remarkable consensus on economic policy emerged in Washington—a convergence of attitudes between the liberal left and the conservative right," Greenspan recalled. "Suddenly everyone was looking to restrain inflation, cut deficit spending, reduce regulation, and encourage investment."[91]

But the old thinking was hard to jettison. The ever-smiling Georgia peanut farmer and former submariner Jimmy Carter reached the White House on the Keynesian pledge of returning America to full employment. In 1978, he approved the Humphrey-Hawkins Full Employment Act,[92] a reprise of the Full Employment Bill of 1945, mandating the president and the Federal Reserve to keep aggregate demand high enough to maintain full employment. In apparent contradiction, the act also directed the president and Congress to balance both the budget and the balance of trade. Like Canute[93] commanding the tides, legislators were proving their impotence. Wishful thinking and majorities in Congress were not enough to beat stagflation. Nor was Carter the person to lead America in a new and painful direction, as was evident from his most conspicuous venture into telling unpalatable truths, the "malaise" speech suggesting the country was suffering from a "crisis that strikes at the very heart and soul and spirit of our national will."[94]

The fact that stagflation was also stalking the rest of the world's leaders, such as the hapless British prime minister James Callaghan, was of little compensation to Carter, for whom time was fast running out. In October 1978 he announced counterinflationary measures, including a new age of austerity, a bonfire of business regulations, tax breaks for industry, a freeze on federal hiring, and a pledge to cut the federal deficit in half.[95] Each would take time to work, and in the meantime the electoral cycle was proving far shorter than the gaps between recessions.

Carter was dealt a death blow in January 1979 when the Islamic Revolution in Iran sparked turmoil in the Middle East. The president became caught up in a second oil crisis that rivaled the OPEC hike of 1973, resulting in severely reduced gasoline supplies. He imposed price controls on fuel, leading to long lines at filling stations. He appointed as chairman of the Federal Reserve a lifelong Democrat, Paul Volcker,[96] with a mission to raise interest rates to choke off the demand that was thought to be the root of inflation. Carter's failure to bring prices under control in time for the November 1980 election was a gift to his Republican rival, the handsome, affable, twinkle-eyed Ronald Reagan, who asked voters, "Are you better off than you were four years ago?" The answer was a resounding no.

It was not only Carter who was on trial, but also John Maynard Keynes. Thirty-four years after the great man's death and more than forty after publication of his *General Theory*, Keynesianism appeared to have run its course. Like the overuse of a wonder drug, dispensers of his remedy appeared to have applied too much of the elixir too often. It was time for the radical reassessment of economic theory that Hayek and his allies had long been plotting.

SIXTEEN

Hayek's Counterrevolution

Friedman, Goldwater, Thatcher, and Reagan, 1963–88

Hayek's darkest hour came just before dawn. He had warned the Mont Pelerin Society that it might take decades before the flaws in Keynes's theories became evident. What he did not grasp was that the prospect of salvation was at hand in the unlikely shape of Milton Friedman, the brother-in-law of Aaron Director. Hayek and Director got on well, perhaps because, with metal-rimmed glasses, thinning hair, and Groucho Marx moustaches, they looked so alike.

In 1943, Hayek's Viennese economist friend Fritz Machlup showed a typescript of *The Road to Serfdom* to Director, who passed it to Frank Knight in Chicago. Despite Knight's skeptical report, the University of Chicago Press agreed to publish it. The decision proved to be highly profitable for the press, with sales of the book still strong nearly seventy years later. Director, a devout, articulate, and persuasive Hayekian who argued against government subsidies, railed against import tariffs, and opposed trade unions, reviewed the book and described Hayek as "our most accomplished historian of the development of economic ideas."[1] But it was a family tie that provided

Director's contribution to the success of Hayek's long march to reburnish economic liberalism. Director's sister Rose had joined him in Chicago, where in her economics class she sat next to, then fell in love with, Milton Friedman, who at that time was a Keynesian. Shortly before the couple married in 1938, Director joked to Rose, "Tell him I shall not hold his very strong New Deal leanings—authoritarian to use an abusive term—against him." Director took Friedman to the first Mont Pelerin meeting.

In the 1930s, Friedman, born in Brooklyn, was a socialist who, after earning degrees at Rutgers, Chicago, and Columbia, followed the migration of young economists eager to take part in Roosevelt's New Deal, finding a job at the National Resources Committee in Washington, D.C. As he was to recall, "The New Deal was a lifesaver for us personally."[2] At the end of the war he returned to Chicago and began to adopt the free-market ideas of Frank Knight and George Stigler. One Mont Pelerin Society member, Stanley Dennison,[3] a Cambridge economist, encouraged Friedman to apply for a Fulbright scholarship, which he received, to study at Cambridge, and that is where he met the Keynesians. Among those he befriended were Richard Kahn, the inventor of the multiplier, Joan Robinson, keeper of Keynes's flame, and Nicholas Kaldor, once Hayek's most-promising pupil.

Like Keynes and Hayek, Friedman became intrigued with the business cycle and began to contemplate the causes of the Great Depression. He studied every peak and trough in America from the mid-nineteenth century on and discovered that each downturn was preceded by an explosion in the supply of money.[4] Looking again at the data of the Great Depression, he reasoned that had the Federal Reserve between 1929 and 1933 increased the supply of money by lowering interest rates rather than sharply contracted it, the slump would have lasted only a couple of years. The Great Depression was, therefore, by Friedman's reckoning, the "Great Contraction," a manmade disaster that might have been avoided. To ameliorate the business cycle, Friedman suggested keeping a tight rein on monetary growth, only allowing the supply of money to grow slowly, a policy that became known as "monetarism."[5]

Friedman concluded that Keynes had misread the situation. "Keynes . . . believed that the Great Contraction . . . occurred despite aggressive expansionary policies by the monetary authorities," Friedman wrote. "The facts are precisely the reverse. . . . The Great Contraction is tragic testimony to the power of monetary policy—not, as Keynes . . . believed, evidence of its impotence."[6] Keynes's prescription for unemployment was public works. Hayek had attempted to show that such a policy directed labor into industries that failed as soon as the stimulus was withdrawn. Friedman approached Keynes from another direction: an economy deep in recession did not so much need more demand than an adequate, but not too generous, supply of money. Setting the right level of money would result in a "natural level of employment," which may or may not be full employment, while too much or too little money in the system would cause unemployment and/or inflation.

Despite Friedman's revelation, in the 1960s America remained in thrall to Keynesianism. Keynesianism was "marvelously simple," Friedman wrote. "What a wonderful prescription: for consumers, spend more out of your income, and your income will rise; for governments, spend more, and aggregate income will rise by a multiple of your additional spending; tax less, and consumers will spend more with the same result."[7] While Friedman regretted that Keynes had given politicians a blank check, he was not as tough on Keynes as Hayek. "I believe that Keynes's theory is the right kind of theory in its simplicity, its concentration on a few key magnitudes, its potential fruitfulness," he wrote. "I have been led to reject it . . . because I believe that it has been contradicted by evidence."[8]

Friedman believed that "Keynes's bequest to technical economics was strongly positive" but that his political legacy was strongly negative. "It has contributed greatly to the proliferation of overgrown governments increasingly concerned with every phase of their citizens' daily lives,"[9] he wrote. Friedman coupled his economic analysis, which owed little to Hayek, with a Hayekian dislike of state intervention. Friedman was in favor of cutting taxes not only because he believed individuals knew better than politicians how their money should be spent, but also because when taxes were cut, government spending had to be reduced.

Friedman echoed Hayek's pessimism about the likely consequences of intervention. "Whatever the economic analysis," he wrote, "benevolent dictatorship is likely sooner or later to lead to a totalitarian society." But he believed Keynes's final letter to Hayek, suggesting that whether intervention led to tyranny depended on whether a country was underpinned by a strong sense of fairness, explained why the welfare state in Britain and in Scandinavian countries had not led to totalitarianism. According to Friedman, Britain had "an aristocratic structure" tempered by "if not . . . a complete meritocracy, at least some way in that direction—one in which *noblesse oblige* was more than a meaningless catchword." Moreover, Britain enjoyed "a largely incorruptible civil service" and "a law-obedient citizenry." He was less optimistic that a benign welfare state could take root in America. "[America] has no tradition of an incorruptible or able civil service," he wrote. "The spoils system formed public attitudes. . . . As a result, Keynes's political bequest has been less effective in the United States."[10]

Friedman could be generous to a fault about Hayek's many achievements. "Friedrich Hayek's influence has been tremendous," he gushed after the 1975 Mont Pelerin Society meeting in Hillsdale, Michigan. "His work is incorporated in the body of technical economic theory; has had a major influence on economic history, political philosophy and political science; has affected students of the law, of scientific methodology, and even of psychology. . . . [And above all strengthened] the moral and intellectual support for a free society." Friedman was happy to credit Hayek with inspiring endless "fellow believers in a free society," yet he was at pains to point out that "I cannot say that for myself, since I was influenced in this direction by my teachers at the University of Chicago before I had come to know Hayek or his work."[11]

Friedman's economic thinking did not stem from the Austrian School's capital theory that Hayek espoused; indeed, Friedman was critical of much of Hayek's work in economics. By contrast, he was always free with his praise of Keynes, for his originality of mind and his invention of macroeconomics. But whatever he thought of Hayek as an economist, he eagerly took up the challenge Hayek threw down to work to reduce the size of government. Friedman's libertarianism, which respected the virtues of individualism and was wary of state powers, chimed perfectly with Hayek's innate distrust of government. Both men believed that inflation was a more invidious affliction than unemployment.

Hayek had long cautioned his followers to stay aloof from politics, for fear they would be compromised. Friedman was more pragmatic. "We must act within the system as it is," he wrote. "We may regret that government has the powers it does; we may try our best as citizens to persuade our fellow citizens to eliminate many of those powers; but so long as they exist, it is often, though by no means always, better that they be exercised efficiently than inefficiently."[12]

Friedman attached himself to the 1964 presidential campaign of the conservative libertarian and Arizona senator Barry Goldwater, who, rare among leading Republicans of the time, railed against the powers of the federal government. From Goldwater's vantage point in Phoenix, the sophisticated worlds of Washington, D.C., and the Eastern Seaboard seemed a long way off. His western frontier outlook led him to believe that a centralized state should not interfere too closely in the affairs of individuals.

In his manifesto, *Conscience of a Conservative*, Goldwater declared, "I have little interest in streamlining government or in making it more efficient, for I mean to reduce its size."[13] He was "much influenced by"[14] *The Road to Serfdom* and detested Keynes's influence, particularly on Republican administrations. Like Hayek, who opposed progressive taxation because it entailed the state not treating every citizen equally, Goldwater believed that "government has a right to claim an equal percentage of each man's wealth, and no more."[15]

Friedman was introduced to Goldwater in 1961 or 1962 by the senator's adviser Bill Baroody of the conservative American Enterprise Institute, and the three often discussed how to put Hayek's notions into practice. Friedman contributed to Goldwater's speeches and found himself in great demand to explain the senator's platform. "Centralized governmental control over the economy . . . has never been able to achieve either freedom or a decent standard of living for the ordinary man," Friedman wrote in a Goldwater campaign submission to *The New York Times*. While declaring that Goldwater "fully supports" the 1946 Employment Act "to promote full employment and stable prices," Friedman cautioned that he "would call first on monetary policy" to fulfill those ends.[16]

Friedman's contribution elicited a sharp response from Paul Samuelson, the chief proselytizer of Keynesianism, who traced his ideas to *The Road to Serfdom* and suggested that the "freedom" philosophy contained a fatal flaw. "Your elbow's freedom leaves off where my ribs begin," Samuelson argued. "The majority of the electorate in the mixed economies of the Western world do not regard the rules of the road they place upon themselves as coercive power imposed by some outside monster," he wrote. "Only if you belong to the minority who think that majority rule has been working badly in American life can you regard government as something outside the people."[17]

Whoever won that scuffle, there was little doubt who won the election of November 1964: Johnson defeated Goldwater in a landslide. The crushing loss appeared to deal a fatal blow to the hope of translating Hayek and Friedman's ideas into action. Yet some good came of it from Friedman's point of view. As the public voice of Goldwater's economic policy, he earned a place in the public mind as the thinking man's conservative and Hayek's natural heir. And the campaign that was born in Phoenix gave rise to a phoenix of its own in the shape of Ronald Reagan.[18]

For years Reagan had preached to factory workers on behalf of General Electric a philosophy of self-help and small government. During the Depression, his father, Jack, had taken a New Deal job in Dixon, Illinois, helping unemployed neighbors find work. The young Ronnie watched his father's pain as the contradictions of the welfare payment system kicked in: when Jack found someone a job, that person was docked unemployment benefits, leaving him worse off than when he was not working.

On top of this life lesson, on reaching Hollywood Reagan learned another, that progressive taxation provided a disincentive to work. As an actor earning over $5 million a year, he was taxed a stinging 79 percent on his income in 1937, rising to 94 percent in 1943. "I know what I did," he explained. "I would be offered scripts of additional pictures and, once I had reached that bracket, I just turned 'em down. I wasn't going to go to work for six cents on the dollar."[19]

When the fashion in Hollywood leading men switched after World War II from the clean-cut, soft-hearted type like Reagan to hard-bitten heroes like William Holden, Reagan found he was no longer in demand, yet he owed an enormous tax bill from the years he had been earning big money. Facing financial ruin, he concluded that tax was not so much an evil necessity as an outright evil and bolstered a rotten system of waste and dependence.

At Eureka College in Illinois, Reagan had learned orthodox economics long before Keynes. Though in no sense an intellectual, Reagan was an avid reader, a habit formed during the interminable hours of waiting on the movie set and, because he feared flying, on long train journeys. Despite his joking demeanor, his taste in books was anything but frivolous. "I have read the economic views of von Mises and Hayek," he explained.[20]

Reagan first met Goldwater at the home of his wife Nancy's parents, who had retired to Phoenix. There was little rapport between the two men, yet Reagan found that Goldwater's take on politics resonated with his own. He agreed in 1964 to become the California state cochairman of the Goldwater campaign, and after delivering his customary assault on high taxation and big government at the Cocoanut Grove nightclub in Los Angeles, he was asked to deliver a nationwide television address to bolster Goldwater's faltering presidential bid.

Reagan's "Time for Choosing" broadcast[21] came too late to save Goldwater from the drubbing that ensued, but it proved a great hit with the conservative faithful, transforming Reagan overnight into a conservative darling and launching him on a trajectory that would start in the governor's mansion in Sacramento and end in the White House.

Friedman met Governor Reagan in Los Angeles in 1967. Reagan knew of Friedman from his 1962 book *Capitalism and Freedom*, and he recruited him to help reduce the size of California's government. Reagan campaigned for an amendment to the state constitution to limit the amount the state could spend and tax annually, and he recruited Friedman to go on the stump with him to sell the idea. Although the initiative failed in 1973 to win the requisite majority, Reagan and Friedman took heart from the fact that they had started a movement that prospered in other states, such as Maine, Michigan, Missouri, Montana, Nebraska, Oklahoma, and Oregon.

Reagan's extraordinary powers as a communicator gave a popular boost to Hayek and Friedman's message. "Reagan knew Hayek personally. He knew Milton Friedman personally," explained Newt Gingrich.[22] "I don't think you'd ever get Hayek on the *Today* show, but you could get Reagan explaining the core of Hayek with better examples and in more understandable language."[23]

Reagan had to wait his turn for the presidency. He made a run in 1968, but Richard Nixon held prior rights to the candidacy. Reagan was hampered, too, by what appeared to be Goldwater's jealousy over the mantle "Leader of the American Conservative Movement." In

June 1968, Goldwater wrote Reagan urging him to fold his delegates in with those of Nixon so the Republicans could unite. Nancy Reagan felt the letter such a betrayal that she ensured that over the eight years of the Reagan presidency, Goldwater did not receive a single invitation to the White House.

Friedman became an informal economic adviser to Nixon. "[Nixon] was intensely ambitious and seemingly ready to jettison his professed principles at the slightest sign of political advantage,"[24] recalled Friedman. During the 1968 presidential campaign, in Mission Bay, California, Nixon told Friedman and the others on his economic advisory panel, who to a man believed in free trade, that he intended to back protective tariffs on textiles imported into America. "He believed that his position on textile protection would determine whether he won or lost one or two crucial southern states," recalled Friedman. "He knew that economically it was the wrong thing to do."[25] When Nixon was elected president, Friedman remained an adviser.

In June 1971, notwithstanding Friedman's views on keeping the money supply on a tight rein, Nixon asked him to recommend to the chairman of the Federal Reserve Board, Arthur Burns, an increase in the money supply. "I protested, saying that faster monetary growth was not desirable because it would lead to later inflation," Friedman recalled. "Nixon agreed but said that it would first promote economic growth and assure that the economy was expanding before the 1972 election. I replied that it might not be worth winning the election at the cost of a major inflation subsequently. Nixon said something like, 'We'll worry about that when it happens.'"[26]

In August 1971, Nixon brought to an end the Bretton Woods fixed-currency regime. If Friedman, an inveterate opponent of Bretton Woods, was given cause to celebrate, it was short-lived: Nixon also imposed a legally binding price and income freeze. "The last time I saw Nixon in the Oval Office, with George Shultz," Friedman recalled, "President Nixon said to me, 'Don't blame George for this silly business of wage and price control.' . . . I said to him, 'Oh, no, Mr.

President, I don't blame George, I blame you."[27] Friedman blanched at Nixon's record: he had failed to cut federal spending as a percentage of national income and introduced rules governing the environment to a raft of new government agencies. As Herbert Stein, Nixon's chief economic adviser, recalled, "Probably more new regulation was imposed on the economy during the Nixon administration than in any other presidency since the New Deal."[28]

As we have seen, the year 1974 was an annus horribilis for Keynesians. Hayek's reputation, however, was in the ascendant. His quest to restore the influence of economic liberalism was given a major boost that year when he was awarded the Nobel Prize for economics. The award came as a surprise, not least to Keynesians. As Samuelson recalled, "In the 1974 senior common rooms of Harvard and MIT, the majority of the inhabitants there seemed not to even know the name of this new laureate."[29]

The reasoning behind the Nobel committee's decision to recognize Hayek's contribution to "pioneering work in the theory of money and economic fluctuations" was not quite the endorsement it seemed. Hayek had to share the honor with Gunnar Myrdal,[30] a Swedish Keynesian economist and social democratic politician. According to Friedman,[31] by yoking Myrdal to Hayek the Nobel committee hoped to avoid the charge of sympathizing with the Left. In the event, the double bill provoked substantial controversy, with Hayek declaring that Nobel Prizes for economics were absurd and worth neither giving nor receiving, and Myrdal condemning the Nobel committee for honoring Hayek.

Nonetheless conservatives and libertarians widely welcomed Hayek's accolade as evidence that his decades of working against the grain had paid off. The prize was a considerable personal boost to Hayek, whose years of clinical depression seemed to vanish on receiving the award. "The Nobel Prize he got in 1974 was the making of him,"[32] recalled his friend Ralph Harris. According to conservative historian George H. Nash, Hayek's Nobel had a threefold effect: "It gave the elderly professor a new lease on life, it gave American conservatives a sense of buoyancy and of having 'arrived,' and it renewed public interest in the little book [*The Road to Serfdom*] that had made him famous."[33]

Delivering his Nobel address, "The Pretence of Knowledge,"[34] in white tie and tails before international dignatories, was the high point of Hayek's life. In true Hayek style, he ignored the convention to stay away from controversy and presented a heartfelt justification for why he had never fallen for the Keynesian Revolution. He extolled the virtues of Austrian capital theory and drew attention to the threats to freedom he warned of in *The Road to Serfdom*.

It was with some satisfaction that Hayek declared, "As a profession we have made a mess of things." He offered a short course in the perils of Keynesianism. "The theory which has been guiding monetary and financial policy during the last thirty years," he explained, was "fundamentally false" and "charlatanism." He described stagflation as a self-inflicted wound that "has been brought about by policies which the majority of economists recommended and even urged governments to pursue." Curing stagflation would require painful readjustments, such as even higher unemployment and widespread bankruptcies, but exactly how "an equilibrium will establish itself" was beyond the knowledge of all economists, including himself. The Keynesian belief that there was a solution to every economic problem had only conspired to make inflation and unemployment worse.

He invited the Stockholm audience to think of the market as a ball game, to demonstrate that no one could know its interminable intricacies. If key facts were established about the players, such as "their state of attention, their perceptions and the state of their hearts, lungs, muscles etc. at each moment of the game, we could probably predict the outcome," he suggested. "But we shall of course not be able to ascertain those facts and in consequence the result of the game will be outside the range of the scientifically predictable." The best an economist could do was to behave like a gardener and "cultivate a growth by providing the appropriate environment."[35]

Hayek began to receive widespread acclamation. With Keynesianism in full retreat, the world appeared to be coming around to his way of thinking. He declared, "When I was a young man, only the very old men still believed in the free market system. When I was in my middle ages [*sic*] I myself and nobody else believed in it. And now I have the pleasure of having lived long enough to see that the young people again believe in it."[36]

Two years after Hayek received his Nobel prize, Friedman too was awarded the Nobel Prize for economics. In his address to the Nobel committee, Friedman donned his cap at Hayek, describing his Austrian mentor's insights into the role prices played in determining individual choices as "brilliant."[37]

In Britain at this time the climate suddenly looked considerably brighter for Hayek. The Conservatives, the most successful electoral party in the Western World, began a fundamental reevaluation of their raison d'être. This rare resort to self-examination by a party that traditionally shunned conceptual thinking of any sort was prompted by two stinging electoral defeats in February and October 1974. The double blow that had wrenched Prime Minister Edward Heath from Downing Street had triggered a bruising leadership contest in which Heath was defeated by Margaret Thatcher, an avowed Hayekian. Her surprise victory was predicated not so much on a preference among Conservatives for Hayek's philosophy but on the fact that she was not Heath.[38]

Thatcher's philosophy was based on convictions learned at the knee of her shopkeeper father, but she had also searched for an intellectual justification for her views. At Oxford, where she studied chemistry, she had read *The Road to Serfdom*,[39] and in 1974 she found the book newly relevant. Soon after assuming the Conservative leadership, when meeting the party's left-leaning research department, she reached into her bag and slammed a copy of Hayek's *Constitution of Liberty* on the table. "This is what we believe!" she cried.[40]

Thatcher was determined to unpick the postwar political consensus[41] in which, in an attempt to capture the middle ground on which elections are won and lost, the Conservatives had compromised with Labour over the welfare state and the management of the economy. This had led to the state owning the railways and buses, the coal mines, all shipbuilders, all steel-makers, the telephone network, the electricity, gas, and water utilities, British Airways, British Petroleum, the ports and airports, and much else besides. Thatcher, a Methodist, declared war on the consensus: "The Old Testament prophets did not say, 'Brothers, I want a consensus.' They said, 'This is my faith. This is what I passionately believe. If you believe it too, then come with me.'"[42]

Thatcher knew that Hayek made an annual visit to the Institute of Economic Affairs in London, headed by Mont Pelerin member Ralph Harris. "Thatcher's office came on [in 1976] and said could she come and drop in to see him," recalled Harris. "And so she called by, and there was a period of unaccustomed silence from Margaret Thatcher as she sat there, intense, attending to the master's words."[43] Hayek and Friedman became regular visitors to her office in 10 Downing Street.

In June 1979, Thatcher was elected prime minister. By coincidence, it was Hayek's eightieth birthday. He wrote her a telegram: "Thank you for the best present to my 80th birthday that anyone could have given me." Thatcher wrote back: "I am very proud to have learned so much from you over the past few years. I am determined that we should succeed. If we do so, your contribution to our ultimate victory will have been immense."[44]

Thatcher set about shrinking the size of the public sector, reducing the supply of money, cutting taxes, freeing businesses from regulations, repaying the national debt, and selling off state assets in a process known as "privatization." It was pure Hayek with a dash of Friedman. "The spirit of enterprise had been sat upon for years by socialism, by too-high taxes, by too-high regulation, by too-high public expenditure," she recalled. "The philosophy was nationalization, centralization, control, regulation. Now this had to end."[45] Thatcher faced considerable opposition to her monetarist ideas, not least from members of her own government who cited growing unemployment and violence in the streets as evidence that the policy was wrong. Nicholas Kaldor, Hayek's star pupil at the London School of Economics, now emeritus professor of economics at Cambridge, scoffed at the Hayekian notions behind Thatcher's counterrevolution and published a tract that invoked the spirit of Keynes, *The Economic Consequences of Mrs. Thatcher*.[46] To no avail.

Thatcher had the bit between her teeth. In 1980, after little more than a year in office, she told the annual Tory conference, "Those who urge us to relax the squeeze, to spend yet more money indiscriminately in the belief that it will help the unemployed and the small businessman, are not being kind or compassionate or caring. They are not the friends of the unemployed or the small business. They are asking us to do again the very thing that caused the problems in the first place." She insisted there was no going back to Keynesianism: "You turn if you want to. The lady's not for turning."[47]

Ever the evangelist, Thatcher told the House of Commons, "I am a great admirer of Professor Hayek. Some of his books . . . would be well read by some honorable members."[48] To encourage her cabinet opponents to fall into line, she invited Friedman to dine with them. "The meeting generated an interesting and spirited discussion," Friedman recalled, "especially after Mrs. Thatcher left, asking me to instruct some of the 'wets'[49] in her cabinet." As the first major economy to try monetarist solutions to end stagflation, there was a certain amount of experimentation, false leads, and errors in implementation in Britain's Friedmanite experiment.[50] Through a conservative think tank,[51] she sought the advice of the Swiss monetarist Jürg Niehans,[52] who told her she was controlling the supply of money too tightly and setting interest rates too high, causing the pound sterling to rise and making British exports too expensive. Friedman blamed the initial failure of monetarism in Britain on the "gyrations" in money supply that had been allowed to occur. "It's gone down, it's gone up, it's gone down, it's gone up," he explained. The result, said Friedman, was "a much more severe recession than would have been necessary."[53]

Thatcher's election and her Hayekian ideas were an encouragement to Reagan in his 1980 White House run. Reagan campaigned on the Hayekian slogan, "We can get government off our backs, out of our pockets"[54] and promised tax cuts, a smaller federal government, and strong defense. On November 4, 1980, Reagan trounced Jimmy Carter. Friedman was invited to join the president's new Economic Policy Advisory Board, or EPAB, with George Shultz at its head. "What [the EPAB] did for [Reagan] more than anything else was to reassure him that the course he was following was right," recalled Reagan adviser Martin Anderson.[55] "It was they who pressed him to resist any tax increases, it was they who strongly urged more and more cuts in federal spending, it was they who pushed for more deregulation."[56]

Friedman was particularly concerned that Reagan should stay true to a sound monetary policy and was much relieved by the chairman of the Federal Reserve, Paul Volcker, who, visiting the LSE as an undergraduate, had become enamored with Austrian School capital theory. Volcker considered stagflation "a dragon that was eating at our innards"[57] and believed Friedman was right: regulating the money supply was the key. "It came to be considered part of Keynesian doctrine that a little bit of inflation is a good thing," Volcker recalled. "What happens then, you get a little bit of inflation, then you need a little more, because it peps up the economy. People get used to it, and it loses its effectiveness. Like an antibiotic, you need a new one."[58]

Volcker had started imposing a tight money policy by sharply raising interest rates halfway through Carter's presidency, causing thousands of jobs to be shed from businesses that depended on borrowing. The ensuing recession contributed to Carter's unpopularity and defeat in 1981. With Reagan in the White House, Friedman and Shultz agreed with Volcker that the remedy for inflation was to deepen the recession. But Reagan was a man who liked to be liked. When

Thatcher had brought on a similar recession in Britain, it had made her the most unpopular prime minister since polling began. Would Reagan be prepared to weather the political storm? "Obviously, who wants a recession?" recalled Shultz. "But I can remember President Reagan using those famous words: 'If not now, when? If not us, who?'"[59]

The imposition of tight money to curb inflation was only one element in a basket of policies that together became known as "Reaganomics," each of which owed their inspiration in some part to Hayek or Friedman. Reagan's personal experience of high income taxes led him to believe tax cuts would inspire Americans to work harder, a policy advocated by EPAB member Arthur Laffer.[60] Over dinner in December 1974 with President Ford's chief of staff, Donald Rumsfeld, and his deputy, Dick Cheney, Laffer had argued that there was an optimum income tax rate that would reap the maximum revenue. He illustrated his reasoning by drawing a bell curve on a napkin, showing where the sweet spot might lie.

The "Laffer curve" instantly became the hastily drawn device used by economists around Reagan to convince others that tax cuts would boost revenues. Sharply cutting income taxes, the Reaganites argued, would increase personal spending, which would in turn increase demand through a "trickle-down" effect on the whole economy. A third key element to Reaganomics, also promoted by Laffer, was "supply-side economics," the notion that a booming economy could best be achieved by encouraging producers to supply more and cheaper goods by cutting industry regulations and corporate taxes rather than relying on "demand-led" growth spurred by Keynesian public spending.

Laffer was graceful enough to point out that, despite his name being attached to it, the Laffer curve was not his invention and that others, notably Keynes, had beaten him to the punch. "Nor should the argument seem strange that taxation may be so high as to defeat its object," Keynes had written in 1933, "and that, given sufficient time to gather the fruits, a reduction of taxation will run a better chance than an increase of balancing the budget." Keynes likened those who kept raising taxes to a manufacturer who, "wrapping himself in the rectitude of plain arithmetic," kept raising his prices, even though no one was buying because prices were too high.[61]

The "trickle-down effect" had a Keynesian derivation too, drawing on the logic of Richard Kahn's multiplier, that those who bought goods created jobs and more spending down the line. However, Reagan's tax cuts made Hayek distinctly nervous. "On the scale on which it is being tried, I'm a little apprehensive," he said in 1982. "I'm all for reduction of government expenditures, but to anticipate it by reducing the rate of taxation before you have reduced expenditure is a very risky thing to do."[62]

There was also general skepticism about Reagan's economic exper iment among Keynesians. John Kenneth Galbraith, in his usual droll drawl, caricatured the argument of supply-siders as, "The poor do not work because they have too much income; the rich do not work because they do not have enough income. You expand and revitalize the economy by giving the poor less, the rich more." He dismissed "trickle down" as "the horse-and-sparrow theory: If you feed the horse enough oats, some will pass through to the road for the sparrows." But he conceded that a tightening of the money supply "will work against inflation, in its own grim fashion."[63] Walter Mondale, Reagan's Democratic opponent in the 1984 presidential election, made "trickle down" a social class issue, scoffing that "the idea behind Reaganomics is this; a rising tide lifts all yachts."[64]

While Volcker's monetary squeeze led to a deep recession that lasted sixteen months in 1981–82, inflation fell dramatically, from 11.8 percent through 1981 to 3.7 percent in 1983. But the price was high. Unemployment rose to its highest level since the Great Depression. In 1980, Reagan inherited a jobless rate of 7.1 percent; by 1983 and 1984 it had reached 9.7 and 9.6 percent. The much derided Phillips curve, which appeared to have lost its relevance when stagflation struck in the mid-1970s, seemed to be back in business.

By Laffer's reckoning, Reagan's tax cuts proved every bit as effective as the Kennedy tax cuts. In the four years after Kennedy's cuts reduced the top rate from 90 percent to 70 percent, growth in real federal income tax revenue leapt from 2.1 percent in the previous four years to 8.6 percent. Real GDP growth rose from 4.6 percent to 5.1 percent in the same period, and the unemployment rate fell from 5.8 percent in January 1962 to 3.8 percent in December 1966.

Reagan's tax cuts were deeper. He sliced income taxes 25 percent across the board, with tax rates for the highest earners slashed from 70 percent in 1981 to 28 percent in 1988. Corporate taxes fell from 28 to 20 percent. According to Laffer, the results were impressive. While between 1978 and 1982 the economy grew at 0.9 percent in real terms, between 1983 and 1986 it soared to 4.8 percent. That growth, in turn, translated into jobs, and by the time Reagan left office in January 1989 the jobless figure was at 5.3 percent.[65]

But that was not the whole story. Despite the Laffer curve, the income tax cuts took a sharp toll on revenue. In 1982, Reagan, alarmed by the fast-increasing budget deficit, rescinded various tax breaks on high earners, increasing taxation by a postwar record of $37 billion, or 0.8 percent of GDP.[66]

The monetarists claimed victory nonetheless. Inflation had been purged from the system and the free forces of capitalism had been released. "Those actions of Reagan, lowering tax rates plus his emphasis on deregulating, unleashed the basic constructive forces of the free market, and from 1983 on, it's been almost entirely up,"[67] crowed Friedman. But there was an important element that Friedman did not mention: Reagan also hosed taxpayers' money into the economy at an unprecedented rate. Reagan trimmed welfare programs for the poor, but that was small change compared to his increased spending on defense, which soared from $267 billion in 1980 to $393 billion in 1988 in constant dollars.[68] Public debt grew from a third of GDP in 1980 to more than half of GDP by the end of 1988, from $900 billion to $2.8 trillion.[69]

The budget imbalance was paid for by public borrowing. When Reagan entered the White House, America was the world's largest creditor; by the time he retired to his Santa Barbara horse ranch, it had become the world's largest debtor, owing foreign lenders about $400 billion.[70] Nixon economic adviser Herbert Stein observed that "the most distinctive feature of Reagan economic policy—aside from its language—was the size of its budget deficits."[71] Reagan, basking in the warmth of a booming economy, shrugged off the record deficit. "I don't worry about the deficit," he quipped. "It's big enough to take care of itself."[72]

For many Keynesians, Reaganomics was little more than a thimblerig, a political gimmick that, behind the macho Hayekian rhetoric about slashing the size of the government, set off a public spending spree on defense that boosted aggregate demand and economic growth. According to the Nobel Prize–winning MIT economist Robert Solow, "The boom that lasted from 1982 to 1990 was engineered by the Reagan administration in a straightforward Keynesian way by rising spending and lowered taxes, a classic case of an expansionary budget deficit."[73]

Galbraith agreed. "[Reagan] came into the presidency as the country was experiencing a rather disagreeable recession and [implemented] lots of strong Keynesian policy," he said. "One of the results was an improving economy in the Eighties under Ronald Reagan. And one of the amusing facts of that was that this was done by people who didn't really understand Keynes and who were critical of him. We had involuntary anonymous Keynesianism."[74]

SEVENTEEN

The Battle Resumed

Freshwater and Saltwater Economists, 1989–2008

The next two decades saw Hayek's warning about the potential for tyranny in government intervention growing in popularity. The collapse of the Soviet Union in 1991 ended the murderous seventy-five-year communist experiment in expunging the free market from the lives of Russians. The leaders of the new democratic governments, such as Václav Havel and Václav Klaus, the first Czech Republic presidents, and Leszek Balcerowicz, Poland's deputy premier, hailed Hayek as an inspiration in their darkest days.[1] With the retreat from Keynesian notions and a return of free-market ideas and the fall of Marxist-Leninism, Hayek lived just long enough to feel vindicated. Watching events unfold, he remarked, "I told you so."[2] He died, at aged ninety-two, on March 23, 1992, in Freiburg im Breisgau, Germany.

While in America the public debate over the role of the government in the nation's affairs was increasingly painted in stark colors, the black-and-white choices in which the academic argument had once been waged turned to shades of gray. There was a respite from what Britain's Labour chancellor Denis Healey[3] called "sado monetarism"[4] and from what the *Economist* came to term "crude Keynesianism."[5] Strict monetary measures were found to be such unreliable indicators that interest rates became the favored device by which inflation was kept under control. The key economic arguments were conducted around commonly perceived issues: the size of the public deficit and how to reduce it; the desirability of free trade; the extent and nature of taxation; and the removal of state entitlements from the undeserving.

The debate about central management of the economy, itself a Keynesian notion, evolved into a prolonged "post-Keynesian" phase, an accommodation between Keynesian and Hayekian ideas. Although there was general agreement among stewards of the national economy that a Keynes and Friedman cocktail should be employed to maximize economic growth and choke off inflation, there remained a profound difference between academic economists, who from the 1970s onward were divided roughly along the lines of the old Keynes-Hayek debate. On one side were the "freshwater economists," so called because their universities clustered around the Great Lakes; on the other, the "saltwater economists" who hailed from schools on the coasts. Freshwater economists considered, like Hayek, inflation to be a country's worst curse; saltwater economists thought, like Keynes, unemployment more serious.

The freshwater group believed the economy should be thought of as a sentient organism ruled by the rational decisions of those who participate in the market. While government should ensure that a market was free and fair, government spending and taxation perverted the natural order of an economy. They assumed that individuals made rational decisions based on what they understood the future to hold; that businessmen held back from new investments when they feared that state spending to spur economic growth would lead to higher taxes and inflation; and that globalization and the rise of electronic communications led to more efficient markets that benefited all. Recessions, they claimed, were routine aspects of an economic cycle that must be endured, not cured. They preferred "supply-side" remedies that encouraged businesses to provide cheaper goods and thereby boost demand by removing government inhibitions such as regulations and business taxes.

The saltwater tribe believed that an economy left to its own devices would not suit everyone. They considered recessions symptoms of an economy in poor health, or the result of unforeseen shocks, and sought to cure unemployment at the bottom of the business cycle. They believed markets, particularly in unionized labor, to be slow to respond to changes, and competition to be imperfect. They acknowledged the logic of supply-side reforms, but put more emphasis on "demand-pull" remedies that concentrated on putting more money into the system to make goods more affordable.

The wheel had turned full circle. Hayek was now up and Keynes down. Many saltwater economists became reluctant to acknowledge their debt to Keynes. "By about 1980, it was hard to find an American academic macroeconomist under the age of forty who professed to be a Keynesian,"[6] reported Alan S. Blinder, a Keynesian Nobel economics laureate at Princeton. The University of Chicago Nobel Prize–winning economist Robert Lucas,[7] who did much to undermine traditional Keynesian concepts, found that "people even take offense if referred to as 'Keynesians.' At research seminars, people don't take Keynesian theorizing seriously any more. The audience starts to whisper and giggle to one another."[8] The Hayekian counterrevolution seemed complete. James K. Galbraith, son of the Keynesian pope John Kenneth Galbraith, recalled that "suddenly it was the conservatives who were the brave and brash bad boys of American culture, while liberals like myself had become the country's killjoys, young fogies hopelessly in the grip of old ideas."[9] According to Blinder, by 2004 Keynesianism was so redundant that "virtually every contemporary discussion of stabilization policy by economists . . . is about monetary policy, not fiscal [tax and spending] policy."[10]

Hayek declared in 1978, "As for the movement of intellectual opinion is concerned [sic], it is now for the first time in my life moving in the right direction."[11] Between 1978 and 2008 the free market ruled the roost. However many doubts an economist might privately have about the efficacy and justice of market forces, they were heralded as virtuous by economists and politicians on all sides. As Hayek had predicted at Mont Pelerin, after roaming the wilderness for thirty years, the Hayekians had overcome Keynes's influence. The Age of Hayek succeeded the Age of Keynes. An air of triumphalism pervaded those who believed that the new post-Keynesian consensus had solved the conundrum that both Keynes and Hayek had set themselves in the 1920s: whether the business cycle—and the endless series of booms and busts—could or should be tamed.

Lucas was in no doubt. The cyclical dragon had been vanquished. "Macroeconomics . . . has succeeded," he announced. "Its central problem of depression-prevention has been solved, for all practical purposes."[12] When the Cold War ended, the American political economist Francis Fukuyama[13] declared that the evolutionary stages of societal development, from feudalism through agricultural and industrial revolutions to a modern capitalist democracy, had come to an end; the world had reached "the end of history."[14] It was with a similar confidence that economists announced "the end of economic history": the world economy was cured of the prospect of a return to depression. Friedman, not Keynes, was credited with solving the mystery of why the Great Depression of the 1930s occurred and how it could be prevented from happening again. In a ninetieth birthday tribute to Friedman, Ben Bernanke,[15] the Federal Reserve chairman at the time, offered a belated apology for the Fed's shortcomings in the 1920s. "Regarding the Great Depression," he declared, "you're right. We did it. We're very sorry. But, thanks to you, we won't do it again."[16]

The individual who bound together the whole of this period, dubbed the "Great Moderation," and who came to personify the bipartisan approach of a largely Friedmanite monetary policy within a generally managed economy, was Alan Greenspan. His stewardship of the Federal Reserve from 1987 to 2006 was hailed as masterly. If he made false steps, they did not become apparent until long after he had departed. In his youth Greenspan learned the saxophone alongside Stan Getz, played sideman in a jazz band with the pop artist Larry Rivers, and flirted with both the termagant Ayn Rand and her libertarian ideas. It was above all the confidence with which Greenspan expressed his inscrutable take on events that convinced four presidents in succession that he was the man to ensure economic stability. As the American journalist Michael Kinsley[17] put it, "Greenspan took the newfound importance of monetary policy, mixed in his number-crunching talents on the one hand and his social and business prestige on the other, topped it off with his soon-to-become-legendary mumbo jumbo at hearings, stirred the mixture, drank it and turned into a wizard."[18]

Greenspan was what the poker world calls a percentage player. He summed up his ultra-cautious philosophy thus: "I always ask myself the question, What are the costs to the economy if we are wrong? If there is no downside risk, you can try any policy you want. If the cost of failure is potentially very large, you should avoid the policy even if the probability of success is better than fifty–fifty, because you cannot accept the cost of failure."[19]

The arrival of the tall, starchy former U.S. Navy aviator George H. W. Bush[20] in the White House in 1989 brought little change to the economic course set by Ronald Reagan. A number of lessons had been learned from the two-term experiment with Reaganomics. Adjustments were made and priorities altered. The freewheeling Reagan years had altered the mood in America. Private enterprise replaced communal action as the preferred way to change society. The free-loving flower children of the 1960s' "Love Generation" had given way to the self-centered "Me Generation" of the '80s and '90s. Bob Dylan's call to action "The Times They Are a-Changin'" had been superceded by Gordon Gekko's mantra "Greed Is Good."[21] The national battle for civil rights for minorities was replaced by a demand for smaller government, states' rights, and more individual rights.

By the early 1990s, Taylor's rule, showing the trade-off between interest rates and the rate of inflation, named after the Stanford economist John Taylor,[22] came to replace the Phillips curve, the trade-off between employment and inflation, as the equation of choice for those running the economy. Bush, a Northeasterner turned Texan patrician who had majored in pre-Keynesian economics at Yale,[23] had dismissed monetarism during the 1978 Republican primaries as "voodoo economics,"[24] but he kept his skepticism to himself when Reagan put him on the ticket as vice president. By the time Bush ran for president against Democrat Michael Dukakis[25] in the 1988 election, he had adopted the Reaganite tax-cutting, small-government rhetoric Republicans wanted to hear. On the stump, in a sound bite that would come back to chomp him, he promised, "Read my lips. No new taxes."[26]

Bush headed straight into an economic storm. The ninety-two months of the Reagan boom, the longest since the Kennedy/Johnson prosperity of the 1960s and the second longest period of uninterrupted economic expansion since 1854, came to an abrupt end in July 1990, and Bush was left carrying the can. Inflation rose to 6.1 percent by the end of the year, and unemployment climbed to 6.7 percent in 1991 and 7.4 percent in 1992. The budget deficit doubled from $152 billion in 1989 to $290 billion in 1992.

Obliged to strike a deal with a Democratic Congress, Bush's compromise was to raise taxes rather than cut spending, a decision that undermined his credibility with many Republicans, including Friedman. Still smarting from Bush's contemptuous dismissal, Friedman was scathing about Bush's about-face, dismissing the administration's economic policy as "Reaganomics in reverse" and "oodoov economics" ("oodoov" being "voodoo" backward). "Mr. Bush may have strong principles in some areas like foreign policy. He clearly has none on economic policy,"[27] sniped Friedman.

The economic cycle was out of step with the electoral cycle, and with Greenspan at the Fed, Bush was powerless to align them. Bush was aware that a too tight money policy threatened his reelection, and he said as much. "I do not want to see us move so strongly against inflation that we impede growth,"[28] he told reporters. But Greenspan was not prepared to loosen the money supply to foment a preelection boom. As the 1992 presidential election loomed, Bush's plight was made terminal by the emergence of a third-party candidate, the diminutive Ross Perot, a Texan Don Quixote tilting at open-trade borders and the federal deficit. The ultimate beneficiary of Perot's intercession was the handsome former Arkansas governor Bill Clinton,[29] whose campaign mantra was "It's the economy, stupid." Clinton advocated a balanced budget and progress toward reducing the national debt; educating Americans with skills to make them more employable; and free trade.

Once in the White House, Clinton was eager not to be perceived as a Keynesian tax-and-spend liberal. Mindful of the fact that under Reagan and Bush the national debt had rocketed to $3 trillion, he advocated a "third way" that melded conservative economic measures with progressive social policies. He tempered a tight monetary policy with specific social programs that cost the government little, such as granting maternity and sick leave without loss of pay. He urged selective tax cuts for the "middle class" and higher income taxes for the wealthy. To broaden the market for American goods, he pushed ratification of a free-trade deal with Canada and Mexico he inherited from Bush.

The core Hayekian belief that the size of government should be kept to a minimum manifested itself in the early 1990s in the ambitions of Newt Gingrich, a university professor turned congressman from Georgia. In 1993, Clinton introduced a bill aimed at lowering the deficit by $125 million a year for four years by reversing Reagan's tax breaks for the rich[30] and cutting $255 billion from social programs. The impatient Gingrich, however, harbored far grander plans for reducing the federal government and "wanted to turn the ship of state on a dime."[31] He contributed to the Hayekian Republican manifesto for the 1994 midterms elections, "Contract with America," which pledged to bring about "the end of government that is too big, too intrusive, and too easy with the public's money"[32] by balancing the budget, reducing business regulations, and cutting taxes. In the elections, both Houses fell to the Republicans for the first time in forty years. Gingrich and others claimed a popular mandate to halt the encroachment of the state.

Gingrich wasted little time in setting up a showdown with the president, proposing deep cuts across the board, from Medicare and Medicaid to education and environmental controls. The new House Majority Whip, Tom DeLay, felt that "big government had been feeding at the public trough too long, and we were in a position to put it on a diet—a drastic diet if necessary."[33] The Republican plan was to shut down the federal government by depriving it of funds if the president did not comply. As Gingrich explained, "It was like the alcoholic going cold turkey. You had to have the shock effect of doing something like that to get this city to take it seriously."[34] In mid-November 1995 the inessential elements of the government duly ground to a halt for five days. Eight hundred thousand federal employees were laid off.

But what Gingrich intended as a principled confrontation soon turned to farce. Earlier in the month, the president had ferried congressional leaders to the funeral of the Israeli leader Yitzak Rabin aboard *Air Force One*, and Gingrich loudly complained at being seated at the back of the plane. Even Gingrich's allies, like DeLay, realized that the leader of the grandly dubbed "Republican Revolution" had "made the mistake of his life." "It was pitiful," remembered DeLay. "Newt had been careless to say such a thing, and now the whole moral tone of the shutdown had been lost. What had been a noble battle for fiscal sanity began to look like the tirade of a spoiled child."[35]

When Gingrich provoked a second shutdown, casting 260,000 federal employees onto the street for twenty-one days over the Christmas holidays, moderate Republicans like Senator Bob Dole, who was weighing a presidential run, abandoned the fight. Gingrich's Hayekian uprising collapsed. The long march from Mont Pèlerin to Capitol Hill faltered. As DeLay concluded, Gingrich "was beset with the classic academic's dysfunction: He thought that ideas were alone enough, that thinking made it so."[36]

Gingrich's failed revolution caused the submarine debate between freshwater and saltwater economists to break surface. Clinton was committed to using tax revenues to pay off the national debt, a policy Keynes advocated in times of prosperity. "We must look to a bold Government program to lift us out of the rut," Keynes argued in 1930, and "if it has the effect of restoring business profits, then the machine of private enterprise might enable the economic system to proceed once more under its own steam."[37] The money government borrowed to stimulate a sluggish economy should be paid back as soon as the economy began booming and tax revenues started pouring in.

In 1993, Clinton had inherited a $290 billion federal deficit, and the Congressional Budget Office warned that it would grow to $455 billion by 2000. As Greenspan recalled, "The hard truth was that Reagan had borrowed from Clinton, and Clinton was having to pay it back."[38] Clinton pledged to halve the deficit and, according to Greenspan, was intent on fulfilling that promise. To that end, Clinton appointed economic advisers who were reluctant to add to taxes and spending. He was lucky too. He benefited from the "peace dividend," the ability to cut defense spending as the Cold War wound down, and he presided over the advent of the digital age, in which computers boosted business efficiency.

In 1997, Clinton introduced the Balanced Budget Act, mostly cutting Medicare costs to balance the budget by 2002. In the summer of 2000 he announced a budget current account surplus for the third year in a row, $69 billion in financial year 1998, $124 billion in 1999, and an estimate of at least $230 billion in 2000, the first surplus in three consecutive years since 1947–49, when Harry Truman was president. The debt had been reduced by $360 billion in three years, with $223 billion paid in 2000, the largest one-year debt reduction in American history.[39] At this rate, the $5.7 trillion national debt would be completely paid off by 2012.[40] Greenspan hailed Clinton as "the best Republican president we've had in a while"[41] and "as far from the classic tax-and-spend liberal as you could get and still be a Democrat."[42]

Clinton's apparent conservative virtue, however, provoked an unlikely response from his opponents. The chasm in economic thinking that had been papered over since the end of the Reagan era was revealed in arguments over how to spend the proceeds of a boom. Congressional Republicans, bolstered by lines of reasoning honed by New Classical economists like Robert Lucas Jr. who based macroeconomic models on microeconomic foundations, favored spending the surplus on tax cuts to encourage Americans to work harder. Clinton preferred to spend the surplus on clearing the national debt and underwriting the mounting costs of Medicare and Social Security. Greenspan favored paying off the national debt rather than cutting taxes.

In his 1996 State of the Union address, Clinton proudly sang from the Hayek hymnal: "We know big government does not have all the answers. The era of big government has ended."[43] Clinton followed Hayekian thinking by easing business regulations. In a move favored by Treasury Secretary Robert Rubin, and strongly endorsed by Greenspan, in 1999 he approved the Gramm-Leach-Bliley Act, abandoning the rules on banking, insurance, and financial companies that Franklin Roosevelt set during the Great Depression. For the first time in sixty years, investment banks were allowed to merge with depository banks. On advice from Rubin, Greenspan, the Securities and Exchange Commission chairman Arthur Levitt, and Rubin's successor Lawrence Summers, Clinton also declined to regulate the growing trade in credit derivatives that speculated on the credit risk of bonds and loans.

The former Texas governor and oil man George W. Bush[44] was elected president in January 2001, after a photofinish election. Thanks to his predecessor's caution, Bush inherited a budget surplus of $128 billion in tax year 2000–1 that was due to reach $280 billion the following year. The Congressional Budget Office reckoned the surplus would amount to $5.6 trillion over the ensuing decade, of which $3.1 trillion was already allocated to cover Social Security and Medicare obligations. By 2006 the Office expected the $3.4 trillion national debt to be paid off completely, with a $500 billion surplus due in each subsequent year. Bush did not think long about how to spend this rare legacy: he wanted to blow the whole of the surplus—and more— on cutting personal taxation. With a Republican majority in both Houses, he was free to announce $1.35 trillion in tax cuts, stretching to the end of 2010, with an instant rebate of $400 billion, or $600 per American household.

But in his first weeks in office the new president found he was facing an imminent recession, the delayed result of the collapse of the grossly inflated market in Internet companies and the price-reducing effects of the heightened competition that resulted from globalization. Greenspan began cutting interest rates to minimize the effect of the inevitable slowdown in economic growth. There was worse to come. By July, federal tax revenues began to plunge as a 20 percent collapse in the Standard & Poor's index between January and September caused capital gains tax receipts from stock transactions to plummet. A bear was stalking Wall Street and the once gargantuan surplus was becoming a will-o'-the-wisp. Then came the Al Qaeda attacks on America on September 11.

Al Qaeda leader Osama bin Laden's stated aim was to bankrupt America through terror, just as, he claimed, he had bankrupted the Soviet Union for occupying Afghanistan. Bush met this threat with a large Keynesian stimulus. After a meeting between Greenspan, former Clinton Treasury secretary Rubin, Bush adviser Larry Lindsey, and congressional leaders, massive new federal spending was swiftly approved. Expenditures to strengthen America's borders, such as tightening airport security, were accompanied by pork barrel projects, such as the building of fire stations in Maine, that had nothing to do with keeping America safe. Greenspan reduced interest rates to 1 percent to pump money into the economy fast, the prospect of the resulting inflation considered far preferable to a terrorist-inspired slump.

Yet these Keynesian measures to bolster the economy did not appear to work. By the end of 2002, growth was sluggish, profits were weak, the stock market was in the doldrums, unemployment was on the rise, and the budget deficit had reached $158 billion, a turnaround of $250 billion since the previous year's surplus of $127 billion. In September 2002, the Budget Enforcement Act of 1990, which ensured that all new federal spending was matched by taxation to pay for it, was allowed to lapse. America appeared to be facing a new danger: chronic deflation along the lines that Japan had endured throughout the 1990s, when a combination of interest rates set at zero and lavish public spending failed to reignite the once booming Japanese economy.

Bush continued pressing the case for tax cuts and increased defense spending, and added a costly extension of prescription drug benefits for those on Medicare.[45] "These goals had not been unrealistic in the light of large and projected surpluses," recalled Greenspan. "But the surpluses were gone six to nine months after George W. Bush took office."[46] After Republican victories in the 2002 midterms, Bush cut taxes on dividends from stocks by 50 percent, a move his Treasury secretary, Paul O'Neill, resisted. At a meeting in December 2002, when Vice President Dick Cheney pushed for the dividend tax breaks and a further cash stimulus to the economy, O'Neill said the deficit was already too large and that the country was "moving toward a fiscal crisis." "Reagan proved deficits don't matter," Cheney interrupted. "We won the mid-terms. This is our due."[47] Shortly after, O'Neill resigned.

The launch of the Iraq War, ongoing military operations in Afghanistan, and antiterrorism measures proved costly: $120 billion in financial year 2006 out of the more than $2 trillion federal budget. But they represented a small proportion of the total $13 trillion economy compared to previous wars.[48] The Hayekian ideals of the Contract with America in 1994 dribbled into the sand as corporate malfeasance, such as the unprecedented scale of the Enron and WorldCom frauds, combined with pork barrel spending by the Republicans in Congress. Congressman John Boehner of Ohio, an architect of Contract with America, wrote in 2003, "It turned out the American people did not want a major reduction of government."[49] Brian Riedl, a budget analyst at the conservative think tank the Heritage Foundation, concluded that "the Republican party is simply not interested in small government now."[50] As Nixon's Council of Economic Advisers chairman Herbert Stein observed back in 1985, "The radical conservative revolution is the dream of conservatives out of office, but not the practice of conservatives in office."[51] Discretionary spending by the federal government increased 22 percent in two years, from $734 billion in 2002 to $873 billion in 2004. By 2004 the federal current deficit was heading toward $400 billion.

In November 2006, the Republicans lost their majority in both Houses. The defeat, according to Dick Armey, the House majority leader from 1995 to 2002, marked the end of the Hayekian small-government revolution of 1994. Looking back on Contract with America, he wrote, "Our primary question in those early years was: How do we reform government and return money and power back to the American people? Eventually, the policy innovators and the 'Spirit of '94' were largely replaced by political bureaucrats driven by a narrow vision. Their question became: How do we hold onto political power?"[52] Hayek's idealistic vision had been defeated by old-school politics.

Another strand of Hayekian thinking, that the free market, left to its own devices, would correct its own mistakes and ensure prosperity for all, suffered a near mortal blow in the summer of 2007. Fearful at the dubious value of bundled debt containing high-risk "subprime" mortgages on homes that had sharply lost their value, banks began seizing up, incapable or unwilling to lend even to other banks. The nervousness among bankers frightened bank customers and prompted the first run on a bank in Britain since the mid-nineteenth century. Northern Rock, a savings and loan turned bank that borrowed extensively on the open market, could not obtain enough credit to satisfy savers' withdrawals. Crowds besieged the bank's branches, demanding their savings be returned. To prevent the panic from spreading to other financial institutions, the British government nationalized Northern Rock. It was a warning to banks around the world, most of which held tainted bundles of debt. Widespread panic ensued in financial institutions, and among savers and investors, on both sides of the Atlantic.

The mayhem suggested that the decades-long experiment in allowing barely restrained markets to generate growth and prosperity had failed. "The whole intellectual edifice collapsed," Greenspan told Congress. "I made a mistake in presuming that the self-interests of organizations, specifically banks and others, were such as that they were best capable of protecting their own shareholders and their equity in the firms. . . . I was shocked."[53] Greenspan's remarks echoed those of Keynes, eighty years before, when commenting on the Great Depression. "We have involved ourselves in a colossal muddle, having blundered in the control of a delicate machine, the working of which we do not understand," wrote Keynes. "The result is that our possibilities of wealth may run to waste for a time—perhaps for a long time."[54]

In response to what Greenspan called "the type of wrenching financial crisis that comes along only once in a century,"[55] Bush spent little time considering whether to allow the unhindered market to continue to do its worst. He reached for Keynes, who said, "I do not understand how universal bankruptcy can do any good or bring us nearer to prosperity."[56] "For about thirty years Keynes's reputation had languished," wrote Keynes biographer Peter Clarke. "In about thirty days the defunct economist was rediscovered and rehabilitated."[57] Asked in 2000 whether the Age of Keynes had been lost forever, John Kenneth Galbraith had declared, "If we were to have another recession, which is possible, we would be back to using some of the crude government surplus to create employment and to get the economy moving again."[58] He little imagined how prophetic his remark would be. In February 2008, Bush demanded from Congress a $168 billion Keynesian economic stimulus in income tax rebates. The Treasury bought from banks $700 billion in "troubled assets," a euphemism for bad debts. The state, the spender of last resort, was intervening wholesale to stop the economy from slipping into the void. In Britain, banks were bailed out in exchange for stocks; in America the banks were given the money outright, lest the president be accused of "socialism."

Bush's stimulus package was accompanied by a basket of actions by Ben Bernanke, who succeeded Greenspan as chairman of the Fed, to encourage banks to resume lending. Interest rates were halved between September 2007 and April 2008, huge short-term loans were made to banks, and the Fed bought bad mortgage debt. In March 2008, Bear Stearns, a leader in subprime mortgage lending, was sold in a fire sale to JPMorgan Chase. The following September, Lehman Brothers went bankrupt. Neither collapse was popular, not even among those who professed to believe the market should take its course. On the contrary, the most common criticism was that the administration had "allowed" Lehman to stop trading. In October 2008, Treasury Secretary Henry Paulson was given $700 billion by Congress to bail out other failing financial companies. On December 16, 2008, the Fed reduced interest rates to zero. Similar actions were taken by governments and central banks around the world.

Keynes was back, with a vengeance. *Time* magazine welcomed the old boy's return with the heading "The Comeback Keynes."[59] "What we are seeing now," wrote the journalist Justin Fox, "is fear we might be headed for an economic collapse caused by a collapse of demand caused by a collapse of credit. Confronted with that threat, governments seemingly cannot help turning to the remedy formulated by Keynes during the dark years of the early 1930s: stimulating demand by spending much more than they take in, preferably but not necessarily on useful public works like highways and schools."[60] Robert Lucas, the Nobel Prize winner who had done more than most Chicago economists to bury Keynes, declared, "I guess everyone is a Keynesian in a foxhole."[61] While the resurgent Keynesian tide engulfed the Treasury and the Fed, and saltwater economists regained prestige and control, freshwater economists were conspicuously silent. "I thought we all agreed that Keynesianism doesn't work," complained a lone voice, Chris Edwards of the conservative Cato Institute. "But now, with the new stimulus package before Congress, all these Keynesians have come out of the woodwork and I'm wondering where all the theorists are that oppose the Keynesian system."[62]

President Barack Obama[63] in February 2009 urged Congress to pass a $787 billion stimulus bill, in tax breaks and spending on unemployment benefits and infrastructure. "We acted because failure to do so would have led to catastrophe," he explained. "It is largely thanks to the Recovery Act that a second Depression is no longer a possibility."[64] But a change of president brought with it a return of the old ideological divisions. Not a single Republican voted for the stimulus. And, with barely a semi-quaver rest, the old Keynes-Hayek arguments broke out again. It was as if the intervening eighty years had not taken place.

From 2009 onward, a new debate emerged questioning the effectiveness of the stimulus and whether it was large enough. For Keynesians, the nub of the argument was the case Keynes made in 1936 about the fallacious nature of Say's Law, which asserted that income is always automatically spent. As tax breaks in the midst of a recession were banked rather than spent, and companies began hoarding cash, saving rather than spending ensured that Kahn's multiplier had little effect. There was a need to pump cash into the economy as fast as possible, yet much of the Obama stimulus package was backloaded, with money dribbling into the economy months, sometimes years later. Rather than the "shovel-ready" projects requested by the administration that would quickly translate into jobs for the unemployed, legislators often proposed long-term projects in their own states that would have little immediate effect on the economy.

The notion that what was good for General Motors was good for America was taken literally. Americans, fearful for their jobs, were delaying the decision to buy a new car, leaving three of the four largest domestic car companies, and their long chain of suppliers, on the edge of bankruptcy. They were given cash aid from the Treasury, in exchange for equity stakes.

In November 2008, world leaders at the G-20 meeting in Washington agreed on a common policy to avoid the looming Great Recession. They pledged to cut interest rates and allow public spending to outstrip taxation. By the time they met in Pittsburgh in September 2009, the prospect of a prolonged recession appeared to have been averted. By early summer 2010, the mood among world leaders had turned turtle. No sooner had the Keynesian spending remedies begun to work than there was buyer's remorse. The scale of national debt was threatening currencies as creditors feared governments would default. The debt-ridden state of the ramshackle Greek economy forced the European Union in May 2010 to muster a hurriedly assembled loan to prevent the Greek government from reneging on its debts. In November 2010, Ireland, too, was bailed out, followed in April 2011 by Portugal. Similar sovereign debt doubts were expressed about the the economies of Italy, Spain, Belgium, even France. To have allowed Greece, Ireland, and Portugal to go bankrupt would have threatened the viability of the European Union's currency, the euro, which would in turn undermine the movement toward European political integration. At the June 2010 G-20 meeting in Toronto, Canada, the same world leaders that backed Keynesian solutions just eighteen months before insisted on sharply reducing government spending and paying off national debt. Their turnaround was like giving an aspirin to someone with a headache, then immediately pumping their stomach.

Two years after Obama's stimulus package was passed, there was little evidence that it had succeeded. The unemployment rate rose to 9.8 percent in November 2010, with more than fifteen million out of work. Home foreclosures continued at a fast pace. Opponents of the stimulus, including all congressional Republicans, claimed it was not working, that recovery was being deterred by the "rational expectations" of those who believed that the extra federal spending and borrowing would lead to higher taxes and less clement conditions for business. They wanted the federal deficit reduced as soon as possible. *The New York Times*'s Nobel Prize economics laureate Paul Krugman[65] reminded those who wanted an immediate return to a policy of lowering taxes and spending that they were inviting a double-dip recession, just as Franklin Roosevelt had prompted the Roosevelt Recession of 1937.

Before long, Keynesians like Krugman, who had always doubted that the stimulus was large or urgent enough, were demanding a second, larger injection of cash and credit into the economy. "We are now, I fear, in the early stages of a third depression," he wrote. "Around the world . . . governments are obsessing about inflation when the real threat is deflation, preaching the need for belt-tightening when the real problem is inadequate spending."[66]

When the Democrats lost the midterms in November 2010, elections that were dominated by "Tea Party"[67] demands that government borrowing be halted and the deficit be paid off without delay, the Obama administration found managing the economy severely limited by the views of the Republican leadership, who insisted on the perpetuation of the Bush tax cuts for the rich as well as the middle class and targeted the government-mandated universal health care. The tax cuts and the tit-for-tat extension of unemployment benefits provided a further Keynesian stimulus that added $858 billion over two years to the federal deficit. Meanwhile, the Federal Reserve continued buying back government bonds to keep long-term interest rates low, causing the dollar's value to diminish. Adding to the nation's supply of money when companies were already awash with cash only confirmed the admonition by Marriner Eccles, Franklin Roosevelt's Federal Reserve chairman, about the impotence of monetary policy as a stimulus; "You cannot push on a string," that is, however much money you make available, you cannot force businesses to make investments.

EIGHTEEN

And the Winner Is . . .

Avoiding the Great Recession, 2008 Onward

So, eighty years after Hayek and Keynes first crossed swords, who won the most famous duel in the history of economics? For a number of decades Keynes appeared to emerge from the scuffle a little battered but triumphant, yet it was hardly a decisive victory. As his biographer Robert Skidelsky explained, "Hayek was defeated by Keynes in the economic debates of the 1930s, not, I think, because Keynes 'proved' his point, but because, once the world economy had collapsed, no one was very interested in the question of what exactly had caused it."[1]

Although Keynesianism has been declared dead a number of times since the mid-1970s, Friedman's acknowledgment in 1966 that "in one sense, we are all Keynesians now; in another, nobody is any longer a Keynesian"[2] is a more accurate, if teasingly ambiguous, assessment of the state of economics in the early twenty-first century. One key difference between the two men, whether an economy is best understood from the top down or the bottom up, through macroeconomics or microeconomics, left Keynes in the ascendant. His big-picture approach is universally used today, as are such concepts as gross domestic product, key tools by which economists measure an economy. As Friedman put it, "We all use many of the analytical details of the *General Theory*; we all accept at least a large part of the changed agenda for analysis and research that the *General Theory* introduced."[3]

Friedman, by his monetarist prescriptions, refined Keynes, but he did not replace him. "[Monetarism] has benefited much from Keynes's work," he wrote in 1970. "If Keynes were alive today, he would no doubt be at the forefront of the [monetarist] counter-revolution."[4] Keynes was looking for a cure for mass unemployment. His remedy was to increase total aggregate demand. He suggested a number of routes: through monetary means, by lowering interest rates and funneling new money into the economy; by tax breaks; and through public works.

Friedman persuaded economists that when on an even keel, the economy would be served better by a gradual, moderate, predictable increase in the supply of money. It was Friedman, not Keynes, whom most economists and politicians from the mid-1970s on adopted as their guide, after the application of all three of Keynes's remedies simultaneously for three decades resulted in stagflation. From the moment in 1979 when Paul Volcker, the Fed chairman, rebooted the economy by deliberately inducing a recession, Friedman's principles were widely applied. Friedman adopted Keynes's idea of running an economy through macroeconomics, and politicians have gone along with it, whatever Hayekian rhetoric they may sometimes employ.

Friedman's position offers clues on how best to gauge who won the Keynes-Hayek contest. In economics, Friedman was closer to Keynes and often praised Keynes's economics, in particular *A Tract on Monetary Reform*. Hayek conceded that "Milton's monetarism and Keynesianism have more in common with each other than I have with either."[5] When it came to politics, however, Friedman was closer to Hayek. Keynes believed state intervention was a suitable means for improving the lives of citizens. Friedman agreed with Hayek that whenever the state intervened in the economy, it hampered the free market's ability to create wealth. Friedman approved of cutting taxes, not to pump more money into the economy, as Keynes recommended, but because he believed that government would shrink as a result. In this respect, Hayek made great strides. The communist tyrannies eventually collapsed, egged on by those inspired by Hayek's antistatist sentiments.

While Hayek celebrated the demise of Soviet communism, he felt he had been defeated by Keynes in the widespread introduction of economic planning. According to Friedman, speaking in 2000, "There is no doubt who won the intellectual argument. . . . The intellectual opinion of the world today is much less favorable towards central planning and controls than it was in 1947. What's much more dubious is who won the practical argument. The world is more socialist today than it was in 1947. Government spending in almost every Western country is higher today than it was in 1947. . . . Government regulation of business is larger."[6]

Hayek took an absolutist position, that because no one could know what was in the minds of every member of society, and that the best indicator of their conflicting needs was market prices, all attempts to direct an economy were misplaced. Over time his failure to attract support during the Keynesian hegemony appeared to drive him into arguing his case ad absurdum. Eventually Hayek wanted state power to withdraw to a minimal citadel, and he wished to see every last element of the economy, even the issuance of money, in private hands because he challenged the state's monopoly of money-creating powers. This put him in direct opposition to Friedman, who, while wishing for the government to be minimized, believed that an economy should be managed to provide steady growth. Friedman's chosen instrument, monetary policy, required a state-run central bank. Hayek believed the issuance of money was the key to ending the business cycle that was the common concern of him and Keynes. "I believe that if it were not for government interference with the monetary system, we would have no industrial fluctuations and no periods of depression," Hayek declared. "If you place the issue of money in the hands of firms whose business depends upon their success in keeping the money they issue stable, the situation changes completely."[7]

The two leaders who promoted Hayek's notions, Ronald Reagan and Margaret Thatcher, went some way to shrinking the state to allow free enterprise to flourish. On his ninetieth birthday, Thatcher wrote to Hayek, "It is ten years this week since I was privileged to become Prime Minister. . . . The leadership and inspiration that your work and thinking gave us were absolutely crucial; and we owe you a great debt."[8] Thatcher awarded Hayek the Companion of Honour, one of Britain's top accolades, as a reward. The compliment was not entirely reciprocated. Interviewed by Mises's stepdaughter, Gita Sereny,[9] in 1985, Hayek was at pains to point out that "it is, of course, not true that I advise Mrs. Thatcher."[10] Hayek's disappointment was evident, too, when a writer for *Forbes* asked him in 1989 to assess Reagan and Thatcher's achievements. He thought their policies "as reasonable as we can expect at this time. They are modest in their ambitions."[11] Neither Thatcher nor Reagan made more than a start on achieving Hayek's ultimate aim to replace the state with private enterprise. Of the two, Thatcher achieved the most, though she started from a lower base, having inherited a mixed economy that was ripe for reform. Reagan's Hayekian rhetoric always outstripped his will to reduce the size of the state, as the ballooning of the federal budget during his presidency testifies.

Hayek wrote *The Road to Serfdom* in wartime, when the struggle against despotism was at its most acute, describing the book forty years later as a "tract for the times."[12] More than sixty years later, however, the book is cited without taking into account the special conditions in which it was written. Even those who might be expected to agree with Hayek readily concede that his apocalyptic view does not do justice to the benignity of the postwar European social democratic governments. The neoconservative thinker Adam Wolfson concluded that "most modern democracies have lived with more extensive welfare states and highly socialized economies than the United States, without somehow reaching a 'tipping point' whereupon they tumble into totalitarianism. There is in fact no road to serfdom through the welfare state."[13] Paul Samuelson, Keynesianism's chief proselytizer, was, as expected, more robust. "As I write in 2007, Sweden and other Scandivanian places . . . are the most 'socialistic' by Hayek's crude definition. Where are their horror camps?" he asked. "Have the vilest elements risen there to absolute power? When reports are compiled on 'measurable unhappiness,' do places like Sweden, Denmark, Finland and Norway best epitomize serfdoms? No. Of course not."[14] Even by Hayek's own measure of well-being, economic growth, the Scandinavian social democracies outperformed their free-market neighbors.[15]

Hayek did not concede the point. He believed Sweden achieved economic success despite, not because of, its large state sector and that the ennui he sensed among Swedes was a symptom of their loss of freedom. "Sweden and Switzerland are the two countries which have escaped the damages [sic] of two wars and have become repositories of a large part of the capital of Europe," he suggested. But such broadly shared prosperity and lack of unemployment came at a heavy price. "There is perhaps more social discontent [by which he perhaps meant suicides] in Sweden than in almost any other country I have been. The standard feeling that life is really not worth living is very strong in Sweden."[16]

Hayek's dismissal of the view among many intellectuals that social democratic countries like Sweden were more civilized than free-market economies caused him to be widely derided. He was treated with disdain by leading figures of both Right and Left. In 1967, when the Hayekian tide had reached its lowest ebb, Anthony Quinton, Thatcher's favorite philosopher, called him a "magnificent dinosaur,"[17] while the British Marxist historian Eric Hobsbawm described him as a "prophet in the wilderness."[18] "For most of his life his economic and political positions were completely out of sync with those of the rest of the intelligentsia," wrote the editor of his collected works, Bruce Caldwell. "He attacked socialism when it was considered 'the middle way,' when seemingly all people of good conscience had socialist sympathies. . . . For much of the century Hayek was a subject of ridicule, contempt, or, even worse for a man of ideas, indifference."[19]

Hayek is still widely considered beyond the pale, particularly in Europe. There have, however, been moves to give him his due since he won the Nobel Prize for economics in 1974. In 2003, *Encyclopaedia Britannica*'s 250-word entry on Hayek was replaced by a longer, more generous account. He has been placed on the social studies syllabus at Harvard, the American wellspring of Keynesianism. But, despite the championing of the political commentator Glenn Beck, who has devoted considerable time to popularizing the message of *The Road to Serfdom*, Hayek remains a little-known figure, paradoxically both a hero to those who define themselves as marginalized and big business's favorite economist.

Hayek was undeterred by his failure to win over those in positions of influence. He appeared to feel that to be cast out from mainstream academia confirmed the truth of his message. It was a startling display of self-confidence that over time brought on loneliness, insularity, and depression. Hayek steamed on, extending *The Road to Serfdom* to its ultimate conclusion: that only by turning over the whole of society to market forces can individuals become truly free. In *The Constitution of Liberty* in 1960, *Law, Legislation and Liberty* in 1973–79, and his final work, *The Fatal Conceit: The Errors of Socialism* in 1988, he proposed a utopia every bit as idealistic and unrealizable as all of the preceding ideal societies envisioned by thinkers ranging from Thomas More to Karl Marx.

He displayed such a strong sense of mission that it left many Hayekians with the feeling that they had inadvertently joined a spiritual sect. This was intentional. Hayek declared in 1949, "What we lack is a liberal Utopia, a program which seems neither a mere defence of things as they are nor a diluted kind of socialism, but a truly liberal radicalism. The main lesson which the true liberal must learn from the success of the socialist is that it was their courage to be Utopian which gained them the support of the intellectuals and thereby an influence on public opinion."[20]

Hayek's utopianism often spilled over into religiosity. As his disciple Ralph Harris described it, "Once . . . you understand there is no other way to preserve the substance of individual freedom except through dispersed property ownership, . . . you can say it's almost like a religious belief. . . . I have said—and it's offended some of my other Christian friends; they have said this is awful, sacrilege— . . . that the market is almost god-ordained."[21] In Hayek's vision, government would be left to manage only those elements of society that could be run by no one else, such as defense. Among the services Hayek believed should be privatized were "all those from education to transport and communications, including post, telegraph, telephone and broadcasting services, all the so-called 'public utilities,' the various 'social' insurances and, above all, the issue of money."[22] Tellingly, and perhaps surprisingly for those who subscribe to Hayek's general aims today, he advocated mandatory universal health care and unemployment insurance, enforced, if not directly provided, by the state, and he believed there should be free movement of labor across national borders.

Hayek, never a conservative, had become a libertarian, but he did not propose a state of anarchy. In place of government he suggested that private companies carry out communal duties. There was "no need for central government to decide who should be entitled to render different services, and it is highly undesirable that it should possess mandatory powers to do so."[23] Instead he envisioned "quasi-commercial corporations competing for citizens."[24] Those who did not like what the company offered should move elsewhere.

He concluded that representative democracy too often provided a "tyranny of the majority" that reduced individual freedoms and imposed unnecessary costs. He insisted that "the free market is the only mechanism that has ever been discovered for achieving participatory democracy."[25] In the light of this ultimate aim, to replace representative government, with all its interest groups, lobbies, and parties, with a privatized society, it is then not surprising that Hayek felt that Reagan and Thatcher did not go nearly far enough.[26]

Reagan and Thatcher had successfully managed representative democracy. To have expounded Hayek's full vision would have opened them to the electorally poisonous accusation that they were undemocratic. Other postwar politicians were mostly concerned with ensuring that everyone was given a chance to exercise the freedoms promised to them. While Hayek concentrated on an abstract utopia, progressives were winning battles over civil rights for African-Americans, women, homosexuals, and the disabled. Many political campaigns, such as the environmental movement and the seismic cultural shift that emanated from the changed mores of the 1960s, were not inspired by notions of governance at all. To many, Hayek's heroic materialism seemed anything but heroic.

Yet the public debate slowly moved in Hayek's favor. In Chile in the 1970s, Hayek was invoked to counter communism. While most of Western Europe held to the mixed economy and the welfare state, in Britain Thatcherism offered a new direction, albeit by his lights "Hayek lite," that Tony Blair's New Labour government embraced. It was in America, where free enterprise has always been a national creed, that Hayek's beliefs made the most progress, partly because the nation was founded on the notion that individuals should be free from government. Generations of Americans had practiced Hayek's philosophy long before he articulated it. Belief in the unbridled market was important to the eighteenth-century gentlemen who wrote the Constitution. Representative democracy, however, has over time encroached on absolute freedoms. As the conservative political scientist Adam Wolfson put it, citing Alexis de Tocqueville, "Big Government is, as it were, written into the political DNA of democracy."[27]

Hayek drew attention to the paradox at the core of the American

Constitution, that it appeared to endorse both individual rights and the powers of a strong federal government. Irritation at the ratchet effect of the government's creeping influence underpinned the message of leaders like Goldwater and Reagan. The Republican Party, once home to the conservatives Hayek so despised, has become the principal agent of Hayekian libertarianism. Shorn of Northeastern patricians, such as Nelson Rockefeller, who believed Keynesianism facilitated a corporatist marriage between state spending and private profit, the Republicans, egged on by the Tea Party, have adopted Hayek's cry for smaller government and have challenged Democrats to defend the status quo. In that sense, American politics has become increasingly Hayekian.

The Republicans' 1994 Contract with America was an attempt to remove powers from the federal government. It failed. Any move to dismantle a democratic system inevitably runs into problems. Politicians remain politicians. Those who have worked hard to be elected, even those who believe that government is too large, find it inconvenient to vote away their hard-won powers. Popular campaigns to reduce the government's reach by legislation or state constitutional amendment have similarly led to contradictions: limiting tax-raising powers by law is at odds with a legal commitment to pay off a budget deficit.

While Hayek may have risen in influence in the last thirty years, Keynes has never been far from economists' thoughts. The federal government's urgent response to the financial crisis of 2007–8, initiated by George W. Bush and continued by Barack Obama, was thoroughly Keynesian, with both administrations intervening in the marketplace to head off the economy's collapse. America faced an existential threat, and as in the 1930s, a failure to act was considered so foolhardly it was barely contemplated.

At the height of the crisis there were few in the short run who countered this resurgence of Keynesianism, even fewer who with a straight face promoted the Hayekian solution, to let the market find its own level. The view of Austrian-American political philosopher Joseph Schumpeter that the free market must from time to time endure a period of "creative destruction" was not allowed to be put to the test. Having so markedly been proved wrong, the widely held assumption that the free market always righted itself over time was not given a second chance. Few have tried to plot the dire consequences that would accompany the collapse of the economy: how many made unemployed; how many deprived of their homes; how many declared bankrupt; how many businesses shuttered.

Yet Bush and Obama received little credit for taking precipitate action to avoid an economic armageddon. And Keynesianism proved to be no panacea. As the stimulus failed to quickly reduce the numbers of unemployed, and the tales of "wasted" money for contentious public programs began to spread, many Americans became alarmed at the extent of government borrowing. For some, like Harvard economics professor Robert Barro, Keynes became a figure of derision, a pied piper who lured the children of future generations into a dark cave of intolerable indebtedness. Others accused Obama and his economic advisers of being closet socialists. Hayek's Austrian School argument that public money put into investments would be wasted was dusted off.

Describing the battle in the 1930s between Keynes and Hayek, Nixon's economic adviser Herbert Stein wrote in 1986, "Conventional conservatives have regarded Keynes as a dark and evil influence bent on undermining the free economic system. In fact, however, he helped to save the free system at a time when much more radical changes in it were being seriously advocated."[28] Twenty-five years on, Stein's words still rang true, but a growing number of Americans appeared more prepared to gamble that Hayek's painful prescriptions were preferable to paying the price of Keynes's remedies.

A similar sense of anxiety affected the Europeans. To them, however, it was not so much choosing Keynes over Hayek as a means of heading off a further financial crisis to ensure the survival of the euro and maintain the pace of European political integration. Led by the Germans, who had been paying disproportionately for sixty years to ensure the success of the European Union, the Europeans became fearful that sovereign debt crises in Greece, Ireland, Portugal, and elsewhere might prompt an irreversible run on the euro. The Germans acted, but at the expense of the Keynesian measures that had tempered the worst effects of the 2008 financial crisis. The price of continuing with European political integration was a tighter money supply and deep cuts in public expenditures.

Britain, too, came under pressure to impose cuts or face a run on sterling. After the 2010 general election in which no party won a majority, the David Cameron coalition of Conservatives and Liberal Democrats announced an unprecedented experiment in reducing Britain's public sector: cuts of 10 percent in spending identified in the first year; a target of 25 percent cuts by the end of the five-year parliament. The excuse to embrace a Hayekian solution was not lost on British Conservatives, such as Foreign Secretary William Hague and Work and Pensions Secretary Iain Duncan Smith, who had long harbored a dream to complete the Thatcher revolution. The revival of the Second Age of Keynes was short-lived, but the invocation of the name Hayek remained so divisive that few of those who advocated a smaller state could bring themselves to name their inspiration. Nor would they acknowledge their debt to Keynes for having saved capitalism twice in eighty years.

Hayek had no such inhibitions about expressing his admiration for Keynes, whom he considered "one of the most influential and colorful minds of his generation" who had had a "profound influence . . . on the development of ideas."[29] While Hayek believed "the 'Keynesian Revolution' will appear as an episode during which erroneous conceptions of the appropriate scientific method led to the temporary obliteration of many important insights," he thought him "so many-sided that when one came to estimate him as a man it seemed almost irrelevant that one thought his economics to be both false and dangerous. . . . He would have been remembered as a great man by all who knew him even if he had never written on economics."[30]

Like Keynes and Hayek, John Kenneth Galbraith did not live to see the Great Recession, but he had an explanation for why conservatives could not applaud Keynes for saving capitalism a second time. "Keynes was exceedingly comfortable with the economic system he so brilliantly explored," observed Galbraith. "So the broad thrust of his efforts, like that of Roosevelt, was conservative; it was to help ensure that the system would survive. But such conservatism in the English-speaking countries does not appeal to the truly committed conservative. . . . Better to accept the unemployment, idled plants, and mass despair of the Great Depression, with all the resulting damage to the reputation of the capitalist system, than to retreat on true principle. . . . When capitalism finally succumbs, it will be to the thunderous cheers of those who are celebrating their final victory over people like Keynes."[31]

ACKNOWLEDGMENTS

I am grateful to my friend and mentor A. O. H. Quick, headmaster of Rendcomb College, for first encouraging me to study political economy, and for my University of York economics professors, Alan T. Peacock and Jack Wiseman, for defying the common wisdom by suggesting there was more to economic theory than John Maynard Keynes. I am grateful to those, such as Enoch Powell, Alfred Sherman, John Hoskyns, Keith Joseph, and Margaret Thatcher, whose injection of free-market thinking into a reluctant British Conservative Party obliged me to reappraise the work of Friedrich Hayek.

In writing this volume I am deeply indebted to Bruce Caldwell, whose knowledge of Hayek's life and work is unparalleled, for reading through a final draft, suggesting amendments, and allowing me an early look at his most recent contribution to Hayek's *Collected Works* published by the University of Chicago Press. I would also like to thank Sidney Blumenthal for his detailed and thoughtful appraisal. Tom Sharpe, who was taught by and then taught alongside members of the Cambridge Circus, offered an original and critical eye, as did Rockwell Stensrud. I was delighted that my research led to a reinvigoration of my long-standing friendship with Paul Levy, a distinguished historian of the Bloomsbury Group. I should hasten to add that I am wholly responsible for what errors of fact or judgment may remain in the final text.

I would also like to thank Patricia McGuire, the archivist at King's College, Cambridge, and her colleague Jane Clarke; Carol A. Leadenham, assistant archivist for reference at the Hoover Institution Archives, Stanford, California; and Sue Donnelly, archivist at the London School of Economics. They all provided prompt and detailed responses to my queries, as did staff at various Manhattan branches of the New York Public Library. Thanks also to Dominick Harrod, Andrew Gilmour, Philip Zabriskie, Dominique Lazanski, Guy Sorman, and David Johns at *The New York Times*.

I could not have hoped for a more intelligent and sympathetic editor than Brendan Curry at W. W. Norton. Assistant editor Melanie Tortoroli was a constant help and guide. Mary Babcock's copyediting was thorough and appropriate, not least when suggesting how best to translate my English-English into American-English.

I offer profound thanks to my literary agent, Raphael Sagalyn, for grasping from our first brief conversation about Keynes that there was a good story to be told if only I could find it. He has gone a long way to replacing the late Giles Gordon, of fondest memory, the exceptional and gifted London and Edinburgh author and agent for my first five books.

Once again I am indebted to Fern Hurst and to Beverly Zabriskie for their generous hospitality and warm encouragement. At key moments in the writing of this volume they offered a bucolic haven that inspired fresh thinking and renewed vigor.

Finally, I owe an apology to my wife, Louise Nicholson, and two sons, William and Oliver, who have been obliged over the past several years to attend a series of impromptu domestic seminars on the relative merits of Keynes and Hayek. I thank them for their interminable patience, good humor, and understanding. I would achieve little without them.

NICHOLAS WAPSHOTT
New York, February 2011

NOTES

Preface

1 "Obituary: Laurence Joseph Henry Eric Hayek," in *King's College, Cambridge, Annual Report 2008*, p. 142. Laurence was Friedrich Hayek's son and, like Keynes, was a Kingsman. His obituary states that Keynes and Hayek "even took shifts on the roof of the King's Chapel on fire-watch during the War." Some doubt has been cast on the truth of this suggestion. At the least, both men fire-watched from the roof of King's.

2 Quoted by John Cassidy, "The Economy: Why They Failed," *New York Review of Books*, December 9, 2010, pp. 27–29.

Chapter One: The Glamorous Hero

1 Francis Ysidro Edgeworth was at the end of a long line of Anglo-Irish land-owners, writers, and eccentrics and became one of the most colorful, original, and brilliant men to have practiced economics in the nineteenth century. His origins were so romantic they deserved a place in one of the best-selling mor-alistic novels penned by his aged aunt Maria Edgeworth, whose vivid depic-tions of Irish life, both upstairs and downstairs, had inspired Sir Walter Scott to write the Waverley novels. Francis's father, Francis Beaufort Edgeworth, an undergraduate studying philosophy at Cambridge, was passing through London en route to Germany when, on the steps of the British Museum, he literally stumbled across Rosa Florentina Eroles, a sixteen-year-old Catalonian girl who was taking refuge in London from the persistent violence that was sweeping her native country. Edgeworth père fell in love on the spot and spon-taneously decided to shun the stern protocol demanded by his sub-aristocratic

family by eloping with his newfound love. The pair were married within three weeks. The fifth child of this unlikely union was Ysidro Francis Edgeworth, who transposed his Christian names in adulthood when there was no longer a chance of being mistaken for his father. Francis did not marry, though for a while he wooed in vain Beatrix Potter, the creator of Peter Rabbit, and instead devoted his energies to applying mathematical formulae to better understand human problems. While Edgeworth's contribution to economic theory was barely acknowledged in his lifetime, his work was commandeered, without adequate credit, by Alfred Marshall, the dominant British economist at the end of the nineteenth century and the resident economics giant at Cambridge who personally taught both John Maynard Keynes and Keynes's economist father, Neville.

2 Alfred Marshall (1842–1924), the most influential economist of his time, brought together the fundamental economic concepts of supply and demand, of marginal utility, and of the costs of production in his textbook *Principles of Economics* (1890), which formed the foundation of economics knowledge at the time.

3 Ludwig Heinrich Edler von Mises (1881–1973), Austrian School economist who fled Nazi Germany for Switzerland in 1934 and emigrated to America in 1940. Inspired by Carl Menger and Eugen von Böhm-Bawerk, he became the most influential economic liberal, inspiring F. A. Hayek, Ayn Rand, Wilhelm Röpke, Fritz Machlup, and Lionel Robbins and the American libertarian movement.

4 Ludwig Wittgenstein's grandmother was the sister of Hayek's great grandfather. Hayek quoted in Oral History Collection, Department of Special Collections, University Library, University of California, Los Angeles, 1983, p. 139.

5 Letter from Wittgenstein to Keynes, sent from K.u.k. Art. Autodetachement, "Oblt. Gurth," Feldpost No 186 on January 25, 1915. Quoted in Ludwig Wittgenstein, *Ludwig Wittgenstein Cambridge Letters*, ed. Brian McGuinness and Georg Henrik Wright (Wiley-Blackwell, Hoboken, N.J., 1997), p. 52.

6 Keynes, who made little attempt to repress his sense of humor even in these black circumstances, had made an entirely pertinent existentialist joke to Wittgenstein in a letter dated January 10, 1915, acknowledging receipt of Wittgenstein's first missive. "I am astonished to have got a letter from you. Do you think it proves that you existed within a short time of my getting it? I think so."

7 F. A. Hayek, *The Collected Works of F. A. Hayek*, vol. 9: *Contra Keynes and Cambridge: Essays and Correspondence*, ed. Bruce Caldwell (University of Chicago Press, Chicago, 1995), p. 58. Hereafter abbreviated "*Collected Works*."

8 George Clemenceau (1841–1929), French prime minister (1906–9, 1917–20).

9 David Lloyd George (1863–1945), British Liberal prime minister (1916–22) and founder of the welfare state.

10 First reference to the "Bloomsbury Group" was by Lytton Strachey. See Stanford Patrick Rosenbaum, *The Bloomsbury Group* (University of Toronto Press, Toronto, 1995), p. 17.

11 Giles Lytton Strachey (1880–1932), biographer of Queen Victoria whose *Eminent Victorians* introduced a new critical edge to the lives of great Britons.

12 Adeline Virginia Woolf née Stephen (1882–1941), innovative English modernist author and essayist whose influential novels included *Mrs. Dalloway* (1925), *To the Lighthouse* (1927), and *Orlando* (1928). She founded, with her husband, Leonard Woolf, the Hogarth Press in 1917.

13 Edward Morgan Forster (1879–1970), English author and fellow of King's College, Cambridge, whose novels include *Where Angels Fear to Tread* (1905), *A Room with a View* (1908), *Howards End* (1910), and *A Passage to India* (1924).

14 Duncan James Corrowr Grant (1885–1978), Scottish painter and lover of Lytton Strachey and John Maynard Keynes who formed an unlikely partnership with the painter Vanessa Bell, the sister of Virginia Woolf.

15 Vanessa Bell née Stephen (1879–1961), English artist who married the art critic Clive Bell before establishing an unconventional ménage with Duncan Grant and his lover David Garnett at their farmhouse, Charleston, in East Sussex.

16 Roger Eliot Fry (1866–1934), English artist and art critic who championed modernism and coined the term "Post-Impressionism." Fry enjoyed a brief love affair with Vanessa Bell.

17 George Edward Moore (1873–1958), English moral philosopher whose 1903 *Principia Ethica* inspired Keynes and the other members of the Bloomsbury Group.

18 *Collected Works*, vol. 9: *Contra Keynes and Cambridge*, p. 240.

19 R. F. Harrod, *The Life of John Maynard Keynes* (Macmillan, London, 1952), p. 200.

20 Letter from Keynes to Grant, April 25, 1915, in ibid., p. 201.

21 Sir Roy Forbes Harrod (1900–78), English economist and Oxford economics don whose *Life of John Maynard Keynes* (1952) remained the definitive biography of Keynes until Robert Skidelsky's three volumes (1983, 1992, 2000).

22 Harrod, *Life of John Maynard Keynes*, p. 206.

23 The Bloomsburys were not pacifists; they believed, however, that they should not be drafted to wage a war they did not agree with. For a full account, see Robert Skidelsky, *John Maynard Keynes*, vol. 1: *Hopes Betrayed 1883–1920* (Viking Penguin, New York, 1986), pp. 315–327.

24 Ibid., p. 324.

25 Ibid.

26 Robert Jacob Alexander, Baron Skidelsky (1939–), British historian of economic thought, emeritus professor of political economy at the University of Warwick, England, and founding member of the Social Democratic Party (1981), whose three-volume biography of John Maynard Keynes remains the definitive account of Keynes's life.

27 Skidelsky, *John Maynard Keynes*, vol. 1: *Hopes Betrayed*, p. 353.

28 Allies' memorandum to President Wilson, in U.S. Department of State, *Papers Relating to the Foreign Relations of the United States, 1918. Supplement 1, The World War* (Government Printing Office, Washington, D.C., 1918), pp. 468–694.

29 Rosalia "Rosa" Luxemburg (1871–1919), German Marxist and leader of the Spartacus League who was executed after the failed Spartacist uprising in Berlin of January 1919.

30 Carl Melchior (1871–1933), German banker for M. M. Warburg who led the contingent representing the defeated German government at the Paris Peace Conference. Despite Keynes's professed "love" for Melchior, there is no evidence that their close friendship was anything but platonic. Melchior had a long-standing mistress, the French author Marie de Molènes, whom he eventually married. They had a child.

31 Skidelsky, *John Maynard Keynes*, vol. 1: *Hopes Betrayed*, p. 374.

32 Letter from Keynes to mother, May 14, 1919, quoted in Harrod, *Life of John Maynard Keynes*, p. 249.

33 Letter from Keynes to Grant, May 14, 1919, quoted in ibid., p. 250.

34 Letter from Keynes to Chamberlain, May 26, 1919, quoted in ibid., p. 251.

35 Letter from Chamberlain to Keynes, May 21, 1919, quoted in ibid., p. 250.

36 Field Marshal Jan Christiaan Smuts (1870–1950), South African statesman and prime minister of the Union of South Africa (1919–24, 1939–48).

37 Letter from Keynes to mother, June 3, 1919, quoted in Harrod, *Life of John Maynard Keynes*, p. 252.

38 Letter from Keynes to Lloyd George, June 5, 1919, quoted in ibid., p. 253.

39 J. M. Keynes, *The Economic Consequences of the Peace* (Harcourt, Brace & Howe, New York, 1920), p. 5.

40 Ibid., p. 3.

41 Ibid., p. 30.

42 Ibid., p. 35.

43 Harrod, *Life of John Maynard Keynes*, p. 256.

44 Keynes, *Economic Consequences of the Peace*, p. 94.

45 Ibid., p. 96.

46 Ibid., p. 158.

47 Ibid., p. 167.

48 Ibid., p. 168.

49 Letter from Strachey to Keynes, Skidelsky, *John Maynard Keynes*, vol. 2: *The Economist as Savior 1920–1937* (Viking Penguin, New York, 1994), p. 392.
50 Letter from Keynes to Strachey, quoted in ibid., p. 392.
51 Ibid., p. 393.
52 Harrod, *Life of John Maynard Keynes*, p. 255.
53 Skidelsky, *John Maynard Keynes*, vol. 1: *Hopes Betrayed*, p. 384.
54 *Collected Works*, vol. 9: *Contra Keynes and Cambridge*, p. 58.

Chapter Two: End of Empire

1 "Nobel Prize–Winning Economist, Friedrich A. von Hayek," Oral History Program, University of California Los Angeles, 1983 (interviews with Hayek conducted on October 28 and November 4, 11, and 12, 1978), p. 475, http://www.archive.org/stream/nobelprizewinnin00haye#page/n7/mode/2up (accessed February 2011). Hereafter "UCLA Oral History Program."
2 F. A. Hayek, *Hayek on Hayek*, ed. Stephen Kresge and Leif Wenar (University of Chicago Press, Chicago, 1994), p. 35.
3 Erich Streissler, ed., *Roads to Freedom: Essays in Honour of Friedrich A. von Hayek* (Augustus M. Kelley, New York, 1969), p. xi.
4 UCLA Oral History Program, p. 387.
5 Ibid., p. 177.
6 Ibid., p. 57.
7 Ibid.
8 Ibid., p. 59.
9 Ibid., p. 434.
10 Keynes, *Economic Consequences of the Peace*, p. 240.
11 Ibid., p. 241.
12 Ibid., p. 233.
13 Ibid., p. 263.
14 Ibid., p. 258 footnote 1.
15 UCLA, Oral History Program, p. 41.
16 Ibid.
17 Carl Menger (1840–1921), Polish-born Austrian-Hungarian economist who developed the theory of marginal utility and founded the Austrian School of economics. His key work, *Principles of Economics* (1871), inspired Eugen von Böhm-Bawerk and generations of market economists, notably Mises and Hayek.
18 Friedrich Freiherr von Wieser (1851–1926), Viennese economist who, with Eugen von Böhm-Bawerk, developed the Austrian School theories of Carl Menger.
19 Hayek, *Hayek on Hayek*, p. 54.

20 Ibid., p. 55.

21 Maximilian Carl Emil "Max" Weber (1864–1920), German sociologist and political economist who, alongside Karl Marx and Émile Durkheim, revolutionized the theory and study of sociology. His *Protestant Ethic and the Spirit of Capitalism* suggested that the austerity inherent in Protestantism allowed the setting aside of consumption in investment that led to modern capitalism. He codrafted the Weimar Constitution, including the notorious article 48 allowing the German president to adopt emergency powers, which provided Adolf Hitler with the means to establish totalitarianism.

22 Hayek, *Hayek on Hayek*, p. 55.

23 UCLA Oral History Program, p. 583.

24 Hayek, *Hayek on Hayek*, p. 60.

25 Richard M. Ebeling, "The Great Austrian Inflation," *Freeman: Ideas on Liberty*, April 2006, pp. 2–3, http://www.fee.org/pdf/the-freeman/0604RMEbeling.pdf.

26 Keynes, *Economic Consequences of the Peace*, pp. 246–247.

27 Ibid., p. 134.

28 Ibid., p. 224.

29 *Collected Works*, vol. 9: *Contra Keynes and Cambridge*, p. 58.

30 J. M. Keynes, *A Tract on Monetary Reform* (1923), p. 54, reprinted in J. M. Keynes, *The Collected Writings of John Maynard Keynes*, vol. 4: *A Tract on Monetary Reform* (1923) (Macmillan for the Royal Economic Society, London, 1971). Hereafter abbreviated "*Collected Writings*." Author's italics.

31 *Collected Works*, vol. 9: *Contra Keynes and Cambridge*, p. 58 and footnote.

32 Skidelsky, *John Maynard Keynes*, vol. 2: *Economist as Savior*, p. 102.

33 Walter Lippmann (1889–1974), Pulitzer Prize–winning American journalist who introduced the notion of the Cold War.

34 It was a problem Keynes was to attempt to address throughout his life, culminating in his contribution to the Bretton Woods conference of 1944, which established the international fixed-currency regime agreed to after World War II.

35 *Collected Writings*, vol. 4: *Tract on Monetary Reform*, p. 16.

36 Ibid., p. 36.

37 Ibid., p. 134.

38 Ibid., p. 136.

39 Ibid., p. 65.

40 Ibid.

41 There was little that was revolutionary or adventurous in the experts' proposed remedy: they advocated a two-year vacation from paying war reparations, a modest foreign loan, and balancing the national budget. Donald Edward Moggridge, *Maynard Keynes: An Economist's Biography* (Routledge, New York, 1992), p. 380.

42 Milton Friedman was later to study under Wesley Clair Mitchell.

Chapter Three: The Battle Lines Are Drawn

1 F. A. Hayek, 1978 foreword to new edition of Ludwig von Mises, *Socialism: An Economic and Sociological Analysis* (LibertyClassics, Indianapolis, 1981), pp. xix–xx.

2 Ludwig von Mises, "Economic Calculation in the Socialist Commonwealth," trans. S. Alder, p. 14, http://mises.org/pdf/econcalc.pdf (accessed February 2011).

3 Both Harrod and Skidelsky consider this raise in the bank rate to have prompted the start of the Keynesian Revolution. "Never, perhaps, was the decision of the Bank of England Court more fraught with far-reaching consequences; for it set Keynes' [*sic*] mind working upon a line of thought which has had a world-wide influence lasting until this day." Harrod, *Life of John Maynard Keynes*, p. 338. "It was the start of the Keynesian Revolution." Skidelsky, *John Maynard Keynes*, vol. 2: *Economist as Savior*, p. 147.

4 J. M. Keynes, "Note on Finance and Investment," *Nation*, July 14, 1923.

5 *Collected Writings*, vol. 19: *Activities 1922–9: The Return to Gold and Industrial Policy* (Macmillan for the Royal Economic Society, London, 1981), pp. 158–162.

6 This is the first hint by Keynes at what was to become the notion of "the multiplier," a theoretical explanation of how the spending of money has a cumulative effect on an economy that was later developed by Keynes's colleague Richard F. Kahn. It was a concept that was to play a large part in the argument of Keynes's *General Theory*. Once again Keynes's intuition was running far ahead of his theory.

7 *Collected Writings*, vol. 19: *Activities 1922–9*, p. 220.

8 *House of Commons Debates*, 5th series (HMSO, London, 1924), vol. 176, July 30, 1924, cols. 2091–2092.

9 *Collected Writings*, vol. 19: *Activities 1922–9*, p. 283.

10 Ibid., p. 229.

11 John Locke (1632–1704), English Enlightenment thinker known as the "Father of Classical Liberalism," whose theories on empiricism, the social contract, and the rule of law informed the Enlightenment that inspired America's Founding Fathers.

12 David Hume (1711–76), Scottish philosopher and economist, key figure in the Scottish Enlightenment.

13 Edmund Burke (1729–97), Irish philosopher and Whig member of Parliament known as the "Father of Modern Conservatism."

14 Jean-Jacques Rousseau (1712–78), Swiss philosopher, author of *The Social Contract*.

15 William Paley (1743–1805), British Christian philosopher.

16 Jeremy Bentham (1748–1832), English philosopher.

17 J. M. Keynes, *The End of Laissez-Faire* (Hogarth Press, London, 1926), p. 11.

18 Charles Dickens, *Hard Times* (Harper & Brothers, New York, 1854), chap. 23, p. 281.

19 Charles Robert Darwin (1809–82), English naturalist who propounded the theory of evolution through natural selection. Keynes's brother Geoffrey married Darwin's granddaughter Margaret.

20 Keynes, *End of Laissez-Faire*, p. 40.

21 Ibid., p. 44.

22 Ibid., p. 45.

23 Ibid., p. 47.

24 *Collected Writings*, vol. 19: *Activities 1922–9*, pp. 267–272.

25 Quoted in Skidelsky, *John Maynard Keynes*, vol. 2: *Economist as Savior*, p. 198.

26 Ibid., p. 202.

27 J. M. Keynes, *The Economic Consequences of Mr. Churchill* (Hogarth Press, London, 1925), p. 9.

28 Ibid., p. 19.

29 *Collected Writings*, vol. 9: *Essays in Persuasion* (1931) (Macmillan for the Royal Economic Society, London, 1972), p. 223.

30 "The Monetary Policy of the United States after the Recovery from the 1920 Crisis," in F. A. Hayek, *Money, Capital, and Fluctuations: Early Essays*, ed. Roy McCloughry (Routledge & Kegan Paul, London, 1984), pp. 5–32.

31 Ibid., p. 17.

32 Knut Wicksell (1851–1926), Swedish economist whose book *Interest and Prices* was an early contribution to what was to become known as "monetarism."

Chapter Four: Stanley and Livingstone

1 Hayek is contradictory about exactly when he first met Keynes. In a lecture given at the University of Chicago in 1963, "The Economics of the 1930s as Seen from London" (published in *Collective Works*, vol. 9: *Contra Keynes and Cambridge*, p 59), he said "I met him at an international conference . . . in 1929." In an essay in the *Oriental Economist* (vol. 34, no. 663, January 1966, pp. 78–80, reproduced in ibid., p. 240), he wrote, "I met him first in 1928 in London." There is no record in Keynes's *Collected Writings* of their first meeting.

2 The London and Cambridge Economic Service (LCES) was directed by an executive committee consisting of William Beveridge and Arthur Bowley from the London School of Economics and Political Science (LSE) and John Maynard Keynes and Hubert Henderson from Cambridge. It aimed to support business by providing existing statistics in a usable form and developing new indicators such as share prices, money wages, and industrial production.

3 Lionel C. Robbins, later Lord Robbins (1898–1984), British economist.

4 "Economics of the 1930s as Seen from London," in *Collected Works*, vol. 9: *Contra Keynes and Cambridge*, p. 59.

5 Hayek, *Hayek on Hayek*, p. 78.

6 Eugen Ritter von Böhm-Bawerk (1851–1914), Viennese economist, disciple of Carl Menger, teacher of Ludwig von Mises, and a persistent contemporary critic of Karl Marx. Böhm-Bawerk was born in Brno, Czechoslovakia, when it was part of Austro-Hungary.

7 William Henry Beveridge, Lord Beveridge (1879–1963), British economist whose 1942 report *Social Insurance and Allied Services* inspired Labour's establishment of the Welfare State and the National Health Service.

8 Lionel Robbins, *Autobiography of an Economist* (Macmillan/St. Martin's Press, London, 1971), p. 150.

9 Hayek, *Hayek on Hayek*, p. 75.

10 Ibid.

11 F. A. Hayek, "The 'Paradox' of Saving," first published in 1929 in *Zeitschrift für Nationalökonomie*, vol. 1, no. 3. See note 15 below.

12 Waddill Catchings (1879–1967), American banker turned economist, and William Trufant Foster (1879–1950), American economist and first president of Reed College, Portland, Oregon.

13 W. T. Foster and W. Catchings, "The Dilemma of Drifts," published by the Pollak Foundation, Newton, Mass., 1926.

14 Herbert Clark Hoover (1874–1964), secretary of commerce (1921–28) and 31st president of the United States (1929–33).

15 Hayek, "The 'Paradox' of Saving," translated by Nicholas Kaldor and George Tugendhat, was published in *Economica*, vol. 11, May 1931, and reproduced in *Collected Works*, vol. 9: *Contra Keynes and Cambridge*, p. 88.

16 Ibid., pp. 118–119.

17 Ibid., p. 119.

18 Ibid.

19 Hayek, *Hayek on Hayek*, p. 77.

20 Hayek, "'Paradox' of Saving," in *Collected Works*, vol. 9: *Contra Keynes and Cambridge*, pp. 74–120.

21 Jörg Guido Hülsmann, *Mises: The Last Knight of Liberalism* (Ludwig von Mises Institute, Auburn, Ala., 2007), p. 514.

22 Margit von Mises, *My Years with Ludwig von Mises* (Arlington House, New Rochelle, N.Y., 1976), p. 44.

23 Ibid., p. 85.

24 Tilton is on the estate of Lord Gage, whose ancestor General Gage lost the first battle of the American War of Independence, the Battle of Bunker Hill.

25 See J. M. Keynes and Lydia Lopokova, *Lydia and Maynard: The Letters of Lydia Lopokova and John Maynard Keynes*, ed. Polly Hill and Richard Keynes (Charles Scribner's Sons, New York, 1989).

26 Skidelsky, *John Maynard Keynes*, vol. 2: *Economist as Savior*, p. 285.

27 Harrod, *Life of John Maynard Keynes*, p. 403.

28 Skidelsky, *John Maynard Keynes*, vol. 2: *Economist as Savior*, p. 314.

29 J. M. Keynes, *A Treatise on Money* (Macmillan, London, 1930), p. vi.

30 *Collected Writings*, vol. 13: *The General Theory and After, Part 1, Preparation* (Macmillan for the Royal Economic Society, London, 1973), pp. 19–22.

31 Ibid.

32 Although Keynes credited Wicksell for defining the different interest rates, he had come to this conclusion independent of Wicksell's work.

33 Keynes, *Treatise on Money*, p. 408.

34 Harrod, *Life of John Maynard Keynes*, p. 413.

35 Keynes, *Treatise on Money*, p. 376.

36 Skidelsky, *John Maynard Keynes*, vol. 2: *Economist as Savior*, p. 297.

37 *Collected Writings*, vol. 19: *Activities 1922–9*, p. 765.

38 Skidelsky, *John Maynard Keynes*, vol. 2: *Economist as Savior*, p. 302.

39 *Collected Writings*, vol. 9: *Essays in Persuasion*, p. 91.

40 *Collected Writings*, vol. 19: *Activities 1922–9*, p. 825.

41 *Collected Writings*, vol. 9: *Essays in Persuasion*, p. 93.

42 Ibid., p. 106.

43 *Collected Writings*, vol. 20: *Activities 1929–31: Rethinking Employment and Unemployment Policies* (Macmillan for the Royal Economic Society, London, 1981), p. 148.

44 Ibid., p. 76.

45 Harrod, *Life of John Maynard Keynes*, p. 416.

46 *Collected Writings*, vol. 20: *Activities 1929–31*, p. 64.

47 Ibid., p. 318.

48 Ibid., p. 102.

49 Ibid., p. 144.

50 Robbins, *Autobiography of an Economist*, p. 187.

51 Harrod, *Life of John Maynard Keynes*, p. 429.

52 Skidelsky, *John Maynard Keynes*, vol. 2: *Economist as Savior*, p. 368.

53 Harrod, *Life of John Maynard Keynes*, p. 427.

54 *Collected Writings*, vol. 13: *General Theory and After, Part 1*, p. 185.

55 Robbins, *Autobiography of an Economist*, p. 151.

56 Susan Howson and Donald Winch, *The Economic Advisory Council, 1930–1939: A Study in Economic Advice during Depression and Recovery* (Cambridge University Press, Cambridge, U.K., 1977), p. 63.

57 Robbins, *Autobiography of an Economist*, p. 152.

58 Norman Mackenzie and Jeanne Mackenzie, eds., *The Diary of Beatrice Webb*, vol. 4: *"The Wheel of Life," 1924–1943* (Virago, London, 1985), p. 260.

Chapter Five: The Man Who Shot Liberty Valance

1 F. A. Hayek, "The 'Paradox' of Saving," *Zeitschrift für Nationalökonomie*, vol. 1, no. 3, 1929.

2 Joan Robinson eventually went one better. She believed, "Everything can be found in Marshall, even [Keynes's] General Theory." Joan Robinson, *Economic: An Essay on the Progress of Economic Thought Philosophy* (Aldine Transaction, Piscataway, N.J., 2006), p. 73.

3 Richard Ferdinand Kahn, Baron Kahn (1905–89), British economist. Kahn was a pupil of Keynes whose work on the consequences of injecting public money into an economic system, as suggested by Keynes, led to his assertion that the addition of sums would increase aggregate demand and result in consistent and measurable increases in economic activity, a notion Keynes dubbed "the multiplier."

4 Richard F. Kahn, *The Making of Keynes' General Theory* (Cambridge University Press, Cambridge, U.K., 1984), p. 171.

5 Joan Violet Robinson née Maurice (1903–83), the first woman fellow of King's College, Keynes's most virulent disciple, and a prominent member of the "Cambridge Circus." She went on to conceive the notion of imperfect competition; cofound the Neo-Ricardian and Post-Keynesian Schools; develop, with Nicholas Kaldor, theories of economic growth, particularly with respect to underdeveloped countries; and revive the study of Karl Marx's economic theories. She married Austin Robinson in 1925.

6 Piero Sraffa (1898–1983), Italian economist saved by Keynes from the threats of Mussolini's fascism to become a Cambridge economics lecturer and the Marshall librarian, a post Keynes specially created for him. Sraffa was cofounder, with Joan Robinson, of the Neo-Ricardian School. Ludwig Wittgenstein credited discussions with Sraffa for many of the breakthroughs in his thoughts on philosophy.

7 James Edward Meade (1907–95), British economist, first at the LSE, later at Cambridge, and cowinner (with Bertil Ohlin) of the 1977 Nobel Prize in economics. He wrote the first draft of the British White Paper on full employment (1944) and the first outline of GATT, the General Agreement on Tariffs and Trade. Between 1945 and 1947 he was chief economist to Clement Attlee's Labour government.

8 Quoted in Marjorie Shepherd Turner, *Joan Robinson and the Americans* (M. E. Sharpe, Armonk, N.Y., 1989), p. 51.

9 Ibid., p. 62.

10 *Collected Writings*, vol. 13: *General Theory and After, Part 1*, p. 339.

11 Joseph Alois Schumpeter (1883–1950), Czech-born Austrian economist and political scientist who studied under Böhm-Bawerk and whose theories of "creative destruction" in economics complemented the Austrian School's notions. He fled Nazism for America in 1932, finding safe haven at Harvard.

12 Kahn, *Making of Keynes' General Theory*, p. 170.

13 Letter from Keynes to Pigou, quoted in Charles H. Hession, *John Maynard Keynes* (Macmillan, New York, 1984), p. 263.

14 Joseph Alois Schumpeter and Elizabeth Boody Schumpeter, *History of Economic Analysis* (Oxford University Press, Oxford, U.K., 1954), p. 1118. For his part, the level-headed Kahn dismissed such an extravagant claim as "clearly absurd." "Perhaps it was inspired by unconscious hostility to Keynes. . . . His friendship with Keynes . . . was towards the end tainted by a trace of jealousy. Keynes found a solution to the basic problem for which Schumpeter had, for a great part of his life, searched in vain. Schumpeter used to say to his friends: 'When I was young I had three ambitions: to become a great lover, a great horseman, and a great economist. I realised only two.'" Kahn, *Making of Keynes' General Theory*, p. 178.

15 Schumpeter and Schumpeter, *History of Economic Analysis*, p. 1152.

16 Michael Senzberg, ed., *Eminent Economists: Their Life Philosophies* (Cambridge University Press, Cambridge, U.K., 1993), p. 204.

17 Ibid., p. 205.

18 Ibid., p. 211.

19 Skidelsky, *John Maynard Keynes*, vol. 2: *Economist as Savior*, p. 703.

20 G. C. Harcourt, "Some Reflections on Joan Robinson's Changes of Mind and Their Relationship to Post-Keynesianism and the Economics Profession," in Joan Robinson, Maria Cristina Marcuzzo, Luigi Pasinetti, and Alesandro Roncaglia, eds., *The Economics of Joan Robinson*, Routledge Studies in the History of Economics, vol. 94 (CRC Press, London, 1996), p. 331.

21 Letter from Keynes to Lydia, February 1, 1932, King's College, Cambridge, U.K.

22 F. A. Hayek, "Preface to the Second Edition" (1935), in *Prices and Production* (Augustus M. Kelley, New York, 1967), p. ix, http://mises.org/books/prices production.pdf.

23 Kahn, *Making of Keynes' General Theory*, pp. 181–182.

24 Joan Robinson, "The Second Crisis of Economic Theory," *History of Political Economy*, vol. 8, Spring 1976, p. 60.

25 Robbins, *Autobiography of an Economist*, p. 127.

26 F. A. Hayek, *Prices and Production and Other Works: F. A. Hayek on Money, the Business Cycle, and the Gold Standard* (Ludwig von Mises Institute, Auburn, Ala., 2008), p. 197, http://mises.org/books/hayekcollection.pdf. First published by Routledge & Sons, London, 1931.

27 Ibid., p. 198.

28 Ibid., p. 199.

29 Richard Cantillon (1680–1734), Irish-French economist who referred to the "natural" behavior of the economy and the notion that economies tended toward an equilibrium.

30 Hayek, *Prices and Production*, p. 205.

31 Henry Thornton (1760–1815), English economist and member of Parliament.

32 David Ricardo (1772–1823), English economist.

33 Thomas Tooke (1774–1858), English economist who lent his name to the chair of economics that Hayek was awarded as a result of his LSE lectures.

34 Thomas Malthus (1766–1834), English economist.

35 John Stuart Mill (1806–73), English philosopher, political theorist, economist, and member of Parliament.

36 Marie-Esprit-Léon Walras (1834–1910), French economist.

37 It is not known whether Hayek had read Keynes's *Treatise,* published in December 1930, by the time he delivered his first lecture at the LSE in February 1931.

38 Hayek, *Prices and Production*, p. 215.

39 Ibid., pp. 217–218.

40 Ibid., p. 219.

41 Ibid., pp. 220–221.

42 Ibid., p. 241.

43 Ludwig von Mises, *Theorie des Geldes und der Umlaufsmittel* (Duncker & Humblot, Munich, 1912) p. 431.

44 Hayek, *Prices and Production*, p. 272.

45 Ibid., p. 273.

46 Ibid., p. 275.

47 Ibid., p. 299.

48 Ibid., p. 288.

49 Ibid.

50 Ibid., p. 290.

51 Ibid., p. 298.

52 Ibid.

53 Robbins, *Autobiography of an Economist*, p. 127.

54 John Cunningham Wood and Robert D. Wood, eds., *Friedrich A. Hayek: Critical Assessments of Leading Economists* (Routledge, London, 2004) p. 201.

55 There is some confusion about how much of a role Robbins played in the appointment. Though it was clear that Robbins was delighted, and some sources, such as Daniel Yergin and Joseph Stanislaw in *The Commanding Heights: The Battle for the World Economy* (Simon & Schuster, New York, 2002), describe the appointment "at the specific instance of Lionel Robbins,"

Robbins claimed in his *Autobiography of an Economist* (p. 127) that "greatly to my surprise, Beveridge asked if we would care to invite the lecturer to join us permanently as holder of the Tooke Chair. . . . There was a unanimous vote in favor."

56 Robbins, *Autobiography of an Economist*, p. 127.

Chapter Six: Pistols at Dawn

1 BBC radio, January 14, 1931, in *Collected Writings*, vol. 9: *Essays in Persuasion*, p. 138.
2 Ibid.
3 Ibid., p. 139.
4 Skidelsky, *John Maynard Keynes*, vol. 2: *Economist as Savior*, p. 384.
5 Howson and Winch, *Economic Advisory Council*, p. 82.
6 Royal Commission on Unemployment Insurance, *Minutes of Evidence* (HMSO, London, 1931), p. 381.
7 There is no evidence Churchill said such a thing. The quote is not cited by Keynes's biographers Roy Harrod and Robert Skidelsky nor by Churchill's biographers Martin Gilbert and Roy Jenkins.
8 Nor is there evidence that Keynes made this remark often attributed to him. Again, it can be found in neither Harrod nor Skidelsky.
9 Hubert Henderson Papers, Nuffield College, Oxford, file 21, June 17, 1931.
10 Skidelsky, *John Maynard Keynes*, vol. 2: *Economist as Savior*, p. 390.
11 Oswald Toynbee "Foxy" Falk (1881–1972), City of London stockbroker and Keynes's friend and investment partner whom he invited to become a member of the 1917 Treasury team.
12 O. T. Falk's papers, British Library, London, June 22, 1931.
13 *Collected Writings*, vol. 20: *Activities, 1929–31*, p. 563.
14 *Collected Writings*, vol. 13: *General Theory and After, Part 1*, p. 343.
15 Ibid., p. 355.
16 Philip Quincy Wright (1890–1970), member of the social sciences department of the University of Chicago from 1923 onward.
17 Skidelsky, *John Maynard Keynes*, vol. 2: *Economist as Savior*, p. 392.
18 J. M. Keynes, *Daily Herald*, September 17, 1931.
19 In an article for the *New Statesman*, republished in John Maynard Keynes, *Essays in Persuasion* (W. W. Norton, New York, 1963), p. 161.
20 Harrod, *Life of John Maynard Keynes*, p. 438.
21 Hayek, *Prices and Production*, p. 425.
22 Ibid.
23 Ibid., p. 426.
24 Ibid.

25 Ibid.

26 Ibid.

27 Ibid.

28 Ibid., p. 427.

29 Ibid., p. 429.

30 Ibid.

31 Ibid., p. 447.

32 Ibid., p. 430.

33 Robbins, *Autobiography of an Economist*, p. 128.

34 Hayek, *Prices and Production*, p. 434.

35 Hayek, *Prices and Production*, p. 436.

36 Frank William Taussig (1859–1940), American economist.

37 Hayek, *Prices and Production*, p. 436.

38 Ibid., p. 455.

39 Ibid., pp. 455–456.

41 Hayek, "Preface to the Second Edition" (1935), in *Prices and Production* (Augustus M. Kelly, New York, 1967), p. xiv, http://mises.org/books/prices production.pdf.

41 Keynes, *Essays in Persuasion* (W. W. Norton, 1963), p. 1.

Chapter Seven: Return Fire

1 Bertrand Russell (1872–1970), British philosopher, mathematician, and historian.

2 Bertrand Russell, *Autobiography* (Allen & Unwin, London, 1967), p. 61.

3 Kenneth Clark, Baron Clark (1903–83), art historian and director of the National Gallery, London.

4 Kenneth Clark, *The Other Half: A Self Portrait* (Harper & Row, New York, 1977), p. 27.

5 Harrod, *Life of John Maynard Keynes*, p. 644.

6 *Collected Writings*, vol. 5: *A Treatise on Money, i: The Pure Theory of Money* (1930) (Macmillan for the Royal Economic Society, London, 1971), p. xviii.

7 Sir Arthur Quiller-Couch (1863–1944), English writer.

8 Arthur Quiller-Couch, *On the Art of Writing* (G. P. Putnam's Sons, New York, 1916), p. 281.

9 *Collected Writings*, vol. 13: *General Theory and After, Part 1*, p. 243.

10 Ibid., p. 252.

11 By far the clearest and most cogent attempt to reconcile the two lines of thought can be found in Bruce Caldwell's exemplary introduction to *Contra Keynes and Cambridge*, p. 25, vol. 9 of *Collected Works* (Hayek). But also see Heinz-Dieter Kurz, "The Hayek-Keynes-Sraffa Controversy Reconsidered,"

in Kurz, *Critical Essays on Piero Sraffa's Legacy in Economics* (Cambridge University Press, Cambridge, U.K., 2000), pp. 257–304.

12 *Collected Writings*, vol. 13: *General Theory and After, Part 1*, p. 244.

13 Ibid., p. 247.

14 Ibid.

15 Ibid., p. 248.

16 Quoted by Robert Skidelsky, "Ideas and the World," *Economist*, November 23, 2000.

17 Arthur Cecil (A. C.) Pigou (1877–1959).

18 The 1932–33 Ashes cricket test between Australia and England was marred by accusations that the English team indulged in "body-line bowling," aiming the ball at the batsman rather than the wicket. This was the ultimate English public school insult from Pigou, that what Keynes had inflicted on Hayek was simply "not cricket."

19 Arthur Pigou, *Economics in Practice* (Macmillan, London, 1935), pp. 23–24.

20 Ibid., p. 24.

21 *Collected Works*, vol. 9: *Contra Keynes and Cambridge*, p. 159.

22 Ibid.

23 Ibid., p. 160.

24 Ibid.

25 Ibid.

26 Ibid., pp. 162–163.

27 *Collected Writings*, vol. 13: *General Theory and After, Part 1*, p. 257.

28 Ibid., pp. 257–258.

29 Ibid., p. 258.

30 Ibid.

31 Ibid., p. 259.

32 Ibid.

33 Ibid., pp. 259–260.

34 Hayek, Prices and Production, p. 434.

34 Ibid., p. 260.

35 Ibid., pp. 262–263.

36 Ibid., pp. 263–264.

37 Ibid., p. 265.

38 Ibid.

39 Ibid., p. 470.

40 Don Patinkin and J. Clark Leith, eds., *Keynes, Cambridge and the General Theory* (University of Toronto Press, Toronto, 1978), p. 74.

41 Ibid., p. 40.

42 Joan Robinson, *Contributions to Modern Economics* (Blackwell, Oxford, U.K., 1978), p. xv.

43 *Collected Writings*, vol. 14: *General Theory and After, Part 2, Defence and Development* (Macmillan for the Royal Economic Society, London, 1973), p. 148.

44 Kahn's 1932 remark quoted by Paul Samuelson, "A Few Remembrances of Friedrich von Hayek (1899–1992)," *Journal of Economic Behavior and Organization*, vol. 69, no. 1, January 2009, pp. 1–4.

45 Hugh Gaitskell (1906–63), leader of the Labour Party.

46 Quoted in Elizabeth Durbin, *New Jerusalems: The Labour Party and the Economics of Democratic Socialism* (Routledge & Kegan Paul, London, 1985), p. 108.

Chapter Eight: The Italian Job

1 BBC radio, January 14, 1931, in *Collected Writings*, vol. 9: *Essays in Persuasion*, p. 138.

2 Ibid.

3 *Collected Works*, vol. 9: *Contra Keynes and Cambridge*, p. 193.

4 Ibid.

5 Ibid., p. 195.

6 Ibid., p. 197.

7 Ibid., p. 182.

8 John Cunningham Wood, ed., *Piero Sraffa: Critical Assessments* (Psychology Press, Hove, U.K., 1995), p. 34.

9 Ludwig Wittgenstein, *Philosophical Investigations* (Wiley-Blackwell, London, 2001), preface.

10 Wood, *Piero Sraffa*, p. 34.

11 Ludwig M. Lachmann, *Expectations and the Meaning of Institutions: Essays in Economics*, ed. Don Lavoie (Psychology Press, Hove, U.K., 1994), p. 148.

12 Jean-Pierre Potier, *Piero Sraffa, Unorthodox Economist (1898–1983): A Biographical Essay* (Psychology Press, Hove, U.K., 1991), p. 9.

13 Bernard Berenson (1865–1959).

14 Sraffa reported this telegram from Mussolini in a letter to Keynes dated Christmas 1922, in the Keynes Papers, the Marshall Library, Cambridge, quoted by Nicholas Kaldor, "Piero Sraffa (1898–1983)," *Proceedings of the British Academy*, vol. 71, 1985, p. 618.

15 Terenzio Cozzi and Roberto Marchionatti, eds., *Piero Sraffa's Political Economy: A Centenary Estimate* (Psychology Press, Hove, U.K., 2001), pp. 31–32.

16 Known as the Investment Saving/Liquidity preference Money supply (IS-LM) model, which charts the relationship between interest rates and real output.

17 John Richard Hicks, *Critical Essays in Monetary Theory* (Clarendon Press, Oxford, U.K., 1967), p. 204.

18 Frank Hyneman Knight (1885–1972), cofounder of the Chicago School of

economics, whose reluctant preference for laissez-faire over state intervention was principally because it was marginally less inefficient.

19 Letter from Knight to Morgenstern, quoted in Michael Lawlor and Bobbie Horn, "Notes on the Hayek-Sraffa Exchange," *Review of Political Economy*, vol. 4, 1992, p. 318, footnote.

20 Piero Sraffa, "Dr. Hayek on Money and Capital," *Economic Journal*, vol. 2, March 1932, pp. 42–53.

21 Ibid.

22 F. A. Hayek, "Money and Capital: A Reply," *Economic Journal*, vol. 2, June 1932, pp. 237–249.

23 Piero Sraffa, "A Rejoinder," *Economic Journal*, vol. 42, June 1932, pp. 249–251.

24 Letter from Knight to Oskar von Morganstern, May 4, 1933, Oskar von Morganstern papers, Duke University, Durham, N.C.

25 John Cunningham Wood and Robert D. Wood, eds., *Friedrich A. Hayek* (Taylor & Francis, London, 2004), p. 200.

26 Lachmann, *Expectations and the Meaning of Institutions*, p. 148.

Chapter Nine: Toward *The General Theory*

1 As late as December 1933, Keynes's provisional title for what became *The General Theory* was "The Monetary Theory of Production." He may have been encouraged to change the title for fear of being confused with Hayek's *Monetary Theory and the Trade Cycle* published the same year.

2 Skidelsky, *John Maynard Keynes*, vol. 2: *Economist as Savior*, p. 459.

3 Letter from Keynes to Lydia, March 5, 1933, quoted in ibid.

4 Foreword, in Gerald O'Driscoll, *Economics as a Coordination Problem* (Andrews & McMeel, Kansas City, 1977), p. ix.

5 Mark Blaug, *Great Economists since Keynes: An Introduction to the Lives and Works of One Hundred Modern Economists* (Edward Elgar, Cheltenham, U.K., 1998), p. 94.

6 Harrod, *Life of John Maynard Keynes*, p. 452.

7 Ibid., p. 453.

8 Kahn, *Making of Keynes' General Theory*, p. 178.

9 Don Patinkin and J. Clark Leith, eds., *Keynes, Cambridge and "The General Theory,"* Proceedings of a Conference at the University of Western Ontario (Macmillan, London, 1977).

10 Kahn, *Making of Keynes' General Theory*, p. 106.

11 Austin Robinson, "John Maynard Keynes, 1883–1946," *Economic Journal*, March 1947, p. 40.

12 *Collected Writings*, vol. 5: *Treatise on Money*, p. 125.

13 Kahn, *Making of Keynes' General Theory*, p. 107.

14 *Collected Writings*, vol. 13: *General Theory and After, Part 1*, p. 270.

15 In fact Keynes was already well on his way to addressing what determined the volume of output. In a letter to the Treasury economist Ralph Hawtrey in response to comments on *A Treatise*, he wrote, "I am not dealing with the complete set of causes which determine volume of output. For this would have led me [on] an endlessly long journey into the theory of short-period supply and a long way from monetary theory [the nominal subject of *A Treatise*]. . . . If I were to write the book again, I should probably attempt to probe further into the difficulties of the latter." Ibid., pp. 145–146.

16 Kahn, *Making of Keynes' General Theory*, p. 175.

17 Ibid., p. 178.

18 Ibid., p. 177.

19 *Collected Writings*, vol. 9: *Essays in Persuasion*, p. 106.

20 Ibid.

21 Kahn, *Making of Keynes' General Theory*, p. 93.

22 Ibid.

23 Ibid., p. 94.

24 Ibid., p. 95.

25 Ibid., p. 98.

26 Letter from Dennis Robertson to Keynes, in *Collected Writings*, vol. 29: *The General Theory and After: A Supplement* (Macmillan for the Royal Economic Society, London, 1979), p. 17.

27 Kahn, *Making of Keynes' General Theory*, p. 100.

28 Ibid., p. 104.

29 L. Tarshis, "The Keynesian Revolution: What It Meant in the 1930s," unpublished typescript, quoted in Skidelsky, *John Maynard Keynes*, vol. 2: *Economist as Savior*, p. 460.

30 Ibid.

31 Quoted in Turner, *Joan Robinson and the Americans*, p. 55.

32 J. M. Keynes, *The Means to Prosperity* (Macmillan, London, 1933), p. 6.

33 Ibid., p. 10.

34 Ibid., p. 12.

35 Ibid., p. 15.

36 Ibid., p. 14.

37 Ibid., p. 16.

38 Harrod, *Life of John Maynard Keynes*, p. 441.

39 Keynes, *Means to Prosperity*, p. 19.

40 Harrod, *Life of John Maynard Keynes*, p. 443.

41 Keynes, *Means to Prosperity*, p. 27.

42 Ibid., p. 31.

43 Ibid., p. 22.

Chapter Ten: Hayek Blinks

1 *Collected Works*, vol. 9: *Contra Keynes and Cambridge*, p. 173.

2 J. M. Keynes, *A Treatise on Money* (Macmillan, London, 1930), p. 199, footnote.

3 P. M. Toms correspondence with Alan Ebenstein, quoted in Alan Ebenstein, *Friedrich Hayek: A Biography* (Palgrave, New York, 2001), p. 75.

4 John Richard Hicks, *Money, Interest, and Wages*, vol. 2 of *Collective Essays on Economic Theory* (Harvard University Press, Cambridge, Mass., 1982), p. 3.

5 Theodore Draimin correspondence with Alan Ebenstein, August 2 1995, quoted in Ebenstein, *Friedrich Hayek*, p. 75.

6 Ralph Arakie letter in the LSE archive, quoted in ibid., p. 74.

7 Aubrey Jones (1911–2003), British Conservative minister who in 1965 became head of the Labour government's Prices and Incomes Board regulating pay and prices.

8 Joan Abse, ed., *My LSE* (Robson Books, London, 1977), p. 35.

9 F. A. Hayek, "Monetary Theory and the Trade Cycle," Ludwig von Mises Institute, September 27, 2008, http://mises.org/daily/3121.

10 Though, as Milton Friedman was later to contend, this was, indeed, the case.

11 F. A. Hayek, *Monetary Theory and the Trade Cycle* (Jonathan Cape, London, 1933), p. 19.

12 Ibid., p. 23.

13 D. H. Macgregor, A. C. Pigou, J. M. Keynes, Walter Layton, Arthur Salter, and J. C. Stamp, Letter to the Editor, *The Times* (London), October 17, 1932.

14 T. E. Gregory, F. A. von Hayek, Arnold Plant, and Lionel Robbins, Letter to the Editor, *The Times* (London), October 18, 1932.

15 Hayek Archive, Hoover Institution, Stanford, Calif., box 105, folder 10. The memorandum is dated "Spring 1933."

16 Hayek, *Hayek on Hayek*, p. 102. Here Hayek dated his memo 1939, but Bruce Caldwell, in *Collected Works*, vol. 2: *The Road to Serfdom: Text and Documents, The Definitive Edition* (University of Chicago Press, Chicago, 2007), p. 5, believes he was mistaken and that the memo was most probably written in May or June 1933.

17 F. A. Hayek, *Individualism and Economic Order* (University of Chicago Press, Chicago, 1948), p. 87.

18 Hayek, *Hayek on Hayek*, p. 100.

19 *Collected Writings*, vol. 13: *General Theory and After, Part 1*, p. 492.

20 J. M. Keynes, *The General Theory of Employment, Interest and Money*, English edition (Macmillan, London, 1936), preface.

21 Paul Anthony Samuelson (1915–2009), MIT professor of economics, prominent post-Keynesian, and first American to win the Nobel Prize in economics, in 1970. Author of the all-time best-selling economics textbook, *Economics:*

An Introductory Analysis (McGraw-Hill, New York, 1948), and adviser to Presidents John F. Kennedy and Lyndon B. Johnson.

22 Paul A. Samuelson, *The Collected Scientific Papers of Paul A. Samuelson*, ed. Joseph E. Stiglitz, vol. 2 (MIT Press, Cambridge, Mass., 1966), p. 1521.

23 John Kenneth Galbraith (1908–2006), Canadian-born Harvard economist and key adviser to John F. Kennedy.

24 John Kenneth Galbraith, "General Keynes," *New York Review of Books*, November 22, 1983.

25 Harrod, *Life of John Maynard Keynes*, p. 451.

26 J. M. Keynes, *The General Theory of Employment, Interest and Money* (Macmillan, 1936; facsimile reprinted by Harcourt, Orlando, Fla.), p. 34.

27 Ibid., p. 3.

28 Ibid., p. 16.

29 In the words of the philosophy that underpins the plot of the 1989 movie *Field of Dreams*, "If you build it, they will come."

30 Keynes, *General Theory* (Macmillan, 1936; facsimile reprinted by Harcourt, Orlando, Fla.), p. 19.

31 Ibid., p. 21.

32 Ibid., p. 179.

33 Ibid., p. 211.

34 Ibid., p. 129.

35 Ibid., p. 130.

36 Ibid., p. 379.

37 J. M. Keynes, *The General Theory of Employment, Interest and Money*, German edition (Duncker & Humblot, Berlin, 1936), preface.

38 Keynes, *General Theory* (Macmillan, 1936), p. 379.

39 Ibid., p. 380.

40 Interview of Robert Skidelsky, July 18, 2000, for *Commanding Heights: The Battle for the World Economy*, PBS, http://www.pbs.org/wgbh/commanding heights/shared/minitext/int_robertskidelsky.html.

41 Keynes, *General Theory*, (Macmillan, 1936), p. 378.

42 Ibid., p. 60.

43 Ibid., p. 80.

44 Ibid., p. 214.

Chapter Eleven: Keynes Takes America

1 Harrod, *Life of John Maynard Keynes*, p. 448.

2 Keynes, *Economic Consequences of the Peace*, p. 84.

3 Ibid., p. 85.

4 Ibid.

5 Ibid., p. 41.

6 J. M. Keynes, "The Consequences of the Banks Collapse of Money," *Vanity Fair*, January 1932.

7 Roosevelt coined the term when accepting the 1932 Democratic nomination for president, promising "a new deal for the American people."

8 Jonathan Alter, *The Defining Moment: FDR's Hundred Days and the Triumph of Hope* (Simon & Schuster, New York, 2006), p. 2.

9 Arthur M. Schlesinger Jr. (1917–2007), American historian of liberal causes and "court historian" of the Kennedy family, whose *A Thousand Days* (1968) romanticized JFK's brief reign.

10 Arthur M. Schlesinger Jr., *The Coming of the New Deal* (Mariner Books, New York, 2003), p. 3.

11 Felix Frankfurter (1882–1965), associate justice of the U.S. Supreme Court.

12 Skidelsky, *John Maynard Keynes*, vol. 2: *Economist as Savior*, p. 492.

13 Letter from Frankfurter to Roosevelt, December 6, 1933, in Max Freedman, ed., *Roosevelt and Frankfurter: Their Correspondence, 1928–1945* (Atlantic-Little, Brown, Boston, 1976), p. 177.

14 Keynes's open letter in full, in Freedman, *Roosevelt and Frankfurter*, pp. 178–183.

15 "Professor" in this sense is the American term denoting simply a university teacher. Keynes was not nor ever became a professor in the English sense. As he once remarked to a filmmaker in 1930, "Don't let them put 'professor' on the screen. I don't want the indignity without the emoluments." Quoted in Milo Keynes, ed., *Essays on John Maynard Keynes* (Cambridge University Press, Cambridge, U.K., 1975), p. 249, footnote.

16 Letter from Roosevelt to Frankfurter, December 22, 1933, in Freedman, *Roosevelt and Frankfurter*, pp. 183–184

17 At the encouragement of O. T. Falk and Geoffrey Marks, Keynes became a member of the board of the National Mutual Life Assurance Society in London in 1919 and chairman two years later, a position he held until 1938. In 1923, Keynes also joined the board of the Provincial Insurance Company and directed investment policy, a position he held until he died.

18 Letter from Frankfurter to Roosevelt, May 7, 1934, in Freedman, *Roosevelt and Frankfurter*, p. 213.

19 Note from Roosevelt to Miss LeHand, in ibid., p. 215.

20 Skidelsky, *John Maynard Keynes*, vol. 2: *Economist as Savior*, p. 505.

21 Harrod, *Life of John Maynard Keynes*, p. 20.

22 Herbert Stein, *On the Other Hand—Essays on Economics, Economists, and Politics* (AEI Press, Washington, D.C., 1995), p. 85.

23 Frances Perkins, *The Roosevelt I Knew* (Viking Press, New York, 1946), p. 226.

24 Ibid.

25 Ibid.

26 Ibid., p. 225.

27 Letter from Frankfurter to Roosevelt, in Freedman, *Roosevelt and Frankfurter*, p. 222.

28 Letter from Roosevelt to Frankfurter in ibid.

29 Letter from Lippmann to Keynes, April 17, 1934, quoted in Harrod, *Life of John Maynard Keynes*, p. 450.

30 Ronald Steel, *Walter Lippmann and the American Century* (Bodley Head, London, 1981), p 308.

31 Ted Morgan, *FDR: A Biography* (Simon & Schuster, New York, 1985), p. 409.

32 Skidelsky, *John Maynard Keynes*, vol. 2: *The Economist as Savior*, p. 508.

33 J. M. Keynes, Speech to the American Political Economy Club, quoted in *Collected Writings*, vol. 13: *General Theory and After, Part 1*, p. 462.

34 William Rogers Louis, *Adventures with Britannia: Personalities, Politics, and Culture in Britain* (I. B. Tauris, London, 1997), p. 191.

35 John Kenneth Galbraith, *A Life in Our Times* (Houghton Mifflin, Boston, 1981), p. 68.

36 Galbraith was to be disappointed. Keynes was absent from Cambridge, recovering from one of what was to be a series of ominous heart attacks.

37 Galbraith, *Life in Our Times* (Houghton Mifflin, 1981), p. 70.

38 Marriner Stoddard Eccles (1890–1977), chairman of the Federal Reserve (1934–48).

39 U.S. Senate, *Evidence to the Senate Finance Committee Investigation of Economic Problems: Hearings, 72nd Congress, 2nd Session. February 13–28, 1933* (Government Printing Office, Washington, D.C., 1933), p. 8.

40 Ibid., p. 9.

41 Ibid., p. 21.

42 Richard Parker, *John Kenneth Galbraith: His Life, His Politics, His Economics* (Farrar, Straus & Giroux, New York, 2005), p. 95.

43 Keynes, *Essays on John Maynard Keynes*, p. 135.

44 William Breit and Roger W. Spencer, eds., *Lives of the Laureates: Seven Nobel Economists* (MIT Press, Cambridge, Mass., 1986), p. 98.

45 Ibid.

46 Ibid.

47 Keynes, *Essays on John Maynard Keynes*, p. 136.

48 Paul A. Samuelson in Robert Lekachman, ed., *Keynes' General Theory: Reports of Three Decades* (St. Martin's Press, New York, 1964), pp. 315–316.

49 Keynes, *Essays on John Maynard Keynes*, p. 136.

50 Ibid.

51 Robert Broughton Bryce (1910–97), Canadian deputy minister of finance (1963–68).

52 Galbraith, *Life in Our Times* (Houghton Mifflin, 1981), p. 90.

53 Keynes, *Essays on John Maynard Keynes*, p. 136.

54 John Kenneth Galbraith, *The Essential Galbraith*, ed. Andrea D. Williams (Mariner Books, Boston, 2001), p. 242.

55 According to JSTOR, quoted in Parker, *John Kenneth Galbraith*, p. 94.

56 Keynes, *Essays on John Maynard Keynes*, p. 138.

Chapter Twelve: Hopelessly Stuck in Chapter 6

1 F. A. Hayek, "The Economics of the 1930s as Seen from London," Lecture at the University of Chicago, 1963, published in *Collected Works*, vol. 9: *Contra Keynes and Cambridge*, p. 60.

2 Robbins, *Autobiography of an Economist*, p. 151.

3 Pigou, *Economics in Practice*, pp. 23–24.

4 Arthur Pigou, "Mr. J. M. Keynes' General Theory of Employment, Interest and Money," *Economica* (New Series), vol. 3, no. 10, May 1936, pp. 115–132.

5 *Collected Writings*, vol. 29: *General Theory and After: Supplement*, p. 208.

6 *Collected Works*, vol. 9: *Contra Keynes and Cambridge*, p. 241.

7 Ibid.

8 Ibid.

9 F. A. Hayek, "The Keynes Centenary: The Austrian Critique," *Economist*, June 11, 1983, pp. 45–48, reproduced in *Collected Works*, vol. 9: *Contra Keynes and Cambridge*, p. 247.

10 *Collected Works*, vol. 9: *Contra Keynes and Cambridge*, p. 251.

11 The Rockefeller Research Fund Committee was already funding one research assistant, E. S. Tucker, whom Hayek shared with Robbins.

12 Minutes of Rockefeller Research Fund Committee meetings of December 14, 1933, LSE Archives, London.

13 Gottfried von Haberler (1900–95), Austrian-born economist and student of Mises who advocated free trade and moved to Harvard University in 1936, where he worked closely with Joseph Schumpeter.

14 Letter from Hayek to Haberler, February 15, 1936, Haberler, Hoover Institution, Stanford, Calif., box 67, quoted in Susan Howson, "Why Didn't Hayek Review Keynes's *General Theory*? A Partial Answer," *History of Political Economy*, vol. 33, no. 2, 2001, pp. 369–374.

15 Letter from Hayek to Haberler, March 15, 1936, Haberler Papers, box 67.

16 Ibid.

17 Ibid., May 3, 1936, Haberler Papers, box 67.

18 For a fuller account of Hayek's grand scheme, see Lawrence H. White's introduction to *Collected Works*, vol. 12: *The Pure Theory of Capital* (University of Chicago Press, Chicago, 2007), pp. xvii–xxi.

19 Fritz Machlup (1902–83), Austrian-born economist and student of Mises who fled from Nazism to America in 1933. He introduced the notion of "knowledge" as a key dimension in understanding economics.

20 Hayek, *Individualism and Economic Order*, p. 43.

21 Ibid.

22 *Collected Works*, vol. 9: *Contra Keynes and Cambridge*, p. 62.

23 Ebenstein, *Friedrich Hayek*, p. 79.

24 John Kenneth Galbraith, *A Life in Our Times* (Houghton Mifflin, New York, 1981), p. 78.

25 Ibid.

26 Ebenstein, *Friedrich Hayek*, p. 64.

27 Paul Samuelson, "A Few Remembrances of Friedrich von Hayek (1899–1992)."

28 Milton Friedman (1912–2006), Nobel Prize–winning father of monetarism and prominent member of the Chicago School of economics.

29 Ebenstein, *Friedrich Hayek*, p. 81.

30 F. A. Hayek, *The Pure Theory of Capital* (University of Chicago Press, Chicago, 2009), p. vi.

31 Ibid., p. viii.

32 Hayek, *Hayek on Hayek*, p. 142.

33 Ibid., p. 141.

34 Hayek, *Pure Theory of Capital*, p. 5.

35 Ibid., p. 374.

36 Ibid.

37 Ibid., p. 406, footnote.

38 Ibid., p. 408.

39 Ibid., p. 452.

40 Ibid., p. 441.

41 Ibid., p. 410.

42 Ibid., p. 440.

43 Ibid.

44 Friedrich August von Hayek, "The Pretence of Knowledge," prize lecture to the Nobel Awards committee, December 11, 1974, nobelprize.org/nobel_prizes/economics/laureates/1974/hayek-lecture.html (accessed February 2011).

45 Hayek, *Pure Theory of Capital*, p. 471.

Chapter Thirteen: The Road to Nowhere

1 Patrick J. Maney, *The Roosevelt Presence: The Life and Legacy of FDR* (University of California Press, Berkeley, 1992), pp. 102–103.

2 The federal deficit was cut from $4.6 billion in 1936 to $2.7 billion in 1937.

Franklin Delano Roosevelt, *FDR's Fireside Chats*, ed. Russell D. Buhite and David W. Levy (University of Oklahoma Press, Norman, 1992), p. 111.

3 Thomas Emerson Hall and J. David Ferguson, *The Great Depression: An International Disaster of Perverse Economic Policies* (University of Michigan Press, Ann Arbor, 1998), p. 151.

4 Franklin D. Roosevelt, "On the Current Recession," broadcast April 14, 1938, *Roosevelt's Fireside Chats,* New Deal Network, http://newdeal.feri.org/chat/chat12.htm.

5 Letter from Keynes to Roosevelt, February 1, 1938, in *Collected Writings,* vol. 21: *Activities 1931–39: World Crises and Policies in Britain and America* (1982) (Macmillan for Royal Economic Society, London, 1982).

6 Murray Newton Rothbard, *America's Great Depression* (Ludwig von Mises Institute, Auburn, Ala., 2000), p. xv.

7 Ibid.

8 Ibid.

9 F. D. Roosevelt, speech in Boston, October 1940, in Robert Dallek, *Franklin D. Roosevelt and American Foreign Policy, 1932–1945* (Oxford University Press, New York, 1979), p. 250.

10 J. M. Keynes, "Will Rearmament Cure Unemployment?" BBC broadcast, June 1939, reproduced in *Listener*, June, 1, 1939, pp. 1142–1143.

11 Hall and Ferguson, *Great Depression*, p. 155.

12 Interview of J. K. Galbraith, September 28, 2000, *Commanding Heights*, PBS, http://www.pbs.org/wgbh/commandingheights/shared/minitext/int_john kennethgalbraith.html.

13 Some have cast doubt on the link between war expenditure and the end of the Great Depression, chief among them Christina Romer, President Obama's chair of the Council of Economic Advisers in 2009–10. See Christina D. Romer, "Changes in Business Cycles: Evidence and Explanations," *Journal of Economic Perspectives*, vol. 13, no. 2, Spring 1999, pp. 23–24.

14 *Collected Works*, vol. 10: *Socialism and War: Essays, Documents, Review,* ed. Bruce Caldwell (Liberty Fund, Indianapolis, 1997), p. 36.

15 Hayek, *Hayek on Hayek*, p. 94.

16 Robert Skidelsky, *John Maynard Keynes*, vol. 3: *Fighting for Freedom 1937–1946* (Viking, New York, 2000), p. 47.

17 Collected Writings, vol. 9: *Essays in Persuasion*, p. 410.

18 John Allsebrook Simon, 1st Viscount Simon (1873–1954), home secretary, foreign secretary, chancellor of the exchequer, and lord chancellor. His support of Chamberlain's appeasement policy toward Hitler ensured that Churchill did not invite him into the British wartime cabinet.

19 Skidelsky, *John Maynard Keynes*, vol. 3: *Fighting for Freedom*, p. 52.

20 Hayek, "Mr Keynes and War Costs," *Spectator*, November 24, 1939, in *Collected Works*, vol. 10: *Socialism and War*, p. 164.

21 Ibid., p. 171.

22 Ibid., p. 164.

23 Ibid., p. 166.

24 Ibid., pp. 167–168.

25 Hayek, *Hayek on Hayek*, p. 91.

26 Ibid., p 98.

27 Ibid., p. 91.

28 Hayek took the title from Tocqueville, "who speaks about the road to servitude. I would like to have chosen that, but it doesn't sound good. So I changed 'servitude' to 'serfdom,' for merely phonetic reasons." *Collected Works*, vol. 2: *Road to Serfdom*, p. 256, footnote.

29 Ebenstein, *Friedrich Hayek*, p. 114.

30 Hayek Archive, Hoover Institution, quoted in ibid., p. 129.

31 Letter from Hayek to Lippmann, quoted in Gary Dean Best, "Introduction," in Walter Lippmann, *The Good Society* (Transaction Publishers, Piscataway, N.J., 2004), p. xxxi.

32 *Collected Works*, vol. 2: *Road to Serfdom*, p. 137. For a full account of how Hayek intended *The Road to Serfdom* to fit into his broader *Abuse of Reason* schema, see *Collected Works*, vol. 13: *Studies on the Abuse and Decline of Reason*, ed. Bruce Caldwell (University of Chicago Press, Chicago, 2010).

33 Ibid., p. 67.

34 Ibid., p. 58.

35 Hayek quoted Keynes, "The Economics of War in Germany," *Economic Journal*, vol. 25, September 1915, p. 450, referring to the "nightmare" of reading a German author advocating the continuation of the military ethos in peacetime industrial life. *Collected Works*, vol. 2: *Road to Serfdom*, p. 195, footnote.

36 F. A. Hayek, Preface to the original edition of *The Road to Serfdom*, in *Collected Works*, vol. 2: *Road to Serfdom*, p. 37.

37 *Collected Works*, vol. 2: *Road to Serfdom*, pp. 148–149.

38 Ibid.

39 Ibid., p. 214.

40 Hayek, Preface to the 1976 edition of *The Road to Serfdom*, in *Collected Works*, vol. 2: *Road to Serfdom*, p. 55.

41 *Collected Works*, vol. 2: *Road to Serfdom*, pp. 58–59.

42 Ibid., p. 105.

43 Hayek, Preface to the 1956 American edition of *The Road to Serfdom*, in *Collected Works*, vol. 2: *Road to Serfdom*, p. 37.

44 Letter from Keynes to Hayek, April 4, 1944, LSE Archives, London.

45 *Collected Writings*, vol. 17: *Activities 1920–2: Treaty Revision and Reconstruction* (Macmillan for the Royal Economic Society, London, 1977), pp. 385–387.

46 Chicago Round Table, quoted in Ebenstein, *Friedrich Hayek*, p. 126.

47 *Collected Works*, vol. 2: *Road to Serfdom*, p. 148.

48 *Collected Writings*, vol. 17: *Activities 1920–2*, pp. 385–387.

49 Interview of Hayek by Thomas W. Hazlitt, 1977, published in *Reason*, July 1992, http://reason.com/archives/1992/07/01/the-road-from-serfdom.

50 *Collected Works*, vol. 2: *Road to Serfdom*, p. 118.

51 Ibid., p. 148.

52 Ibid., pp. 249–250.

53 Henry Hazlitt, "An Economist's View of 'Planning,'" review of *The Road to Serfdom*, by F. A. Hayek, *The New York Times*, September 24, 1944, Sunday Book Review, p. 1.

54 Max Forrester Eastman (1883–1969), wide-ranging American author who condemned Soviet communism after a visit there in 1923 but remained committed to leftist views until 1941, when he began writing conservative commentaries for *Reader's Digest*.

55 George Orwell, nom de plume of English author and socialist political campaigner against totalitarianism Eric Arthur Blair (1903–50).

56 George Orwell, "Grounds for Dismay," *Observer*, London, April 9, 1944.

57 Barbara Wootton née Adam, Baroness Wootton of Abinger (1897–1988), British economist, sociologist, and criminologist. In 1968 Harold Wilson's government commissioned her to officially investigate the implications of cannabis use. Her recommendation in the "Wootton Report" (1969) that possession of small amounts of the drug should not be a crime was ignored.

58 UCLA Oral History Program, p. 229.

59 Barbara Wootton, *Freedom under Planning* (G. Allen & Unwin, London, 1945).

60 Harold Macmillan wrote in his memoir that Churchill was "fortified in his apprehensions by reading Professor Hayek's 'The Road to Serfdom.'" *Tides of Fortune* (Macmillan, London, 1969), p. 32.

61 Clement Richard Attlee, Earl Attlee (1883–1967), British politician, leader of the Labour Party (1935–55), Churchill's deputy in the wartime coalition, and prime minister (1945–51) who presided over the foundation of the comprehensive welfare state and the decolonization of India, Pakistan, Sri Lanka, Burma, Palestine, and Jordan.

62 Quoted in Martin Gilbert, *Churchill: A Life* (Henry Holt, New York, 1991), p. 846.

63 Roy Harris Jenkins, Baron Jenkins of Hillhead (1920–2003), British Labour home secretary (twice), chancellor of the exchequer, and president of the Euro-

pean Union. He left the Labour Party to found the Social Democratic Party, which he led from 1982 to 1983.

64 Roy Jenkins, *Churchill* (Macmillan, London, 2001), p. 791.

65 Roy Jenkins, ed., *Purpose and Policy: Selected Speeches of C. R. Attlee* (Hutchinson, London, 1947), p. 3.

66 Tony Benn, in *Commanding Heights*, PBS, http://www.pbs.org/wgbh/commandingheights/shared/minitext/tr_show01.html.

67 F. A. Hayek, in ibid.

68 Alvin Hansen, "The New Crusade against Planning," *New Republic*, vol. 12, January 1, 1945, pp. 9–10.

69 Professor T. V. Smith (1890–1964), professor of philosophy at University of Chicago and House of Representative congressman from Illinois.

70 T. V. Smith, "*The Road to Serfdom*," book review, *Ethics* (University of Chicago Press, Chicago), vol. 55, no. 3 April 1945, p. 226.

71 Ibid., pp. 225–226.

72 Russell Kirk, James McClellan, and Jeffrey Nelson, *The Political Principles of Robert A. Taft* (Transaction Publishers, Piscataway, N.J., 2010), p. 86.

73 Ibid.

74 Herman Finer (1898–1969), British political scientist who taught at the universities of Chicago and Harvard.

75 Herman Finer, *The Road to Reaction* (Little, Brown, Boston, 1945), preface.

76 Ibid., p. ix.

77 Ayn Rand O'Connor, née Alissa Zinov'yevna Rosenbaum (1905–82), Russian-born American author, anticollectivist, polemicist, and screenwriter. She is best known for her didactic novels *The Fountainhead* (1943), filmed by King Vidor in 1949 starring Gary Cooper and Patricia Neal, and *Atlas Shrugged* (1957), filmed by Paul Johansson in 2010 starring himself.

78 Rand to Theodore J. Lowi, quoted in Theodore J. Lowi, *The End of the Republican Era* (University of Oklahoma Press, Norman, 2006), p. 22, footnote.

79 Rand quoted in Ayn Rand, *Ayn Rand's Marginalia: Her Critical Comments on the Writings of Over 20 Authors*, ed. Robert Mayhew (Second Renaissance Books, New Milford, Conn., 1995), pp. 145–160.

80 Hayek, *Hayek on Hayek*, p. 90.

81 *Collected Works*, vol. 9: *Contra Keynes and Cambridge*, p. 232.

82 UCLA Oral History Program, p. 117.

83 He suffered from bacterial endocarditis, an infection of the heart valves, an incurable condition before the era of antibiotics.

84 Skidelsky, *John Maynard Keynes*, vol. 3: *Fighting for Freedom*, p. 472.

85 Quoted in Ebenstein, *Friedrich Hayek*, p. 344.

86 Hayek, *Hayek on Hayek*, p. 143.

87 Ibid., p. 103.

Chapter Fourteen: The Wilderness Years

1 UCLA Oral History Program, p. 463.

2 Helen Elna Hokinson (1893–1949), American staff cartoonist at *The New Yorker* who specialized in portraying portly, proper, prim matrons of a certain age.

3 UCLA Oral History Program, p. 463.

4 Interview of Ralph Harris, July 17, 2000, *Commanding Heights*, PBS, http://www.pbs.org/wgbh/commandingheights/shared/minitext/int_ralphharris.html.

5 Hayek, *Hayek on Hayek*, p. 143.

6 Ralph Harris (1924–2006), ennobled by Margaret Thatcher as Baron Harris of High Cross, founder of the free-market think tank Institute of Economic Affairs, London.

7 Interview of Ralph Harris, July 17, 2000, *Commanding Heights*, PBS.

8 Ibid.

9 UCLA Oral History Program, p. 10.

10 *Collected Works*, vol. 4: *The Fortunes of Liberalism: Essays on Austrian Economics and the Ideal of Freedom*, ed. Peter G. Klein (University of Chicago Press, Chicago, 1992), p. 191.

11 Raymond-Claude-Ferdinand Aron (1905–83), French sociologist and social scientist, and friend of Jean-Paul Sartre.

12 Michael Polanyi, born Polányi Mihály (1891–1976), Hungarian-born English economist, chemist, and philosopher of science who fled Nazi Germany in 1933 to avoid Jewish persecution.

13 Wilhelm Röpke (1899–1966), the German economist whose ideas about the need to temper the depridations of the free market with "economic humanism" led to him help establish the highly successful postwar German social-market economy that underpinned the "German miracle."

14 Now the Hôtel Mirador.

15 Albert Hunold (1899–1981).

16 Philip Mirowski and Dieter Plehwe, *The Road from Mont Pèlerin: The Making of the Neoliberal Thought Collective* (Harvard University Press, Cambridge, Mass., 2009), p. 15.

17 George H. Nash (1945–), American historian, authority on Herbert Hoover, and author of *The Conservative Intellectual Movement in America since 1945* (Basic Books, New York, 1976).

18 Nash, *Conservative Intellectual Movement in America*, p. 26.

19 George Joseph Stigler (1911–91) who, after researching for the Manhattan Project, became a leading member of the University of Chicago School of Economics and protégé of Frank Knight, who won a Nobel Prize for economics in 1982.

20 John Jewkes (1902–88), professor of economic organization at Merton College, Oxford.

21 Sir Karl Raimund Popper (1902–94), former Marxist Viennese-born British scientific philosopher and advocate of the hypercritical liberal democratic tradition that forms the "open society."

22 Dame (Cicely) Veronica "C. V." Wedgwood (1910–97), English historian and biographer of leading figures of the sixteenth and seventeenth centuries, particularly the English Civil War and the Thirty Years' War.

23 Aaron Director (1901–2004), former leftist radical whose teaching at the University of Chicago Law School influenced leading right-leaning American justices, including Robert Bork, Richard Posner, Justice Antonin Scalia, and Chief Justice William Rehnquist.

24 Milton Friedman and Rose D. Friedman, *Two Lucky People: Memoirs* (University of Chicago Press, Chicago, 1998), p. 158.

25 Ibid.

26 Ibid., p. 159. After 1957, when his children were old enough to be left alone in the United States, Milton Friedman, often accompanied by his wife, Rose, made the annual Mont Pelerin meeting his summer vacation. He became president of the society in 1971.

27 Quoted in Friedman and Friedman, *Two Lucky People*, p. 159.

28 Ibid.

29 Paul Samuelson, "A Few Remembrances of Friedrich von Hayek (1899–1992)."

30 Interview of Milton Friedman, October 1, 2000, *Commanding Heights*, PBS, http://www.pbs.org/wgbh/commandingheights/shared/minitextlo/int_mil tonfriedman.html.

31 Samuelson, "A Few Remembrances of Friedrich von Hayek (1899–1992)."

32 Robbins's full Statement of Aims, April 8, 1947, The Mont Pelerin Society, http://www.montpelerin.org/montpelerin/mpsGoals.html.

33 *Collected Works*, vol. 4: *Fortunes of Liberalism*, p. 192.

34 Interview of Milton Friedman, October 1, 2000, *Commanding Heights*, PBS.

35 Quoted by William Buckley in his address to the Mont Pelerin Society, Hillsdale College, Hillsdale, Mich., August 26, 1975, in William F. Buckley Jr., *Let Us Talk of Many Things: The Collected Speeches* (Basic Books, New York, 2008), p. 224.

36 Stephen Kresge, "Introduction," in Hayek, *Hayek on Hayek*, p. 22.

37 UCLA Oral History Program, p. 395.

38 Ibid.

39 Hayek, *Hayek on Hayek*, p. 127.

40 Jacob Viner (1892–1970), cofounder of the Chicago School of economics who advised FDR's secretary of the Treasury, Henry Morgenthau, against attempting Keynesian remedies during the Great Depression. Viner taught Milton Friedman.

41 Quoted in Ebenstein, *Friedrich Hayek*, p. 174.

42 John Ulric Nef, *The Search for Meaning: The Autobiography of a Nonconformist* (Public Affairs Press, Washington, D.C., 1973), p. 37.

43 Ebenstein, *Friedrich Hayek*, p. 196.

44 F. A. Hayek, *The Constitution of Liberty* (University of Chicago Press, Chicago, 1960), p. 6.

45 Ibid., p. 87.

46 Ibid., p. 13.

47 Ibid., pp. 86–87.

48 Ibid., p. vi.

49 Ibid., p. 42.

50 Ibid., pp. 46–47.

51 Ibid., p. 397.

52 Ibid., p. 400.

53 Ibid., p. 402.

54 Ibid., p. 401.

55 Ibid., p. 403.

56 Ibid., p. 405.

57 Ibid.

58 Ibid.

59 Lionel Robbins, "Hayek on Liberty," *Economica* (New Series), vol. 28, no. 109, February 1961, p. 67.

60 Jacob Viner, "Hayek on Freedom and Coercion," *Southern Economic Journal*, vol. 27, no. 3, January 1961, p. 231.

61 Ibid., p. 235.

62 Ibid., p. 232.

63 Ibid., p. 235.

64 Ibid., pp. 235–236.

65 Ibid., p. 235.

66 Robbins, "Hayek on Liberty," p. 68.

67 Ibid., p. 80.

68 Ibid., pp. 79–80.

69 F. A. Hayek in *Commanding Heights*, PBS, http://www.pbs.org/wgbh/commandingheights/shared/minitextlo/tr_show01.html#1.

70 Robbins, *Autobiography of an Economist*, p. 154.

71 Ibid., p. 155.

72 Ralph Harris, in *Commanding Heights*, PBS, http://www.pbs.org/wgbh/commandingheights/shared/minitextlo/tr_show01.html#1.

73 Lawrence Hayek, in ibid.

74 Hayek–North/Skouken interview, quoted in Ebenstein, *Friedrich Hayek*, p. 252.

Chapter Fifteen: The Age of Keynes

1 Keynes had asked in his will for his ashes to be interred at King's College, but the executor, his brother Geoffrey, decided to scatter the ashes in Sussex.

2 Alexander Kerensky (1881–1970), prime minister of the Russian Provisional Government superceded by Vladimir Lenin after the October Revolution.

3 Alan Peacock, *Liberal News*, February 23, 1951.

4 Martin Gilbert, *Winston Churchill, the Wilderness Years* (Houghton Mifflin, New York, 1982), p. 31.

5 William Beveridge, *Full Employment in a Free Society* (Allen & Unwin, London, 1944), p. 135.

6 UCLA Oral History Project, p. 111.

7 Ibid., pp. 111–112.

8 Ibid., p. 111.

9 Articles 55 and 56, Charter of the United Nations, 1945, http://un.org/en/documents/charter/index.shtml.

10 Johannes Morsink, *The Universal Declaration of Human Rights: Origins, Drafting, and Intent* (University of Pennsylvania Press, Philadelphia, 2000), p. 160.

11 Robert J. Donovan, *Conflict and Crisis: The Presidency of Harry S. Truman, 1945–1948* (University of Missouri Press, Columbia, 1996), p. 112.

12 Franklin D. Roosevelt, "State of the Union Message to Congress," January 11, 1944, The American Presidency Project, http://www.presidency.ucsb.edu/ws/index.php?pid=16518.

13 James Murray (1876–1961), Canadian-born American who was a five-term senator for Montana.

14 Leon H. Keyserling (1908–87), economist who was taught by Rexford Tugwell, an architect of the New Deal and a member of Franklin Roosevelt's brain trust. See W. Robert Brazelton, "The Economics of Leon Hirsch Keyserling," *Journal of Economic Perspectives*, vol. 11, no. 4, Fall 1997, pp. 189–197.

15 Oral history interview with Leon Keyserling by Jerry N. Hess, Washington, D.C., May 3, 1971, Harry S. Truman Library, Independence, Mo., pp. 25–26.

16 Full Employment Bill of 1945, in Stephen Kemp Bailey, *Congress Makes a Law: The Story behind the Employment Act of 1946* (Vintage, New York, 1964), p. 57.

17 U.S. Senate, *Assuring Full Employment in a Free Competitive Economy. Report from the Committee on Banking and Currency*, S. Rept. 583, 79th Congress, 1st session (Government Printing Office, Washington, D.C., September 22, 1945), p. 81.

18 Harry S. Truman (1884–1972), 33rd president of the United States (1945–53).

19 Full Employment Bill of 1945, section 2 (b–c).

20 Seymour E. Harris, "Some Aspects of the Murray Full Employment Bill," *Review of Economics and Statistics*, vol. 27, no. 3, August 1945, pp. 104–106.

21 Gottfried Haberler, "Some Observations on the Murray Full Employment Bill," *Review of Economics and Statistics*, vol. 27, no. 3, August 1945, pp. 106–109.

22 Employment Act of 1946, section 2.

23 Edwin Griswold Nourse (1883–1974), agricultural economist and chairman of the Council of Economic Advisers (1946–49).

24 Oral history interview with Edwin Nourse by Jerry N. Hess, Washington, D.C., March 7, 1972, Harry S. Truman Library, Independence, Mo., pp. 24–26.

25 David McCullough, *Truman* (Simon & Schuster, New York, 1992), p. 633.

26 Oral history interview with Leon Keyserling by Jerry N. Hess, Washington, D.C., May 10, 1971, p. 117.

27 Silvia Nasar, interview with Paul Samuelson, "Hard Act to Follow?" *The New York Times*, March 14, 1995.

28 Dwight David "Ike" Eisenhower (1890–1969), supreme commander of the Allied forces in Europe who directed the invasion of Nazi-occupied France and Germany in 1944 and became the 34th president of the United States (1953–61).

29 John W. Sloan, *Eisenhower and the Management of Prosperity* (University Press of Kansas, Lawrence, 1991), p. 13.

30 Arthur Frank Burns (1904–87), chairman of the Council of Economic Advisers under Eisenhower (1953–56) and chairman of the Federal Reserve (1970–78).

31 Burns speech, June 16, 1955, Dwight D. Eisenhower papers, Dwight D. Eisenhower Presidential Library and Museum, Abilene, Kans., Ann Whitman File, Administrative Series, box 10.

32 Parker, *John Kenneth Galbraith*, p. 319.

33 Editorial, "People's Success Story," *Life*, August 1, 1960, p. 20.

34 Defense spending amounted to at least half of all federal spending throughout the 1950s. In the 1960s the figure was $48.1 billion in a $92.2 billion federal budget. U.S. Office of Management and Budget, *Historical Tables: Budget of the United States Government, 2006* (Government Printing Office, Washington, D.C., 2005).

35 James Oberg, *NBC News*, April 27, 2004.

36 Richard Hofstadter, *American Perspective*, vol. 4 (Foundation for Foreign Affairs, Washington, D.C., 1950), p. 35.

37 Federal defense contracts were awarded to large corporations such as Lockheed, Grumman, Hughes, Litton Industries, TRW, General Motors, IBM, and General Electric.

38 Dwight D. Eisenhower, "Farewell Address," January 17, 1961, The American Presidency Project, www.presidency.ucsb.edu.

39 Eisenhower news conference, November 5, 1958, The American Presidency Project, http://www.presidency.ucsb.edu/ws/index.php?pid=11286.

40 Richard Milhous Nixon (1913–94), 36th vice president (1953–61) and 37th president of the United States (1969–74).

41 John Fitzgerald "Jack" Kennedy (1917–63), 35th president of the United States (1961–63).

42 Stein, *On the Other Hand*, p. 85.

43 John Kenneth Galbraith, *Ambassador's Journal* (Houghton Mifflin, New York, 1969), p. 48.

44 William McChesney Martin Jr. (1906–98), longest-serving chairman of the Federal Reserve, from April 1951 to January 1970, and the son of the architect of the Federal Reserve Act, William McChesney Martin.

45 When Leon Keserling complained to Kennedy that he was appointing too many conservatives to key positions, Kennedy retorted, "You don't realize that I only got elected by one half of one per cent," to which Keserling responded, "I suppose that if Dick Nixon had been elected by one half of one percent, he would have appointed me Secretary of the Treasury to please the liberals." Oral history interview with Leon Keyserling by Jerry N. Hess, Washington, D.C., May 10, 1971, p. 94.

46 Walter Wolfgang Heller (1915–87), chair of economics at the University of Minnesota. Helped design the Marshall Plan of 1947 that reinvigorated Europe after World War II. Suggested to Lyndon Johnson the "War on Poverty."

47 Kermit Gordon (1916–76), later president of the Brookings Institution who oversaw the first budget of Johnson's Great Society.

48 John F. Kennedy, "State of the Union Message to Congress," February 2, 1961, The American Presidency Project, http://www.presidency.ucsb.edu/ws/index.php?pid=8111&st=kennedy&st1=congress.

49 Michael O'Brien, *John F. Kennedy: A Biography* (Macmillan, London, 2006), p. 637.

50 Arthur M. Schlesinger Jr., *A Thousand Days: John F. Kennedy in the White House* (Houghton Mifflin, New York, 1965), p. 630.

51 Quoted from various sources in Parker, *John Kenneth Galbraith*, p. 340.

52 Oral history interview with Leon Keyserling by Jerry N. Hess, Washington, D.C., May 10, 1971, p. 94.

53 JFK speech to the Economic Club of New York, December 14, 1962, John F. Kennedy Presidential Library and Museum, http://www.jfklibrary.org/Historical+Resources/Archives/Reference+Desk/Speeches/Speeches+of+John+F.+Kennedy.htm.

54 Michael M. Weinstein, "Paul A. Samuelson, Economist, Dies at 94," *The New York Times*, December 13, 2009.

55 Robert M. Collins, *The Business Response to Keynes, 1929–1964* (Columbia University Press, New York, 1981), p. 192.

56 Evsey Domar (1914–97), Polish-born American economist who studied the link between deficits and economic growth.

57 Robert Merton Solow (1924–), American economist, at Columbia and MIT, and winner of the 1987 Nobel Prize for economics who identified the importance of technical innovation in economic growth.

58 William Phillips (1914–75), electrical engineer turned LSE economist who built an early analog computer and in 1958 postulated a link between changes in unemployment and inflation in his "Phillips curve."

59 Douglass Cater Oral History Interview II, by David G. McComb, May 8, 1969, Lyndon Baines Johnson Library and Museum, Austin, Tex., Oral History Collection, p. 16.

60 S. Douglass Cater (1923–95), special assistant to President Johnson.

61 "Kennedy Tax Cuts Boosted Revenue," Heritage Foundation, http://www .heritage.org/static/reportimages/1326E87331F4B5FC87405FF5C1BFC7EE .gif.

62 Bureau of Labor Statistics figures, www.bls.gov.

63 *Time*, December 31, 1965. Uncredited author.

64 "President Lyndon B. Johnson's Remarks at the University of Michigan," May 22, 1964, Lyndon Baines Johnson Library and Museum, http://www.lbjlib .utexas.edu/johnson/archives.hom/speeches.hom/640522.asp.

65 Barry Goldwater (1909–98), a conservative and libertarian thinker who was a five-term senator for Arizona and Republican presidential candidate in 1964.

66 Wilbur Mills (1909–92), congressman from Arkansas, chairman of the House Ways and Means Committee in the 1960s, and putative Democratic presidential candidate who lost to George McGovern at the 1972 convention.

67 Wilbur Mills Oral History Interview I, by David G. McComb, February 11, 1971, Lyndon Baines Johnson Library and Museum, Austin, Tex., Oral History Collection, p. 15.

68 Richard Nixon, "State of the Union Address," January 22, 1970, Miller Center of Public Affairs, University of Virginia, http://millercenter.org/scripps/ archive/speeches/detail/3889.

69 Paul McCracken (1915–), American economist.

70 Herbert Stein (1916–99) pro-welfare free-marketeer journalist and chairman of Nixon's Council of Economic Advisers.

71 George Shultz (1920–), Nixon's secretary of labor (1969–70), director of the Office of Management and Budget (1970–72), secretary of the Treasury (1972–74), then Ronald Reagan's secretary of state (1982–89).

72 U.S. Bureau of Labor Statistics (BLS): Current Population Survey (CPS) [Household Survey – LNS14000000], http://zimor.com/chart/Unemployment_Rate.

73 Stein, *On the Other Hand*, p. 96.

74 Nixon, "State of the Union Address," January 22, 1970.

75 Stein, *On the Other Hand*, p. 101.

76 Ibid.

77 Ibid., p. 105.

78 Interview of Milton Friedman, October 1, 2000, *Commanding Heights*, PBS, http://www.pbs.org/wgbh/commandingheights/shared/minitextlo/int_miltonfriedman.html.

79 John Connally (1917–93), nimble politician who played both sides of the aisle. He was JFK's secretary of the Navy; then the governor of Texas, who was wounded traveling in the same car as John F. Kennedy when he was assassinated in Dallas in November 1963; then Nixon's Treasury secretary.

80 Stein, *On the Other Hand*, p. 101.

81 Ibid., p. 102.

82 William Safire, "Do Something!" *The New York Times*, February 14, 1974.

83 Richard Nixon, *The Memoirs of Richard Nixon* (Arrow Books, London, 1979), p. 971.

84 George Shultz, in *Commanding Heights*, PBS, http://www.pbs.org/wgbh/commandingheights/shared/minitextlo/tr_show01.html#1.

85 The word is believed to have been coined by the British Conservative Party finance spokesman Iain Macleod in 1965, though its first use has also been credited to Paul Samuelson.

86 Gerald Ford (1913–2006), born Leslie Lynch King Jr., long-standing member of the House who was elevated to vice president, then became 38th president of the United States (1974–77) after Richard Nixon resigned in the wake of the Watergate scandal.

87 Alan Greenspan (1926–), chairman of the Federal Reserve (1987–2006).

88 Greenspan's confirmation hearings were held on the day Nixon resigned.

89 "Historical Inflation," InflationData.com, http://inflationdata.com/inflation/Inflation_Rate/HistoricalInflation.aspx?dsInflation_currentPage=2.

90 Interview of Milton Friedman, October 1, 2000, *Commanding Heights*, PBS.

91 Alan Greenspan, *The Age of Turbulence: Adventures in a New World* (Penguin, London, 2008), p. 72.

92 Officially known as the "Full Employment and Balanced Growth Act."

93 Canute (985–1035), Viking king of Denmark, England, Norway, and parts of Sweden.

94 Jimmy Carter, "'Crisis of Confidence' Speech," July 15, 1979, Miller Center of Public Affairs, University of Virginia, http://millercenter.org/scripps/archive/speeches/detail/3402.

95 Jimmy Carter, "Anti-Inflation Program Speech," October 24, 1978, Miller Center of Public Affairs, University of Virginia, http://millercenter.org/scripps/archive/speeches/detail/5547.

96 Paul Volcker (1927–), chairman of the Federal Reserve (1979–87) under

Presidents Carter and Reagan and chairman of President Obama's Economic Recovery Advisory Board (2008–).

Chapter Sixteen: Hayek's Counterrevolution

1 Aaron Director, "Review of F. A. Hayek, *The Road to Serfdom*," *American Economic Review*, vol. 35, no. 1, March 1945, p. 173.

2 Friedman and Friedman, *Two Lucky People*, p. 58.

3 Stanley Dennison (1912–92), lecturer in economics at Cambridge (1945–57) and vice-chancellor of the University of Hull (1972–80).

4 Milton Friedman and Anna D. Schwartz, *A Monetary History of the United States, 1867–1960* (Princeton University Press, Princeton, N.J., 1963).

5 Friedman's definitive account of his monetary theory was "The Quantity of Money—A Restatement, an Essay in Studies in the Quantity Theory of Money," in Friedman, ed., *Studies in the Quantity Theory of Money* (University of Chicago Press, Chicago, 1956).

6 Milton Friedman, "The Role of Monetary Policy," American Economic Association presidential address, December 29, 1967, in *American Economic Review*, vol. 58, no. 1, March 1968.

7 Milton Friedman, "John Maynard Keynes," in J. M. Keynes, *The General Theory of Employment, Interest and Money* (facsimile of 1936 edition reprinted by Verlag Wirtschaft und Finanzen GmbH, Düsseldorf, 1989), p. 11.

8 Robert J. Gordon, ed., *Milton Friedman's Monetary Framework: A Debate with His Critics* (University of Chicago Press, Chicago, 1974), pp. 133–134.

9 Friedman, "John Maynard Keynes," p. 20.

10 Ibid., pp. 21–22.

11 Friedman, "Foreword," in Fritz Machlup, *Essays on Hayek* (Routledge, London, 2003), p. xxi.

12 Friedman, "John Maynard Keynes," p. 21.

13 Barry M. Goldwater, *Conscience of a Conservative* (Victor, New York, 1960), p. 17.

14 Barry M. Goldwater with Jack Casserley, *Goldwater* (St. Martin's Press, New York, 1988), p. 140.

15 Goldwater, *Conscience of a Conservative*, p. 44.

16 Milton Friedman, "The Goldwater View of Economics," *The New York Times*, October 11, 1964.

17 Paul Samuelson, *The New York Times*, October 25, 1964.

18 Ronald Reagan (1911–2004), Hollywood actor, California governor, and 40th president of the United States.

19 Rowland Evans and Robert Novak, *The Reagan Revolution* (E. P. Dutton, New York, 1981), p. 237.

20 Ibid.

21 Ronald Reagan, "Time for Choosing," address broadcast on television, October 27, 1964.

22 Newton Leroy "Newt" Gingrich (1943–), born Newton Leroy McPherson. After completing a doctoral dissertation on Belgian education policy in the Congo from 1945 to 1960, he taught at West Georgia College before being elected to the House of Representatives in 1978. Speaker of the House of Representatives (1995–99).

23 Interview of Newt Gingrich, Spring 2001, *Commanding Heights*, PBS, http://www.pbs.org/wgbh/commandingheights/shared/pdf/int_newtgingrich.pdf.

24 Friedman and Friedman, *Two Lucky People*, p. 388.

25 Ibid., p. 386.

26 Ibid., pp. 386–387.

27 Milton Friedman, in "*Commanding Heights*, PBS, http://www/pbs.org/wgbh/commandingheights/shared/minitextlo/tr_show01.html#1.

28 Herbert Stein, *Presidential Economics* (Simon & Schuster, New York, 1985), p. 255.

29 Paul Samuelson, "A Few Remembrances of Friedrich von Hayek (1899–1992)."

30 Gunnar Myrdal (1898–1987), Swedish economist and government minister whose pioneering work on the living conditions of African-Americans is credited with the campaign to educate all Americans that culminated in the *Brown v. Board of Education* Supreme Court decision. Friedman, who met him a number of times at Columbia, thought him "awfully charming and intelligent." Friedman and Friedman, *Two Lucky People*, p. 78.

31 Ibid.

32 Interview of Ralph Harris, July 17, 2000, *Commanding Heights*, PBS, http://www.pbs.org/wgbh/commandingheights/shared/minitextlo/int_ralphharris.html.

33 George H. Nash, "Hayek and the American Conservative Movement," lecture given to the Intercollegiate Studies Institute Indianapolis Conference, Indianapolis, Ind., April 3 2004, www.isi.org/lectures/text/pdf/hayek4-3-04.pdf.

34 Hayek gave his Nobel address on December 11, 1974.

35 F. A. Hayek, "The Pretence of Knowledge," quoted in Assar Lindbeck, ed., *Nobel Lectures in Economic Sciences 1969–1980* (World Scientific, Singapore, 1992), p. 179.

36 UCLA Oral History Program, p. 195.

37 Milton Friedman, "Inflation and Unemployment," Nobel Memorial Lecture,

December, 13, 1976, http://nobelprize.org/nobel_prizes/economics/laureates/1976/friedman-lecture.pdf.

38 A full account of the leadership contest can be found in Nicholas Wapshott, *Ronald Reagan and Margaret Thatcher: A Political Marriage* (Sentinel, New York, 2007), pp. 76–82.

39 Ralph Harris doubts that this is the case, telling PBS *Commanding Heights* researchers in his interview on July 17, 2000, "I would be surprised whether a student of science at Oxford would have had on her reading list 'The Road to Serfdom' by Hayek. It wasn't widely available; it wasn't widely reviewed. It was [only] in certain intellectual papers."

40 John Ranelagh, *Thatcher's People: An Insider's Account of the Politics, the Power, and the Personalities* (HarperCollins, London, 1991), p. ix.

41 The consensus was dubbed "Butskellism" as it conflated two nearly identical approaches to government, that of the Conservative R. A. Butler and of Hugh Gaitskell, the Labour leader.

42 Nicholas Wapshott and George Brock, *Thatcher* (Macdonald/Futura, London, 1983), p. 176.

43 Interview of Ralph Harris, July 17, 2000, *Commanding Heights*, PBS.

44 Laurence Hayek, in *Commanding Heights*, PBS, http://www.pbs.org/wgbh/commandingheights/shared/minitextlo/tr_show01.html#1.

45 Margaret Thatcher, in ibid.

46 Nicholas Kaldor, *The Economic Consequences of Mrs. Thatcher: Speeches in the House of Lords, 1979–82*, ed. Nick Butler (Duckworth, London, 1983).

47 Margaret Thatcher, "The Lady's Not for Turning," *Guardian*, April 30, 2007, full text at http://www.guardian.co.uk/politics/2007/apr/30/conservatives.uk1. The phrase "The lady's not for turning" was adapted by Thatcher's chief phrase maker, the dramatist Ronald Millar, from the title of Christopher Fry's 1948 play *The Lady's Not for Burning*.

48 Thatcher, House of Commons, February 5, 1981. www.margaretthatcher.org/document/104593.

49 Thatcher, a state school pupil, adopted terms of abuse that her privately educated Tory opponents traditionally hurled at her. Thus she dismissed those with patrician values who resisted her hard-nosed economic policy as "wets," while those who agreed with her were called "dries." To discover on which side of the divide a Tory was, she would ask, "Is he one of us?"

50 For a full account of the implementation of Thatcher's monetarist policies, see Wapshott and Brock, *Thatcher*, pp. 183–212.

51 The conservative think tank is the Centre for Policy Studies, founded by Sir Keith Joseph and Margaret Thatcher and run by the former Marxist Alfred Sherman.

52 Jürg Niehans (1919–2007), Swiss monetarist economist and economic histo-

rian, and professor at the University of Bern and Johns Hopkins University (1966–77).

53 Milton Friedman, BBC interview, March 1983, quoted in Hugo Young, *The Iron Lady: A Biography of Margaret Thatcher* (Noonday Press, New York, 1990), p. 319.

54 Ronald Reagan, in *Commanding Heights*, PBS, http://www.pbs.org/wgbh/commandingheights/shared/minitextlo/tr_show01.html#1.

55 Martin Anderson (1936–), economist, senior policy adviser to the Reagan presidential campaigns of 1976 and 1980, and member of the Foreign Intelligence Advisory Board (1980–86).

56 Martin Anderson, *Revolution: The Reagan Legacy* (Harcourt Brace Jovanovich, San Diego, 1990), p. 267.

57 Paul Volcker, in *Commanding Heights*, PBS, http://www/pbs.org/wgbh/commandingheights/shared/minitextlo/tr_show01.html#1.

58 Ibid.

59 George Shultz, in *Commanding Heights*, PBS, http://www.pbs.org/wgbh/commandingheights/shared/minitextlo/tr_show01.html#1. Reagan stood firm on the need for a recession, but his Treasury secretary Donald Regan hedged his bets in case Reagan changed his mind, running a "Fed bashing" whispering campaign to the press and Congress that put blame for the bad economic news on Volcker.

60 Arthur Laffer (1940–), American fiscal conservative economist and libertarian and professor at the University of Chicago Graduate School of Business.

61 *Collected Writings*, vol. 9: *Essays in Persuasion*, p. 338.

62 Interview of Hayek, "Business People; A Nobel Winner Assesses Reagan," *The New York Times*, December 1, 1982.

63 John Kenneth Galbraith, "Recession Economics," *New York Review of Books*, February 4, 1982.

64 Mondale speech in Springfield, Ill., in Steven M. Gillon, *The Democrats' Dilemma: Walter F. Mondale and the Liberal Legacy* (Columbia University Press, New York, 1995), p. 371.

65 All figures from Arthur Laffer, *The Laffer Curve: Past, Present and Future*, Executive Summary Backgrounder No. 1765 (Heritage Foundation, Washington, D.C., June 2004).

66 Jerry Tempalski, "Revenue Effects of Major Tax Bills," OTA Working Paper 81, Office of Tax Analysis, U.S. Treasury Department, Washington, D.C., July 2003.

67 Milton Friedman, in *Commanding Heights*, PBS, http://www.pbs.org/wgbh/commandingheights/shared/minitext/tr_show01.html.

68 Defense figures expressed in constant 2000 dollars. U.S. Office of Management and Budget, *Historical Tables: Budget of the United States Government, 2006* (Government Printing Office, Washington, D.C., 2005), table 6.1.

69 Ibid.

70 John Case, "Reagan's Economic Legacy," *Inc.*, October 1, 1988.

71 Stein, *Presidential Economics*, p. 308.

72 Reagan speech to Gridiron Club, March 24, 1984, quoted in Lou Cannon, *President Reagan: The Role of a Lifetime* (PublicAffairs, New York, 2000), p. 100.

73 Quoted in Holcomb B. Noble, "Milton Friedman, Free Market's Theorist, Dies at 94," *The New York Times*, November 16, 2006.

74 Interview of John Kenneth Galbraith, September 28, 2000, *Commanding Heights*, PBS, http://www.pbs.org/wgbh/commandingheights/shared/minitext lo/int_johnkennethgalbraith.html.

Chapter Seventeen: The Battle Resumed

1 According to Tom G. Palmer, "The one name that you hear more than any other throughout Central and Eastern Europe is Friedrich Hayek. Underground, or samizdat, editions and rare English copies of *The Road to Serfdom* are widely read," Tom G. Palmer, "Why Socialism Collapsed in Eastern Europe," *Cato Policy Report*, September/October 1990.

2 John Cassidy, "The Price Prophet," *The New Yorker*, February 7, 2000.

3 Denis Winston Healey, Baron Healey (1917–), British chancellor of the exchequer (1974–79).

4 Denis Healey, *The Time of My Life* (Michael Joseph, London, 1989), p. 491.

5 Quoted in "Austerity Alarm," *Economist*, July 1, 2010, www.economist.com/node/16485318.

6 Alan S. Blinder, "The Fall and Rise of Keynesian Economics," *Economic Record*, December 1988.

7 Robert Emerson Lucas Jr. (1937–), University of Chicago economist, winner of the 1995 Nobel Prize for economics, and founder of New Keynesianism. He emphasized the importance of rational expectations in individual economic decisions and of microeconomic decisions in determining macroeconomic aggregates.

8 Quoted in Brian Snowdon and Howard R. Vane, *A Macroeconomics Reader* (Routledge, London, 1997), p. 445.

9 James K. Galbraith, *The Predator State: How Conservatives Abandoned the Free Market and Why Liberals Should Too* (Free Press, New York, 2008), p. 4.

10 Quoted in Kevin A. Hassett, "The Second Coming of Keynes," *National Review*, February 9, 2009.

11 UCLA Oral History Program, p. 195.

12 Robert E. Lucas Jr., "Macroeconomic Priorities," presidential address to the American Economic Association, January 10, 2003, http://home.uchicago .edu/%7Esogrodow/homepage/paddress03.pdf.

13 Yoshihiro Francis Fukuyama (1952–), American political economist.

14 Francis Fukuyama, *The End of History and the Last Man* (Simon & Schuster, New York, 1992).

15 Ben Bernanke (1953–), chairman of the Federal Reserve (2006–), chairman of George W. Bush's Council of Economic Advisers (2005–6).

16 Ben Bernanke, remarks at "A Conference to Honor Milton Friedman," University of Chicago, Chicago, November 8, 2002.

17 Michael Kinsley (1951–), American political journalist.

18 Michael Kinsley, "Greenspan Shrugged," *The New York Times*, October 14, 2007.

19 Greenspan, *Age of Turbulence*, p. 68.

20 George H. W. Bush (1924–), ambassador to the UN, director of the CIA, and 41st president of the United States (1989–93).

21 The "Greed Is Good" speech by Gordon Gekko, the hero of Oliver Stone's 1987 movie *Wall Street*, was based on a commencement address at the University of California, 1986, by the convicted inside-dealing stock trader Ivan Boesky, who said, "I think greed is healthy. You can be greedy and still feel good about yourself."

22 John Brian Taylor (1946–), American economist and Robert Raymond Professor of Economics at Stanford University.

23 George H. W. Bush attended Yale from 1945 to 1948.

24 A phrase coined by Bush's press secretary Peter Teeley and used by Bush in a speech before the Pennsylvania primary, in April 1978.

25 Michael Stanley Dukakis (1933–), governor of Massachusetts (1975–79, 1983–91) and Democratic presidential nominee (1988).

26 The line delivered by Bush to the 1988 Republican National Convention in New Orleans is credited to Reagan speechwriter Peggy Noonan.

27 Milton Friedman, "Oodoov Economics," *The New York Times*, February 2, 1992.

28 Quoted in Greenspan, *Age of Turbulence*, p. 113.

29 William Jefferson "Bill" Clinton, born William Jefferson Blythe III (1946–), governor of Arkansas and 42nd president of the United States (1993–2001).

30 This was subsequently described as "the biggest tax increase in history," though at $32 billion and 0.5 percent of GDP, it was a little less than Reagan's 1982 tax hike. See Tempalski, "Revenue Effects of Major Tax Bills."

31 Quoted in Tom DeLay with Stephen Mansfield, *No Retreat, No Surrender: One American's Fight* (Sentinel, New York, 2007), p. 115.

32 Newt Gingrich, Ed Gillespie, and Bob Schellhas, *Contract with America* (Times Books, New York, 1994), p. 7.

33 DeLay with Mansfield, *No Retreat, No Surrender*, p. 112.

34 Interview of Newt Gingrich, Spring 2001, *Commanding Heights*, PBS, http://

www/pbs.org/wgbh/commandingheights/shared/minitext/int_newtgingrich
.html.

35 DeLay with Mansfield, *No Retreat, No Surrender*, p. 112.

36 Ibid., p. 115.

37 *Collected Writings*, vol. 20: *Activities 1929–31*, p. 147.

38 Greenspan, *Age of Turbulence*, p. 147.

39 Kelly Wallace, "President Clinton Announces Another Record Budget Surplus," CNN report, September 27, 2000.

40 White House announcement, September 27, 2000, http://clinton4.nara.gov/WH/new/html/Tue_Oct_3_113400_2000.html.

41 Alan Greenspan, interview with Tim Russert, *Meet the Press*, NBC, September 23, 2000.

42 Greenspan, *Age of Turbulence*, p. 145.

43 William Jefferson Clinton, "State of the Union Address," January 23, 1996, http://clinton2.nara.gov/WH/New/other/sotu.html.

44 George Walker Bush (1946–), 43rd president of the United States (2001–9).

45 The prescription drug act cost an extra $500 billion over ten years.

46 Greenspan, *Age of Turbulence*, p. 233.

47 Ron Suskind, *The Price of Loyalty: George W. Bush, the White House, and the Education of Paul O'Neill* (Simon & Schuster, New York, 2004), p. 291.

48 The Vietnam War cost 9.5 percent of GDP; the Korean War 14 percent.

49 Quoted in Republican senators' newsletter the *American Sound*, November 19, 2003.

50 Gail Russell Chaddock, "US Spending Surges to Historic Level," *Christian Science Monitor*, December 8, 2003.

51 Stein, *Presidential Economics*, p. 313.

52 Dick Armey, "End of the Revolution," *Wall Street Journal*, November 9, 2006.

53 Alan Greenspan, testimony before the House Committee on Oversight and Government Reform, October 23, 2008, quoted in "Greenspan 'Shocked' That Free Markets Are Flawed," *The New York Times*, October 23, 2008.

54 J. M. Keynes, "The Great Slump of 1930" (1930), in *Collected Writings*, vol. 9: *Essays in Persuasion*, p. 126.

55 Alan Greenspan, "Markets and the Judiciary," Sandra Day O'Connor Project Conference, Georgetown University, Washington, D.C., October 2, 2008.

56 *Collected Writings*, vol. 13: *General Theory and After, Part 1*, p. 349.

57 Peter Clarke, *Keynes: The Rise, Fall, and Return of the 20th Century's Most Influential Economist* (Bloomsbury, New York, 2009), p. 19.

58 Interview of John Kenneth Galbraith, September 28, 2000, *Commanding Heights*, PBS, http://www.pbs.org/wgbh/commandingheights/shared/minitext/int_johnkennethgalbraith.html.

59 Justin Fox, "The Comeback Keynes," *Time*, October 23, 2008.

60 Ibid.

61 Ibid.

62 Chris Edwards, on *All Things Considered*, NPR, January 29, 2009.

63 Barack Hussein Obama II (1961–), senator for Illinois and 44th president of the United States, elected in 2008.

64 President Obama, televised address, February 16, 2010, in "Obama Says Stimulus Halted 'Catastrophe,'" *Financial Times*, February 17, 2010.

65 Paul Krugman (1953–), American economist at Princeton and the LSE, and 2008 winner of Nobel Prize for economics.

66 Paul Krugman, "The Third Depression," *The New York Times*, June 27, 2010.

67 The populist Tea Party emerged during 2009 and is a loose coalition of entry-ists into the Republican Party who favor lower taxes, smaller government, and paying off government debt.

Chapter Eighteen: And the Winner Is . . .

1 Robert Skidelsky, "After Serfdom," review of *Hayek: The Iron Cage of Liberty* by Andrew Gamble, Oxford, Polity, in *Times Literary Supplement*, September 20, 1996.

2 Milton Friedman, Letter, *Time*, February 4, 1966.

3 Milton Friedman, "John Maynard Keynes" in J. M. Keynes's *The General Theory of Employment, Interest and Money* (facsimile of 1936 edition reprinted by Verlag Wirtschaft und Finanzen GmbH, Düsseldorf, 1989), p. 6.

4 Milton Friedman, *The Counter-Revolution in Monetary Theory: First Wincott Memorial Lecture, Delivered at the Senate House, University of London, September 16, 1970* (Institute of Economic Affairs, London, 1970), p. 8.

5 Interview of Hayek by Thomas W. Hazlitt, 1977, published in *Reason*, July 1992. http://reason.com/archives/1992/07/01/the-road-from-serfdom.

6 Interview of Milton Friedman, October 1, 2000, *Commanding Heights*, PBS, http://www.pbs.org/wgbh/commandingheights/shared/minitext/int_milton friedman.html.

7 Interview of Hayek by Thomas W. Hazlett, 1977.

8 Richard Cockett, *Thinking the Unthinkable: Think Tanks and the Economic Counter-Revolution, 1931–1983* (HarperCollins, London, 1994), p. 175.

9 Gita Sereny (1921–), Austrian-born British author, biographer of Hitler's architect Albert Speer.

10 Quoted in Gita Sereny, *The Times* (London), May 9, 1985.

11 Interview of F. A. Hayek, *Forbes*, May 15, 1989, pp. 33–34.

12 *Collected Works*, vol. 2: *Road to Serfdom*, preface to the 1976 edition, p. 53. Hayek had described Keynes's *General Theory* in identical terms.

13 Adam Wolfson, "Conservatives and Neoconservatives," in Irwin Stelzer, ed., *The Neocon Reader* (Grove Press, New York, 2004), p. 224.

14 Paul Samuelson, "A Few Remembrances of Friedrich von Hayek (1899–1992)."

15 See Jeffrey D. Sachs, "The Social Welfare State, beyond Ideology: Are Higher Taxes and Strong Social 'Safety Nets' Antagonistic to a Prosperous Market Economy?" *Scientific American*, October 16, 2006.

16 Interview of Hayek by Thomas W. Hazlett, 1977.

17 John Cassidy, "The Price Prophet," *The New Yorker*, February 7, 2000.

18 Ibid.

19 Bruce Caldwell, *Hayek's Challenge: An Intellectual Biography of F. A. Hayek* (University of Chicago Press, Chicago, 2005), p. 3.

20 F. A. Hayek, *Studies in Philosophy, Politics and Economics* (University of Chicago Press, Chicago, 1967), p. 194.

21 Interview of Ralph Harris, July 17, 2000, *Commanding Heights*, PBS, http://www.pbs.org/wgbh/commandingheights/shared/minitext/int_ralphharris.html.

22 F. A. Hayek, *Law, Legislation and Liberty*, vol. 3: *The Political Order of a Free People* (University of Chicago Press, Chicago, 1979), p. 147.

23 Ibid., p. 146.

24 Ibid., p. 147.

25 *Collected Works*, vol. 2: *Road to Serfdom*, p. 260.

26 In fact, through her chancellor Nigel Lawson's ingenious efforts, Thatcher had at least responded to some extent to Hayek's notion of liberating the money supply from state control. Thatcher had always resisted the European Union's persistent demands for the establishment of a single currency, with sterling to join the euro, on nationalistic grounds: it would deprive Britain of her ultimate sovereignty—the means by which the government could fix interest rates to suit the conditions of Britain and Britain alone, and a currency floating in the marketplace reflecting the strengths and weaknesses of the British economy. Lawson, perhaps not entirely seriously, came up with an "alternative form of monetary union . . . based on the Hayekian idea of competing currencies. . . . Currency creation would remain in the hands of competing currencies. . . . With complete interchangeability and no legal impediments, good currencies would threaten gradually to drive out the bad . . . until eventually Europe might theoretically find itself with a single currency, freely chosen." (See Nigel Lawson, *The View from Number 11* [Bantam Press, London, 1992], p. 939.) Lawson's ruse came to nothing, as he fully expected. As Thatcher explained in *The Downing Street Years* (HarperCollins, London, 1995, p. 716), "It was not at all in the statist, centralized model which our European community partners preferred." But even Thatcher and Lawson's ingenious counter to Europe's persistent pressure to build a single enormous state with

a single government and a single currency did not quite pass Hayek's test as it continued to allow government-owned central banks to issue money. Indeed, the prospect of a single currency freely arrived at by market pressures would have provided an endorsement of the monopoly power of the state to issue money that would have been politically difficult and embarrassing to cede to private hands, as Hayek would have preferred.

27 Wolfson, "Conservatives and Neoconservatives," p. 224.

28 Herbert Stein, *Washington Bedtime Stories: The Politics of Money and Jobs* (Free Press, New York, 1986), p. 116.

29 F. A. Hayek, "Review of Harrod's *Life of J. M. Keynes,*" *Journal of Modern History*, vol. 24, no. 2, June 1952, pp. 195–198.

30 F. A. Hayek, "Personal Recollections of Keynes and the 'Keynesian Revolution,'" *Oriental Economist*, vol. 34, no. 663, January 1966, pp. 78–80.

31 J. K. Galbraith, "Keynes, Roosevelt, and the Complementary Revolutions," *Challenge* (New York University Institute of Economic Affairs, M. E. Sharpe, New York), vol. 26, 1983, p. 76.

SELECTED BIBLIOGRAPHY

Abse, Joan, ed. *My LSE* (Robson Books, London, 1977).

Alter, Jonathan. *The Defining Moment: FDR's Hundred Days and the Triumph of Hope* (Simon & Schuster, New York, 2006).

Ambrose, Stephen. *Nixon: Ruin and Recovery, 1973–1990* (Simon & Schuster, New York, 1991).

Anderson, Martin. *Revolution: The Reagan Legacy* (Harcourt Brace Jovanovich, San Diego, 1990).

Beveridge, William. *Full Employment in a Free Society* (Allen & Unwin, London, 1944).

Black, Conrad. *Roosevelt: Champion of Freedom* (PublicAffairs, New York, 2003).

Blaug, Mark. *Great Economists since Keynes: An Introduction to the Lives and Works of One Hundred Modern Economists* (Edward Elgar, Cheltenham, U.K., 1998).

Blinder, Alan S. *Hard Heads, Soft Hearts: Tough-Minded Economics for a Just Society* (Addison-Wesley, Reading, Mass., 1987).

———. "The Fall and Rise of Keynesian Economics," *Economic Record*, December 1988.

Boyer, Paul S., ed. *The Oxford Companion to United States History* (Oxford University Press, New York, 2001).

Breit, William, and Roger W. Spencer, eds. *Lives of the Laureates: Seven Nobel Economists* (MIT Press, Cambridge, Mass., 1986).

Bridges, Linda, and John R. Coyne Jr. *Strictly Right: William F. Buckley Jr. and the American Conservative Movement* (Wiley, Hoboken, N.J., 2007).

Buckley, William F., Jr. *On the Firing Line: The Public Life of Our Public Figures* (Random House, New York, 1989).

———. *Let Us Talk of Many Things: The Collected Speeches* (Basic Books, New York, 2008).

Caldwell, Bruce. *Hayek's Challenge: An Intellectual Biography of F. A. Hayek* (University of Chicago Press, Chicago, 2005).

Cannon, Lou. *President Reagan: The Role of a Lifetime* (PublicAffairs, New York, 1991).

Carter, Jimmy. *Keeping Faith: Memoirs of a President* (Collins, London, 1982).

Clark, Kenneth. *The Other Half: A Self Portrait* (Harper & Row, New York, 1977).

Clarke, Peter. *Keynes: The Rise, Fall, and Return of the 20th Century's Most Influential Economist* (Bloomsbury, New York, 2009).

Cockett, Richard. *Thinking the Unthinkable: Think Tanks and the Economic Counter-Revolution, 1931–1983* (HarperCollins, London, 1994).

Collins, Robert M. *The Business Response to Keynes, 1929–1964* (Columbia University Press, New York, 1981).

Cozzi, Terenzio, and Roberto Marchionatti, eds. *Piero Sraffa's Political Economy: A Centenary Estimate* (Psychology Press, Hove, U.K., 2001).

Dallek, Robert. *Franklin D. Roosevelt and American Foreign Policy, 1932–1945* (Oxford University Press, New York, 1979).

DeLay, Tom, with Stephen Mansfield. *No Retreat, No Surrender: One American's Fight* (Sentinel, New York, 2007).

Dickens, Charles. *Hard Times* (Harper & Brothers, New York, 1854).

Dimand, Robert W. *The Origins of the Keynesian Revolution* (Stanford University Press, Stanford, Calif., 1988).

Dolan, Chris J., John Frendreis, and Raymond Tatlovich. *The Presidency and Economic Policy* (Rowman & Littlefield, Lanham, Md., 2008).

Donovan, Robert J. *Conflict and Crisis: The Presidency of Harry S. Truman, 1945–1948* (University of Missouri Press, Columbia, 1996).

Durbin, Elizabeth. *New Jerusalems: The Labour Party and the Economics of Democratic Socialism* (Routledge & Kegan Paul, London, 1985).

Ebenstein, Alan. *Friedrich Hayek: A Biography* (Palgrave, New York, 2001).

Ebenstein, Lanny. *Milton Friedman: A Biography* (Palgrave Macmillan, New York, 2007).

Edwards, Lee. *Goldwater: The Man Who Made a Revolution* (Regnery, Washington, D.C., 1995).

Evans, Rowland, and Robert Novak. *The Reagan Revolution* (E. P. Dutton, New York, 1981).

Finer, Herman. *The Road to Reaction* (Little, Brown, Boston, 1945).

Freedman, Max, ed. *Roosevelt and Frankfurter: Their Correspondence, 1928–1945* (Atlantic–Little, Brown, Boston, 1967).

Friedman, Milton, ed. "The Quantity Theory of Money—A Restatement, an Essay in Studies in the Quantity Theory of Money," (in Friedman, ed., *Studies in the Quantity Theory of Money* [University of Chicago Press, Chicago, 1956]).

Friedman, Milton, and Rose D. Friedman. *Two Lucky People: Memoirs* (University of Chicago Press, Chicago, 1998).

Friedman, Milton, and Anna D. Schwartz. *A Monetary History of the United States, 1867–1960* (Princeton University Press, Princeton, N.J., 1963).

Fukuyama, Francis. *The End of History and the Last Man* (Free Press, New York, 1992).

Galbraith, James K. *Ambassador's Journal* (Houghton Mifflin, New York, 1969).

———. *A Life in Our Times* (Houghton Mifflin, Boston, 1981).

———. *The Essential Galbraith,* ed. Andrea D. Williams (Mariner Books, Orlando, Fla., 2001).

———. *The Predator State: How Conservatives Abandoned the Free Market and Why Liberals Should Too* (Free Press, New York, 2008).

Gamble, Andrew. *Hayek: The Iron Cage of Liberty* (Westview Press, Boulder, Colo., 1996).

Gilbert, Martin. *Winston Churchill, the Wilderness Years* (Houghton Mifflin, New York, 1982).

———. *Churchill: A Life* (Henry Holt, New York, 1991).

Gillon, Steven M. *The Democrats' Dilemma: Walter F. Mondale and the Liberal Legacy* (Columbia University Press, New York, 1995).

Gingrich, Newt, Ed Gillespie, and Bob Schellhas. *Contract with America* (Times Books, New York, 1994).

Goldwater, Barry M. *Conscience of a Conservative* (Victor, New York, 1960).

Goldwater, Barry M., with Jack Casserley. *Goldwater* (St. Martin's Press, New York, 1988).

Gordon, Robert J., ed. *Milton Friedman's Monetary Framework: A Debate with His Critics* (University of Chicago Press, Chicago, 1974).

Greenspan, Alan. *The Age of Turbulence: Adventures in a New World* (Penguin, New York, 2008).

Hall, Thomas Emerson, and J. David Ferguson. *The Great Depression: An International Disaster of Perverse Economic Policies* (University of Michigan Press, Ann Arbor, 1998).

Hansen, Alvin H. *A Guide to Keynes* (McGraw-Hill, New York, 1953).

———. *Business Cycles and National Income: Expanded Edition* (W. W. Norton, New York, 1964).

Harcourt, G. C. "Some Reflections on Joan Robinson's Changes of Mind and Their Relationship to Post-Keynesianism and the Economics Profession," in Joan Robinson, Maria Cristina Marcuzzo, Luigi Pasinetti, and Alesandro Roncaglia, eds., *The Economics of Joan Robinson,* Routledge Studies in the History of Economics, vol. 94 (CRC Press, London, 1996).

Harrod, R. F. *The Life of John Maynard Keynes* (Macmillan, London, 1952).

Hayek, F. A. *Monetary Theory and the Trade Cycle* (Jonathan Cape, London, 1933).

———. *Individualism and Economic Order* (University of Chicago Press, Chicago, 1948).

———. *The Constitution of Liberty* (University of Chicago Press, Chicago, 1960).

———. *Studies in Philosophy, Politics and Economics* (University of Chicago Press, Chicago, 1967).

———. *Prices and Production* (Augustus M. Kelley, New York, 1967).

———. *Law, Legislation and Liberty*, vol. 3: *The Political Order of a Free People* (University of Chicago Press, Chicago, 1979).

———. *A Tiger by the Tail: The Keynesian Legacy of Inflation* (Cato Institute, San Francisco, 1979).

———. *The Collected Works of F. A. Hayek*, ed. Bruce Caldwell.

Vol. 2: *The Road to Serfdom, Text and Documents, The Definitive Edition*, ed. Caldwell (University of Chicago Press, Chicago, 2007).

Vol. 4: *The Fortunes of Liberalism: Essays on Austrian Economics and the Ideal of Freedom*, ed. Peter G. Klein (University of Chicago Press, Chicago, 1992).

Vol. 9: *Contra Keynes and Cambridge: Essays and Correspondence*, ed. Caldwell (University of Chicago Press, Chicago, 1995).

Vol. 10: *Socialism and War: Essays, Documents, Reviews*, ed. Caldwell (Liberty Fund, Indianapolis, 1997).

Vol. 12: *The Pure Theory of Capital*, ed. Lawrence H. White (University of Chicago Press, Chicago, 2007).

Vol. 13: *Studies on the Abuse and Decline of Reason*, ed. Caldwell (University of Chicago Press, Chicago, 2010).

———. *Hayek on Hayek*, ed. Stephen Kresge and Leif Wenar (University of Chicago Press, Chicago, 1994).

———. *Prices and Production and Other Works: F. A. Hayek on Money, the Business Cycle, and the Gold Standard* (Ludwig von Mises Institute, Auburn, Ala., 2008).

. *The Pure Theory of Capital* (University of Chicago Press, Chicago, 2009).

———. University of California Los Angeles Oral History Project, interviews with Hayek conducted Oct. 28, Nov. 4, 11, 12, 1978. http://www.archive.org/stream/nobelprizewinning00haye#page/n7/mode/2up (accessed Feb 2011).

Healey, Denis. *The Time of My Life* (Michael Joseph, London, 1989).

Hession, Charles H. *John Maynard Keynes* (Macmillan, New York, 1984).

Hicks, John Richard. *Critical Essays in Monetary Theory* (Clarendon Press, Oxford, U.K., 1967).

———. *Money, Interest, and Wages*. Vol. 2 of *Collective Essays on Economic Theory* (Harvard University Press, Cambridge, Mass., 1982).

Howson, Susan, and Donald Winch. *The Economic Advisory Council, 1930–1939:*

A Study in Economic Advice during Depression and Recovery (Cambridge University Press, Cambridge, U.K., 1977).

Hülsmann, Jörg Guido. *Mises: The Last Knight of Liberalism* (Ludwig von Mises Institute, Auburn, Ala., 2007).

Jenkins, Peter. *Mrs. Thatcher's Revolution: The Ending of the Socialist Era* (Harvard University Press, Cambridge, Mass., 1987).

Jenkins, Roy, ed. *Purpose and Policy: Selected Speeches of C. R. Attlee* (Hutchinson, London, 1947).

———. *Churchill* (Macmillan, London, 2001).

Johnson, Elizabeth S., and Harry G. Johnson. *The Shadow of Keynes* (University of Chicago Press, Chicago, 1978).

Jordan, Hamilton. *Crisis: The Last Year of the Carter Presidency* (Michael Joseph, London, 1982).

Judis, John B., and William F. Buckley Jr. *Patron Saint of the Conservatives* (Simon & Schuster, New York, 1988).

Kahn, Richard F. *The Making of Keynes' General Theory* (Cambridge University Press, Cambridge, U.K., 1984).

Kaldor, Nicholas. *The Economic Consequences of Mrs. Thatcher: Speeches in the House of Lords, 1979–82,* ed. Nick Butler (Duckworth, London, 1983).

Keynes, J. M. *The Economic Consequences of the Peace* (Harcourt, Brace and Howe, New York, 1920).

———. *The Economic Consequences of Mr. Churchill* (Hogarth Press, London, 1925).

———. *The End of Laissez-Faire* (Hogarth Press, London, 1926).

———. *A Treatise on Money* (Macmillan, London, 1930).

———. *The Means to Prosperity* (Macmillan, London, 1933).

———. *The General Theory of Employment, Interest and Money* (Macmillan, London, 1936).

———. *The Collected Writings of John Maynard Keynes.*

Vol. 4: *A Tract on Monetary Reform* (1923) (Macmillan for the Royal Economic Society, London, 1971).

Vol. 5: *A Treatise on Money, i: The Pure Theory of Money* (1930) (Macmillan for the Royal Economic Society, London, 1971).

Vol. 9: *Essays in Persuasion* (1931) (Macmillan for the Royal Economic Society, London, 1972).

Vol. 13: *The General Theory and After, Part 1, Preparation* (Macmillan for the Royal Economic Society, London, 1973).

Vol. 14: *The General Theory and After, Part 2, Defence and Development* (Macmillan for the Royal Economic Society, London, 1973).

Vol. 17: *Activities 1920–2: Treaty Revision and Reconstruction* (Macmillan for the Royal Economic Society, London, 1977).

Vol. 19: *Activities 1922–9: The Return to Gold and Industrial Policy* (Macmillan for the Royal Economic Society, London, 1981).

Vol. 20: *Activities 1929–31: Rethinking Employment and Unemployment Policies* (Macmillan for the Royal Economic Society, London, 1981).

Vol. 21: *Activities 1931–9: World Crises and Policies in Britain and America* (1982) (Macmillan for the Royal Economic Society, London, 1982).

Vol. 29: *The General Theory and After: A Supplement* (1979) (Macmillan for the Royal Economic Society, London, 1979).

Keynes, J. M., and Lydia Lopokova. *Lydia and Maynard: The Letters of Lydia Lopokova and John Maynard Keynes*, ed. Polly Hill and Richard Keynes (Charles Scribner's Sons, New York, 1989).

Keynes, Milo, ed. *Essays on John Maynard Keynes* (Cambridge University Press, Cambridge, U.K., 1975).

Kirk, Russell, James McClellan, and Jeffrey Nelson. *The Political Principles of Robert A. Taft* (Transaction Publishers, Piscataway, N.J., 2010).

Lachmann, Ludwig M. *Expectations and the Meaning of Institutions: Essays in Economics*, ed. Don Lavoie (Psychology Press, Hove, U.K., 1994).

Laffer, Arthur. *The Laffer Curve: Past, Present and Future.* Executive Summary Backgrounder No. 1765 (Heritage Foundation, Washington, D.C., June 2004).

Lawson, Nigel. *The View from Number 11* (Bantam Press, London, 1992).

Lekachman, Robert, ed. *Keynes' General Theory; Reports of Three Decades* (St. Martin's Press, New York, 1964).

Lindbeck, Assar, ed. *Nobel Lectures in Economic Sciences 1969–1980* (World Scientific, Singapore, 1992).

Louis, William Rogers. *Adventures with Britannia: Personalities, Politics, and Culture in Britain* (I. B. Tauris, London, 1997).

Lowi, Theodore J. *The End of the Republican Era* (University of Oklahoma Press, Norman, 2006).

Machlup, Fritz. *Essays on Hayek* (Routledge, London, 2003).

Mackenzie, Norman, and Jeanne Mackenzie, eds. *The Diary of Beatrice Webb*, Vol. 4: *"The Wheel of Life," 1924–1943* (Virago, London, 1985).

Macmillan, Harold. *Tides of Fortune* (Macmillan, London, 1969).

Malabre, Alfred L., Jr. *Lost Prophets: An Insider's History of the Modern Economists* (Harvard Business School Press, Boston, 1994).

Maney, Patrick J. *The Roosevelt Presence: The Life and Legacy of FDR* (University of California Press, Berkeley, 1992).

Martin, Kingsley. *Editor: A Second Volume of Autobiography, 1931–45* (Penguin, London, 1969).

McCullough, David. *Truman* (Simon & Schuster, New York, 1992).

Mirowski, Philip, and Dieter Plehwe. *The Road from Mont Pèlerin: The Making of the Neoliberal Thought Collective* (Harvard University Press, Cambridge, Mass., 2009).

Mises, Ludwig von. *Theorie des Geldes und der Umlaufsmittel* (Duncker & Humblot, Munich, 1912).

———. *Socialism: An Economic and Sociological Analysis,* trans. I. Kahane (LibertyClassics, Indianapolis, 1981).

Mises, Margit von. *My Years with Ludwig von Mises* (Arlington House, New Rochelle, N.Y., 1976).

Moggridge, Donald Edward. *John Maynard Keynes* (Penguin Books, New York, 1976).

———. *Maynard Keynes: An Economist's Biography* (Routledge, New York, 1992).

Morgan, Ted. *FDR: A Biography* (Simon & Schuster, New York, 1985).

Morsink, Johannes. *The Universal Declaration of Human Rights: Origins, Drafting, and Intent* (University of Pennsylvania Press, Philadelphia, 2000).

Nash, George H. *The Conservative Intellectual Movement in America since 1945* (Basic Books, New York, 1976).

Nef, John Ulric. *The Search for Meaning: The Autobiography of a Nonconformist* (Public Affairs Press, Washington, D.C., 1973).

Nell, Edward, and Willi Semmler, eds. *Nicholas Kaldor and Mainstream Economics: Confrontation or Convergence?* (St. Martin's Press, New York, 1991).

Niskanen, William A. *Reaganomics: An Insider's Account of the Policies and the People* (Oxford University Press, New York, 1988).

Nixon, Richard. *The Memoirs of Richard Nixon* (Arrow Books, London, 1979).

Noonan, Peggy. *When Character Was King: A Story of Ronald Reagan* (Viking Penguin, New York, 2001).

O'Brien, Michael. *John F. Kennedy: A Biography* (Macmillan, London, 2006).

O'Driscoll, Gerald. *Economics as a Coordination Problem* (Andrews & McMeel, Kansas City, 1977).

Parker, Richard. *John Kenneth Galbraith: His Life, His Politics, His Economics* (Farrar, Straus & Giroux, New York, 2005).

Patinkin, Don, and J. Clark Leith, eds. *Keynes, Cambridge and the General Theory* (University of Toronto Press, Toronto, 1978).

Peacock, Alan T., and Jack Wiseman. *The Growth of Public Expenditure in the United Kingdom* (George Allen & Unwin, London, 1961).

Perkins, Frances. *The Roosevelt I Knew* (Viking Press, New York, 1946).

Pigou, Arthur. *Economics in Practice* (Macmillan, London, 1935).

Potier, Jean-Pierre. *Piero Sraffa, Unorthodox Economist (1898–1983): A Biographical Essay* (Psychology Press, Hove, U.K., 1991).

Rand, Ayn. *Ayn Rand's Marginalia: Her Critical Comments on the Writings of Over Twenty Authors,* ed. Robert Mayhew (Second Renaissance Books, New Milford, Conn., 1995).

Reagan, Ronald. *An American Life* (Simon & Schuster, New York, 1990).

Reeves, Richard. *President Reagan: The Triumph of Imagination* (Simon & Schuster, New York, 2005).

Robbins, Lionel. *Autobiography of an Economist* (Macmillan/St. Martin's Press, London, 1971).

Robinson, Joan. *Contributions to Modern Economics* (Blackwell, Oxford, U.K., 1978).

———. *Economic Philosophy: An Essay on the Progress of Economic Thought* (Aldine Transaction, Piscataway, N.J., 2006).

Rockefeller, David. *Memoirs* (Random House, New York, 2002).

Roosevelt, Franklin Delano. *FDR's Fireside Chats*, ed. Russell D. Buhite and David W. Levy (University of Oklahoma Press, Norman, 1992).

Rothbard, Murray Newton. *America's Great Depression* (Ludwig von Mises Institute, Auburn, Ala., 2000).

Royal Commission on Unemployment Insurance. *Minutes of Evidence*, Vol. 2 (HMSO, London, 1931).

Russell, Bertrand. *Autobiography* (Allen & Unwin, London, 1967).

Samuelson, Paul A. *Economics: An Introductory Analysis* (McGraw-Hill, New York, 1948).

———. *The Collected Scientific Papers of Paul A. Samuelson,* ed. Joseph E. Stiglitz, Vol. 2 (MIT Press, Cambridge, Mass., 1966).

Schlesinger, Arthur M., Jr. *A Thousand Days: John F. Kennedy in the White House* (Houghton Mifflin, New York, 1965).

———. *The Coming of the New Deal* (Mariner Books, New York, 2003).

Schumpeter, Joseph Alois, and Elizabeth Boody Schumpeter. *History of Economic Analysis* (Oxford University Press, Oxford, U.K., 1954).

Senzberg, Michael, ed. *Eminent Economists: Their Life Philosophies* (Cambridge University Press, Cambridge, U.K., 1993).

Shlaes, Amity. *The Forgotten Man: A New History of the Great Depression* (HarperCollins, New York, 2007).

Skidelsky, Robert. *John Maynard Keynes.*
Vol. 1: *Hopes Betrayed 1883–1920* (Viking Penguin, New York, 1986).
Vol. 2: *The Economist as Savior 1920–1937* (Viking Penguin, New York, 1994).
Vol. 3: *Fighting for Freedom 1937–1946* (Viking, New York, 2000).
———. *Keynes: The Return of the Master* (Public Affairs, New York, 2009).

Sloan, John W. *Eisenhower and the Management of Prosperity* (University Press of Kansas, Lawrence, 1991).

Snowdon, Brian, and Howard R. Vane. *A Macroeconomics Reader* (Routledge, London, 1997).

Steel, Ronald. *Walter Lippmann and the American Century* (Bodley Head, London, 1981).

Stein, Herbert. *Presidential Economics* (Simon & Schuster, New York, 1985).

————. *Washington Bedtime Stories: The Politics of Money and Jobs* (Free Press, New York, 1986).

————. *On the Other Hand—Essays on Economics, Economists, and Politics* (AEI Press, Washington, D.C., 1995).

Stelzer, Irwin, ed. *The Neocon Reader* (Grove Press, New York, 2004).

Stigler, George J. *Memoirs of an Unregulated Economist* (Basic Books, New York, 1988).

Streissler, Erich, ed. *Roads to Freedom: Essays in Honour of Friedrich A. von Hayek* (Augustus M. Kelley, New York, 1969).

Suskind, Ron. *The Price of Loyalty: George W. Bush, the White House, and the Education of Paul O'Neill* (Simon & Schuster, New York, 2004).

Tempalski, Jerry. "Revenue Effects of Major Tax Bills," OTA Working Paper 81, Office of Tax Analysis, U.S. Treasury Department, Washington D.C., July 2003.

Thatcher, Margaret. *The Downing Street Years* (HarperCollins, London, 1995).

Turner, Marjorie Shepherd. *Joan Robinson and the Americans* (M. E. Sharpe, Armonk, N.Y., 1989).

U.S. Senate. *Evidence to the Senate Finance Committee Investigation of Economic Problems: Hearings, 72nd Congress, 2nd session. February 13–28, 1933* (Government Printing Office, Washington, D.C., 1933).

————. *Assuring Full Employment in a Free Competitive Economy, Report from the Committee on Banking and Currency,* S. Rep. No. 583, 79th Congress, 1st session (Government Printing Office, Washington, D.C., September 22, 1945).

Wapshott, Nicholas. *Ronald Reagan and Margaret Thatcher: A Political Marriage* (Sentinel, New York, 2007).

Wapshott, Nicholas, and George Brock. *Thatcher* (Macdonald/Futura, London, 1983).

Winch, Donald. *Economics and Policy: A Historical Study* (Walker, New York, 1969).

Wittgenstein, Ludwig. *Ludwig Wittgenstein: Cambridge Letters,* ed. Brian McGuinness and Georg Henrik Wright (Wiley-Blackwell, Hoboken, N.J., 1972).

Wood, John Cunningham, ed. *Piero Sraffa: Critical Assessments* (Psychology Press, Hove, U.K., 1995).

Wood, John Cunningham, and Robert D. Wood, eds. *Friedrich A. Hayek: Critical Assessments of Leading Economists* (Routledge, London, 2004).

Wootton, Barbara. *Freedom under Planning* (G. Allen & Unwin, London, 1945).

Yergin, Daniel, and Stanislaw, Joseph, *Commanding Heights: The Battle for the World Economy* (Simon & Schuster, New York, 2002).

Young, Hugo. *The Iron Lady: A Biography of Margaret Thatcher* (Macmillan, London, 1989).

INDEX

Hayek's views on, xiii, 2, 41–45, 48–49,
  89, 112–13, 138, 140, 143–44,
  179–81, 184–85, 193–205, 209,
  217, 218–23, 240, 241, 247, 250–
  52, 266, 267–68, 275, 278, 286–95
Keynes's views on, xiii, 2, 24–25, 32–34,
  42–45, 52, 60–61, 77–78, 85–87,
  133–37, 143–46, 149–51, 154–70,
  186–97, 194–95, 249–50, 279–87,
  293–95
majority rule in, 252, 291–92
public works projects of, xiii, 31, 33,
  41–42, 48–49, 52, 57–58, 60–61,
  70–71, 82, 89, 94, 112–13,
  123–24, 126, 129–31, 134, 138,
  144, 149–51, 158–59, 161–62,
  163, 180–81, 184–85, 187, 188,
  193–205, 233–34, 280–81, 294
regulation by, 22–23, 145, 151, 180–81,
  186–97, 245, 246, 273, 275
revenues of, 12, 131, 234–35, 262–63,
  264, 267, 274, 276
shutdowns of, 273–74
size of, 251, 254, 261, 270, 272–73, 275,
  278, 291–92
social programs of, 26, 33–34, 49, 50,
  57–58, 60, 61, 77–78, 85, 134,
  199–200, 237, 253, 260, 283–84,
  291
spending cuts by, 26, 85–86, 188–89,
  242, 271, 272–75, 282–83
totalitarian, xiii, 87, 91, 144–45, 150–
  51, 193–205, 218–19, 221, 241,
  266, 287, 288–90
grades, bond, 84
Gramm-Leach-Bliley Act (1999), 275
Gramsci, Antonio, 114
Grant, Duncan, 5, 7, 10, 11, 24, 66, 226,
  301n
Great Britain:
  banking in, 24, 32–33, 37, 39, 59, 61,
    62, 279, 280
  currency of (pound sterling), 24, 38–40,
    55–56, 57, 72, 85–87, 260–61,
    344n–45n
  economy of, 32–34, 38, 39–40, 72–73,
    81–82, 83, 85–87, 106, 111, 131,
    134–35, 223, 260, 266, 279, 280,
    295, 344n–45n

elections in, *see* elections, British
industrial sector of, 60, 62, 86–87
infrastructure of, 57–58, 60, 82, 159
living standards in, 38
Parliament of, 33, 40, 58, 69, 86, 260
postwar period of, 193, 227
public programs in, 159, 160
rearmament of, 189, 190–94
unemployment rate of, 38, 56, 57–58,
  81–82, 85–87, 128, 134, 178–79,
  189, 191, 203, 260
as welfare state, 250, 258–61, 295
Great Depression, xiii, 40, 52–53, 60,
  71–73, 77–78, 81–85, 110–11,
  129–37, 141–44, 154–70, 188–90,
  224, 236, 248–49, 253, 263, 269,
  275, 279, 281, 296, 324n
Great Depression, The (Robbins), 224
"Great Moderation," 269–70
Great Society, 240
Greece, 282, 295
Greenspan, Alan, 244, 269–72, 274, 275,
  276, 277, 279, 280
Grey, Edward, 140, 161
gross domestic product (GDP), 190, 264
"growth gap," 236
Guide to Keynes, A (Hansen), 169

Haberler, Gottfried von, 176–77, 213,
  229–30, 322n
Hague, William, 295
Hampstead Garden Suburb, 139, 215
Hansen, Alvin H., 168–69, 204, 228, 231,
  232
Harcourt, Brace, 139
Harding, Warren G., 49
Hard Times (Dickens), 35
Harris, Ralph, 225, 256, 259, 291, 338n
Harris, Seymour E., 169, 209, 229
Harrod, Roy F., 7, 13, 54, 59, 62, 86, 95,
  125–26, 135, 136, 147, 238,
  301n
Harrod-Domar model, 238
Harvard University, 158, 161, 163, 165,
  166–68, 204, 232, 235, 256, 290
Havel, Václav, 266
Hayek, August, 15, 20
Hayek, Christine Maria Felicitas, 139, 214,
  215